Test Kitchen

A word about the Better Homes and Gardens® Test Kitchen

Our seal assures you that every recipe in *Anyone Can Cook* has been tested in the Better Homes and Gardens® Test Kitchen. This means that each recipe is practical and reliable, and meets our high standards of taste appeal. We guarantee your satisfaction with this book for as long as you own it.

How do I chop fresh mushroom and other vegetables?

How do I make a deep-dish pizza at home?

Better Homes and Gardens ®

anyone CAN COOK

step-by-step recipes just for you

Meredith® Books, Des Moines, Iowa

Editor: Tricia Laning Art Director: Ken Carlson Contributing Project Editor: Shelli McConnell
Contributing Editors: Ellen Boeke, Linda Henry, Jessica Saari, Joyce Trollope, Mary Williams Contributing Writer: Lisa Kingsley
Contributing Designers: Som Inthalangsy, Chad Johnson Contributing Photographers: Scott Little, Andy Lyons, Blaine Moats, Jay Wilde
Food Stylists: Greg Luna, Jill Lust, Dianna Nolin, Janet Pittman, Charles Worthington Contributing Prop Stylists: Andrea McGahuey, Sue Mitchell
Contributing Copy Editor: Sarah Oliver Watson Contributing Proofreaders: Gretchen Kauffman, Susan J. Kling
Contributing Indexer: Elizabeth T. Parson Test Kitchen Director: Lynn Blanchard Test Kitchen Product Supervisor: Lori Wilson
Test Kitchen Home Economists: Elizabeth Burt, R.D.,L.D.; Marilyn Cornelius, Juliana Hale, Laura Harms, R.D.;
Maryellyn Krantz; Jill Moberly; Colleen Weeden Copy Chief: Terri Fredrickson Copy Editor: Kevin Cox
Publishing Operations Manager: Karen Schirm Senior Editor, Asset & Information Management: Phillip Morgan
Edit and Design Production Coordinator: Mary Lee Gavin Editorial Assistant: Cheryl Eckert
Book Production Managers: Pam Kvitne, Marjorie J. Schenkelberg, Rick von Holdt, Mark Weaver Imaging Center Operator: Leslie Garrett

Meredith₀ Books

Executive Director, Editorial: Gregory H. Kayko Executive Director, Design: Matt Strelecki Managing Editor: Amy Tincher-Durik
Executive Editor: Jennifer Darling Senior Editor/Group Manager: Jan Miller Marketing Product Manager: Toye Guinn Cody

Publisher and Editor in Chief: James D. Blume Editorial Director: Linda Raglan Cunningham
Executive Director, New Business Development: Todd M. Davis Executive Director, Sales: Ken Zagor Director, Operations: George A. Susral
Director, Production: Douglas M. Johnston Director, Marketing & Publicity: Amy Nichols Business Director: Jim Leonard

Vice President and General Manager: Douglas J. Guendel

Better Homes and Gardens₀ Magazine

Editor in Chief: Gayle Goodson Butler Deputy Editor, Food and Entertaining: Nancy Hopkins

Meredith Publishing Group

President: Jack Griffin Senior Vice President: Karla Jeffries

Meredith Corporation

Chairman of the Board: William T. Kerr President and Chief Executive Officer: Stephen M. Lacy

In Memoriam: E.T. Meredith III (1933–2003)

Copyright © 2007 by Meredith Corporation, Des Moines, Iowa. First Edition. All rights reserved. Printed in China.
Library of Congress Control Number: 2007921756   ISBN: 978-0-696-23293-0

All of us at Meredith₀ Books are dedicated to providing you with the information and ideas you need to create delicious foods. We welcome your
comments and suggestions. Write to us at: Meredith Books, Cookbook Editorial Department, 1716 Locust St., Des Moines, IA 50309–3023.

What's in this book?

Something new—for you.

Every time we—as food editors, recipe developers, designers, and photographers—start the process of creating another cookbook, we know the purpose of the end result is to satisfy a hunger. This book does that and more. It satisfies the hunger for something good to eat—and the craving for a new way to learn how to cook.

We know there are millions of you out there—no matter your skill level—who say you really enjoy cooking and want to learn more and get better and better at it. We also recognize that the world has changed dramatically since the last generation pulled a chair up to the kitchen counter to help Mom make dinner. We live and work on the Internet and interact with friends, family, and workmates through texting and technology as much we do face to face.

As wired as we are—and as much time as we spend in cyberspace—we also know that a single great cookbook is still the fastest download for a stellar recipe for stir-fry or for detailed instructions on how to work with fresh garlic. That's the spirit *Anyone Can Cook* was created in. It's published by the same people who have been producing the best-selling cookbook in the country for more than 75 years. It comes from a tradition of reliability and excellence but is anything but traditional. *Anyone Can Cook* is a new kind of cookbook for a new generation of cooks. Its highly visual style and interactive elements (see page 9 for an explanation of those) reflect the highly visual wired world we live in. No other book looks—or cooks—like it. More than 500 recipes and nearly 1,000 photos inspire and show you—step-by-step—how to cook. We wanted to reach cooks at all skill levels, with recipes that are simple and clear— but don't talk down to anyone. You can start with the basics (and stay with them) or go as far beyond them as you want. *Anyone Can Cook* is your ticket to a lifetime of great food and great times. See you in the kitchen!

The recipes in this book were carefully picked with your tastes in mind. There's everything from the comfort foods you crave (mashed potatoes and mini meat loaves) to the world flavors (Indian curries and Thai-style wraps) you enjoy in restaurants.

Tricia Laning

Editor, *Better Homes and Gardens® Anyone Can Cook*

intro to
COOKING

Here's everything you need to know about what to stock, how to shop, how to chop, and more—a starting point you'll return to again and again.

1

How to use this book

Hungry for a home-cooked meal? You're holding the key ingredient here in your hands. There's nothing more basic to living well than eating well—and the best way to do that is to learn to cook. Ready?

Why learn to cook?

Cooking and eating good food nourishes more than just your body. It's a great way to be self-reliant, take care of yourself, and feel a sense of accomplishment—not to mention that it's a lot of fun. Think you're all thumbs in the kitchen? Don't know the difference between a saucepan and a skillet? Never chopped an onion or separated an egg? Don't worry about it. (And that's all about to change.) You're in good hands. Everything you need to know to get started cooking—and to grow as a cook—is right here in this book.

Designed with you in mind

Every recipe in this book has been created to taste great (that's a given) and be easy to make. Check the top of every recipe for a Skill Level icon. Skill Level 1 means you'll be successful even if you've never heard of a skillet. As you work your way up to Skill Levels 2 and 3, you'll still find these recipes simple to make, but you'll build on the skills you acquired in the easier recipes.

1 Skill Level

2 Skill Level

3 Skill Level

The first section of this book includes all the information you need to bone up on your vocabulary, ingredient knowledge, and skills. These pages will walk you through your kitchen arsenal and describe the gear you need and the extra stuff you might want as you discover how and what you like to cook. Next you'll learn how to choose and prepare fruits and vegeta-

bles for cooking. You'll find essential information on pantry items and how to store ingredients. Once you're familiar with tools and ingredients, you'll see step-by-step examples of basic cooking techniques you need to know—and a few fancy tricks only the pros know. But here's the best part. At the bottom of every recipe page there's an "Ask Mom" feature that covers the questions you might have about a recipe. So even if you've never touched a chef's knife or don't know what "mincing" means, you won't be stuck for long. Just find your question, flip to the page number that follows, and you'll find the answer. (You may be telling your own mom a thing or two before long.)

Ask Mom How do I measure butter? pages 58, 42 / How do I cut in butter? page 63 / What is the be How do I separate an egg yolk? page 62 / How do I m

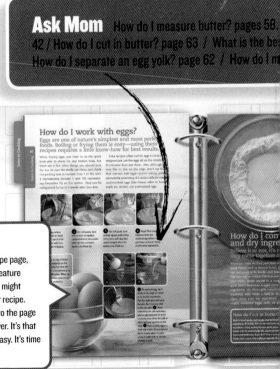

Ask Mom

At the bottom of each recipe page, you'll find an "Ask Mom" feature that covers questions you might have about that particular recipe. The question directs you to the page where you'll find the answer. It's that comprehensive. It's that easy. It's time to get cooking.

Kitchen Toolbox

Whether you are moving into your first kitchen or have committed to cooking and eating at home more often, you'll need the right culinary gear. Here are the essentials—and a few extras too.

A. Slotted spoon You can use a slotted spoon to stir, but it's also great for straining. Use it to remove cooked ground meat from a skillet, for instance, and leave the grease behind.

B. Scrapers Use these to get the last bits of anything from a bowl, jar, or pan. They're also great for folding wet and dry ingredients together. Silicone scrapers stand up to high heat better than those made of rubber.

C. Wooden spoons The classic cook's tool, wooden spoons are great for all kinds of stirring, and they won't scratch nonstick cookware. Hand wash them to avoid cracking.

D. Turner/spatula Flip your Saturday morning pancakes with this tool or use it to serve anything you've grilled, broiled, or panfried.

E. Whisk A wire whisk is a must for beating eggs, but it has lots of other uses too. It's perfect for blending sauces to make them smooth and terrific for mixing dry ingredients when baking.

F. Ladle The most obvious use for a ladle is serving soups. It's also handy for transferring soups, stews, sauces, and other liquidy foods from the cooking vessel to the serving bowl or to storage containers.

A Slotted spoon

B Scrapers

C Wooden spoons

D Turner/spatula

E Whisk

F Ladle

Mix & Measure

Measuring accurately is the first step to successful cooking. Unless you have a perfect sense of proportion, you need measuring tools—and something in which to stir what you've measured.

A A set of three mixing bowls will carry you through almost any kind of cooking. Generally a $1\frac{1}{2}$-, 3-, and 5-quart will do nicely. Stainless steel won't scratch, stain, or absorb flavors.

A Mixing bowls

B Most sets of measuring spoons have a tablespoon, teaspoon, $\frac{1}{2}$ teaspoon, and $\frac{1}{4}$ teaspoon. (You'll have to guess at a pinch.)

B Measuring spoons

C You'll be pulling out the glass measuring cups just about every time you cook or bake anything. A 1-cup and a 2-cup measure are essential.

C Glass measuring cups

D Use dry measuring cups only for dry goods such as flour, sugar, rice, and dry pasta. Most sets have a cup, $\frac{1}{2}$ cup, $\frac{1}{3}$ cup, and $\frac{1}{4}$ cup.

Nice to Have

You can certainly fill your 1- and 2-cup measures multiple times, but it is handy to have larger measures—such as a 4-cup and 8-cup—for measuring large amounts of broth when making soup or for mixing multiple liquids when making sauces.

D Dry measuring cups

Cookware

Here's where the pot meets the heat. The right pan opens up the possibilities for the foods you can cook.

The materials and sizes and shapes of cookware can make your head spin. Materials include aluminum, stainless steel, aluminum coated with stainless steel, anodized aluminum, copper, nonstick, cast iron, and cast iron coated with enamel porcelain. Buy the best cookware you can afford. It will last far into the future and give you the best results. Wash and dry all types of cookware by hand.

A. Stockpot The original purpose of this generously sized pot may have been for making stocks and broths, but it has many other uses. Use it to cook pasta or to make large batches of soup, stew, or chili. Look for one that has a volume of 6 or 8 quarts.

B. Large saucepan Saucepans have tall, straight sides and tight-fitting lids. Use a large saucepan (3 to 4 quarts) to cook vegetables or make sauces. It's nice to have a medium saucepan (2 to 2½ quarts) for other uses.

C. Small saucepan Use this smallest saucepan (1 to 1½ quarts) to melt chocolate or

A Stockpot

B Large saucepan

C Small saucepan

D Large skillet

E Small nonstick skillet

butter, to heat syrup or chocolate sauce, or to make a cup of hot chocolate.

D. Large skillet Skillets have wide surface areas and sloping or short, straight sides for quick cooking over high heat and easy-access flipping. Use a skillet to fry eggs, fish fillets, boneless chicken breasts, or vegetables. A large skillet is generally 10 or 12 inches across.

E. Small nonstick skillet Want to make just one fried egg for breakfast? A small (6- to 8-inch) nonstick skillet is ideal. Also use it to toast nuts and seeds on top of the stove.

F. Dutch oven One of the coolest things about this hot pot is how it easily goes from the stovetop into the oven. It's great for quick-browning a pot roast, for instance, and then cooking it slowly or braising it in the oven. Most Dutch ovens have a 4- to 6-quart capacity and they always have a lid. The one shown below is made of brushed stainless steel; the one on page 20 is made of porcelain enamel-coated cast iron.

G. Saute pan Although a skillet and a saute pan are interchangeable in many ways, each has its own uses. The saute pan, with a lid and deep, straight sides, is better for slowly braising meats, such as bone-in chicken pieces, on the stovetop. But either one can handle most quick panfrying jobs.

H. Roasting pan Whole birds and large roasts require a roasting pan that is large, shallow, and sturdy.

Nice to Have

A vegetable steamer insert makes it a snap to cook your veggies in the most healthful way possible. The accordion-fold design fits in several pan sizes and sits just above the boiling water. The handle makes it easy to pull out of the pan.

F Dutch oven

G Saute pan

H Roasting pan

EAU CLAIRE DISTRICT LIBRARY

A Kitchen tongs

B Ruler

C Pastry blender

D Spatula/spreader

E Custard cups

F Rolling pin

Nice to Have

Use pastry brushes to oil a baking pan, to brush barbecue sauce or glaze on meat, or to "paint" (technically to baste) a chicken or turkey with pan juices and drippings as it roasts.

A. Kitchen tongs These function like a second set of hands—heatproof hands—that can pick up a hot potato or turn over a chicken breast in a hot skillet. You can also use them to toss a salad or serve spaghetti.

B. Ruler Use a standard ruler to measure the distance between the broiler and the food under it, the thickness of rolled cookie dough, or the size of a piecrust.

C. Pastry blender If you like to bake pies or biscuits, this is a helpful tool for cutting cold butter or shortening into flour. You can use two butter knives—moved in a crisscross motion—but it's much easier and more efficient with a pastry blender.

D. Spatula/spreader Use this handy dual-function tool to neatly remove cut bars or brownies from a baking pan—or to easily spread frosting prettily on a cake.

E. Custard cups These small heatproof bowls serve as cooking and serving vessels (for individual custards or puddings) or as small prep bowls to hold premeasured ingredients.

F. Rolling pin There are two basic types of rolling pins. Above is the classic roller style. The other is the French-style rolling pin—an elongated rod with tapered ends. Rolling pins come in a variety of materials including wood, ceramic, metal, silicone, and marble. Use them to roll out piecrust, pizza dough, or puff pastry.

B Perfect for cleanly slicing juicy, ripe tomatoes, this serrated utility knife is also great for cutting all fruits and vegetables.

C This is the big kahuna—the all-purpose knife for cutting meat, slicing, and dicing. Chef's knives come in blade lengths ranging from 6 to 12 inches.

D This knife's serrated blade easily cuts through the hard crust of European-style breads without squashing the loaf.

A This smallest knife, with a 3- to 4-inch blade, is ideal for peeling and coring foods such as apples.

E Keep a pair strictly for kitchen use: cutting up a chicken, snipping fresh herbs in a small bowl, or opening packages.

B Tomato knife

D Serrated/bread knife

A Paring knife

C Chef's knife

E Kitchen scissors

Nice to Have

A boning knife (left) is useful for cutting around and removing the bone in a cut of meat. A santoku knife (right) is a Japanese-style knife with a thinner blade than a chef's knife that cuts easily through some of the denser vegetables.

Cutting Edge
A set of good knives and knowing how to use them correctly—and safely—are crucial in the kitchen.

Good knives are expensive. You can skimp on the dinner plates, but kitchen knives are all about function. Invest in the very best ones you can afford—then hand wash and dry them and keep them professionally sharpened. Look for those that have high-carbon stainless-steel blades. The good news: High-quality knives, well cared for, will last for years.

Baker's Dozen

Baking requires precision. Having the right bakeware will help you get impressive results.

Bakeware comes in several materials, including aluminum, nonstick coated aluminum or steel, silicone, and glass. Aluminum—nonstick or not—is a good choice. It is lightweight and conducts heat well, which ensures even baking and browning of your baked goods. Know this: You should wash and dry aluminum bakeware by hand.

A. Muffin pan The standard muffin pan has 12 cups. Most muffin and cupcake recipes make more than 12, so you can bake in stages or buy more than one.

B. Round cake pan All birthday cake bakers should have two of these. Pans are generally 8 or 9 inches across. Most layer-cake recipes work with either size.

A Muffin pan

B Round cake pan

C Springform pan

F Pie plate

D Wire cooling rack

E Cookie sheet

C. Springform pan This pan has a latch that opens so you can remove the sides; it's crucial for cheesecake and deep-dish pizza. The most common sizes are 9 and 10 inches across.

D. Wire cooling rack You'll wind up with soggy cakes and cookies if you don't have a couple of these. They allow air to circulate around baked goods as they cool.

E. Cookie sheet This sideless pan allows heat to circulate around the cookies and makes it easy to transfer them to a wire rack. Buy two.

F. Pie plate Whether it's aluminum or glass, 9 or 10 inches, this is a must-have.

G. Square baking pan You'll need one of these for bar cookies, cakes, and corn bread. Choose either 9×9×2 inches or 8×8×2 inches.

H. Loaf pan If you love banana bread or meat loaf, you'll need at least one. The most common size is 8×4×2 inches, though it's a good idea to stock the larger 9×5×3-inch size too.

I. Rectangular baking pan A standard 9×13×2-inch pan is indispensable for baking nonlayer cakes.

J. Jelly-roll pan Whether you never make a jelly roll, you'll use this pan to toast nuts, bake a pizza, and roast veggies.

Nice to Have

If you discover a knack for baking, you might want to add a couple of pieces to your bakeware collection. A 10-inch fluted tube pan makes beautiful tube cakes, pound cakes, and coffee cakes. A 9-inch tart pan with a removable bottom enables you to make authentic fruit and nut tarts—and to easily get them out of the pan and onto a plate.

G Square baking pan

H Loaf pan

I Rectangular baking pan

J Jelly-roll pan

(A) Round casserole

(B) Square baking dish

(C) Rectangular baking dish

Baking Dishes

From an egg strata in the morning to a one-dish dinner at night, these workhorses aim to serve.

Baking dishes and casseroles (incidentally, the name of the type of dish and not just the food you make in it) function for baking and serving. They are often made of glass, ceramic, stoneware, or enamel-coated cast iron. Most of the glass varieties are oven-, microwave-, and freezer-safe; check the brand you buy to be sure. Baking dishes can be round, oval, square, or rectangular and range in capacity from about 1 quart to more than 6 quarts.

A. Round casserole The most common sizes are $1\frac{1}{2}$-, 2-, and 3-quart. Round casseroles usually come with lids—which makes them handy for storing leftovers in the refrigerator.

B. Square baking dish These small dishes (usually 2-quart) are perfect for baking small casseroles and fruit crisps and cobblers.

C. Rectangular baking dish A 3-quart rectangular dish is the right size when cooking for a crowd.

Kitchen Toolbox continued ...

A Large colander

B Can/bottle opener

C Egg separator

D Can opener

E Meat mallet

F Vegetable peeler

Nice to Have

You can use a paring knife to slice cheese, but your slices will be more uniform if you use a cheese slicer—not to mention that it's easier with the right tool. Most have an adjustable wire so you can make slices as thick or thin as you prefer.

A. Large colander Colanders can be made of fine-wire mesh—like the one above—or of stainless steel or enamel-coated steel. The latter type is usually dotted with small holes. Use a colander to drain vegetables or pasta after cooking—or to hold raw vegetables or fruits under running water as you wash them.

B. Can/bottle opener This handy tool opens soda and beer bottles and punches holes in cans with one quick motion.

C. Egg separator This gadget makes quick work of separating the yolk from the white. Handles suspend it over a cup that catches the white while the separator cradles the yolk.

D. Can opener There's no mystery here: A sharp, round, rotating blade cuts into the edges of the can and continues around as you turn the handle. Be careful: The edges of the can lid are as sharp as a knife.

E. Meat mallet It may look like something that belongs on the basement workbench, but the purpose of this hammer is to tenderize and/or flatten meat. The spiked side tenderizes and flattens; the smooth side flattens.

F. Vegetable peeler Its obvious function is to peel potatoes and carrots, but a vegetable peeler also makes large, attractive strips of lemon and orange peel for cooking or for garnishing.

Kitchen Toolbox continued ...

B Meat thermometer

C Instant-read thermometer

D Box grater

Nice to Have

A citrus juicer makes juicing lemons, limes, and oranges a cinch. The sieve strains pulp and seeds; the spout makes pouring easy.

E Kitchen timer

F Potato masher

A. Dutch oven Use this versatile pot on top of the stove and in the oven. A 4- or 6-quart size with lid will handle most jobs.

B. Meat thermometer Use a dial-type thermometer that is ovensafe; insert it into meat before roasting. Keep it in the entire time.

C. Instant-read thermometer Dial or digital thermometers, such as this one, give an immediate reading upon insertion outside the oven.

D. Box grater A grater is used for shredding and grating ingredients. Most have fine and coarse sides; some may have a knuckle guard.

E. Kitchen timer Underdone or overdone can mean a matter of minutes. Go digital, like the timer above, or use the classic wind-up kind.

F. Potato masher For light, fluffy mashed potatoes, this low-tech tool is essential. Use it to mash ripe bananas for banana bread too.

Small Appliances

Why do manual labor when the push of a button and a little electricity can take care of the work for you? You don't need every fancy plug-in gadget in the world, but a few of them do make life easier.

A. Food processor This chopping, mincing, pureeing machine is arguably a cook's best friend. Most food processors have settings for continuous running or pulsing—intermittent hits of power. An 8- to 10-cup bowl is a good size—buy larger if you plan to make yeast bread dough in it.

B. Slow cooker The ultimate unwatched pot, a slow cooker can conveniently fit home-cooked meals into a busy schedule. Slow cookers come in $3\frac{1}{2}$-, 4-, 5-quart, and even larger sizes. It's recommended you fill the cooker at least half full and not more than two-thirds full. Be sure to use a cooker that's within the size range given in a recipe so your foods cook properly and leave the lid on while it's cooking. Slow cookers can be round, as shown, or oval, which is better for roasts and crowd-size dishes. Either shape works for nearly all recipes though.

C. Hand mixer Whipping up a batch of chocolate chip cookies, a birthday cake, or a bowl of whipped cream can be done effortlessly with a hand mixer. The most useful type has at least five speeds and enough power to mix reasonably stiff cookie dough.

D. Blender Give the smoothie stand down the street a run for its money. For slurp-and-run breakfasts and postworkout power shakes, blended margaritas, and pureed soups (in the absence of an immersion blender, pictured below) a blender is essential. Most have multiple speeds. Be sure yours is tough enough to crush ice.

A Food processor

B Slow cooker

C Hand mixer

D Blender

Nice to Have

Making grilled cheese is a breeze in a panini press or electric grill, left. Conveniently puree creamy soups in the pot with an immersion blender, right.

Kitchen Toolbox continued ...

A Fine-mesh sieve

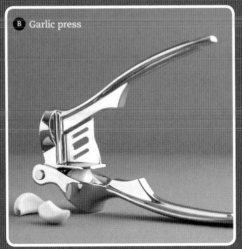

B Garlic press

C Pepper grinder

D Melon baller

Nice to Have

There's nothing quite like the flavor of freshly ground herbs and spices. Crush them yourself in a mortar and pestle—and taste the difference.

A. Fine-mesh sieve Use this finely screened sieve to drain small amounts of cooked pasta or vegetables. It's also great for straining seeds out of fresh berries and preserves for use in dessert sauces. Crush and press the berries with a wooden spoon, then push the juice through. Here's another trick: Use a fine-mesh sieve to dust powdered sugar over baked goods such as cookies and cakes. Put a small amount of powdered sugar in the strainer, then tap one side of it gently with your hand, moving it back and forth.

B. Garlic press Minced garlic is an ingredient in many recipes. A garlic press makes it easy to mince—no knife or chopper needed. Just pop the peeled cloves in the hopper and squeeze: Presto! Minced garlic emerges.

C. Pepper grinder Many serious cooks believe that by using good salt (fine kosher salt or sea salt) and freshly ground black pepper, cooking improves dramatically. You don't want to crush fresh peppercorns every time you need them in a mortar and pestle (see above). What you need is a pepper grinder. They come in several materials, including wood, stainless steel, and acrylic, and can be manual or battery powered. All have mechanisms to adjust the grind from coarse to fine.

D. Melon baller You can cut your melon into chunks, but it's aesthetically pleasing to serve sweet little orbs of fruit. This tool functions like an ice cream scoop: Drag it across the surface of the melon until a tidy ball forms.

Shopping & Pantry

Get to know your grocery store. With a little planning, you'll be one step ahead in the cooking game.

If you have a deep knowledge of the frozen pizza case at your grocery store—and that's about it—you have a little exploring to do. Take a trip to the market some day when you aren't in a hurry and learn where everything is stocked and what's available there. Familiarity with your supermarket is really the first step to learning to cook.

Ingredients: The Building Blocks

There's a dizzying array of ingredients available at the modern supermarket. They come fresh, frozen, canned, dried, and otherwise preserved. And there are all kinds of ethnic ingredients—curry pastes, hot sauces, wonton wrappers—that make cooking so much fun. If you want to eat well, buy the best ingredients your budget will allow. Watch newspaper ads and inserts for weekly specials and coupons. And when it comes to produce, learn what's in season at any given time of the year. Your food will not only taste better but also will be more affordable. Compare the flavor and price tag of June strawberries or August tomatoes to those you can get in mid-January, and you'll begin to appreciate the difference.

Nice to Know

Every meal you make doesn't have to be entirely from scratch. Sometimes you might need to depend on a roasted chicken from the deli, with a simple vegetable side dish. When you shop, stock up on shortcut ingredients such as frozen meatballs, frozen vegetables, pizza shells, pasta sauce, shredded cheese, rice mixes, precut fruits and vegetables, and packaged salad greens.

Smart Shopping

Getting organized means more than having tidy cabinets. It means organizing your shopping too. Here are a few things you can do to streamline the grocery-gathering process:

● Keep a running list of what you need. Post it somewhere in the kitchen so you can jot things down as you think of them.

● Include on your list things you'll need for several days' worth of meals.

● Shop when the market isn't crowded. You can take your time to read nutrition labels and discover new foods you might want to try.

Put it in Order

To ensure that your strawberries don't get squished or your bread broken, start off with heavier canned goods in the bottom of the basket or cart—then visit the produce section and bakery last, right before you check out.

Stock It & Store It

You're much more likely to veer off into that fast-food drive-through if your cupboard is bare. After you figure out where everything is at the supermarket, here's what to bring home—and where to put it.

The Prepared Pantry

The pantry isn't just one cupboard in your kitchen. It's your freezer, your refrigerator, and your cupboards. Check out the following lists for the types of things to have on hand. You don't want to get in the middle of a recipe and discover you're experiencing a personal butter shortage.

Smart Storage

To make meal prep go as smoothly as possible, have an organizational system for storing your ingredients. Keep all of the dry goods, such as flour and sugar, together. The same goes for canned goods, such as chicken broth and tomatoes. When you get home from the store, go through the refrigerator and toss less-than-fresh produce and any meat, dairy products, eggs, or condiments that have expired dates. Wipe the refrigerator shelves and inside the door with a warm, soapy sponge or clean kitchen cloth. Store fresh items such as leftover grated cheese or lunchmeat in tightly sealed containers.

Staples: Dry Goods, Canned Goods & Condiments

Essentials	Where do I find it?	Where do I store it?	How long will it keep?
Baking powder	Baking aisle	Cupboard	6 months after opening
Baking soda	Baking aisle	Cupboard	6 months after opening
Bread crumbs (dry)	Baking aisle	Cupboard	6 months after opening
Broth or bouillon granules (beef, chicken, vegetable)	Soup aisle	Unopened: cupboard Opened: refrigerator	Check expiration date
Chocolate (cocoa powder, semisweet chocolate pieces, unsweetened)	Baking aisle	Cupboard	1 year
Cornmeal	Baking aisle	Cupboard or freezer	6 months; freeze for up to 1 year
Cornstarch	Baking aisle	Cupboard	2 years after opening
Couscous	Pasta/grain aisle	Cupboard	2 years
Flour (all-purpose white)	Baking aisle	Airtight container	1 year
Fruit, canned	Canned goods aisle	Cupboard	1 year unopened
Garlic (bulb)	Produce section	Cool, dry place	1 month
Ketchup	Condiments aisle	Refrigerator	6 months after opening
Maple syrup	Ask grocer	Refrigerator	1 year after opening
Mustard (Dijon-style, yellow)	Condiments aisle	Refrigerator	6 months
Nonstick cooking spray	Baking aisle	Cupboard	Check expiration date
Nuts (almonds, cocktail peanuts, pecans, walnuts)	Baking aisle or produce section	Freezer	8 months
Oats (quick cooking, rolled)	Cereal aisle	Airtight container	6 months; freeze for up to 1 year
Oils (olive, vegetable)	Baking aisle	Cupboard	6 months
Onions (yellow or white and red)	Produce section	Cool, ventilated place	Several weeks
Pasta, dried	Pasta/grain aisle	Cupboard	2 years
Peanut butter	Ask grocer	Cupboard	2 months after opening
Potatoes	Produce section	Cool, ventilated place	Several weeks
Rice (converted brown and white, long grain white, rice mixes, wild)	Pasta/grain aisle	Cupboard	2 years

Staples: Dry Goods, Canned Goods & Condiments *(continued)*

Essentials	Where do I find it?	Where do I store it?	How long will it keep?
Roasted red sweet peppers	Condiment aisle	Refrigerator	2 weeks after opening
Salsa	Ethnic food aisle	Refrigerator	1 month after opening
Soy sauce	Ethnic food aisle	Refrigerator	1 year after opening
Spaghetti sauce	Pasta/grain aisle	Refrigerator	2 weeks after opening
Sugar (brown, granulated, powdered)	Baking aisle	Cupboard	brown: 4 months; granulated/powdered: 18 months
Tomatoes, canned (diced, stewed, whole, tomato paste, tomato sauce)	Canned goods aisle	Cupboard	1 year unopened
Tomatoes (dried, oil packed)	Condiment aisle	Refrigerator	1 month after opening
Vegetable shortening	Baking aisle	Cupboard	6 months after opening
Vegetables, canned	Canned goods aisle	Cupboard	1 year unopened
Vinegar (balsamic, cider, distilled red or white)	Baking aisle	Cupboard	Indefinitely
Worcestershire sauce	Condiment aisle	Refrigerator	Check expiration date

Nice to Have	Where do I find it?	Where do I store it?	How long will it keep?
Beans, canned and dried (black, cannellini, garbanzo, kidney, pinto)	Canned goods or pasta/grain aisle	Cupboard	1 year unopened
Corn syrup (light color)	Ask grocer	Cupboard	1 year after opening
Dried fruit (apricots, cherries, cranberries, raisins)	Baking aisle	Cupboard	Check expiration date
Green chiles, canned	Ethnic food aisle	Cupboard	1 year unopened
Honey	Ask grocer	Cupboard	1 year
Hot pepper sauce	Condiment aisle	Cupboard	1 year after opening
Milk (evaporated, sweetened condensed)	Baking aisle	Cupboard	Check expiration date
Molasses	Ask grocer	Cupboard	6 months after opening
Olives (green, kalamata, ripe)	Condiment aisle	Refrigerator	1 month after opening
Sherry (dry)	Liquor department	Cool, dry place	Indefinitely
Tuna, canned	Canned fish aisle	Cupboard	Check expiration date
Wines (dry red, dry white)	Liquor department	Cool, dry place	1 week after opening
Yeast	Baking aisle	Cool, dry place	Check expiration date

Nice to Know

Ingredients like flour and brown sugar don't do well if they're left in their original packaging after they're opened—too much air gets to them. See-through storage jars keep things fresh—and allow you to see exactly what's in them.

Staples: Fresh, Refrigerated & Frozen Items

Essentials	Where do I find it?	Where do I store it?	How long will it keep?
Butter	Dairy section	Refrigerator	3 months
Carrots	Produce section	Refrigerator	2 weeks
Celery	Produce section	Refrigerator	2 weeks
Cheese (American, cheddar, Parmesan, Swiss)	Dairy section or deli	Refrigerator	2 to 3 weeks
Eggs	Dairy section	Refrigerator	4 to 5 weeks
Lemons	Produce section	Refrigerator	Several weeks
Limes	Produce section	Refrigerator	Several weeks
Mayonnaise	Condiment aisle	Refrigerator	2 months after opening
Milk	Dairy section	Refrigerator	Check expiration date
Oranges	Produce section	Refrigerator	Several weeks
Salad greens	Produce section	Refrigerator	2 to 5 days

Nice to Have	Where do I find it?	Where do I store it?	How long will it keep?
Capers	Condiment aisle	Refrigerator	I year after opening
Fruit, frozen (blueberries, raspberries, strawberries)	Frozen foods aisle	Freezer	I year
Prepared horseradish	Ask grocer	Refrigerator	Check expiration date
Salad dressing	Condiment aisle	Refrigerator	3 months after opening
Tortillas	Ask grocer	Refrigerator	Check expiration date
Vegetables, frozen (broccoli, corn, green beans, spinach)	Frozen foods aisle	Freezer	I year

Staples: Herbs & Spices

Essentials	Where do I find it?	Where do I store it?	How long will it keep?
Basil	Baking aisle	Cupboard	Check expiration date
Bay leaves	Baking aisle	Cupboard	Check expiration date
Chili powder	Baking aisle	Cupboard	Check expiration date
Cinnamon (ground)	Baking aisle	Cupboard	Check expiration date
Cloves (ground)	Baking aisle	Cupboard	Check expiration date
Cream of tartar	Baking aisle	Cupboard	Check expiration date
Cumin (ground)	Baking aisle	Cupboard	Check expiration date
Dillweed (dried)	Baking aisle	Cupboard	Check expiration date
Garlic powder	Baking aisle	Cupboard	Check expiration date
Ginger (ground/fresh)	Baking aisle/ Produce section	Cupboard/ Refrigerator	Check expiration date/ 2 to 3 weeks
Mustard (dry)	Baking aisle	Cupboard	Check expiration date
Nutmeg (ground)	Baking aisle	Cupboard	Check expiration date
Onion powder	Baking aisle	Cupboard	Check expiration date
Oregano	Baking aisle	Cupboard	Check expiration date
Paprika	Baking aisle	Cupboard	Check expiration date
Pepper (black, cayenne, crushed red pepper)	Baking aisle	Cupboard	Check expiration date
Poppy seeds	Baking aisle	Cupboard	Check expiration date
Rosemary	Baking aisle	Cupboard	Check expiration date
Sage	Baking aisle	Cupboard	Check expiration date
Salt (regular, kosher)	Baking aisle	Cupboard	Indefinitely
Thyme	Baking aisle	Cupboard	Check expiration date
Vanilla	Baking aisle	Cupboard	4 to 5 years

Fruits & Vegetables

Mom always said to eat your fruits and veggies. Wise advice. But before you can eat them, you have to know what to do with them. Here's your guide for choosing and prepping the most common produce.

Feeling a little lost in the produce section? This section is all about helping you pick the freshest fruits and vegetables, giving you information on how to store them so they stay that way, and then showing you how to prepare them for eating them raw or for cooking. This doesn't cover every exotic pear or plum there is, but it does cover most common fruits and vegetables in detail. Prepping may simply entail washing and peeling, or it may involve washing, peeling, mincing, or making a chiffonade or a julienne. What's that, you say? You'll find the answers in one of the most helpful features of this book.

How Do I Do That?

You may have read about the "Ask Mom" feature on page 9. It works like this: If you're mak-

Nice to Know

Although there's no question that fresh fruits and vegetables are ideal in terms of flavor, sometimes there's no time to peel and chop. Suffer no guilt: Frozen fruits and vegetables are flash-frozen soon after harvesting. Flash-freezing helps retain vitamins and minerals at levels that are equal to (or even greater than!) fresh. They're available year-round and store in the freezer.

ing the Herbed Leek Gratin on page 136 and you need to know how to clean, trim, and cut leeks, an "Ask Mom" question on that page will direct you to page 43 in this section, where you'll see—step-by-step—exactly how to do it.

Growing as a Cook

The more you become familiar with—and even master—the techniques of working with fresh fruits and vegetables, the more you'll be able to concentrate on the fun, creative aspects of cooking. You may only have to read about how to remove the seed from an avocado (see page 36) once or twice. It's sort of like practicing the scales before you can learn to play the piano.

Mix It Up

Because fruits and vegetables contain different kinds and amounts of vitamins and minerals, eating a varied diet is one of the keys to good health. Don't be boring; try something new today.

Apples

An apple isn't just an apple. Flavors range from sweet to tart; certain varieties are best for eating out of hand and in salads, others are for baking and cooking, and some are all-purpose.

Select apples that are firm with smooth and shiny skin and no bruises or breaks. Handle apples gently to prevent bruising. Store apples in a plastic bag in the refrigerator crisper so they maintain their crispness and flavor; at room temperature they get mushy and mealy. Just don't store them near foods with strong odors—they'll absorb the smells.

1 Rinse apples with water and scrub with a produce brush. To peel, use a vegetable peeler or paring knife; start at the stem end and circle around to the blossom end. **2** To remove the core, cut the apple into four pieces through stem and blossom ends. Cut away core and seeds, stem, and blossom ends. **3** For smaller wedges, place quarters on a cutting board, cut sides down, and start by cutting through the skin. **4** For bite-size pieces, cut up wedges with the knife.

Nice to Have

An apple corer makes quick work of removing the core without cutting the apple into wedges. Another handy tool is a round disk that cuts away the core and cuts the apple into wedges at the same time.

How do I cut up a cantaloupe?

1 Before cutting, thoroughly scrub melon with a clean produce brush. Use a large chef's knife to cut the cantaloupe in half, cutting through the stem and blossom ends; steady the melon with your other hand. Be sure to use a cutting board. **2** Using a large spoon, scoop out the seeds and fiber in the center of the melon halves; discard the seeds.

Melon Math:

1 medium cantaloupe or honeydew (2½ pounds) = about 6 cups cubed or about 5½ cups melon balls

3 Cut the melon halves in half again and then, if you want, into smaller wedges. Use a boning knife to cut between the rind and fruit of each wedge; discard the rind. **4** Serve the melon in wedges, cut the wedges into large chunks, or chop the melon into smaller pieces.

Cantaloupes

There are several theories on choosing a cantaloupe. Some say thump it; some say squeeze it. A good place to start is on the outside: Choose a cantaloupe (sometimes referred to as a muskmelon) that has a cream-color netting over a rind that is green, yellow, or gray. The blossom end should yield to gentle pressure; the rest of the melon should be firm and free from decay, bruises, and cuts. Smell it at the stem end—it should have a sweetly aromatic scent. If it seems underripe, store it at room temperature for up to 2 days. For honeydew melon,* choose one that is firm and ripe and has a creamy yellow color. Store ripe melons in the refrigerator.

*Note: Cut a honeydew melon using the same technique.

Citrus

Lemons, limes, oranges, and grapefruit are rare exceptions to the rule that summer fruit is best. They're in season during winter—and provide sunny color and refreshing flavor when you need it most.

At most supermarkets, a lemon is a lemon and a lime is a lime—but you will see several types of oranges. The two most common ones are juicy Valencia oranges and easy-to-peel navel oranges. Valencias are small to medium in size and have a smooth, thin peel. Navel oranges generally are larger and have a pebbly, thicker peel and a button shape at the end opposite the stem; they're seedless and easy to section.

Look for well-formed citrus fruits that are heavy for their size and have a colorful skin. Bruised and wrinkled fruit is past its prime. A slight greenish tinge found on the surface of some oranges doesn't affect the eating quality.

Store citrus fruit in the refrigerator crisper for up to several weeks for best flavor and nutrient value. Be sure to rinse the fruit thoroughly, scrub with a clean produce brush, and dry with paper towels before cutting it up or shredding the peel.

Citrus Math:

1 medium lemon = 2 teaspoons finely shredded peel = 3 tablespoons juice

1 medium lime = $1\frac{1}{2}$ teaspoons finely shredded peel = 2 tablespoons juice

1 medium orange = 1 tablespoon finely shredded peel = $\frac{1}{3}$ cup juice = $\frac{1}{3}$ cup sections

Shredding: Use a shredder, making sure you remove just the colored part of the peel (called the zest). Avoid the bitter white stuff. Shred onto a sheet of waxed paper for easy cleanup.

Wedging: Use a paring knife to cut the citrus fruit through the stem end, then cut into smaller wedges if desired.

Slicing: Use a paring knife to cut the lemon crosswise into rounds. To make an easy garnish, make a cut to the center of the slice and twist ends in opposite directions to make a citrus twist.

Juicing: To get the most juice from the fruit, leave it out at room temperature about 30 minutes. Then roll each fruit on the counter under the palm of your hand before squeezing the fruit half on a citrus juicer.

How do I section an orange?

If you pack an orange in your lunch box, you'll likely peel it and eat the sections, membrane and all. But if you want the sections to be prettier—and a little more pleasant to eat—you can cut it in such a way that you don't get any stringy membranes (see how to do it, below). This is especially important if you're using the orange sections in a salad or even sauteeing them for a sauce (yes, it's done). You can cut grapefruit using the same method.

1 Start by cutting off a thin slice from both ends of the orange using a paring knife.
2 Place the flat end of the orange on a cutting board. Using the knife, cut away the peel and the white part of the rind, working from top to bottom of the orange. **3** Cut into the center of the peeled orange between one section and the membrane. Cut along the other side of the section next to the membrane, freeing each section. If you prefer, work over a bowl to catch the juices.

Pears

You'll get the juiciest, finest-textured pears during the fall, their peak season. Want the simplest autumn appetizer ever? Put out a platter of ripe pear wedges, blue cheese, and walnuts. You'll be wildly applauded.

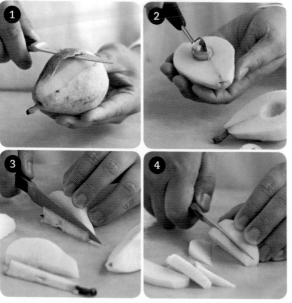

Look for pears that are fresh and firm and without bruises or cuts. The ripeness test depends on the variety. Green Bartletts turn bright yellow and red Bartletts turn a brilliant red. To test ripeness for other varieties, gently press near the stem end—if it yields, it's ready to eat. Be careful—they bruise easily.

Store unripe pears at room temperature until ripe. To ripen pears more quickly, place in a paper bag and check daily. Keep ripe pears in the refrigerator for up to 5 days. Refrigeration slows ripening.

Pears brown quickly once they're peeled and cut; to slow browning, dip the cut surfaces in a mixture of lemon juice and water.

1 Before cutting, thoroughly rinse pears. If desired, peel pears. Use a paring knife to remove the skin. One technique is to start cutting at the stem end and cut toward the blossom end. **2** To remove the core from pears while leaving the pear half intact, use a melon baller to scoop out the seeds, then cut away the stem. **3** To remove the core if cutting up the pear, cut peeled or unpeeled pear in half, then cut each half in half again and cut away the center core. **4** To slice or chop the pear, place cored peeled or unpeeled quarters side by side and thinly slice, then chop if desired.

Pear Math: 1 medium pear = 1 cup sliced or chopped

Pick pineapples that look fresh and have top leaves that are green, not brown. They should have a fragrant aroma and should be plump and heavy for their size. Avoid those with bruises or soft spots or that are dry and old looking. Handle them gently; ripe pineapples bruise easily.

Pineapple Math: 1 medium pineapple (4 pounds) = 4½ cups peeled and cubed

How do I cut up a pineapple?

1 Before cutting, thoroughly rinse pineapple and scrub with a clean produce brush. Use a knife to cut off the bottom stem end and the green top crown of the pineapple. **2** Stand the pineapple on one end and slice off the peel in strips from top to bottom. If desired, make narrow wedge-shape grooves into the pineapple to remove as many "eyes" as possible. **3** With the peeled pineapple standing on end, cut it into four pieces from top to bottom. Then cut the fruit away from the core on each quarter; discard core. **4** Cut the quarters into spears or chunks or chop the pineapple into desired pieces.

Pineapples

If you've never tasted a fresh pineapple, you're in for a treat. Store a fresh whole pineapple in the refrigerator for up to 2 days. If you cut up the pineapple, place it in a tightly covered container and chill it in the refrigerator for up to another day or two.

Asparagus

How do you know it's spring? When the weather warms, the flowers bloom, and the best asparagus of the year appears in the supermarket. The season's first crop is the thinnest and most tender.

Other than eating asparagus at the peak of its season, there are a few other ways to ensure you get the good stuff. Choose asparagus spears that are crisp, straight, and firm with tightly closed tips. They should have good color (whether that's green or white). Avoid wilted asparagus. Pick spears that are the same size so that they will cook more evenly.

Store asparagus in the refrigerator. It tastes best if it's cooked the same day you buy it, but you can store it for a little while. Wrap the bases of the spears in wet paper towels and place in a plastic bag or in your refrigerator's crisper. For best quality, store in the refrigerator for up to 3 days.

Before you cook it, wash it well. Asparagus is grown in sandy soil—and you don't want to eat grit along with this delicately flavored vegetable. It also has a woody lower stem that you don't want to eat—it's really fibrous. There is a point in the stem at which it will easily snap, leaving the woody part behind. If the lower end of the stem still seems tough, you can remove the outer layer of that bottom part of the stem with a vegetable peeler. If you find yourself loving asparagus, consider an asparagus steamer. It's a special pot with a basket insert so you can cook a bunch of asparagus upright. It cooks the stems in boiling water and lightly steams the tender tips.

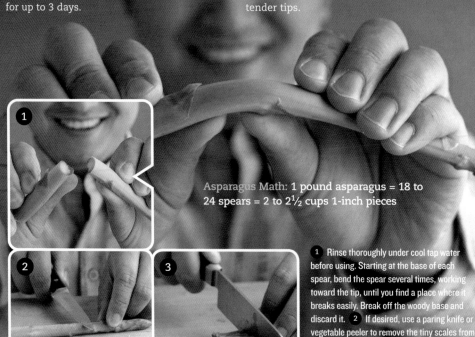

Asparagus Math: 1 pound asparagus = 18 to 24 spears = 2 to $2\frac{1}{2}$ cups 1-inch pieces

1 Rinse thoroughly under cool tap water before using. Starting at the base of each spear, bend the spear several times, working toward the tip, until you find a place where it breaks easily. Break off the woody base and discard it. **2** If desired, use a paring knife or vegetable peeler to remove the tiny scales from each stalk. **3** Leave spears whole or line up the tips of several spears on a cutting surface. Starting at the tip ends, cut the spears into bite-size pieces about 1 inch long, using a small chef's knife (such as a santoku).

Roasted Asparagus (*see recipe, page 125*)

Avocado

They're so creamy and rich, you hardly know you're eating a fruit when you eat an avocado. Look for those that are not bruised or overly soft and that have no gouges or broken skin. Choose very firm avocados if you won't be using them for 3 or 4 days or ripe avocados if you plan to use them immediately. Firm, ripe avocados that are ready to eat and good for slicing yield to gentle pressure when cradled in your hands. A very ripe avocado feels soft (but not too soft) and is good for mashing.

Store avocados at room temperature until they ripen, then refrigerate and use within 3 days. Refrigeration slows ripening. To ripen avocados more quickly, put them in a brown paper bag with an apple or banana.

1 Rinse the avocado under cool tap water. Use a knife to make a lengthwise cut around the seed, cutting through the fruit and skin.

2 Holding the avocado in your hands, gently twist the two halves in opposite directions to separate them.

3 To remove the seed, use a quick, hard motion to whack the blade of the knife into the pit; twist and pull to remove it.

4 On a cutting surface, cut each half in half again and peel away the skin from each of the quarters using your fingers or a small knife.

Broccoli

Broccoli is one of those vegetables that is equally good raw or cooked. However you plan to eat it, you clean and prepare it the same way—and of course you want the best you can find. Pick bunches of broccoli that have firm stems and dark green or purplish green heads that are packed tightly and whose florets (the little tiny flowerlike buds in the heads) are tightly closed. Pass up broccoli with heads that are light green or yellowing—that means its time has come and gone.

Wash broccoli right before you plan to use it. Store unwashed broccoli in a covered container or bag in the refrigerator for up to 4 days.

Broccoli Math:
1 pound broccoli =
4 cups florets

1 Rinse broccoli thoroughly under cool tap water and drain. Lay a broccoli stem on a cutting surface and cut off the stem end with a small chef's knife.

2 If the stems seem tough, use a knife to peel away the tough outer portion. Use your hands to break apart the stem into large clusters of florets.

3 If desired, use a small knife to cut up the larger broccoli clusters into smaller florets.

Carrots

When you need a quick veggie fix, there's nothing easier than grabbing a crunchy carrot. Carrots keep well and are a good thing to have in the crisper. Choose well-shaped, straight, rigid, bright orange carrots that aren't cracked and dried out and that don't have tiny rootlets growing off the sides. Carrots are generally sold without tops; however, if you buy them with tops attached, be sure the tops look fresh and are not wilted or slimy. Generally carrots with tops (like radishes that have their greens attached) are a little fresher and sweeter tasting than those without. Also the more slender the carrots, the sweeter they are. Store carrots (without tops) in a plastic bag in the refrigerator for up to 2 weeks.

1 Rinse carrots under cool tap water and scrub with a clean produce brush. Use a vegetable peeler to remove peel. Trim off tip and stem end. (Peeling is optional.)

2 To slice carrots, use a small chef's knife. If carrots are small, you might be able to line up several side by side on a cutting surface, then cut into 1/4-inch slices.

3 To make julienne sticks, cut carrot crosswise in half or thirds. Make lengthwise cuts into 1/4-inch slices. Stack slices and cut lengthwise strips 1/8 to 1/4 inch wide.

4 To cut chunks for dishes such as stew, cut large carrots in half lengthwise; place the flat side on a cutting surface and cut crosswise into chunks. You don't need to halve thinner carrots.

4

Carrot Math:
1 pound carrots = 6 to 8 medium carrots
1 medium carrot = 1/2 cup sliced, chopped, julienned, or finely shredded

Cauliflower

This knobby, crunchy veggie is delicious steamed or roasted. Choose a head of cauliflower that is solid and heavy for its size. It should be creamy white with no brown bruises or speckles. The leaves should be green, crisp, and fresh looking, not yellow or withered.

1 Rinse the head of cauliflower thoroughly under cool tap water. Snap or cut off the lower green leaves and discard.

2 Cut off the stem. Remove core with the knife. If you want the head whole, angle the blade to avoid cutting into the florets. Or cut the head in half and cut out the core from each half.

3 Use your hands to break the head into large clusters of florets.

4 For smaller florets, use a paring knife to cut the clusters of florets into bite-size pieces.

Celery

The delicate flavor of celery adds so much to soups, sauces, and stuffing. Eaten raw, it satisfies the need for something crunchy to munch on. To get the best, most beautiful celery, choose a bunch of crisp, firm, shiny stalks (sometimes called ribs). Look for unblemished stalks that are not cracked. The leaves that are attached should be fresh and green, not yellow and droopy.

Packaged celery hearts are the tender innermost stalks of celery.

Store celery in a plastic bag or container in the refrigerator for up to 2 weeks. Celery freezes easily so don't store in the coldest part of the refrigerator.

If you don't like the strings, run a vegetable peeler down the back of the stalk.

Celery Math:
1 stalk celery =
½ cup sliced
or chopped

1 To remove stalks from the bunch, break away one stalk at a time from the base and rinse thoroughly under cool tap water to remove dirt and sand. Cut off the leaves.

2 To make slices, use a small chef's knife on a cutting surface to trim off the base. Place the stalk, hollow side down, and cut across the stalk into slices of desired thickness.

3 To chop celery into smaller pieces, cut each stalk into three lengthwise narrow strips.

4 Line up the strips side by side and cut them across into the desired size.

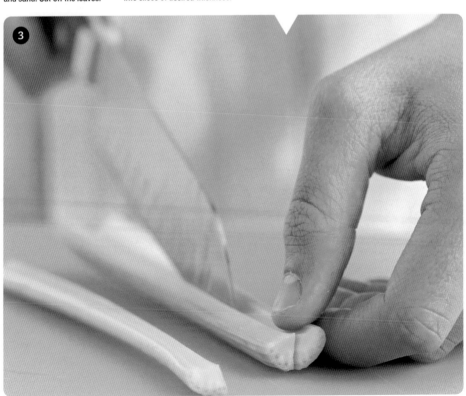

How do I peel and mince garlic?

1 To peel a garlic clove, press down on the unpeeled clove using the heel of your hand placed on the flat side of a broad-bladed knife. This loosens the papery skin.

2 Use your fingers to peel off the skin. Cut off the tough stem end with a knife.

3 To mince garlic, use a chef's knife to make lengthwise cuts through the clove, then cut the strips crosswise into tiny pieces. Anchor the knife tip to the cutting board and use a rocking motion to cut the pieces into yet smaller pieces.

4 Another method for mincing or crushing the garlic is to use a garlic press. Place an unpeeled garlic clove in the press and force it through the tiny holes. (For some presses, you'll need to remove the peel first.)

Garlic Math: **1 clove garlic = ½ teaspoon minced = ⅛ teaspoon garlic powder**

Clove of garlic

Bulb or head of garlic

Garlic

You don't even want to think about what food would taste like without garlic. It has to be one of the best flavors on the planet. It starts out strong when it's raw and mellows and sweetens as it cooks.

There is no substitute for fresh garlic. Jars of minced garlic are convenient, but you'll get the best flavor if you buy a bulb of garlic and prepare your own. Pick bulbs that are firm and plump. Their skin should be papery and dry.

Store garlic in a cool, dry, dark place such as a brown paper bag in the pantry or a garlic keeper on the counter. Leave the bulbs whole so that the individual cloves won't dry out quickly. Garlic can be stored for up to several months.

Ginger

Along with onions and garlic, ginger is considered an aromatic—it adds great flavor to food, whether it's an Asian-style stir-fry or a gingerbread cake.

Look for fresh ginger (sometimes called gingerroot) that is firm and has smooth, slightly shiny, fresh-looking skin that isn't shriveled or wrinkled. Store unpeeled ginger loosely wrapped in a paper towel in the refrigerator for up to a week. Or wrap the unpeeled piece of ginger in plastic wrap and store in the freezer for up to several months. You can grate or cut off what you need from the frozen root.

Preparing: To prepare fresh ginger, rinse thoroughly under cool tap water. Cut off one end of the root and use a vegetable peeler or sharp knife to remove the thin brown peel, cutting away from your hand.

Mincing: To mince or finely chop the peeled fresh ginger on a cutting surface, cut lengthwise slices with the grain of the root. Stack the slices and cut slices into narrow strips. Cut across the pile of tiny strips into very tiny pieces using a small chef's knife.

Grating: To grate the fresh peeled ginger, rub a piece of ginger across a fine grating surface. You can use a grater as shown or a special ginger grater. To save on cleanup, grate onto a piece of waxed paper.

Stripping: Thoroughly rinse fresh herbs under cool water. Blot dry with paper towels or use a salad spinner. Remove tiny leaves of herbs such as thyme from the stem by holding onto the stem with one hand and stripping the leaves into a bowl using the other hand.

Snipping: To cut larger clean and dry fresh herbs, place leaves in a measuring cup or bowl and snip them with kitchen scissors, using short, quick strokes. For herbs with tough stems, as with rosemary, strip the leaves from the stem first.

Chiffonade: A chiffonade is bunch of thin strips or shreds. To create a chiffonade of herbs, roll up larger leaves, such as basil, and cut across the roll. This works for shredding spinach leaves too.

Storing: To store fresh herbs, cut a ½ inch from the stems. Stand stem ends in a small jar with some water. Loosely cover leaves with a plastic bag and store in the refrigerator. (Don't refrigerate basil—it may blacken.) Discard wilted leaves as they appear.

Sage

Italian (flat-leaf) parsley

Basil

Thyme

Oregano

Rosemary

Cilantro

Herb Math (in an emergency):
1 tablespoon snipped fresh herb =
1 teaspoon dried leaf herb

Herbs

Fresh herbs add spark and life to food. Choose herbs that have fresh-looking leaves without brown spots. Fresh herbs are highly perishable, so buy as you need them—or, better yet, grow them in your garden or in a pot on your windowsill.

Leeks & Green Onions

Mild green onions (sometimes called scallions) are delicious sauteed in butter but are most often used raw as a final topping or garnish. Buy green onions that have fresh-looking green tops and clean white ends. Leeks look like large green onions but have a more distinctive flavor. The leaves of leeks should also be crisp and healthy looking. Leeks that are 1½ inches or smaller in diameter are more tender than larger leeks. Wash them well before using.

How do I slice and clean leeks?

1 Using a chef's knife and a cutting surface, cut a thin slice from the root end of the leek. Cut off the dark green leaves and remove any wilted outer leaves. Continue cutting into slices.

2 To wash, rinse leek slices in a colander under cool running water. Drain leeks on paper towels.

3 Or, to cut a leek lengthwise, cut all the way through the root end.

4 To wash, hold the leek halves under the faucet with the root ends up. Rinse leek under cool running water, separating and lifting the leaves with your fingers to make sure that all the dirt is flushed out and removed.

Green Onion & Leek Math
1 medium green onion = 2 tablespoons sliced
1 medium leek = ⅓ cup sliced

How do I slice green onions?

1 Rinse onions under cool tap water and remove any wilted or damaged tops or slimy skins on the white parts. Trim off the root ends and about 2 inches from the green tops. Lay several onions on a cutting surface and cut across into slices. **2** For larger pieces, line up the trimmed onions and cut into 1-inch or longer pieces.

Shiitake mushroom

These have a meaty flavor and texture. Discard the rough stems and use only the caps of this variety.

White mushrooms

These are all-purpose mushrooms with a mild, woodsy flavor; small ones sometimes are called button mushrooms.

Cremini mushroom

Similar to white mushroom creminis have an earthier flavor and a tan to rich brown color. They are also called brown mushrooms.

Portobello mushrooms

These hearty and meaty mushrooms come in large, medium, and small sizes.

Mushrooms

These lowly fungi add a meaty texture and earthy flavor to so much good food. What would pizza, red sauce, and grilled steak be without mushrooms?

If you're foraging for mushrooms in the produce aisle of your supermarket, freshness is key. Here's how to tell if mushrooms are fresh: They'll be firm, plump, and free from bruises with no visible moisture on the outside. Steer clear of slimy or spotted mushrooms. On white mushrooms—the most common type, also called button mushrooms—the gills on the underside of the mushrooms should be tightly closed. Once you get fresh mushrooms home, store them, unwashed, in the refrigerator for up to 2 days in a paper bag or the original packaging. Don't store mushrooms in a plastic bag or they will deteriorate more quickly—they need to breathe. Wash them right before you intend to use them according to the method shown below.

Mushroom Math: 8 ounces = 3 cups sliced or chopped

How do I clean and slice fresh mushrooms?

1 The best way to clean fresh mushrooms is to use a damp paper towel or a soft mushroom brush and wipe them one at a time. Or lightly rinse the mushrooms and gently pat dry with paper towels. (Don't soak mushrooms. They will become waterlogged.) **2** After cleaning, trim thin slices from the ends of the stems before using a knife to cut mushrooms into halves or quarters on a cutting surface—or slice or chop as needed.

Onions

If the French—who know a thing or two about cooking—can build an entire soup around the onion, there has to be something to its popularity. The onion's strong, sweet flavor enhances so many dishes.

But not just any old onion will do. Choose those that are firm, are heavy for their size, and have papery outer skins and short necks. They should be free of blemishes and soft spots. Avoid those that are starting to sprout. You'll find spring/summer onions (March through August) have a milder, sweeter, and less pungent flavor than fall/winter storage onions (August through April). The fall/winter storage onions have thicker, darker outer skins and a more pungent flavor. Spring/summer onions have thin, light-color outer skins, a higher water content, and are more delicate.

In general you don't want to refrigerate onions. Store them loosely (not too packed) in a container in a cool, dry, well-ventilated place for several weeks. Since spring/summer onions are more delicate, they have a fairly short storage life and sometimes are refrigerated to stay their best.

Does chopping onions make you weep? You're not alone. Here's a trick: Put the onion in the freezer for 20 minutes before you chop it. Freezing it will cut down on the sulfuric compounds the cut onion releases into the air. (It's the stuff that makes you cry.)

Red onions
Pretty in purple-red, these generally have a sharp but sweet flavor; they add great color when used fresh.

White onions
These often have a sharp flavor; smaller varieties include pearl onions (about ½ inch in diameter) and boiling onions (⅞ to 1½ inches in diameter).

Shallots
The flavor of a shallot is kind of a cross between onion and garlic. Though they tend to lean more to the milder flavor of onion, they grow more like garlic—in heads that contain two or three large cloves wrapped in papery skins. You can use shallots the same way you use onions. Store shallots in a cool, dry place for up to a month.

How do I chop an onion?

1 Rinse the onion thoroughly under cool tap water. To chop an onion, use a chef's knife to slice off the stem and root ends on a cutting surface.

2 Remove the papery outer skins. Cut the onion in half from top end to root end.

3 Place each onion half, flat side down, on the cutting surface and make side-by-side vertical slices from stem end to root end. Holding the slices together, cut across the slices, making tiny pieces.

Slicing and Wedging

1 To slice a peeled onion, place it on its side and use a chef's knife to cut it crosswise, making slices as thin as desired. Discard the top and root end slices. **2** To make wedges, cut the onion in half from stem end to root end. Place the flat side of a half down and cut from end to end, angling toward the center to make desired-size wedges.

Yellow onions
These are the most common type of onion; they're full of flavor and are most often used for cooking.

Onion Math:
1 small onion = ⅓ cup chopped
1 medium onion = ½ cup chopped
1 large onion = 1 cup chopped

Peppers

Peppers are bold in many ways. Mild-tasting sweet peppers come in eye-popping shades of green, orange, yellow, and red. And hot peppers—with their wide range of heat levels—add a touch of fire to food.

All peppers—whether they're sweet or hot (also called chile peppers)—are botanically in the *Capsicum* family. So when you're buying either type, you want to look for the same things. Pick peppers that are glossy, have bright color, and are a good shape for the variety (see the photos, below). Steer clear of peppers that are shriveled or bruised or have soft spots.

Refrigerate sweet peppers, covered, for up to 5 days.

Store most chile peppers in the refrigerator, unwashed and wrapped in paper towels in a plastic bag, for up to 10 days. (There is an exception. Serrano chiles shouldn't be stored in plastic but instead kept in the vegetable crisper.) Wash sweet or hot peppers right before you use them. Rinse them thoroughly and scrub with a clean produce brush, then prep as needed. Chile peppers take a bit of extra precaution (see "Hot Stuff," below).

Hot Stuff

When working with fresh chile peppers, wear disposable plastic or rubber gloves. Chiles contain volatile oils that can burn your skin and eyes; avoid contact with them as much as possible. If your bare hands do touch the chiles, wash your hands and nails well with soap and hot water. If you get some of the oils in your eyes, flush them with cool water. Cut the chiles in half; remove seeds and membrane, then cut up. The seeds and membrane are the hottest parts of the pepper; some people choose to leave them in because they like the heat.

Hot

A Poblano chile

B Banana wax pepper

C Serrano chile

D Red serrano

E Jalapeño chile

Sweet

F Green sweet pepper

F Orange sweet pepper

F Red sweet pepper

F Yellow sweet pepper

A Poblano chile—dark green; flavor ranges from mild to medium hot **B** Banana wax pepper—also called Hungarian wax; has a milder flavor than some chile peppers **C** Serrano chile—flavor ranges from very hot to extremely hot (green skin turns red as pepper ripens) **D** Red serrano chile **E** Jalapeño chile—round tip; flavor ranges from medium hot to hot **F** Sweet peppers—green, yellow, red, and orange; sometimes called bell peppers because of their bell-like shape

1 To remove seeds and stem from sweet peppers, hold the pepper upright on a cutting surface. Slice each of the sides using a sharp knife. You should have 4 large flat pieces that are free of seeds and stem. (Stem, seeds, and ribs should all be in one unit you can discard.) If there is enough pepper left, trim it from the seeds and ribs.

2 To cut into strips, cut larger flat pieces into lengthwise or crosswise pieces.

3 To chop, line up the strips on a cutting surface; cut across strips into the size you want.

Potatoes

There are few foods that provide as much comfort as the humble potato. Ever crave a simple baked potato? Has a plate of Mom's mashed ever made something right that was wrong? Potatoes are a good thing to have around the house. Here's how to get the best ones: Choose those that have smooth, unblemished skins, have a firm texture, and are a good shape for the variety. Avoid those that are soft, moldy, shriveled, or green (see below). Store potatoes, unwashed, in a cool, well-ventilated, dark place for up to several weeks. If kept at room temperature, use within a week. (Don't refrigerate potatoes—they tend to get sweet.)

Russet potatoes
These are fluffy when cooked. They have netted dark brown skin and are good for baking, mashing, and french fries.

Sweet potatoes
These have pale yellow to dark orange flesh that's not as sweet as yams, which are deeper in color.

Round white potatoes
These have firm, waxy flesh and hold their shape well after cooking. They are an all-purpose potato but are especially good in salads.

Red round potatoes
This is also a potato with firm, waxy flesh. Red potatoes have a moist texture and are good for salads, boiling, roasting, and steaming.

Yellow round potatoes
These all-purpose potatoes have a creamy texture when cooked. Yukon gold is a popular variety.

New red potatoes
New potatoes are simply young, thin-skinned potatoes that are harvested before they're mature; they can be of any variety.

Yukon gold potatoes
This yellow-flesh potato has a creamy texture; it's a good all-purpose potato.

Nice to Know

Avoid buying potatoes that have green on them (see potato on the right). Green coloring on the skin is a buildup of solanine in the potato, which is caused when potatoes are exposed to too much light. Solanine gives potatoes a bitter flavor and can be harmful if too much is eaten.

Potato Math: 1 pound potatoes = 3 cups cubed, unpeeled, or 2¾ cups cubed, peeled

Potatoes are one of nature's most perfect foods. They can be creamy or crispy—mashed, baked, boiled, roasted, or fried. Check out the different kinds, left, to see which ones are best for which purpose.

Peeling: Rinse thoroughly and scrub potatoes with a clean produce brush. If desired, use a vegetable peeler or paring knife to remove the skin, cutting away from your hand.

Cubing: To cube or chop unpeeled or peeled potatoes, slice potatoes into desired thickness, depending on the size of cubes or pieces you want. Stack several slices and cut across several times in both directions.

Removing Eyes: To remove eyes or sprouts, cut them out using the tip of the vegetable peeler or use a small sharp knife.

Slicing: After removing the eyes, place potato on a cutting surface and use a small chef's knife to slice the unpeeled or peeled potatoes.

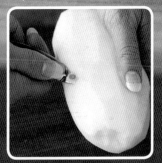

Tomatoes

In a salad, on a sandwich, or cooked into a sauce, tomatoes are one of nature's most delicious and versatile fruits (yes, technically, they're a fruit).

A good tomato is a beautiful thing; a bad one is a real bummer. Pick ripe or not quite ripe tomatoes that feel heavy for their size and that are well shaped and plump (not bruised, cracked, or soft). A ripe tomato yields to slight pressure and smells like a tomato. Store tomatoes at room temperature out of direct sunlight until ripened and then up to 3 days in a cool place. Don't refrigerate whole tomatoes; it changes their flavor and makes them mushy and mealy. (Cut tomatoes should be refrigerated and used as soon as possible.)

Slicing: To slice a cored tomato, use a serrated knife to cut away very thin slices from stem and bottom ends; slice tomato into desired thickness.

Wedging: To cut cored tomatoes into wedges, halve the tomato. Place, cut side down, on a cutting surface. Using the serrated knife, cut at an angle into wedges.

Seeding: To remove seeds from cored wedges or halves, hold tomato over a bowl and use the tip of a spoon to scoop away the seeds.

Chopping: To chop tomatoes, core, seed if desired, and cut into narrow slices from stem end to bottom. Holding slices together, cut across the slices into desired pieces.

Roma tomato
(also called plum tomato)

Common tomato

Red cherry tomato

Grape tomato

Nice to Know

Commercially dried tomatoes have an intense flavor and a chewy texture and are available in halves or pieces. Some are packed dry and others are packed in olive oil. Look for these products in the produce section or with canned tomato products in the supermarket. Follow package directions for preparing dried tomatoes. If there are no directions, cover dried tomatoes with boiling water; let stand about 20 minutes or until pliable. Drain well and pat dry. Use a kitchen scissors to snip into pieces.

Some people love tomatoes so much they want to eat them year-round, but the best time to buy tomatoes is when they're sweet, juicy, and in season—at the height of summer. For the best year-round tomatoes, buy roma tomatoes.

Tomato Math: **1 medium tomato = $\frac{1}{2}$ cup peeled, seeded, and chopped**

Zucchini & Yellow Squash

Although it's available year-round, the best time to enjoy summer squash such as zucchini and yellow squash is—you guessed it—during the summer. Green or yellow, it's great sauteed or grilled.

Intro to Cooking

Summer squash is differentiated from winter squash (see page 56) by its thin skin, soft seeds, and high water content. Summer squash takes very little time to cook. Choose summer squash that are firm, heavy for their size, and free of cuts and soft spots. Don't panic over a few blemishes: Since they are so tender skinned, sometimes the exteriors aren't perfect. Smaller squash are more delicately flavored than larger ones. Avoid summer squash that is shriveled.

Store wrapped summer squash in the refrigerator for up to 5 days.

Cleaning: Rinse thoroughly under cool tap water. No need to peel summer squash. Using a chef's knife, cut a slice off the stem end (along with the stem) and blossom end. For larger summer squash, cut squash in half lengthwise through the center.

Slicing: To slice, place halved squash, flat side down, on a cutting surface and make crosswise slices that are about ¼ inch thick. Or, for smaller squash, don't halve; just cut across into rounds.

Julienne: To make julienne sticks, trim ends and cut squash into 2- to 3-inch chunks. Cut into ¼-inch slices. Stack slices and cut into lengthwise sticks.

Zucchini
These are usually slender and elongated with green skin; the smaller the zucchini, the thinner its skin.

Yellow squash
These are available straight neck (shown) or crookneck. Both have bright yellow skin and off-white flesh.

Winter Squash

At the end of the long growing season, your patience is rewarded with something sweet: a crop of squash with gorgeous color and sugary flesh.

Winter squash starts appearing in the markets in the fall. It's differentiated from summer squash (see pages 54 and 55) by its hard shell, hard seeds, and meaty flesh. Select winter squash that is firm, has a dull sheen, and feels heavy for its size. Avoid those with soft spots or cracks. The stem, if it's still on the squash, should be rounded and dry.

Store unwashed winter squash in a cool, dry, well-ventilated place for up to 2 months. If you buy a cut piece of a larger squash, store it, wrapped, in the refrigerator for up to 4 days.

1 Thoroughly rinse squash (this one's butternut) under cool tap water and scrub with a clean produce brush. Cut off the stem end of the squash with a large chef's knife.

2 Cut squash in half lengthwise through the neck and down to the bottom using a large chef's knife. Use a large spoon to remove the seeds and fibrous material from each half of the squash.

3 To peel winter squash before cubing or slicing, start with a seeded squash half. Use a sturdy vegetable peeler to cut off long strips of the peel, cutting away from you. The squash can then be cut into cubes for cooking.

Baking a squash: If you're baking a whole squash (this one's acorn), simply trim the stem and bottom ends and scoop out the seeds. After it's baked you can easily remove the soft cooked flesh from the hard rind.

Spaghetti squash
This squash is named for the long, toothsome spaghettilike strands you can pull with a fork from the cooked squash.

Winter Squash Math: 2 pounds acorn or butternut winter squash = 4 cups chopped or 2 cups mashed

Acorn squash
This has a deep, furrowed, acorn-shape shell that can be green, gold, or white.

Butternut squash
This deep-orange-fleshed squash has a tan-color shell and a bulbous bottom.

Cooking Techniques & Tricks

Every discipline has its fundamentals. This section covers all of the basic skills you need to know to start cooking—and to keep cooking better and better.

You've heard the phrase: You have to walk before you can run. The same concept can be applied to cooking. Before you decide to dive in and bake a cake or stir up a big pot of soup, you might want to know the best way to measure flour or crack an egg—or the difference between minced garlic and chopped garlic. Those techniques—plus a lot more—are spelled out, step-by-step, in this section.

Just Ask

More often than not—because recipe writers want recipes to be as short and streamlined as possible—not absolutely every detail is spelled out. There are a few assumptions made about how some things are done. Language is sometimes trimmed from a recipe to keep it from becoming gargantuan. It may, for example, call for "½ cup almonds, toasted." But that may leave you wondering: "How do I toast almonds?" (See page 65.) Or it may call for "2 cloves garlic, minced." Again: "What does minced look like?" (See page 64.)

If you have a question on a technique, this section will answer it.

Timing Is Everything
One of the most challenging things about cooking is timing everything right so your whole meal is ready at the same time. Getting it right comes with experience, but if you're unsure, start with the time you want to eat. Carefully read through the recipes and back up the time you have to start cooking each dish from that time—then add the prep time too.

Dinner @ 7:00

Chicken Thighs and Orzo
Roasted Asparagus
Phyllo Cups with honey filling and berries

5:30 pm Start all prep work
6:00   Bake phyllo cups
          Start chicken
6:30   Simmer chicken
          Trim asparagus
6:45   Put asparagus in oven
7:00   EAT !!

7:30   Make honey filling
8:10   Fill phyllo cups
8:15   DESSERT !!

Safety Concerns

The kitchen is a happy place, but it's also a place that bears some caution. Not only are there fire, hot liquid, and sharp objects involved in cooking, but the food you're preparing can present health and safety issues. Read through the information on Kitchen Safety (page 82) and Food Safety (pages 83 and 84) to keep your cooking experience injury- and illness-free.

Be Prepared

There is a French cooking term, mise en place, that translates into "setting in place." It means that before you start cooking, all of your ingredients should be prepped, washed, chopped, and measured so once you start cooking, you don't have to stop. Makes things go smoothly.

How do I measure things?

Although it's crucial to measure ingredients precisely when baking, learning to accurately measure for any kind of cooking helps ensure optimum results.

The first step to proper measuring is having the right tools. Check out page 11 for the specifics, but here's the most fundamental thing to know: Use dry measuring cups for dry ingredients and liquid measuring cups for liquids.

It's especially important when measuring flour to fluff it a little by gently stirring it with a spoon before spooning it into the cup. Use a spatula/spreader or a knife to level it rather than shaking off the excess. Shaking compacts the flour and you'll have too much.

Eventually—except for when you're baking—you won't have to measure everything. You'll have a feel for how much oil to add to the skillet when sauteeing or how much salt to add to the soup to season it.

Measuring Math:

3 teaspoons = 1 tablespoon
16 tablespoons = 1 cup
1 tablespoon = $\frac{1}{2}$ fluid ounce
1 cup = $\frac{1}{2}$ pint = 8 fluid ounces

Flour

Before measuring, stir through the flour in the canister to loosen it. Lightly spoon flour into a dry measuring cup, then level it off with a spatula or knife.

Brown Sugar
Spoon brown sugar into a dry measuring cup. Pack it firmly into the cup until it is level.

Shortening
Spoon shortening into a dry measuring cup. Pack it firmly into the cup and level off the top.

Liquids
Measure liquids into glass measuring cups. Get at eye level with the cup and fill just to the measuring line.

Butter
Butter sticks have tablespoon markings on the wrapper—8 per stick. Just cut off what you need.

What does it mean when a recipe calls for softened butter?

Most recipes for baked goods such as cookies and cakes start out with butter being beaten in a bowl with an electric mixer. This is difficult to do if the butter is cold and hard right from the refrigerator. You'll wind up with lumps of butter instead of smooth, whipped butter that easily incorporates with the remaining ingredients. If you've forgotten to set the butter out to soften, you can speed-soften it this way: Put it in a microwave-safe dish; microwave on 30 percent power (defrost) for 15 seconds. Check and repeat, if necessary. Don't let it melt though.

Butter Math:
4 tablespoons = $\frac{1}{4}$ cup
$\frac{1}{2}$ stick = $\frac{1}{4}$ cup
1 stick = $\frac{1}{2}$ cup

Cold Butter
Cold butter is firm and slices easily. Use it when the recipe just calls for "butter" in the ingredient list.

Softened Butter
Softened butter has been allowed to come to room temperature. It is spreadable and blends easily into recipes.

Melted Butter
It's for more than just popcorn! Melted butter is sometimes used instead of cooking oil in a recipe.

How do I make sweetened whipped cream?

Easy. Forget the canned stuff; fresh is so much better.

1 In a chilled mixing bowl combine 1 cup whipping cream, 2 tablespoons sugar, and $\frac{1}{2}$ teaspoon vanilla. Beat with an electric mixer on medium speed until soft peaks form (tips curl). **2** If desired, add one of the following with the vanilla: $\frac{1}{2}$ teaspoon finely shredded citrus peel; 2 tablespoons unsweetened cocoa powder plus 1 tablespoon sugar; 2 tablespoons amaretto, coffee, or hazelnut liqueur; or $\frac{1}{4}$ teaspoon ground cinnamon, nutmeg, or ginger.

How do I keep baked goods from sticking to the pan?

There's nothing much worse than having a home-made cake stuck in the pan. Here's how to ensure yours pop out, beautifully intact, every time.

There are three ways to get baked goods to release easily from a pan. The first one is to grease the pan with solid shortening, butter, or nonstick cooking spray and then line it with waxed paper—a method used mostly for cakes. The second, used most often for brownies, bar cookies, and fudge, is to line the pan with foil, leaving some hanging over the edge. The additional advantage of this method is that it allows you to easily lift the bars out of the pan before cutting them. The third method, also used mostly for cakes, is to grease or butter and then flour the pan. Follow the directions for preparing the pan in the recipe you're making.

How to line a pan with waxed paper

1 Grease the bottom and sides of the pan with shortening. Set the pan on a piece of waxed paper and trace around the pan with a pencil.

2 With a clean pair of kitchen scissors, cut just inside the traced line on the paper.

3 Fit the cut piece of waxed paper in the pan, pressing it into the corners and smoothing out any wrinkles or bubbles.

How to line a pan with foil

1 Tear a piece of foil that is larger than the pan. Shape the foil over the outside of the pan bottom. Cut slits at the corners to make it fit neatly.

2 Gently lift the shaped foil off of the pan.

3 Turn the pan over and fit the shaped foil into it. Leave an inch or two of overhang to use as "handles" to lift the baked good out of the pan.

How to grease and flour a pan

1 With a pastry brush or paper towel, brush shortening evenly over the bottom of the pan, taking care not to leave any uncoated shiny spots.

2 When greasing the sides and corners of the pan, turn the pan on that end so you can better see what you're doing. You don't have to go all of the way to the top of the pan.

3 When the pan is completely greased, sprinkle a couple of spoonfuls of all-purpose flour in the bottom of it.

4 To distribute the flour over the pan, hold it on one edge and rap the other with your free hand. The flour will "skate" over the greased surface and stick to it. When the pan bottom is coated, tilt the pan, tapping it to move the flour over the sides. Tap out any extra flour into the sink.

How do I work with eggs?

Eggs are one of nature's simplest and most perfect foods. Boiling or frying them is easy—using them in recipes requires a little know-how for best results.

When buying eggs, do a quick once-over to check for any broken ones, but there are a few other things you should look for too. Be sure the shells are clean and check the packing date (a number from 1 to 365, with 1 representing January 1 and 365 representing December 31) on the carton. The eggs can be refrigerated for up to 5 weeks after that date.

Some recipes call for eggs to be at room temperature. Let the eggs sit on the counter for 30 minutes before using them. Also, although you may like to live on the edge, don't eat foods that contain raw eggs—you'll risk getting salmonella poisoning. If a recipe calls for raw or undercooked eggs (like Caesar salad or homemade ice cream), use pasteurized eggs.

1 Beat egg whites in a clean glass or metal bowl. Even a speck of fat (including the yolk) can prevent proper whipping.

2 For soft peaks, beat with a mixer on medium speed until the egg whites form peaks with tips that curl when beaters are lifted.

3 For stiff peaks, beat on high speed until egg whites form peaks with tips that stand straight when the beaters are lifted.

4 Oops! This is what happens when you overbeat egg whites—they get lumpy and won't blend in with other ingredients.

Whether an egg is brown or white depends on the breed of the hen that laid it. There is no nutritional or flavor difference. What you choose comes down to your sense of aesthetics.

1

2

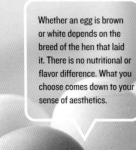

3

1 To crack an egg, tap it firmly on the edge of a bowl or on a flat countertop. Pull the shell open with your thumbs. Don't let any shell get into the raw eggs (see Trick #8, page 80). **2** When separating the yolk and white, use an egg separator. A slotted spoon also works well for this task. **3** Beat a whole egg in a bowl with a fork. It's considered lightly beaten when it's pale yellow with no streaks of white or yolk.

How do I combine wet and dry ingredients?

Believe it or not, it's not just a matter of stirring; how they come together can make or break your recipe.

When you make muffins, pancakes, waffles, or quick breads such as banana bread, you want the result to be tender and fine grained. The best way to ensure this is to not overmix your batter, which produces a tough texture. Here's how to do it right: Once your dry ingredients (flour, leavening, salt) are stirred together, make a well in the center. Then, when your wet ingredients (eggs, milk, oil) are thoroughly combined, gently pour them into the well you've made in the dry ingredients. The best tool for mixing is a rubber scraper. Start by running the scraper around the edge of the bowl, gently knocking the dry ingredients into the center. Reach to the bottom of the bowl and pull the dry ingredients over and into the wet ingredients. Stop when the mixture is just barely combined. It's okay—good, even—to leave a few streaks of flour here and there. They will be absorbed during baking.

How do I cut in butter?

Buttery baked goods, such as piecrust or biscuits, call for cutting cold butter into the dry ingredients. To do this, first cut the cold butter in $\frac{1}{2}$- to I-inch chunks, then add it to the dry ingredients. Using a pastry blender, gently press and cut the butter into smaller and smaller pieces until the mixture looks like coarse crumbs. These bits of butter create flaky layers and tenderness. If you don't have a pastry blender, use two table knives. Move the blades next to each other, pulling in opposite directions while cutting through the butter.

How do I use my knives?

With the right knife and a little practice, you can reduce anything to the proper size and shape for cooking—and keep your fingers intact too.

First know which knife to use (see page 15). Then observe the cardinal rule of knife skills: Know where your fingers are. The best way to cut efficiently and be safe is to keep the tip of the knife down against the cutting board and use a rocking motion from the tip to the heel, or back, of the knife. The tip of the knife—about the first third of the blade—is used for more delicate work, while the back of the blade is best for heavier tasks.

What's the difference in mincing, chopping, dicing, and cubing?

Mincing
Use a paring knife or small chef's knife to cut foods into tiny irregular pieces. Garlic is usually minced.

Chopping
Use a chef's knife to cut foods that can't be cut uniformly into fine, medium, or coarse irregular pieces.

Dicing
Use a chef's knife to cut foods into uniform pieces that are about $1/8$ to $1/4$ inch on all sides.

Cubing
Use a chef's knife to cut foods into uniform pieces that are about $1/2$ inch on all sides.

How do I use a serrated knife?

Serrated knives are useful for cutting foods with tough exteriors and soft interiors, like breads, cakes, or tomatoes. They easily slice through the exterior without crushing or tearing the interior of the food. Serrated knives are usually very sharp, so not much pressure is needed to cut foods. Gently saw back and forth and let the knife's teeth do the work.

How do I work with nuts & seeds?

Left raw or toasted to bump up their flavor, nuts and seeds add crunch and richness to all kinds of foods.

You can buy most nuts—including walnuts, pecans, peanuts, and almonds—already chopped (often labeled as "pieces"). If you buy whole nuts, you can chop them the size your recipe specifies. Almonds come prechopped in more shapes than any other kind of nut. They come whole; slivered, without skin and cut into narrow quarter-moon-shape slices; and sliced, with skin and shaved lengthwise down through the nut into very thin slices.

Ground nuts are sometimes added to crumb crusts for cheesecake and to some cake and cookie recipes. If you have a food processor, you can use it to grind nuts—just be careful that you don't overdo it and end up with nut butter. You can avoid this by using a quick start-and-stop motion on the machine and by adding 1 tablespoon of the sugar or flour from the recipe to the nuts to absorb some of the oil that is released as the nuts are processed.

Coarsely Chopped
Large irregular pieces more than 1/4 inch in size

Chopped
Medium irregular pieces about 1/4 inch in size

Finely chopped
Small irregular pieces about 1/8 inch in size or smaller

1 To toast whole nuts or large pieces, spread them in a shallow pan. Bake in a 350°F oven 5 to 10 minutes, shaking pan once or twice. You can toast coconut the same way, but watch it closely so it doesn't burn.

2 Toast finely chopped or ground nuts or sesame seeds in a dry skillet over medium heat, stirring often so they don't burn.

How do I remove the skins from tomatoes and peaches?

If you're eating a tomato in a salad or a peach out of your hand, leaving the skin on isn't such a big deal (though some people never like eating fuzzy peach skin). But if you're making tomato sauce and don't want tomato skins floating around in your food—or if you're mak-ing peach pie—you'll probably want to remove the skins. You can use the method shown below to remove the skin from peaches too. You won't need to score the peach skin first. After it's skinned, cut it in half and remove the pit.

1 Using a paring knife, make small Xs in the tomato bottoms. Dunk them in boiling water about 30 seconds to loosen the skins.

2 Using a slotted spoon, transfer the tomatoes to a bowl of ice water. This stops the cooking process and makes the tomatoes easy to handle.

3 Using a paring knife, peel the skins away from the tomatoes. Start from where you scored the skin. Cut out the core on the other side.

How do I caramelize onions?

You might have seen "caramelized onions" on a restaurant menu. Sounds fancy, but it's really simple.

Caramelizing is a method of cooking that turns onions soft, golden, and supersweet—with a few crusty and yummy brown bits here and there. The process involves cooking them slow-ly over medium-low or low heat so that their natural sugars break down and brown. The result is rich flavor and melt-in-your-mouth texture. Use caramelized onions to top a baked potato, a burger, or a plate of sauteed spin-ach—or in a frittata (see page 170).

1 Melt 2 tablespoons butter in a 10-inch skillet over medium-low heat. Add 2 thinly sliced onions. Cook, covered, about 15 minutes or until tender. **2** Uncover. Cook and stir over medium-high heat for 3 to 5 minutes more or until onion is golden.

How do I roast garlic and peppers?

Roasting vegetables sweetens and intensifies their flavors. Smear roasted garlic on bread as an appetizer—or toss sliced roasted peppers with pasta.

How to roast garlic

1 Using a chef's knife, cut off the top ½ inch of the garlic bulbs to expose the ends of cloves. Remove loose, papery outer layers.

2 Place bulbs, cut ends up, in muffin cups. Drizzle each bulb with about I tablespoon olive oil. Sprinkle with salt and ground black pepper.

3 Cover bulbs with foil. Roast in a 400°F oven about 25 minutes or until tender. Cool; squeeze from the bottom of papery husk and cloves will pop out.

How to roast sweet peppers

2 Bake in a 425°F oven for 20 to 25 minutes or until peppers are charred and very tender. Bring the foil up around peppers and fold edges together to enclose. Let stand about 15 minutes or until cool enough to handle. Letting the peppers steam in this way loosens the skin.

1 Halve peppers lengthwise; remove stems, seeds, and membranes. Place pepper halves, cut sides down, on a foil-lined baking sheet.

3 Using a paring knife, gently pull off the skin in strips and discard. Use peppers as directed in recipe.

What are the different methods of cooking?

All cooking involves heat. Whether it's low or high, moist or dry—whether food is flash-fried or slow simmered—is determined by the size and type of food and the result you're after.

What does it mean to broil?

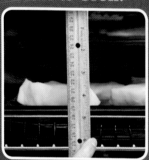

To broil is to cook food a measured distance below direct, dry heat. When broiling, position the broiler pan and its rack so that the surface of the food (not the rack) is the specified distance from the heat source. Use a ruler to measure this distance in a cold oven.

What does it mean to roast?

To roast is to cook food with dry heat, uncovered, in an oven. Large items, like poultry or beef roast, are often placed on a rack in a roasting pan to allow melted fat to drip away. This method works best with tender meats that have internal or surface fat to keep them moist.

What does it mean to sear?

To sear is to brown a food, usually meat, on all sides using high heat. This gives the meat color and flavor, but it does not seal in juices as is commonly thought. Usually you sear meats that will finish cooking covered, as in a slow cooker, since they might not brown otherwise.

What does it mean to stew?

To stew is to cook food for a long time in a covered pot with liquid over low heat. This moist-cooking technique helps tough cuts of meat get tender. The liquid in the pot is brought to boiling; then it's covered and the temperature is reduced so the mixture simmers (bubbles gently).

What does it mean to panfry?

To panfry is to cook food, which may have a light breading or coating, in a skillet in a small amount of hot fat or oil. The surface of the food browns and will become crisp if coated. Thin cuts of fish or meat, which can cook quickly, work well for this method.

What does it mean to braise?

To braise is to cook foods in a small amount of liquid in a tightly covered pan on the stovetop or in the oven. Braising is best for less tender cuts of meat, like a pot roast.

What does it mean to saute?

Saute comes from the French word "sauter," which means "to jump." Sauteed food is cooked and stirred in a small amount of fat or oil over fairly high heat in an open, shallow pan. Food that is cut into a uniform size sautes best.

What does it mean to stir-fry?

To stir-fry is to quickly cook small, uniform pieces of food in a little hot oil in a wok or large skillet over medium-high heat. Foods need to be stirred constantly to prevent burning. This technique is usually used to cook vegetables and to prepare Asian-style dishes.

What does it mean to steam?

To steam is to cook foods over boiling water. The steam from the water cooks food, usually vegetables, without washing away any color or nutrients. Food is placed in a steamer basket, set over boiling water, and covered. This is a relatively fast cooking method.

What does it mean to deglaze a pan?

Don't let those crusty little bits on the bottom of your pan go to waste—there's big flavor in there.

After you've browned a piece of meat in a pan, usually bits of crispy meat and a glaze of cooked meat juices remain in the bottom. Deglazing the pan is the process of using liquid—usually broth, wine, or some kind of spirit (or even water)—to loosen those brown bits and dissolve the caramelized meat juices over heat. Both are loaded with rich flavor. The resulting liquid is often used as a base for a sauce (see below) with more liquid and often with minced vegetables, herbs, or spices. Sometimes—particularly in the case of poultry or fish—the meat has first been dusted in flour before frying so that the deglazing liquid thickens slightly to make an instant sauce. Regular—not nonstick—pans are better suited for deglazing.

After adding liquid to the pan, scrape the bottom with a wooden spoon or spatula to loosen the flavorful brown bits.

How (and why) do I make a sauce reduction?

If you can simmer something and stir it once in a while, you can make a reduction.

A reduction, in cooking terms, refers to something—usually wine, stock, or a sauce—that has been gently simmered for a time so that a lot of the liquid evaporates. The result of this process is intensified flavor and a thicker consistency. When you're making a pan sauce, the reduction process usually takes place after you have deglazed the pan (see above). When a recipe has a reducing step, it will usually specify how much of the liquid should evaporate in terms of its volume—which you can just eyeball. Often it will be reduced by half. Depending on the liquid and how high the heat is, reductions can take varying amounts of time. You'll just need to keep an eye on the pot and stir occasionally so that whatever is in it doesn't burn.

The ultimate reduction is something called demi-glace, a sauce made with beef stock and sherry cooked down until it coats the back of a spoon. It's used as a flavorful base for many other sauces.

1 Liquids reduce more quickly in a large shallow skillet than in a deeper saucepan.

2 Let the sauce boil gently to allow it to cook down. Stir occasionally to prevent burning.

Grate
To rub food such as hard cheese
or ginger across a grating
surface to make very fine pieces

Crumble
To gently break foods into
small, irregular pieces

Shred
To push food across a
shredding surface to make
long, narrow strips

...ely Shred
...ush food along a shredding
...ace with very small holes to
...e long, thin strips

How do I shred cheese?

Preshredded cheeses are convenient, but cheese tastes fresher if you shred it yourself.

All you need is a box grater (shown above). This simple and inexpensive piece of equipment is four tools in one: It usually has a grating surface, a large-holed shredding surface, a small-holed shredding surface, and a slicing surface.

Just push the chunk or wedge of cheese downward over the correct surface, taking great care not to catch your knuckles, especially as the piece of cheese gets smaller. (Unless your grater has a knuckle guard.)

What does it mean to dredge?

Culinarily speaking, it means to dip food that's to be fried—such as poultry, fish, or meat—in flour, cornmeal, or bread crumbs to give it a crispy coat.

Dredging is done in specific steps for specific reasons. The first, a drag through the flour, seals in moisture. The second—a dip in a bath of egg, milk, buttermilk, water, or some combination thereof—helps provide a surface onto which the coating will cling. To keep your fingers from getting more coating on them than the food, use one hand for dipping the food into the liquid and the other for dipping it into the breading. Your dry hand can be used to sprinkle the breading onto the food. Set each finished piece on a platter until you're ready to fry.

2 Next dip both sides of the food in egg that has been beaten with milk or water. The egg wash provides a sticky surface so the final coating has something on which to cling.

1 Dredge food such as chicken or fish first in flour. The flour helps seal in the food's moisture to protect it from the high cooking heat.

3 Finally dredge the food in a coating of seasoned bread crumbs, cornmeal, or crushed crackers. Pat coating gently onto both sides.

Prepare the coatings for dredging and place them in separate shallow dishes. Right before cooking, dredge and coat the food in an assembly-line fashion.

How do I thaw frozen poultry, meat, and fish?

Leave frozen poultry, meat, and fish in their original packaging. Place in a dish with sides to catch any juices that may leak out as the foods thaw. Always thaw in the refrigerator.

The most important thing to remember when thawing poultry, meat, or fish is always to thaw in the refrigerator—never at room temperature. How long something takes to thaw depends on its size and density. Thin cutlets or fish fillets taken out of the freezer and put in the refrigerator in the morning will probably be thawed by dinnertime. Steaks, roasts, and bone-in chicken may have to sit in the refrigerator overnight; a 20-pound turkey may take 3 days. You can safely thaw food in your microwave on defrost—but it can start to cook. Check the manufacturer's directions for defrosting. You can also put whatever you're thawing in a leak-proof plastic bag in the sink and immerse it in cold water. Change the water every half hour, turning the bag over occasionally. Cook food immediately after thawing.

What does it mean to marinate?
Soaking foods in a seasoned bath does two things: It infuses them with flavor and tenderizes too.

A marinade is usually made up of an acidic liquid such as vinegar, wine, or citrus juice (or a natural enzyme such as ginger or pineapple); oil; and flavorings such as garlic, seasonings, and fresh herbs. To marinate something is to let it soak in that liquid; it usually penetrates about ¼ inch into the surface of the meat. More tender cuts of meat require up to 2 hours of soaking time. You can marinate less tender cuts for 4 to 24 hours—but don't overdo it. Meats and poultry marinated for more than 24 hours turn mushy. Fish requires only a few hours of marinating time or the acidic ingredients will begin to "cook" it and make it tough. Always marinate in the refrigerator and never reuse marinades. Turn the bag occasionally to distribute the marinade evenly.

Place food to be marinated in a resealable plastic bag. Set it in a bowl or shallow dish. Add the marinade, then seal the bag. Turn the bag to coat. The bowl is a safeguard in case the bag leaks.

How do I use the two sides of my meat mallet?

A few whacks with this cool tool make a tough piece of meat tender or a thick piece of meat nice and thin.

That imposing, sort of medieval-looking tool has two functions. The flat side of the mallet is used to pound pieces of meat and poultry very thin. These thin pieces of meat—called a paillard in French, a scaloppine in Italian, and a cutlet in English—are usually panfried and cooked quickly and evenly. They can also be rolled around fillings—as in French roulade, which is a thin piece of meat rolled around a stuffing of mushrooms, bread crumbs, cheese, and/or vegetables.

The bumpy side of the mallet is used to tenderize tougher cuts of meat—usually beef or pork—by breaking down connective tissues.

Good candidates for tenderizing include top round steak, skirt steak (the meat used in fajitas), and flank steak or London broil.

A tip for even thickness: Start pounding in the center of the piece of meat and gradually move outward toward the edges, making sure you're moving the mallet all over the meat.

To flatten meat for quick, even cooking, place it between two sheets of plastic wrap. Pound with the flat side of the mallet.

The bumpy side of the mallet helps break down connective tissues on tough cuts of meat to tenderize them.

How do I use a meat thermometer?

Whether yours is oven safe or an instant-read model, getting a correct reading is crucial to safe eating.

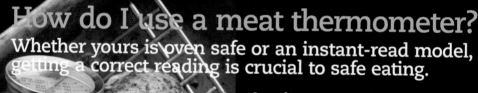

Some thermometers are inserted into the meat and stay there during cooking; others are used to test meats out of the oven. See page 20 to determine which type you have. As a general rule, insert the thermometer into the thickest part of the meat (don't touch bone) and always cook to the temperature the recipe specifies.

Meat Thermometer
For a whole bird, insert the thermometer into the center of an inside thigh muscle. Don't let it touch bone.

For thin foods, insert an instant-read thermometer in from the side, making sure it's at least 2 inches in.

Whichever type of thermometer you use, make sure it's in the thickest part of the meat and is not touching bone.

How do I get the pits out of olives?

Pitted olives from the store are pricey and can be hard to find. It's not hard to pit them yourself.

If you're noshing on olives as an appetizer, it's fine to put out a bowl of olives with pits. If you're cooking with them, though, it's generally nicer not to have to spit an olive pit out onto your dinner plate. Also they're often chopped or sliced—hard to do when there's a pit getting in the way. Gently split the olive open by crushing it with your thumb or the broad side of a chef's knife. The pit will then present itself—just pop it out. Repeat. (And again.)

1 Using your thumb, gently crush the long side of an unpitted olive to break it open. **2** Pull the sides of the olive apart and the pit will pop out.

How do I know when it's done?

Knowing when something is done cooking or baking—whether it's a steak on the grill or a birthday cake for a friend—is one of the keys to avoiding frustrating kitchen situations. For instance, if you take a cake out of the oven that's still batter in the center, it will collapse. And it's certainly a bummer to call everyone to the table and find the fish still opaque in the center and the baked potatoes crunchy. Though there are doneness tests for different foods (see below), one rule applies to all foods: Start testing at the minimum time given in a recipe to avoid overcooking, then test every minute or two after that to ensure you catch the food at its optimum doneness.

Baked goods
Stick a wooden toothpick into the center of the food. When pulled out, it should be clean with no batter.

Fish
Gently place the tines of a fork into the fish. Twist it slightly. The fish should flake (pull apart) easily.

Potatoes
The tines of a fork should easily pierce a done potato all the way to the center.

Cookies
Check the edges first for a golden color. The top of the cookies may be a little lighter than the edges.

What if a recipe calls for bread crumbs or cracker crumbs?

Humble bread and cracker crumbs have many culinary uses. They create crispy coatings on fried foods and add lightness to meat loaf and meatballs.

The fine dry bread crumbs you can buy in a can at the store come both seasoned and plain. They're convenient and work just fine for coating foods, but they've also been sitting around on the shelf for a while and can taste a little stale. With a food processor, you can make your own bread crumbs—either fine dry crumbs or soft fresh crumbs—in a snap. And because bread and crackers are staples you can usually find in your cupboards, you likely have what you need to make them. To make fine dry bread crumbs, you first need to make toasted bread cubes (page 77), but to make fresh crumbs, just toss some slices into the food processor and buzz it a few times. If you don't have a food processor, you can make cracker crumbs by putting crackers in a resealable plastic bag and crushing them with a rolling pin.

How do I make cracker crumbs and bread crumbs?

Cracker Crumbs
Place crackers in a food processor fitted with the blade attachment. Process using on/off pulses until crumbs are of desired consistency. For I cup of crumbs, you'll need 28 saltine crackers, 14 graham crackers, or 24 rich, round crackers.

Bread Crumbs
For fluffy soft bread crumbs, use I slice fresh bread for every $\frac{3}{4}$ cup. For fine dry bread crumbs, see page 77 for making dry bread cubes. Process dried bread cubes until finely ground. One slice of bread yields $\frac{1}{4}$ cup fine dry crumbs.

What's the difference?
This is what coarse cracker crumbs (left) and soft fresh bread crumbs (right) look like.

What's better, fresh or dry bread crumbs?

There are two types of bread crumbs, ideally used for different purposes: fine dry bread crumbs—purchased from the store or made from toasted bread cubes (see page 77)—and fresh crumbs, made from soft bread. Dry bread crumbs are generally used for breading foods that are to be fried. Fresh crumbs are used as crispy toppings on casseroles and as filler in ground-meat dishes such as meat loaf and meatballs.

Fine dry crumbs   Fresh crumbs

How do I toast sandwich buns?

Toasting cut surfaces of sandwich buns makes them a little sturdier and adds a pleasant crispness to each bite of bread. Place buns, cut sides up, on a broiler pan; broil about 4 inches from heat for 1 to 2 minutes until golden. Watch constantly—they can burn in a heartbeat!

What does it mean to toss things together?

Cooking involves some tossing—pasta with sauce and salad with dressing, for instance. All you need is two spoons or a set of salad forks and a gentle touch. If you're tossing salad, pour the dressing over contents of the bowl. With the spoons, start scooping down the edge of the bowl to the bottom; lift and drop ingredients. Repeat until everything is mixed and coated with dressing or sauce.

1 To dress a salad, place the salad ingredients in a bowl. Pour the dressing over the top.

2 Using two spoons or salad forks, gently lift and drop ingredients to mix them and coat them with dressing.

How do I make bread cubes?

Turn bread that's turned the corner into dry bread crumbs used in cooking. First cube the bread.

Some recipes call for toasted bread cubes (like some stuffing recipes) and some recipes call for dry bread crumbs. To make dry bread crumbs, you need to make toasted bread cubes. You can use any kind of bread, as long as you cut it properly. To make croutons, see page 344.

1 Stack a few slices of bread. Using a serrated knife, cut bread into ½-inch strips.

2 Cut strips crosswise into ½-inch cubes. Arrange cubes in a single layer on a baking pan.

Bake cubes in a 300°F oven for 10 to 15 minutes or until golden, stirring once or twice. Let cool.

How do I work with dried herbs?

Though fresh may be best in many cases, intensely flavored dried herbs definitely have their uses.

Crush dried herbs in the palm of your hand by pressing and rubbing them gently with a finger.

Buy dried herbs in small amounts and use them up within a few months to ensure they're fresh. Crush them with your finger or in a mortar and pestle to release their aromatic oils. Add dried herbs at the beginning or middle of cooking; add fresh herbs at the end.

One teaspoon of dried herbs is generally equal to 1 tablespoon (3 teaspoons) of fresh herbs.

Crush seeds such as cumin with a mortar and pestle. The bowl is the mortar and the utensil is the pestle.

How do I use a fine-mesh sieve?

A fine-mesh sieve is used to strain lumps from sauces or to extract liquids from foods. To extract liquids, place the sieve over a bowl. Use the back of a wooden spoon to press out excess liquid, as with draining spinach. Or press the pulp and juices of seedy berries through the sieve, leaving the seeds behind.

What does it mean to drop from a rounded teaspoon?

Most drop cookie recipes call for the dough to be dropped from a rounded teaspoon. All this means is that you scoop a ball of dough with a teaspoon from your flatware set and slide it onto the cookie sheet with another.

Odds and Ends

Stumped on an ingredient you've never heard of—or on a technique you've read about in a recipe? Here are a few terms you may need to know.

Bias-slice To slice a food, such as a carrot, at a 45-degree angle.

Blend To combine two or more ingredients by hand or with an electric mixer or blender until smooth and uniform in texture, flavor, and color.

Brine (noun) A heavily salted water mixture that may contain vinegar and is used to pickle or cure vegetables, meats, fish, or seafood.

Brown To cook food in a skillet, broiler, or oven to add flavor and aroma and develop a rich, desirable color on the outside.

Capers Capers are the buds of a shrub that grows from Spain to China. They have an assertive flavor that is a cross between citrus and olive plus a tang that comes from the salt-and-vinegar brine in which they are packed.

Cheesecloth A thin 100-percent-cotton cloth with a fine or coarse weave. In cooking, cheesecloth is used to bundle herbs, strain liquids, and wrap rolled meats. Look for it among cooking supplies in supermarkets and specialty cookware shops.

Cooking oil A room-temperature liquid made from vegetables, nuts, or seeds. Common types for general cooking include corn, soybean, canola, sunflower, safflower, peanut, and olive. For baking, cooking oils cannot be used interchangeably with solid fats because they do not hold air when beaten.

Crisp-tender The texture of vegetables that have been cooked just until tender but still somewhat crunchy. At this stage, a fork can be inserted into the vegetables with a little pressure.

Dash A small amount of seasoning that is added to food. It is generally between $1/16$ and $1/8$ teaspoon.

Drizzle To randomly pour a liquid, such as icing, in a thin stream over food.

Fold A method of gently mixing ingredients without decreasing their volume. To fold, use a rubber spatula to cut down vertically through the mixture from the back of the bowl. Move the spatula across the bottom of the bowl and bring it back up the other side, carrying some of the mixture from the bottom over the surface. Repeat, rotating the bowl a quarter-turn each time you complete the folding process.

Garnish To add visual appeal to a finished dish, such as sprinkling with snipped fresh herbs or adding a twist of lemon.

Glaze A thin, glossy coating.

Kosher salt A coarse salt with no additives that many cooks prefer for its light, flaky texture and clean taste.

Parchment paper A grease- and heat-resistant paper used to line baking pans, to wrap foods in packets for baking, or to make disposable pastry bags.

Pinch The amount of a dry ingredient that can be pinched between your finger and thumb.

Poach To cook food by partially or completely submerging it in a simmering liquid.

Score To cut narrow slits, often in a diamond pattern, through the outer surface of a food to decorate it, tenderize it, help it absorb flavor, or allow fat to drain as it cooks.

Sea salt A salt variety derived from the evaporation of sea water. It is desired for its clean, salty taste.

Simmer To cook food in a liquid that is kept just below the boiling point; a liquid is simmering when a few bubbles form slowly and burst just before reaching the surface.

Skewer A long, narrow metal or wooden stick that can be inserted through pieces of meat, fruit, or vegetables for grilling. If using bamboo or wooden skewers, soak them in cold water for 30 minutes before you thread them to prevent burning.

Skim To remove a substance, such as fat or foam, from the surface of a liquid, such as homemade broth or stock.

Top 10 tricks only the pros know

Professional cooks pick up lots of cool tricks along the way that help make their jobs easier. This collection of insider secrets gives your everyday cooking the benefits of their experience.

Trick #3

Find yourself without a rolling pin? If there's a wine bottle around, use it to roll out any kind of dough—biscuit, pizza, cookie, or piecrust. It cleans up easily when you're done—and you can celebrate your genius with a toast.

Trick #4

It's difficult to extract much juice from a lemon, lime, or orange without a citrus juicer (see page 20), but if you don't have one, pierce the cut surface of the fruit all over with a fork before squeezing it over a bowl. Piercing will maximize the amount of juice that comes out of the fruit—and so will these two tricks: If the fruit is cold, microwave it on 100 percent power (high) for 10 seconds. Then roll it on the counter a few times to loosen fruit from the skin.

Trick #7

Fresh herbs looking a little bedraggled and not quite up to garnishing much of anything? Refresh them by soaking the sprigs in ice water for a few minutes; thoroughly drain them, wrap them in paper towels, and put them in a plastic bag in the refrigerator for up to a few hours or until you're ready to use them.

Trick #8

Oops! If you drop a shell into a bowl of raw eggs, it can be tricky to get it out of the sticky stuff: It's a mess with your fingers and slippery with a spoon. Use one half of a clean eggshell to scoop it out.

Trick #1

Sticky or greasy ingredients—such as honey, molasses, and solid shortening—don't always release from the measuring cup easily. Spray the measuring cup (a dry measuring cup for solid shortening and a glass measuring cup for honey or molasses) first with nonstick cooking spray and everything will slide right out.

Trick #2

You may not have a biscuit cutter, but surely you have a drinking glass. You can use one to cut out biscuit dough. Dip the glass in flour before cutting each biscuit to keep the dough from clinging to the glass.

Trick #5

Pouring salt and pepper—and other spices, for that matter—from a larger jar into one with a smaller opening can be a messy proposition. Make a funnel out of waxed paper and the seasonings will go in neat and tidy without spilling as much as a grain.

Trick #6

A spatula is nice to have for icing cakes, but it's not a necessity. If you don't have one, you can use the back of a spoon to spread the frosting and make pretty swirls.

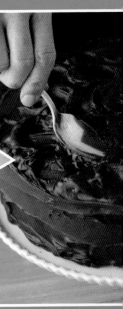

Trick #9

The sides of a tart pan with a removable bottom slip off easily enough, but it's dangerous business to hold the tart pan from the bottom and try to slide the sides off. You'll wind up with the sides around your arm and a just-baked tart slip-sliding off of the bottom. Instead place the tart on a can and let the sides drop to the counter. Transfer the tart to a wire cooling rack, where it can complete cooling.

Trick #10

European-style breads generally don't last much beyond the day they're baked because they contain no fats to stabilize them and keep them moist. You can refresh a day-old loaf of bread by spritzing it with water and warming it in a 375°F oven for 8 to 10 minutes. It will once again have a crisp crust and soft, chewy interior—but eat it immediately. (And don't use that trick on the same loaf more than once.)

Kitchen Safety

The kitchen may be the heart of the home, but it's also a danger zone with heat, fire, sharp objects, and potentially slippery floors. Be safety smart and everyone will wind up full, whole, and happy.

The Hottest Spot in the House

According to the National Fire Protection Association, three out of every 10 house fires start in the kitchen. Most of those are preventable if you observe a few commonsense rules:

● Never leave the stovetop unattended when you're frying, grilling, broiling, or boiling. If you have to walk away for even a minute, turn off the stove.

● If you're simmering or baking something over a long period of time, check on it regularly to be sure it's not boiling over or burning. Stay in the house and, if you have to, use a timer to remind you that the stove or oven is on.

● Don't wear loose clothing or dangling sleeves while cooking. That's just a wick waiting to be lit!

● Keep a fire extinguisher in the kitchen just in case you do have a grease fire. Never, ever throw water on a grease fire; it causes a violent spattering reaction and can spread the flammable grease—and the fire—everywhere.

Nice to Know

There are two kinds of kitchen exhaust systems—updraft and downdraft. An updraft system is usually contained in a hood over the stove. It sucks hot air, grease, and smoke up and vents it out of the house. A downdraft system is usually built into the cooktop and pulls hot air, grease, and smoke down and out of the kitchen. Find out which type your kitchen has—and use it!

● Never use a kitchen towel as a pot holder; it can drag down onto the burner and catch on fire—and never leave a pot holder sitting on top of a pot lid.

Beyond Smoke and Fire

Fire isn't the only hazard in the kitchen. When you're cooking, there are always opportunities for getting burned by hot liquid or a hot utensil. To prevent burns:

● Always turn a pot handle toward the back of the stove so you don't bump into it—or so that a child doesn't grab it.

● Never leave a spoon—wooden, metal, or otherwise—sitting in a pan as it simmers. It can get hot and you can get burned when you go to grab it, or it can flip out of the pan and spatter hot soup or sauce or oatmeal everywhere.

On Other Safety Fronts

● Always store knives in a knife block or on a magnetic wall-mounted strip—never in a kitchen drawer.

● Wipe up spills of any kind immediately. When you're moving fast and are distracted by your kitchen tasks, it's far too easy to slip and fall.

In Case of Fire

Keep a fire extinguisher in the kitchen in case of a grease fire. You can smother a small fire with baking soda, salt, or flour, but never throw water on a grease fire—it will spread the fire elsewhere.

Food Safety

There are three basic rules so food is safe to eat: Keep it clean. Keep it the right temperature. Keep it separate—don't cross-contaminate. Observe those and you'll have a healthy kitchen and peace of mind.

Keep Your Hands Clean

Make sure that your hands and all surfaces and utensils that come into contact with food are clean. Nearly half of all cases of food-borne illness could be eliminated by frequent and thorough hand washing. Remember to wash your hands:

● Before you handle food or utensils—or before you eat.

● After handling food, especially raw meat, poultry, fish, shellfish, or eggs.

● Between tasks—for example, after cutting up a raw chicken and before dicing the vegetables, even if they're going to be cooked.

● After using the bathroom, changing diapers, playing with pets, or touching any unclean item.

Proper hand washing means thoroughly scrubbing your hands—front and back, all the way up to the wrists, over and under your fingernails, and in between fingers—in hot, soapy water for at least 20 seconds. Rinse your hands and use paper towels or a clean cloth to dry them. If you have an open wound or cut, prevent contamination by wearing rubber gloves while handling food.

Keep Dishcloths, Towels, and Sponges Clean

One way to eliminate the bacteria that thrive in sponges and dishcloths is to soak them in a diluted bleach solution (¾ cup bleach per 1 gallon water) three times a week. Sponges should be allowed to air-dry. Change your dishcloth and dish towel daily—and wash them on the hot cycle of your washing machine. Use paper towels to clean up spills, especially those from raw meat, poultry, fish, and shellfish.

> ## Nice to Know
>
> Bacteria thrive at temperatures between 40°F and 140°F—sometimes called "the danger zone" when it comes to food safety. So keep cold foods at 40°F or below and serve hot foods immediately—or keep them at 140°F or above. You may not be able to see, taste, or smell the bacteria that cause food-borne illness, but you can prevent them from growing in the first place.

Keep Surfaces and Utensils Clean

Immediately after preparing raw meat, poultry, fish, shellfish, eggs, and produce, clean any utensils and surfaces with hot, soapy water.

● Take care of your cutting boards. After each use, thoroughly wash them with hot, soapy water, then rinse and allow to air-dry or pat dry with paper towels. Or, if they're dishwasher safe, place them in the dishwasher. As an added safety measure, flood a cutting board's

> ## Clean Slates
>
> Replace cutting boards whenever they have become worn or develop hard-to-clean grooves. Wash dishwasher-safe cutting boards in the dishwasher and let wood ones air-dry after washing them by hand.

surface with a sanitizing solution (1 teaspoon of liquid chlorine bleach per 1 quart of water); allow the board to stand several minutes. Rinse and air-day or pat dry with paper towels.

● Wash the probe of an instant-read thermometer after each use with hot, soapy water and rinse before reinserting it into food.

● Wipe up refrigerator spills immediately. Clean refrigerator surfaces with hot, soapy water and rinse. Once a week throw out perishable foods that should no longer be eaten.

● Keep pets off counters and away from food.

Separate, Don't Cross-Contaminate

Cross-contamination happens when cooked or ready-to-eat foods pick up bacteria from other foods or unclean hands, cutting boards, knives, or other utensils. To avoid cross-contamination, it's especially important to keep raw meat, poultry, eggs, fish, and shellfish and their juices away from other foods. Follow these guidelines:

● When shopping, keep raw meat, poultry, fish, and shellfish separate from other foods in your grocery cart.

● When you get home, store raw meat, poultry, fish, and shellfish in sealed containers or plastic bags so the juices don't drip onto other foods. Place whole poultry and roasts on a tray or pan that is large enough to catch any juices that may leak out.

● Buy two cutting boards, if possible, that are distinctly different from one another. Make one for raw meat, poultry, fish, and shellfish and

Nice to Know

Information on food safety is constantly changing. For the latest information and precautions, call the USDA Meat and Poultry Hotline at 800/535-4555, the U.S. FDA Center for Food Safety and Applied Nutrition Outreach Center at 888/723-3366, or your health care provider. You can also get information by checking the government's food safety website: www.foodsafety.gov.

the other one for ready-to-eat foods such as breads and vegetables.

● Follow guidelines on page 83 to keep your hands and any utensils and surfaces that come into contact with foods clean.

● Place cooked foods on a clean plate—never on an unwashed one that was used to hold raw meat, poultry, fish, or shellfish.

● Don't wash raw poultry, beef, pork, lamb, or veal before cooking. Doing so poses a risk of cross-contamination with other foods and utensils in the kitchen. Any bacteria that might be present are destroyed with proper cooking.

● Marinate foods safely (see page 73).

Chill Out

Cold temperatures keep most harmful bacteria from multiplying. Follow these steps to keep foods cold:

● When shopping, buy perishable foods last. Go straight home and refrigerate them right away. Follow packaging labels for safe handling.

● Refrigerate leftover foods in tightly sealed containers immediately after you have finished eating. Leftovers shouldn't stay out of the refrigerator for longer than 2 hours (1 hour if the temperature is above 80°F).

Nice to Know

If you aren't sure that food has been prepared, served, or stored safely, throw it out. If food has been improperly handled, even cooking it correctly can't make it safe. Never taste food to see if it's safe to eat—contaminated food can look, smell, and even taste perfectly OK, and if it's not, even a small amount can make you sick. It's not worth the risk!

ANY-DAY
appetizers
& SNACKS

Friends coming over with hearty appetites in tow? Get the party started with these nibbles and noshes.

① Skill Level

Avocado-Feta Salsa

2 roma tomatoes, chopped

1 avocado, halved, seeded, peeled, and chopped

¼ cup finely chopped red onion

1 tablespoon snipped fresh parsley

1 tablespoon snipped fresh oregano

1 tablespoon olive oil

1 tablespoon white wine vinegar

1 clove garlic, minced

1 cup coarsely crumbled feta cheese (4 ounces) (see photo I, page 96)

Tortilla chips

Toasted Pita Bread Wedges (optional)

1 In a medium bowl stir together tomato, avocado, onion, parsley, oregano, oil, vinegar, and garlic. Stir gently to mix. Gently stir in feta cheese. Cover and chill for 2 hours or up to 6 hours. Serve with tortilla chips or Toasted Pita Bread Wedges. Makes 12 (¼-cup) servings.

Per serving (dip only): 63 cal., 5 g total fat (2 g sat. fat), 8 mg chol., 106 mg sodium, 3 g carbo., 1 g fiber, 2 g pro.

Tomato Salsa: Prepare as above, except omit avocado, parsley, oregano, and feta cheese. Add 2 additional roma tomatoes, chopped; 3 additional cloves garlic, minced; 2 to 4 fresh jalapeño chile peppers, seeded and finely chopped; 2 tablespoons lime juice; 2 tablespoons snipped fresh cilantro; and ¼ teaspoon salt. Serve with tortilla chips.

Ingredient Info This thoroughly modern salsa is infinitely versatile. If you manage to have a bit left over (or if you make a double batch), you can use it to spruce up other meals. Spoon it on burgers and sandwiches, top lettuce salads, or stir it into cooked pasta for a "satisfying" side dish.

1 Use kitchen scissors to cut pocket-style pitas in half crosswise. Cut along the edge to separate the top and bottom portions of the pita.

2 While holding the top and bottom portions together, cut the pita halves into wedges. Separate wedges and spread on baking sheets.

Toasted Pita Bread Wedges
Preheat oven to 350°F. Halve pita loaves crosswise, then split halves horizontally. Cut halves into wedges. Spread wedges in a single layer on baking sheets. Bake about 10 minutes or until crisp. Cool completely. Store toasted wedges in an airtight container in a cool place.

Ask Mom What is a roma tomato? page 52 / How do I chop a tomato? pages 52, 328 / How do I seed and peel an avocado? page 36 / How do I chop an onion? page 47 / How do I snip fresh herbs? page 42 / What is that vinegar? page 349 / What is a garlic clove? page 40 / How do I mince garlic? page 40 / How do I crumble cheese? pages 71, 96 / How do I handle hot chile peppers? page 48 / How do I juice a lime? pages 30, 80 / How much juice does one lime yield?

(2) Skill Level

Mango Salsa

1½ cups chopped, peeled mango (1 large) or peach (2 medium)
1 medium red sweet pepper, seeded and finely chopped
2 tablespoons thinly sliced green onion (1)
1 fresh jalapeño chile pepper, seeded and finely chopped
1 tablespoon olive oil
½ teaspoon finely shredded lime peel
1 tablespoon fresh lime juice
1 tablespoon vinegar
¼ teaspoon salt
¼ teaspoon ground black pepper
Tortilla chips

Ingredient Info
Mangoes have large, flat pits running their length. A mango looks wider on its face than on its side. To get the most fruit from a mango, cut it through its side close to the pit to remove the faces from the pit, as shown by the dotted lines below.

Face   Side

1 In a medium bowl combine the mango, sweet pepper, green onion, and jalapeño pepper. In a small bowl whisk together the oil, lime peel, lime juice, vinegar, salt, and black pepper. Drizzle lime mixture over mango mixture; stir gently to coat. Serve salsa with chips. Makes 8 (¼-cup) servings.

Per serving (dip only): 41 cal., 2 g total fat (0 g sat. fat), 0 mg chol., 74 mg sodium, 7 g carbo., 1 g fiber, 0 g pro.

1 Place the mango on its end. Using a small chef's knife, slice down along one side of the pit to remove the fleshy face.

2 Turn the mango around and slice off the other face, keeping the knife as close to the pit as you can.

3 Using a paring knife, score the flesh in each half in a checkerboard pattern up to, but not through, the skin.

4 Turn the skin in to the cubes of mango fles Cut the cubes of mango the skin with the paring

Ask Mom How do I peel peaches? page 66 / How do I seed and chop sweet peppers? page 49 / How do I slice green onions? page 43 / How do I handle hot chile peppers? page 48 / How do I shred lemon/lime peel? page 30 / How do I juice a lemon/lime? pages 30, 80 / How much juice does one lemon/lime yield? page 30 / What is that vinegar? page 349 / What does drizzle mean? page 79

1 Skill Level

Guacamole

- 2 medium very ripe avocados, halved, seeded, peeled, and cut up
- 2 tablespoons chopped onion
- 1 tablespoon snipped cilantro or parsley
- 1 tablespoon fresh lime juice
- ¼ teaspoon salt
- 1 clove garlic, minced
- ⅔ cup finely chopped, seeded, peeled tomato (1 large) (optional)
  Tortilla chips

Ingredient Info How do you find fruit that is ripe but not so ripe it's turned to black mush? Avocados always seem to be rock hard or completely squishy. To prevent this, plan ahead. Bring home firm, heavy avocados and let them ripen in a paper bag for 2 to 4 days or until they yield to gentle palm pressure. Perfect!

1 In a food processor or blender combine avocado, onion, cilantro, lime juice, salt, and garlic. Cover and process or blend until mixture is smooth, scraping sides as necessary. If desired, stir in tomato. Transfer to a serving bowl. Serve immediately or cover and chill for up to 24 hours. Serve with tortilla chips. Makes 16 (2-tablespoon) servings.

Per serving (dip only): 37 cal., 3 g total fat (0 g sat. fat), 0 mg chol., 38 mg sodium, 2 g carbo., 1 g fiber, 0 g pro.

Basil Guacamole: Prepare as above, except omit cilantro; add ¾ cup snipped fresh basil.

Spicy Guacamole: Prepare as above, except add 2 fresh jalapeño chile peppers, seeded and chopped; ½ of a 4-ounce can (¼ cup) diced green chile peppers, drained; or several drops of bottled hot pepper sauce.

Supereasy Guacamole: Prepare as above, except place avocado, onion, cilantro, lime juice, salt, garlic, 2 tablespoons sour cream, and, if desired, tomato in a resealable plastic bag (below). Seal bag; knead with your hands to combine ingredients (below). Serve immediately or chill for up to 8 hours. To serve, snip a hole in one corner of the bag. Squeeze guacamole into serving bowl or onto chips (below).

1 Save on dishes and time by placing all the ingredients for guacamole in a resealable plastic bag.

2 Seal the bag, then squeeze and knead it to mash the ingredients into an almost-smooth consistency.

3 When ready to serve, cut a corner of the bag off with scissors; squeeze guacamole into a serving bowl.

Ask Mom How do I seed and peel an avocado? page 36 / How do I chop an onion? page 47 / How do I snip fresh herbs? pages 42, 328 / How do I juice a lemon/lime? pages 30, 80 / How much juice does one lemon/lime yield? page 30 / What is a garlic clove? page 40 / How do I mince garlic? page 40 / How do I peel tomatoes? page 66 / How do I seed tomatoes? page 52 / How do I chop a tomato? page 52 / How do I handle hot chile peppers? page 48

Dilled Onion Cheese Ball

1 8-ounce package cream cheese
1 cup finely shredded Gouda cheese (4 ounces)
¼ cup butter
1 tablespoon milk
½ teaspoon Worcestershire sauce for chicken
2 tablespoons thinly sliced green onion (1)
2 tablespoons snipped fresh dill or 2 teaspoons dried dillweed
½ cup chopped toasted almonds
Assorted crackers and/or flatbread

1 In a large bowl let cream cheese, Gouda, and butter stand at room temperature for 30 minutes. Add milk and Worcestershire sauce. Beat with an electric mixer on medium speed until light and fluffy. Stir in green onion and dill. Cover and chill for 4 to 24 hours.

2 Before serving, shape cheese mixture into a ball. Roll ball in nuts and let stand for 15 minutes. Serve with crackers or flatbread. Makes about 30 (1-tablespoon) servings.

Make-ahead directions: Prepare as above in Step 1. Shape cheese mixture into a ball; wrap in plastic wrap. Freeze for up to 1 month. To serve, thaw the cheese ball in the refrigerator overnight. Unwrap and roll in nuts. Let the cheese ball stand at room temperature for 15 minutes before serving.

Per serving (spread only): 63 cal., 6 g total fat (3 g sat. fat), 16 mg chol., 62 mg sodium, 1 g carbo., 0 g fiber, 2 g pro.

Prosciutto-Basil Cheese Ball: Prepare as above, except substitute finely shredded fontina cheese for the Gouda cheese, stir in 2 ounces chopped prosciutto and 2 tablespoons snipped fresh basil with the green onion, and omit the dill. Substitute chopped toasted pine nuts for the almonds. If desired, serve with apples, crackers, or flatbread.

Spicy Taco Cheese Ball: Prepare as above in Step 1, except substitute finely shredded taco cheese for the Gouda cheese, stir in 2 tablespoons bottled chopped jalapeño chile peppers with the green onion, and omit the dill. Substitute ½ cup crushed corn chips for the almonds.

Good to Know A buttery-rich cheeseball with crackers is a classic party nibble. In addition to the ball shape, you can mold this recipe into little logs by dividing the recipe into four portions and shaping accordingly (you can also make several small cheese balls by dividing the mixture and shaping it this way). Or if you're short on time, just pack the cheese into a small serving bowl, sprinkle with nuts, and serve it that way.

Ask Mom How do I shred cheese? page 71 / How do I measure butter? page 58 / How do I slice green onions? page 43 / How do I snip fresh herbs? pages 42, 328 / How do I toast nuts? page 65 / How do I chop nuts? page 65 / What is prosciutto? page 358 / How do I toast pine nuts? pages 65, 245 / How do I crush cornflakes/chips? page 222 / How do I crack peppercorns? page 22

LOOKING FOR OPTIONS? Give your guests what they want by rolling smaller cheese balls in different coatings. Try different chopped toasted nuts, cracked peppercorns, or snipped fresh herbs, such as dill, basil, or parsley.

Hummus

I 15-ounce can chickpeas (garbanzo beans), rinsed and drained
$\frac{1}{4}$ cup tahini (sesame seed paste)
$\frac{1}{4}$ cup lemon juice
$\frac{1}{4}$ cup olive oil
$\frac{1}{2}$ teaspoon salt
$\frac{1}{4}$ teaspoon paprika
I clove garlic, minced
I tablespoon snipped fresh parsley
2 to 3 teaspoons olive oil (optional)
2 tablespoons pine nuts, toasted (optional)
Toasted Pita Bread Wedges (page 87) and/or assorted cut-up vegetables

1 In a blender or food processor combine chickpeas, tahini, lemon juice, $\frac{1}{4}$ cup oil, the salt, paprika, and garlic. Cover and blend or process until smooth, scraping sides as necessary.

2 Spoon the hummus onto a serving platter. Sprinkle with parsley. If desired, drizzle with 2 to 3 teaspoons oil and garnish with pine nuts. Serve with Toasted Pita Bread Wedges and/or cut-up vegetables. Makes 14 (2-tablespoon) servings.

Per serving (dip only): 97 cal., 6 g total fat (I g sat. fat), 0 mg chol., 178 mg sodium, 8 g carbo., 2 g fiber, 2 g pro.

Stir-ins: Prepare as above, except stir in one or more of the following: $\frac{1}{4}$ cup sliced green onion (2); $\frac{1}{4}$ cup crumbled feta cheese (1 ounce); $\frac{1}{3}$ cup chopped ripe olives or kalamata olives; $\frac{1}{3}$ cup chopped roasted red sweet pepper; 2 to 3 chopped chipotle peppers in adobo sauce; and/or $\frac{1}{3}$ cup purchased basil pesto.

Shopping Savvy Although it sounds exotic, tahini is actually widely available in supermarkets. It's used in all kinds of Middle Eastern dressings, sauces, and dips. Your best bet is to search the condiment aisle or the ethnic foods section of the store—but if you don't have any luck, don't be afraid to ask for help.

Ask Mom How do I rinse and drain canned beans? page 390 / How do I juice a lemon/lime? pages 30, 80 / How much juice does one lemon/lime yield? page 30 / What is a garlic clove? page 40 / How do I mince garlic? page 40 / How do I snip fresh herbs? pages 42, 328 / How do I toast pine nuts? pages 65, 245 / How do I slice green onions? page 43 / How do I crumble cheese? pages 71, 96 / How do I roast sweet peppers? page 87

Skill Level

Creamy Parmesan Dip

1 8-ounce package cream cheese, softened
1 8-ounce carton dairy sour cream
$\frac{1}{3}$ cup grated Parmesan cheese (2 ounces)
2 tablespoons finely chopped green onion (1)
2 teaspoons dried Italian seasoning, crushed
   Milk (optional)
   Sliced green onion (optional)
   Assorted cut-up vegetables, such as baby carrots, cauliflower florets, cherry tomatoes, green onions, jicama or red sweet pepper strips, pea pods, radishes, yellow summer squash slices, and/or zucchini slices; or crackers or chips

Good to Know The quickest way to soften cream cheese is in the microwave. In a microwave-safe bowl, heat unwrapped cheese, uncovered, on 100 percent power (high). Allow 10 to 20 seconds for 3 ounces and 30 to 60 seconds for 8 ounces. Let it stand 5 minutes before using it.

1 In a medium bowl beat cream cheese, sour cream, Parmesan cheese, green onion, and Italian seasoning with an electric mixer on low speed until fluffy. Cover and chill at least 1 hour.

2 If the dip is too thick after chilling, stir in 1 to 2 tablespoons milk. Spoon the dip into a serving bowl. If desired, garnish with sliced green onion. Serve with cut-up vegetables, crackers, and/or chips. Makes about 30 (1-tablespoon) servings.

Make-ahead directions: Prepare dip as above through Step 1. Cover and chill for up to 24 hours. Cut up vegetable dippers and place in resealable plastic bags; chill for up to 24 hours.

Per serving (dip only): 40 cal., 4 g total fat (2 g sat. fat), 11 mg chol., 49 mg sodium, 1 g carbo., 0 g fiber, 1 g pro.

Creamy Dill Dip: Prepare as above, except omit Parmesan cheese, Italian seasoning, and sliced green onion garnish. Stir 2 tablespoons snipped fresh dill or 2 teaspoons dried dillweed and $\frac{1}{2}$ teaspoon seasoned salt or salt into the beaten cream cheese mixture. If desired, garnish with a dill sprig.

Ask Mom How do I soften cream cheese? page 93 / How do I grate cheese? page 71 / How do I crush dried herbs? page 78 / What does garnish mean? page 79 / How do I slice green onions? page 43 / How do I snip fresh herbs? pages 42, 328

Bruschetta

1 8-ounce loaf baguette-style French bread
2 tablespoons olive oil
  Freshly ground black pepper
  Fresh Tomato and Olive Topping, Shrimp Topping, Basil Pesto and White Bean Topping,
    or Dried Fig and Pistachio Topping (page 95)

1 Preheat oven to 425°F. For crostini, bias-slice the bread into ½-inch-thick slices (below). Arrange slices in a single layer on an ungreased baking sheet. Lightly brush one side of each bread slice with olive oil (below). Lightly sprinkle oiled side of bread with pepper. Bake, uncovered, in the preheated oven for 4 minutes. Turn slices over and bake for 3 to 4 minutes more or until crisp and light brown.

2 Prepare one or more of the desired toppings. Spoon onto toasted bread just before serving. Makes 8 to 10 servings.

Make-ahead directions: Cool toasts. Place in an airtight container and store at room temperature for up to 24 hours.

Per serving (Basil Pesto and White Beans): 282 cal., 18 g total fat (4 g sat. fat), 36 mg chol., 503 mg sodium, 24 g carbo., 3 g fiber, 9 g pro.

1 To bias-slice a baguette, cut it at an angle with a serrated knife. This gives you slices with more surface area than straight cuts would.

2 Arrange slices on a baking sheet. Using a pastry brush, brush a light layer of olive oil on the top sides of the baguette slices.

Good to Know

Bruschetta comes from the Italian word "bruscare," which means "to roast over coals." Bruschetta is made by drizzling slices of bread with olive oil and baking them until they're crisp. (Sounds like a fancy name for toast!) Of course, it's so much more than that when spooned with heaping tablespoons of these crowd-pleasing toppings (page 95).

Ask Mom How do I use a serrated knife? page 64 / How do I grind pepper? page 22 / How do I seed and chop tomatoes? page 52 / How do I pit olives? page 75 / How do I chop an onion? page 47 / How do I snip fresh herbs? pages 42, 328 / What is that vinegar? page 349 / How do I mince garlic? page 40 / How do I hard-cook an egg? page 436 / How do I rinse and drain canned beans? page 390 / How do I slice green onions? page 43 / What is a shallot? page 46 / How do I chop nuts? page 65

Fresh Tomato and Olive Topping

In a small bowl stir together 1 cup seeded and finely chopped tomato (2 medium); 1 cup coarsely chopped assorted pitted ripe olives (such as kalamata, Greek, or Mission); 1/3 cup finely chopped red onion; 2 tablespoons snipped fresh cilantro or parsley; 2 tablespoons balsamic vinegar or red wine vinegar; and 2 cloves garlic, minced.

Shrimp Topping

In a medium bowl stir together 8 ounces peeled and deveined cooked shrimp, chopped; 1 tablespoon olive oil; 2 teaspoons white wine vinegar; 1/4 teaspoon salt; and 1/4 teaspoon ground black pepper. Set aside. Halve 2 large cloves of garlic and rub toasts with cut sides before topping with shrimp mixture.

Basil Pesto and White Bean Topping

In a small bowl stir together a 9-ounce container (1 cup) basil pesto; 1 finely chopped hard-cooked egg; and 1 teaspoon lemon juice, sherry vinegar, or red wine vinegar. In another small bowl stir together 1/2 of a 19-ounce can cannellini (white kidney) beans or 1/2 of a 15-ounce can Great Northern beans, rinsed and drained (1 cup); 1 tablespoon thinly sliced green onion or chopped shallot; 1 tablespoon olive oil; and 1/8 teaspoon crushed red pepper.

Dried Fig and Pistachio Topping

In a medium bowl place 3 ounces cream cheese, 2 ounces fontina or provolone cheese, and 3 ounces goat cheese (chèvre); let stand at room temperature for 30 minutes. In a small bowl stir together 1/4 cup snipped dried figs and 1 tablespoon balsamic vinegar; let stand at room temperature for 30 minutes. Beat cheese with an electric mixer on low speed until well combined; stir in figs. Sprinkle with 1/4 cup chopped pistachios.

Skill Level

Greek Layer Dip

- 1 6-ounce carton plain yogurt
- ½ cup finely chopped unpeeled cucumber
- 1 tablespoon finely chopped red onion
- 1 teaspoon snipped fresh mint
- 1 10-ounce container plain hummus
- ½ cup chopped, seeded tomato (1 medium)
- ½ cup crumbled feta cheese (2 ounces)
- 3 large white and/or wheat pita rounds

Good to Know Layer dips are a great way to get a bunch of different flavors crammed into one dish. This recipe calls for purchased hummus, but it's also a good way to use up extra homemade hummus (see page 92). Or if you're feeling ambitious, whip up a batch of homemade just for this recipe. Any leftover hummus can be served on its own.

1 In a small bowl stir together yogurt, ¼ cup of the cucumber, onion, and mint. Set aside.

2 Spread hummus in the bottom of a 10-inch quiche dish or 9-inch pie plate. Spread yogurt mixture evenly over hummus. Sprinkle with tomato, remaining ¼ cup cucumber, and the feta cheese (below). Split each pita bread round in half horizontally; cut each half into eight wedges. Serve pita bread wedges with dip. Makes about 10 servings.

Per serving: 128 cal., 4 g total fat (1 g sat. fat), 6 mg chol., 241 mg sodium, 18 g carbo., 2 g fiber, 5 g pro.

1 To crumble a chunk of feta, gently break it apart with your fingers. You can also buy it precrumbled.

2 Assemble the dip in an attractive dish for serving. After spreading the hummus and yogurt layers, top with tomato.

3 Fill in spaces around the tomato with chopped cucumber and crumbled feta. Use unpeeled cucumber for added color.

Ask Mom How do I chop an onion? page 47 / How do I snip fresh herbs? pages 42, 328 / How do I seed tomatoes? page 52 / How do I chop a tomato? page 52

Turkey Salad
Tartlets

1 $\frac{1}{4}$ cups finely chopped cooked turkey breast*

3 slices packaged ready-to-serve cooked bacon, chopped, or 3 slices bacon, crisp-cooked, drained, and crumbled

2 tablespoons finely chopped shallot (1 medium) or onion

2 tablespoons mayonnaise

2 tablespoons dairy sour cream

2 teaspoons lime juice

1 teaspoon Dijon-style mustard

Salt and ground black pepper

1 avocado, halved, seeded, peeled, and chopped

2 2.1-ounce packages baked miniature phyllo dough shells (30 shells)

8 grape tomatoes, quartered lengthwise

1 In a medium bowl stir together turkey, bacon, and shallot. Set aside.

2 In a small bowl stir together mayonnaise, sour cream, lime juice, mustard, and salt and pepper to taste. Add mayonnaise mixture to turkey mixture, stirring to combine. Add avocado to turkey salad, gently tossing to combine.

3 Spoon turkey salad into phyllo shells. Garnish each tart with a tomato wedge. Makes 30 tartlets.

*Note: To save time, coarsely chop the turkey, put in a food processor, cover, and pulse with several on/off turns until finely chopped.

Make-ahead directions: Prepare as above through Step 2. Cover and chill turkey salad for up to 24 hours. Just before serving, stir in the avocado and spoon the salad into tart shells.

Per tartlet: 52 cal., 3 g total fat (0 g sat. fat), 6 mg chol., 52 mg sodium, 3 g carbo., 0 g fiber, 3 g pro.

Pineapple-Almond Turkey Salad Tartlets: Prepare as above, except omit the mustard and substitute $\frac{1}{2}$ cup drained pineapple tidbits for the avocado and $\frac{1}{4}$ cup toasted sliced almonds for the tomatoes.

Flavor Changes If you're throwing an appetizer party, mini phyllo shells may become your new best friend. They can be used as a vessel for so many foods. You can pack them full of tuna, ham, and seafood salads. Or add a small layer each of cream cheese, crumbled blue cheese, chopped dried cherries, and chopped toasted pecans. For a sweet twist, fill shells with purchased lemon curd or chopped fruit and berries. Top with a little whipped cream and you have tiny tarts!

Ask Mom How do I cook bacon? page 172 / What is a shallot? page 46 / How do I chop an onion? page 47 / How do I juice a lime? pages 30, 80 / How much juice does one lime yield? page 30 / What is Dijon-style mustard? page 379 / How do I seed and peel an avocado? page 36 / What is a grape tomato? page 52 / What does garnish mean? page 79 / How do I toast nuts? page 65

1 Skill Level

Nutty-Sweet Brie

- 1 8-ounce round Brie cheese
- ¼ cup butter or margarine
- ¼ cup packed brown sugar
- ¼ cup chopped nuts
- 1 tablespoon honey
  Assorted crackers

Ingredient Info When you take the Brie out of its package, you'll notice that it has a papery-looking peel on it. Don't waste time trying to scrape this off. It's actually the downy rind of the cheese and it's completely edible. It's not removed before baking, so that's one step you can scratch off your list.

1 Preheat oven to 350°F. Place the cheese in a shallow baking dish or pie plate. Bake, uncovered, in the preheated oven for 10 minutes.

2 Meanwhile, in a small saucepan combine the remaining ingredients except crackers. Bring the butter mixture to boiling over medium heat, stirring constantly. Pour sauce over Brie. Serve with assorted crackers. Makes 8 servings.

Per serving: 204 cal., 16 g total fat (9 g sat. fat), 44 mg chol., 222 mg sodium, 10 g carbo., 0 g fiber, 7 g pro.

2 Skill Level

Bacon and Cheese-Stuffed Dates

- 2 slices bacon, crisp-cooked, drained, and finely crumbled, or ¼ cup chopped prosciutto (2 ounces)
- ¼ cup thinly sliced green onion (2)
- 2 cloves garlic, minced
- ½ cup crumbled blue cheese (2 ounces)
- 1 3-ounce package cream cheese, softened
- 2 teaspoons Dijon-style mustard
- ⅛ teaspoon ground black pepper
- 24 Medjool dates (about 16 ounces unpitted)

1 Preheat oven to 350°F. In a medium bowl stir together bacon, green onion, and garlic. Add blue cheese, cream cheese, mustard, and pepper to bacon mixture. Stir to combine.

2 Using a sharp knife, make a lengthwise slit in each date. Spread each date open slightly. Remove pits (page 99). Fill each date with a rounded teaspoon of the bacon mixture (page 99). Place dates, filling sides up, on a baking sheet. Bake, uncovered, in the preheated oven for 5 to 8 minutes or until heated through. Serve warm. Makes 24 dates.

Make-ahead directions: Prepare as above, except do not bake the dates. Place stuffed dates in an airtight container, cover, and chill for up to 24 hours. Bake as directed just before serving.

Per date: 91 cal., 2 g total fat (1 g sat. fat), 6 mg chol., 66 mg sodium, 18 g carbo., 2 g fiber, 2 g pro.

Ask Mom How do I measure butter? pages 58, 59 / How do I pack brown sugar? page 58 / How do I chop nuts? page 65 / How do I cook bacon? page 172 / What is prosciutto? page 358 / How do I slice green onions? page 43 / What is a garlic clove? page 40 / How do I mince garlic? page 40 / How do I crumble cheese? pages 71, 96 / How do I soften cream cheese? page 93 / What is Dijon-style mustard? page 379

WHAT'S A MEDJOOL DATE?
Big, fat, and flavorful—that's the kind of date you want for stuffing. Dubbed "nature's candy," Medjool dates are the perfect choice. This premium fresh date is at its best from November through March but can be found year-round. Look for it in the supermarket produce section.

1 Use a paring knife to make a lengthwise slit along each date. Remove the pit with the knife tip.

2 Spoon cheese mixture into dates so they are very full. Place stuffed dates, filling sides up, on baking sheet.

GET CREATIVE. The final shape these fun antipasti-on-a-stick take is entirely up to you. Put the long things (salami rolls and banana peppers) on the ends with the short things in the middle. Or alternate long and short.

A 6-inch bamboo skewer will hold a generous number of munchables, but you can also put these kabobs together on all kinds of fun party and/or cocktail picks.

Antipasto Kabobs

16 refrigerated cheese-filled tortellini (about 2 ounces)*

6 ounces thinly sliced salami or other thinly sliced cooked meat

1 14-ounce can artichoke hearts, drained and halved or quartered

16 large pimiento-stuffed green olives

16 pickled banana peppers or small pepperoncini salad peppers

16 red or yellow cherry tomatoes

1 recipe Herb-Balsamic Vinaigrette or ⅔ cup bottled Italian salad dressing

1 Cook pasta according to package directions; drain. Rinse with cold water; drain well. Fold salami slices in half; roll up. On sixteen 6-inch wooden skewers, thread salami rolls, tortellini, artichoke pieces, olives, peppers, and tomatoes. Place kabobs in a single layer in shallow plastic storage containers.

2 Drizzle Herb-Balsamic Vinaigrette or Italian dressing over kabobs. Cover and chill for at least 2 hours or up to 24 hours, turning kabobs occasionally. Drain kabobs to serve. Makes 16 kabobs.

*Note: If desired, substitute 1 cup cubed provolone cheese or mozzarella cheese (4 ounces) for the tortellini.

Herb-Balsamic Vinaigrette: In a screw-top jar combine ⅓ cup olive oil or salad oil; ⅓ cup white balsamic, balsamic, or red wine vinegar; 1 tablespoon snipped fresh thyme, oregano, or basil or ½ teaspoon dried thyme, oregano, or basil, crushed; 1 teaspoon sugar; and 1 clove garlic, minced. Cover and shake well (see photos, page 357).

Per kabob: 89 cal., 6 g total fat (1 g sat. fat), 10 mg chol., 578 mg sodium, 5 g carbo., 1 g fiber, 3 g pro.

Good to Know All kinds of foods are more fun eaten on a stick. Try fruit and cheese—a great combo. Alternate cubes of melon, small strawberries, and grapes with cubed mozzarella or cheddar cheese. Or skip the cheese and just use your choice of small fruit pieces and berries for a fruit wand. Better yet, try a dessert skewer by threading with brownie squares, marshmallows, and strawberries. You can even serve chocolate-flavor syrup for dipping. Or substitute squares of angel food or pound cake for the brownies.

Ask Mom What is a cherry tomato? page 52 / What is a skewer? page 79 / What does drizzle mean? page 79 / What is that oil? page 348 / What is that vinegar? page 349 / How do I snip fresh herbs? pages 42, 328 / How do I crush dried herbs? page 78 / What is a garlic clove? page 40 / How do I mince garlic? page 40

Sweet and Sassy Meatballs

  1 16-ounce can jellied cranberry sauce
  1 18-ounce bottle barbecue sauce
  2 1-pound packages frozen cooked meatballs, thawed (32 per pound)

1 For sauce, in a large skillet stir together cranberry sauce and barbecue sauce. Cook over medium heat until cranberry sauce is melted, stirring occasionally.

2 Add meatballs to sauce. Cook, uncovered, about 10 minutes or until meatballs are heated through, stirring occasionally. Serve immediately or keep meatballs warm in a slow cooker on low setting to serve. Makes 16 servings.

Make-ahead directions: Prepare as directed in Step 1. Stir in frozen or thawed meatballs. Place in an airtight container. Cover and chill for up to 24 hours. To serve, heat meatballs and sauce in a large skillet over medium heat until heated through, stirring occasionally.

Per serving: 60 cal., 4 g total fat (2 g sat. fat), 5 mg chol., 178 mg sodium, 5 g carbo., 1 g fiber, 2 g pro.

Chipotle-Sauced Meatballs: Prepare as above, except substitute one 12-ounce bottle chili sauce for the barbecue sauce and stir in 3 to 4 tablespoons finely chopped canned chipotle peppers in adobo sauce (see photo, page 373).

Hawaiian-Sauced Meatballs Prepare as above, except substitute one 8-ounce can crushed pineapple, undrained, for the cranberry sauce.

Party **Nachos**

8 ounces tortilla chips (about 10 cups)
2 cups shredded cheddar cheese (8 ounces)
2 cups shredded Monterey Jack cheese (8 ounces)
⅓ cup sliced green onion (3)
1 cup chopped seeded tomato (2 medium)
1 4-ounce can diced green chile peppers, drained
1 2.25-ounce can sliced pitted ripe olives, drained
1 15-ounce can black beans, rinsed and drained
   Purchased salsa (optional)
   Dairy sour cream (optional)
   Purchased guacamole or 1 recipe Guacamole (page 89) (optional)

1 Preheat oven to 400°F. Divide tortilla chips between two 12-inch round pizza pans or oven-safe serving platters, spreading to the edges. Top chips with half of the cheddar cheese, half of the Monterey Jack cheese, the green onion, tomato, and chile peppers. Sprinkle with remaining cheeses, the olives, and black beans.

2 Bake, uncovered, one pan at a time, in the preheated oven for 5 to 7 minutes or until cheese melts. Serve immediately. If desired, serve with salsa, sour cream, and/or guacamole. Makes 8 to 10 servings.

Per serving: 414 cal., 27 g total fat (13 g sat. fat), 55 mg chol., 720 mg sodium, 28 g carbo., 5 g fiber, 20 g pro.

Good to Know For every occasion, big or small, nachos are a surefire way to please the masses. Your best bet is to assemble the ingredients on the pans right before the party begins, then bake one pan immediately. When the first one is gone, pop the second pan in the oven and bake it hot and fresh. Just make sure all the wet ingredients—chile peppers, olives, and black beans—are drained well so they don't make the chips on the second pan mushy.

Ask Mom How do I shred cheese? page 71 / How do I slice green onions? page 43 / How do I seed and chop tomatoes? page 52 / How do I rinse and drain canned beans? page 390

Skill Level

Polenta with
Peppers and Olives

 1 16-ounce tube refrigerated cooked polenta
 2 tablespoons olive oil
 1 cup red, green, and/or yellow sweet pepper cut into thin strips
 1/8 teaspoon salt
 1/8 teaspoon crushed red pepper
 1/4 cup pitted kalamata olives, coarsely chopped
 2 tablespoons finely shredded Parmesan cheese
 1 1/2 teaspoons snipped fresh rosemary

Ingredient Savvy
Polenta is basically cornmeal mush. Although that may not trip your trigger, once you get a taste, you'll understand why polenta is a favorite in northern Italy. Although it can be eaten in its "mush" state, it is often cooled until firm and easy to slice. Packaged polenta is always in the firm state. Look for it in the refrigerated produce section.

1 Preheat oven to 350°F. Trim ends of polenta; discard trimmings. Cut polenta into 12 slices (1/2 inch thick) (below). Brush both sides of polenta slices with 1 tablespoon of the oil (below). Place polenta slices on a baking sheet. Bake in the preheated oven for 10 to 15 minutes or until heated through.

2 Meanwhile, in a 10-inch skillet heat remaining 1 tablespoon oil over medium heat. Add sweet pepper strips, salt, and crushed red pepper. Cook and stir until pepper strips are tender (below). Stir in the olives.

3 To serve, spoon the pepper mixture evenly over warm polenta slices. Sprinkle with Parmesan cheese and rosemary. Makes 12 servings.

Per serving: 52 cal., 4 g total fat (1 g sat. fat), 3 mg chol., 124 mg sodium, 4 g carbo., 1 g fiber, 1 g pro.

Parmesan Polenta: Prepare as above, except omit pepper mixture. During the last 5 minutes of baking, sprinkle polenta slices with 1/2 cup finely shredded Parmesan cheese.

1 Use unflavored dental floss to cut polenta. Loop it under the polenta, then cross it over top. Pull ends to tighten the loop and make a slice.

2 Using a pastry brush, lightly brush 1 tablespoon olive oil over both sides of polenta slices. Arrange on an ungreased baking sheet.

3 Cook pepper strips in the remaining 1 tablespoon oil over medium heat. Stir occasionally until pepper strips are tender.

Ask Mom How do I seed sweet peppers and cut them into strips? page 49 / How do I pit olives? page 75 / How do I shred cheese? page 71 / How do I snip fresh herbs? pages 42, 328

COOL ALTERNATIVES. Set up a buffet of hot polenta slices and bowls filled with a variety of toppings so guests can pick and choose. Try drained marinated artichoke heart quarters, slivered pepperoni slices, snipped fresh basil, snipped fresh oregano, chopped kalamata olives, flaked lox-style smoked salmon, and salsa and refried beans.

Hot Artichoke Spread

- ¾ cup finely chopped onion (1 large)
- 2 cloves garlic, minced
- 1 tablespoon butter
- 2 8-ounce packages reduced-fat cream cheese (Neufchâtel), softened
- 1½ cups grated Parmesan cheese
- ¼ cup milk
- ¼ cup light mayonnaise
- ¼ cup light dairy sour cream
- ¼ teaspoon ground black pepper
- 3 cups chopped fresh spinach leaves
- 1 14-ounce can artichoke hearts, drained and chopped
- Bagel chips, crostini, or sliced French bread

1 Preheat oven to 350°F. In a 10-inch skillet cook onion and garlic in hot butter over medium heat for 3 to 4 minutes or until tender, stirring occasionally. Set aside to cool.

2 In a large bowl stir together cream cheese, Parmesan cheese, milk, mayonnaise, sour cream, and pepper. Stir in spinach, artichoke hearts, and the onion mixture. Spread cheese mixture in the bottom of a 10-inch deep-dish pie plate.

3 Bake in the preheated oven for 30 to 35 minutes or until heated and top begins to brown. Serve with bagel chips, crostini, or French bread. Makes about 40 (2-tablespoon) servings.

Make-ahead directions: Prepare as above through Step 2. Cover and chill for up to 24 hours. Uncover and bake as directed about 40 minutes or until bubbly.

Per serving (spread only): 58 cal., 4 g total fat (2 g sat. fat), 14 mg chol., 138 mg sodium, 2 g carbo., 0 g fiber, 2 g pro.

Hot Feta Cheese and Olive Spread: Prepare as above in Step 1. In Step 2, substitute 1 cup crumbled feta cheese with basil and tomato for 1 cup of the Parmesan cheese; substitute ½ cup halved, pitted kalamata olives for the artichoke hearts; and add 2 tablespoons snipped fresh basil. Continue as above in Step 3. If desired, serve with Toasted Pita Bread Wedges (see recipe, page 87).

Hot Sausage and Mushroom Spread (in photo): Prepare as above in Step 1, except omit the butter and cook 8 ounces bulk hot Italian sausage, 2 cups sliced fresh mushrooms, and ½ cup chopped green or red sweet pepper with the onion and garlic; drain off fat. Set sausage mixture aside to cool. For Step 2, substitute 1 cup shredded mozzarella cheese for 1 cup of the Parmesan cheese and omit the artichoke hearts.

Ask Mom How do I chop an onion? page 47 / What is a garlic clove? page 40 / How do I mince garlic? page 40 / How do I measure butter? pages 58, 59 / How do I soften cream cheese? page 93 / How do I grate cheese? page 71 / How do I crumble cheese? pages 71, 90 / How do I pit olives? page 75 / How do I snip fresh herbs? pages 42, 328 / How do I slice fresh mushrooms? page 45 / How do I seed and chop sweet peppers? page 49

3 Skill Level

Spinach-Stuffed Mushrooms

- 24 large fresh mushrooms, 1½ to 2 inches in diameter
- 2 tablespoons olive oil
  Salt and ground black pepper
- 8 ounces bulk hot Italian sausage
- ¼ cup finely chopped onion
- ¼ cup finely chopped red sweet pepper
- 1 clove garlic, minced
- 1 cup fresh spinach, chopped
- ¼ cup finely shredded Parmesan cheese
- ¼ cup fine dry bread crumbs

1 Preheat oven to 425°F. Lightly rinse mushrooms; pat dry with paper towels. Remove stems and chop (below); set aside. Lightly grease a baking sheet. Place mushroom caps on a prepared baking sheet. Brush caps with oil (below). Sprinkle with salt and black pepper. Set aside.

2 In a 12-inch skillet cook chopped mushroom stems, sausage, onion, sweet pepper, and garlic over medium heat until sausage is brown, stirring occasionally. Stir in spinach until wilted. Stir in Parmesan and crumbs. Remove from heat. Spoon sausage mixture into mushroom caps (below).

3 Bake in the preheated oven for 10 to 12 minutes or until stuffing is brown and mushrooms are tender. Makes 24 mushrooms.

Per mushroom: 56 cal., 4 g total fat (2 g sat. fat), 7 mg chol., 179 mg sodium, 2 g carbo., 0 g fiber, 3 g pro.

Chicken-Stuffed Mushrooms: Prepare as above, except substitute ground uncooked chicken for the sausage, Asiago cheese for Parmesan, and golden raisins for the sweet pepper. Add 2 slices bacon, crisp-cooked, drained, and crumbled, and ¼ teaspoon salt with bread crumbs.

1 Remove mushroom stems by bending them to the side until they pop out. Chop them.

2 Using a pastry brush, lightly brush the tops of mushroom caps with olive oil.

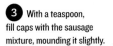

3 With a teaspoon, fill caps with the sausage mixture, mounding it slightly.

Ask Mom How do I clean fresh mushrooms? page 45 / How do I chop an onion? page 47 / How do I seed and chop sweet peppers? page 49 / What is a garlic clove? page 40 / How do I mince garlic? page 40 / How do I shred cheese? page 71 / What are fine dry bread crumbs? page 76 / How do I cook bacon? page 172

Mushroom-Bacon Turnovers

2 tablespoons butter or margarine

2 cups chopped fresh cremini or button mushrooms

1 cup chopped fresh shiitake mushrooms (caps only)

⅓ cup finely chopped red onion (1 small)

3 tablespoons whipping cream

3 slices bacon, crisp-cooked, drained, and crumbled

1 tablespoon snipped fresh thyme or 1 teaspoon dried thyme, crushed

1 tablespoon snipped fresh basil or 1 teaspoon dried basil, crushed

1 17.3-ounce package refrigerated large biscuits (8 biscuits)

1 egg

1 Preheat oven to 350°F. For filling, in a 12-inch skillet melt butter over medium heat. Add mushrooms and onion; cook about 5 minutes or until mushrooms are tender, stirring occasionally. Stir in whipping cream; simmer for 2 minutes more. Remove skillet from heat. Stir in bacon, thyme, and basil.

2 Using your fingers, separate each biscuit in half so you have 16 biscuit rounds (below). On a lightly floured surface, flatten each biscuit round to a 3-inch circle (below). Place about 2 teaspoons of the filling onto one half of each circle of dough (below). Fold dough over filling; seal edges by pressing them together firmly with tines of a fork (below).

3 Place filled turnovers on an ungreased baking sheet. In a small bowl beat egg lightly with a fork; brush egg over turnovers. Bake in the preheated oven for 14 to 17 minutes or until turnovers are golden. Serve warm. Makes 16 turnovers.

Per turnover: 139 cal., 8 g total fat (3 g sat. fat), 22 mg chol., 310 mg sodium, 13 g carbo., 1 g fiber, 3 g pro.

1 Separate each refrigerated biscuit into two halves by pulling it apart with your fingers.

2 On a lightly floured surface, press biscuit halves into 3-inch circles. Make sure they are an even thickness.

3 Using a flatware spoon, spoon about 2 teaspoons mushroom filling in the center of each circle of dough.

4 Fold the dough over filling to make a half-circle. Seal edges by pressing with the tines of a fork.

Ask Mom How do I measure butter? pages 58, 59 / What are some mushroom varieties? page 44 / How do I chop fresh mushrooms? page 45 / How do I chop an onion? page 47 / How do I cook bacon? page 172 / How do I snip fresh herbs? pages 42, 328 / How do I crush dried herbs? page 78 / How do I beat eggs? page 62

Ginger-Glazed Cocktail Ribs

2½ to 3 pounds meaty pork loin back ribs or spareribs*
    Salt and ground black pepper
¼ cup finely chopped onion
 I clove garlic, minced
 2 teaspoons olive oil or cooking oil
⅓ cup bottled chili sauce
⅓ cup apricot or peach preserves
 I tablespoon soy sauce
 I teaspoon grated fresh ginger or ¼ teaspoon ground ginger

1 Preheat oven to 350°F. Cut ribs into single-rib portions (below). Sprinkle ribs with salt and pepper. Arrange ribs, meaty sides up, in a shallow roasting pan (below). Roast in the preheated oven about 1 hour or until tender.

2 Meanwhile, for glaze, in a 1-quart saucepan cook and stir onion and garlic in hot oil over medium heat about 3 minutes or until onion is tender. Stir in chili sauce, apricot preserves, soy sauce, and ginger. Heat and stir until bubbly.

3 Using a pastry brush, brush ribs generously with glaze (below). Roast ribs for 15 minutes more, brushing once or twice with glaze during baking time. Makes about 30 servings.

*Note: Ask butcher to cut ribs in half across the bones to make smaller pieces.

Make-ahead directions: Prepare as above through Step 3. Cool and place in an airtight container; cover and chill for up to 3 days. To serve, preheat oven to 350°F. Place ribs in a large baking pan and bake in the preheated oven about 5 minutes or until heated through.

Per serving: 54 cal., 2 g total fat (I g sat. fat), II mg chol., 95 mg sodium, 3 g carbo., 0 g fiber, 5 g pro.

1 Use a chef's knife to cut the ribs between the bones to make single-rib portions.

2 Place the ribs in a shallow roasting pan with the meaty sides up.

3 Brush the ribs at the end of roasting so they are coated nicely and the glaze doesn't burn.

Ask Mom How do I chop an onion? page 47 / What is a garlic clove? page 40 / How do I mince garlic? page 40 / What is fresh ginger? page 4I / How do I grate fresh ginger? page 4I

(2) Skill Level

Buffalo Wings

12 chicken wings (about 2 pounds)
2 tablespoons butter or margarine, melted
3 tablespoons bottled hot pepper sauce
2 teaspoons paprika
¼ teaspoon salt
¼ teaspoon cayenne pepper
1 recipe Blue Cheese Dip
Celery sticks (optional)

Good to Know This might just be the all-time favorite bar food ever. Created at the Anchor Bar in Buffalo, New York, these spicy, vinegary wings are a popular appetizer, snack—even a meal! Short on time? Substitute bottled blue cheese dressing for the dip.

1 Cut off and discard tips of chicken wings (below). Cut wings at joints to form 24 pieces. Place chicken wing pieces in a plastic bag set in a shallow dish (below).

2 For marinade, stir together butter, bottled hot pepper sauce, paprika, salt, and cayenne pepper. Pour over chicken wings; seal bag. Marinate at room temperature for 30 minutes. Drain chicken wings, discarding marinade.

3 Place the chicken wings on the unheated rack of a broiler pan. Broil 4 to 5 inches from the heat about 10 minutes or until light brown. Turn wings over (below). Broil for 10 to 15 minutes more or until chicken is tender and no longer pink. Serve with Blue Cheese Dip and, if desired, celery sticks. Makes 12 servings.

Blue Cheese Dip: In a blender or food processor place ½ cup dairy sour cream; ½ cup mayonnaise or salad dressing; ½ cup crumbled blue cheese; 1 tablespoon white wine vinegar; and 1 clove garlic, minced. Cover and blend or process until smooth. Transfer dip to a bowl. Cover and chill for up to 1 week. If desired, top with additional crumbled blue cheese before serving.

Per serving (with dip): 221 cal., 19 g total fat (6 g sat. fat), 47 mg chol., 258 mg sodium, 1 g carbo., 0 g fiber, 11 g pro.

1 Use kitchen shears to cut off wing tips between the joints. Discard wing tips.

2 Cut between joints of the meaty portions of wings. Cut over a plastic bag in a bowl so the pieces fall right in.

3 Use long-handled tongs to turn chicken wings halfway through broiling.

Ask Mom How do I measure butter? pages 58, 59 / How do I crumble cheese? pages 71, 96 / What does it mean to marinate? page 73 / What is a garlic clove? page 40 / How do I mince garlic? page 40

Asian Chicken Wings

12 chicken wings (about 2 pounds)
1 ½ cups water
⅔ cup soy sauce
½ cup sliced leek (1 medium)
4 slices fresh ginger
1 tablespoon sugar
1 tablespoon vinegar
2 or 3 dried red chile peppers
½ teaspoon purchased five-spice powder
2 cloves garlic, minced
   Bottled teriyaki sauce (optional)

1 Cut off and discard tips of chicken wings. If desired, cut wings at joints to form 24 pieces (see photos, page 110).

2 For sauce, in a 4-quart Dutch oven stir together water, soy sauce, leek, ginger, sugar, vinegar, chile peppers, five-spice powder, and garlic. Bring to boiling. Add chicken. Return to boiling; reduce heat. Simmer, covered, for 20 to 25 minutes or until chicken is no longer pink.

3 Using a slotted spoon, remove chicken wings from the Dutch oven. If desired, serve wings with bottled teriyaki sauce for dipping. Makes 12 servings.

Per serving: 123 cal., 9 g total fat (2 g sat. fat), 58 mg chol., 204 mg sodium, 0 g carbo., 0 g fiber, 10 g pro.

Shopping Savvy Some may like it hot, but some don't. Keep this in mind when choosing the dried red chiles for this recipe. Here are some options for dried chiles that you can look for in the store:

Anaheim chile: The dried red variety of this pepper is between 2 and 4 out of 10 on the heat scale.
De arbol chile: Long and slender, this one rates 6 on the heat scale.
Thai (bird) chile: Similar to de arbol, these chiles are a 7 on the scale.
Japonés chile: These babies rate around 7 out of 10 on the heat scale.
Habañero chile: Look out for this one. It rates a 10+ (out of 10) on the heat scale and is almost in the danger zone. Never cut one without gloves on.

Ask Mom What is a leek? page 43 / How do I slice a leek? page 43 / What is fresh ginger? page 41 / What is that vinegar? page 349 / What is a garlic clove? page 40 / How do I mince garlic? page 40 / What does simmer mean? page 79

(2) Skill Level

Good to Know
Meat and poultry generally benefit from extended marinating times, but fish and seafood do not. Their delicate flesh tends to break down faster when exposed to the acid in marinade (such as the lemon juice in this recipe). To keep this from happening, get the shrimp mixture out of the marinade within the 2- to 6-hour time frame.

Mediterranean Shrimp

$\frac{1}{4}$ cup olive oil or salad oil

3 tablespoons white wine vinegar

2 tablespoons finely chopped shallot (1 medium)

2 tablespoons snipped fresh oregano

1 teaspoon finely shredded lemon peel

1 tablespoon lemon juice

$\frac{1}{2}$ teaspoon salt

1 clove garlic, minced

1 pound frozen large cooked shrimp (with tails), thawed

4 ounces smoked provolone cheese, cut into $\frac{1}{2}$-inch cubes, or crumbled feta cheese (1 cup)

1$\frac{1}{2}$ cups grape tomatoes and/or yellow pear-shape tomatoes

$\frac{1}{2}$ cup drained capers

1 In a large resealable plastic bag combine oil, vinegar, shallot, oregano, lemon peel, lemon juice, salt, and garlic. Seal bag; mix marinade well. Set bag in a large bowl; add shrimp, cheese, tomatoes, and capers to marinade. Seal bag; marinate in the refrigerator for 2 to 6 hours, turning bag occasionally.

2 Chill 8 margarita glasses or small glass serving dishes in the refrigerator until ready to use. To serve, spoon shrimp mixture into chilled glasses. Makes 8 servings.

Per serving: 179 cal., 11 g total fat (4 g sat. fat), 120 mg chol., 654 mg sodium, 3 g carbo., 1 g fiber, 16 g pro.

Cajun Shrimp: Prepare as above, except for the marinade, in a large resealable bag combine $\frac{1}{4}$ cup lemon juice, $\frac{1}{4}$ cup salad oil, 1$\frac{1}{2}$ teaspoons Cajun seasoning, and 2 cloves garlic, minced. Omit provolone cheese and capers. Add 1 cup chopped red, yellow, and/or green sweet pepper and $\frac{3}{4}$ cup sliced celery to the marinade with the shrimp.

Citrus Shrimp: Prepare as above, except for the marinade, in a large resealable bag combine $\frac{1}{2}$ cup grapefruit juice; $\frac{1}{4}$ cup salad oil; 1 tablespoon honey; 2 teaspoons snipped fresh thyme or $\frac{1}{4}$ teaspoon dried thyme, crushed; $\frac{1}{4}$ teaspoon salt; and $\frac{1}{4}$ teaspoon ground black pepper.

Quick and Easy Shrimp: Prepare as above, except for the marinade, in a large resealable bag use 1 cup purchased Italian vinaigrette or dried tomato vinaigrette.

Ask Mom What is that oil? page 348 / What is that vinegar? page 349 / What is a shallot? page 46 / How do I chop an onion? page 47 / How do I snip fresh herbs? pages 42, 328 / How do I shred lemon peel? page 30 / How do I juice a lemon? pages 30, 80 / How much juice does one lemon yield? page 30 / How do I mince garlic? page 40 / What is a grape tomato? page 52 / What are capers? page 79 / How do I seed/chop sweet peppers? page 49 / How do I seed/peel an avocado? page 36

SHRIMP COCKTAIL GOES GLOBAL. This spirited little saladlike starter is for shrimp lovers everywhere—no matter how you decide to style it. This versatile recipe lets you choose from Mediterranean, Mexican, Cajun, or refreshingly citrusy tropical flavor profiles.

Tequila Shrimp Prepare as on page 112, except for the marinade, in a large resealable bag combine ¼ cup olive oil, ¼ cup lime juice, ¼ cup tequila, 2 tablespoons snipped fresh cilantro, ⅛ teaspoon salt, and 2 cloves garlic, minced. Omit the provolone and capers. Add 1 cup of ¾-inch pieces of red, yellow, and/or green sweet pepper to the marinade with the shrimp. After spooning shrimp mixture into glasses, top with 1 avocado that has been halved, seeded, peeled, and cut into 8 slices.

Double-Quick Shrimp Cocktail

  I 8-ounce carton dairy sour cream
¼ cup prepared horseradish
  2 tablespoons snipped chives or thinly sliced green onion tops
  I tablespoon lemon juice
  I 12-ounce jar seafood cocktail sauce or chili sauce
1½ pounds (60 to 75) frozen peeled and cooked shrimp (with tails), thawed
    Chives and/or lemon wedges

1 In a small bowl stir together sour cream, horseradish, chives, and lemon juice. Place half of the sour cream mixture in one side of a 4-cup shallow serving bowl. Spoon half of the cocktail sauce into the bowl next to the sour cream mixture. Spoon the rest of the sour cream mixture over the sour cream mixture in the bowl and the rest of the cocktail sauce over the cocktail sauce. If desired, cover and chill dip mixture for up to 4 hours before serving.

2 To serve, place the bowl containing the dip mixture on a platter. Rinse shrimp; pat dry with paper towels (see photos 1 and 2, page 277). Arrange shrimp around the bowl. Garnish with chives and/or lemon wedges. Makes 30 servings.

Per serving: 28 cal., I g total fat (I g sat. fat), 27 mg chol., 90 mg sodium, 2 g carbo., 0 g fiber, 3 g pro.

Good to Know
Two sauces and a bucket load of shrimp—sounds like a party! It's simple to get the two sauces into one bowl—just start by pouring half of one sauce on one side, then half of the other sauce on the other side. They will meet in the middle but won't run together. If this makes you nervous, use two separate bowls for the sauces. Nobody will know the difference and the sauces will still taste great!

Ask Mom What is prepared horseradish? page 429 / How do I snip fresh herbs? pages 42, 328 / How do I slice green onions? page 43 / How do I juice a lemon/lime? pages 30, 80 / How much juice does one lemon/lime yield? page 30 / How do I cut lemon/lime wedges? page 30 / What does garnish mean? page 79

1 Skill Level

Crab Cakes with Easy Aïoli

- 1 6- to 9-ounce package frozen crab cakes (about 6 regular or 12 miniature)
- ⅓ cup mayonnaise
- 1 to 2 cloves garlic, minced
- 1 teaspoon water
- ½ teaspoon lemon juice
- ⅛ teaspoon salt or coarse sea salt
- ¼ to ⅓ cup olive oil
- 2 teaspoons snipped fresh basil
  Snipped fresh basil
  Lemon wedges (optional)

Good to Know Aïoli is an aromatic garlic-flavored mayonnaise that can be tricky to make from scratch. This supereasy version starts with purchased mayo as the base. In addition to crab cakes, try aïoli with vegetable dippers or cold cooked shrimp, smeared on a sandwich, or with a piece of grilled fish.

1 Heat crab cakes according to package directions. Meanwhile, for aïoli, in a medium bowl stir together the mayonnaise and garlic. Using a wire whisk, whisk in the water, lemon juice, and salt until smooth (below). Whisk in the olive oil, a few teaspoons at a time, until the mixture reaches desired consistency (below). (If the mixture becomes too thick, whisk in additional water.) Stir in the 2 teaspoons snipped fresh basil.

2 Serve aïoli with hot crab cakes. Sprinkle with additional snipped basil. If desired, serve with lemon wedges. Makes 6 servings.*

*Note: This recipe easily doubles for 12 servings.

Per serving: 236 cal., 22 g total fat (4 g sat. fat), 9 mg chol., 254 mg sodium, 7 g carbo., 0 g fiber, 2 g pro.

1 Have all the ingredients for the aïoli ready to go. Whisk together the mayonnaise, garlic, water, lemon juice, and salt.

2 Drizzle the olive oil slowly into the mayonnaise mixture while quickly whisking. Add only a little at a time so the mayonnaise can absorb it.

Ask Mom What is a garlic clove? page 40 / How do I mince garlic? page 40 / How do I juice a lemon? pages 30, 80 / How much juice does one lemon yield? page 30 / What is sea salt? page 79 / How do I snip fresh herbs? pages 42, 328 / How do I cut lemon wedges? page 30

(2) Skill Level

Beer and Cheddar Fondue

1 clove garlic, halved
1 cup light beer
$\frac{1}{2}$ teaspoon instant chicken bouillon granules
2 tablespoons cornstarch
2 tablespoons cold water
1 cup shredded American cheese (4 ounces)
2 cups shredded sharp cheddar cheese (8 ounces)
  Assorted items for dipping (French or Italian bread cubes, breadsticks, broccoli florets, red sweet pepper pieces, soft pretzels, and/or precooked baby sunburst squash)

1 Rub the bottom and sides of a heavy metal fondue pot* with garlic halves (below); discard garlic. In fondue pot, combine the beer and bouillon. Bring to boiling over medium-high heat.

2 In a small bowl stir together cornstarch and the water. Add cornstarch mixture in a steady stream to beer mixture while stirring with a heat-resistant rubber spatula or wooden spoon (below). Cook and stir until thickened and bubbly. Reduce heat to medium-low. Gradually stir in shredded cheeses, stirring after each addition until cheese melts.

3 Place fondue pot over fondue burner (below). Serve immediately with desired items for dipping. Spear item with a fondue fork or wooden skewer; dip into cheese mixture, swirling to coat. (Fondue will thicken as it holds over the burner.) Makes 6 to 8 servings.

*Note: If you want to use a ceramic fondue pot, prepare fondue in a medium saucepan as above through Step 2. Transfer cheese mixture to ceramic pot and continue as directed in Step 3.

Per serving (fondue only): 258 cal., 18 g total fat (12 g sat. fat), 57 mg chol., 580 mg sodium, 6 g carbo., 0 g fiber, 14 g pro.

1 Cut a garlic clove in half and rub its cut sides all over the inside of the fondue pot.

2 Cornstarch keeps the cheese and liquid from separating as the fondue sits. Add cornstarch mixture all at once, stirring while you pour.

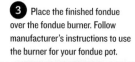

3 Place the finished fondue over the fondue burner. Follow manufacturer's instructions to use the burner for your fondue pot.

Ask Mom What is a garlic clove? page 40 / How do I shred cheese? page 71

Caramel Snack Mix

Good to Know Cereal snack mixes offer a big payoff for not a lot of effort. For just a little bit of mixing and stirring, you end up with a whole lot of food. (And it's very popular. No matter how much you make it usually all disappears.)

117

Appetizers & Snacks

1 12-ounce box crispy corn and rice cereal (about 12 cups)
1 ½ cups mixed nuts, cashews, or almonds
½ cup packed brown sugar
½ cup light-colored corn syrup
½ cup butter
2 cups chocolate-covered raisins, chocolate-covered peanuts, or semisweet or milk chocolate pieces

1 Preheat oven to 300°F. In a large roasting pan combine cereal and nuts; set aside. In a 1-quart saucepan combine brown sugar, corn syrup, and butter. Cook and stir over medium heat until butter is melted and mixture is smooth (below). Pour over cereal mixture; stir gently to coat (below).

2 Bake in the preheated oven for 30 minutes, stirring twice. Remove from oven. Spread mixture in a single layer on a large piece of buttered foil (below). Cool; break into pieces. Stir in chocolate-covered raisins. Store in an airtight container for up to 3 days or freeze for up to 1 month. Makes 30 (½-cup) servings.

Per serving: 186 cal., 9 g total fat (4 g sat. fat), 9 mg chol., 122 mg sodium, 27 g carbo., 1 g fiber, 2 g pro.

Spiced Caramel Snack Mix: Prepare as above, except add 1 teaspoon ground cinnamon and ½ teaspoon ground ginger to the butter mixture.

1 Using a wooden spoon, cook and stir brown sugar mixture until butter is melted and mixture is smooth and a uniform color.

2 Pour caramel sauce over cereal and nuts in the roasting pan, stirring the cereal mixture so everything is evenly coated.

3 Using a heat-resistant spatula or wooden spoon, spread snack mix in a shallow pan lined with buttered foil. Let cool before adding chocolate-covered raisins.

Ask Mom How do I pack brown sugar? page 58 / What's the best way to measure sticky liquids? pages 58, 81 / How do I measure butter? pages 58, 59

Lime-Tea Punch

- 8 individual-size black tea bags
- 6 cups boiling water
- 2 tablespoons honey
- 1 12-ounce can frozen limeade concentrate
- 1 liter (about 4 cups) ginger ale, chilled
    Ice cubes
- 1 lime

1 In a large bowl or heat-proof pitcher steep tea bags in boiling water for 5 minutes; remove tea bags and discard. Let mixture cool for 15 minutes. Stir in honey until dissolved. Stir in limeade concentrate until melted. Cover and chill mixture for at least 4 hours.

2 To serve, if necessary, transfer tea mixture to a large pitcher; add ginger ale and ice. Cut the lime in half lengthwise; cut each half into 8 slices. Garnish each serving with a lime slice. Makes 16 servings.

Make-ahead directions: Prepare tea mixture as above through Step 1. Cover and chill for up to 48 hours. To serve, continue with Step 2.

Per serving: 73 cal., 0 g total fat (0 g sat. fat), 0 mg chol., 9 mg sodium, 19 g carbo., 0 g fiber, 0 g pro.

FLAVOR CHANGES This refreshing punch also is delicious made with green tea. If you like stronger tea flavor, add another tea bag. Don't steep it any longer—tea gets bitter if brewed for more than 5 minutes.

Ask Mom How do I slice lemons/limes? page 30 / What does garnish mean? page 79

Bartending Basics

The nibbles and noshes in this chapter are more fun to eat with something spirited alongside. Here's what you need to know to become a master mixologist.

It's no secret that the cocktail has been undergoing a renaissance of late—and there's no secret to making great drinks at home either. There are just a few simple cocktail-concoting concepts to master. Once you have them down, you can stir up everything from the classics to your own creations. There are two basic types of drinks—sweet and dry. Most drinks consist of three basic parts: bases, modifiers, and accents. Bases are the spirits. Common bases are bourbon, vodka, gin, brandy, and tequila. Modifiers (or mixers) include vermouth, seltzer, juices, colas, and so on. Accents are subtle amounts of powerful ingredients like lime, olives, bitters, and complex liqueurs.

MIX MASTER MATH Since you may make drinks for more than one person, it's helpful to understand the concept of "parts." A drink that consists of 2 ounces tequila, 1 ounce orange liqueur, and 1 ounce lime juice would be 2 parts tequila to 1 part lime juice to 1 part orange liqueur, or 2:1:1. (That's a margarita, by the way.)

This ratio is helpful because as a basic drink formula, if you mix 2 parts of any base (spirit) with 1 part sweetener (liqueur or sugar) and 1 part juice (lemon, lime, or orange), you can mix a multitude of cocktails without a recipe.

A A strainer fits over a shaker and catches the ice and any solids while you pour out the liquid. **B** Use a shaker to combine liquids with ice to chill them fast. **C** A jigger measures liquids. A two-ended jigger may have a 1 ½-ounce (shot) end and a 1-ounce (pony) end. **D** Use a juicer to squeeze juice from citrus fruits. It strains seeds and has a lip for pouring. **E** A long-handled bar spoon is used to mix drinks right in the glass.

A Strainer

B Shaker

C Jigger

D Juicer

E Bar spoon

Nice to Have

While there's nothing saying you can't serve drinks in old jelly jars, there's nothing quite like handing someone a drink served in a classic cocktail glass. The three must-haves are the martini glass, the Collins glass, and the rocks (or old-fashioned) glass.

Gibson

2 ounces gin
¼ to ½ ounce dry vermouth
Cocktail onions

In a cocktail shaker combine gin and vermouth. Add *ice cubes*; cover and shake until very cold. Strain liquid into a chilled martini glass. Garnish with cocktail onions. Makes I serving.

Daiquiri

1½ ounces rum
I ounce lime juice
I teaspoon super-fine sugar
Lime wedge

In a cocktail shaker combine rum, lime juice, and sugar. Add *ice cubes*; cover and shake until sugar is dissolved and drink is very cold. Strain liquid into a chilled glass. Garnish with lime wedge. Makes I serving.

Old-Fashioned

I teaspoon sugar
Dash bitters
Orange slice
2 ounces bourbon
Maraschino cherry

In a rocks glass combine sugar, bitters, and orange slice; crush with the back of a spoon. Add bourbon and *ice cubes*; stir. Garnish with a cherry. Makes I serving.

Martini

2 green olives
2 ounces gin or vodka
¼ ounce dry vermouth
Fresh lemon peel twist

Thread the olives on a cocktail pick; set aside. In a cocktail shaker combine gin and vermouth. Add *ice cubes*; cover and shake until very cold. Strain liquid into a martini glass. Garnish with lemon twist and /or olives. Makes I serving.

Kamikaze

2 ounces vodka
2 ounces lime juice
I ounce orange liqueur
Lime wedge

In a cocktail shaker combine vodka, lime juice, and orange liqueur. Add *ice cubes*; cover and shake until very cold. Strain liquid into a vodka glass set in a bowl of ice or, if desired, into a glass filled with additional ice cubes. Garnish with lime wedge. Makes I serving.

Mint Julep

I teaspoon sugar
I to 2 fresh mint leaves
2 ounces bourbon
Crushed ice

In a cocktail shaker combine sugar and mint leaves; crush with the back of a spoon. Add bourbon and *ice cubes*; cover and shake until sugar is dissolved and drink is very cold. Fill an 8-ounce glass with *crushed ice*. Strain liquid into glass. Garnish with *mint sprigs*. Makes I serving.

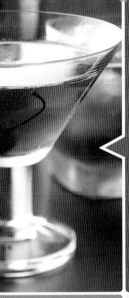

Manhattan

2 ounces bourbon
½ ounce sweet vermouth
Dash bitters
Maraschino cherry

In a cocktail shaker combine bourbon, vermouth, and bitters. Add *ice cubes*; cover and shake until very cold. Strain liquid into a chilled glass or a glass filled with additional ice cubes. Garnish with a cherry. Makes 1 serving.

Margarita

2 limes, halved
Coarse salt
2 ounces tequila
1 ounce orange liqueur

Cut a slice and wedge from one lime half; set wedge aside. Rub rim of glass with slice; dip rim into coarse salt. Juice remaining lime halves to get 1 ounce. In a cocktail shaker combine lime juice, tequila, and liqueur. Add *ice cubes*; cover and shake until very cold. Strain into a glass with additional ice. Garnish with lime wedge. Makes 1 serving.

Tom Collins

2 ounces gin
1½ ounces lemon juice
1½ teaspoons sugar
Lemon slices
Sparkling water

In a cocktail shaker combine gin, lemon juice, and sugar. Add *ice cubes*; cover and shake until sugar is dissolved and drink is very cold. Strain liquid into a glass filled with *crushed ice* and 1 or 2 lemon slices. Add a splash of sparkling water; stir. Makes 1 serving.

Side Car

Superfine sugar (optional)
2 ounces brandy
1 ounce lemon juice
1 ounce orange liqueur
Fresh lemon peel twist

If desired, wet the rim of a chilled glass with water. Dip the rim in sugar. In a cocktail shaker combine brandy, lemon juice, and orange liqueur. Add *ice cubes*; cover and shake until very cold. Strain liquid into prepared glass or a glass filled with additional ice cubes. Garnish with lemon peel twist. Makes 1 serving.

Cosmopolitan

2 ounces vodka
1 ounce orange liqueur
1 ounce cranberry juice
½ ounce lime juice
Fresh lime peel twist

In a cocktail shaker combine vodka, orange liqueur, cranberry juice, and lime juice. Add *ice cubes*; cover and shake until very cold. Strain liquid into a chilled martini glass. Garnish with lime peel twist. Makes 1 serving.

Whiskey Sour

2 ounces bourbon
1 ounce lime juice
1 ounce lemon juice
1 tablespoon sugar
Orange slice
Maraschino cherry

In a rocks glass combine bourbon, lime juice, lemon juice, and sugar. Using a spoon, stir until combined and sugar is dissolved. Add *ice cubes*. Garnish with an orange slice and a cherry. Makes 1 serving.

Shopping Savvy Look for superfine sugar in the baking aisle of your supermarket—it's often called baker's sugar. It's ideal for making cold drinks because the extremely fine grains dissolve easily in cold liquids. It's not only a bartender's friend, but it's great in iced coffee and tea and homemade lemonade too.

Mojito Fresco

2 large limes, cut into wedges (reserve one piece)
4 cups water
⅔ cup sugar
¼ to ½ cup light rum
Superfine sugar
½ cup fresh mint leaves
Ice cubes
Quartered limes (optional)

1 In a blender combine lime wedges, 2 cups of the water, and ⅔ cup sugar. Cover and blend about 30 seconds or until limes are chopped; do not puree (below). Strain through a fine-mesh sieve into a large pitcher (below). Stir in the remaining 2 cups water. Cover and chill for 1 to 12 hours.

2 To serve, stir rum into chilled lime mixture. Moisten the rims of 8 glasses with the reserved lime wedge; dip rims in superfine sugar (below). Place mint leaves in a mortar* and use the pestle to lightly bruise the leaves (below); place some of the bruised leaves in each glass. Fill glasses with ice cubes. Pour chilled lime mixture into glasses. If desired, garnish with quartered limes. Makes 8 servings.

*Note: If you don't have a mortar and pestle, place mint leaves in a small bowl and crush with the back of a spoon.

Per serving: 127 cal., 0 g total fat (0 g sat. fat), 0 mg chol., 4 mg sodium, 29 g carbo., 1 g fiber, 0 g pro.

1 Blend lime wedges, water, and sugar just until limes are chopped up. You don't want a uniform puree.

2 Strain the mixture in the blender through a fine-mesh sieve into a serving pitcher to remove the lime chunks.

3 Run the cut side of a lime wedge around the rims of the serving glasses and dip rims in superfine sugar.

4 Use a mortar and pe to just bruise the mint lea so they release their flavor You don't want a paste.

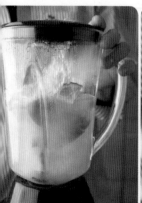

Ask Mom How do I cut lemon/lime wedges? page 30 / What is a mortar and pestle? page 22 / What does garnish mean? page 79

satisfying
SIDES

Go beyond steamed broccoli. These spectacular serve-alongs will spark up the simplest meal.

3

Roasted Asparagus

- 1 pound fresh asparagus, trimmed
- 1/8 teaspoon ground black pepper
- 1 tablespoon olive oil
- 3 tablespoons grated Parmesan cheese

1 Preheat oven to 450°F. Place asparagus in a 2-quart square baking dish. Sprinkle with pepper. Drizzle with olive oil. Toss lightly to coat. Roast, uncovered, in the preheated oven about 15 minutes or until crisp-tender, lightly tossing twice during roasting (below). Transfer asparagus to a warm serving platter. Sprinkle with cheese. Makes 4 servings.

Per serving: 58 cal., 5 g total fat (1 g sat. fat), 3 mg chol., 59 mg sodium, 3 g carbo., 1 g fiber, 3 g pro.

Good to Know Don't want to heat up the oven just for the asparagus? Instead try quick-cooking it on the stovetop. Lay the spears in a skillet and top with an inch of water. Lightly salt the water and bring to a simmer. Cook, covered, for 3 to 5 minutes or until crisp-tender.

Use tongs to grab a bunch of asparagus spears for easier tossing during roasting.

Ask Mom How do I trim asparagus? page 34 / What does drizzle mean? page 79 / What does crisp-tender mean? pages 79, 126 / How do I grate cheese? page 71

Farm-Style Green Beans

8 ounces fresh green beans

2 slices bacon, cut up

I medium onion, cut into thin wedges (about I cup)

½ cup sliced fresh mushrooms

1½ cups chopped tomato or one 14.5-ounce can diced tomatoes, drained

¼ teaspoon salt*

1 Trim green beans and leave whole or cut into 1-inch pieces (below). In a 3-quart saucepan cook beans, covered, in a small amount of boiling salted water about 10 minutes or until crisp-tender (below); drain.

2 Meanwhile, in a 10-inch skillet cook bacon over medium heat until crisp, stirring occasionally. Remove bacon, reserving drippings in skillet. Drain bacon on paper towels; set aside. Cook and stir onion and mushrooms in reserved drippings over medium heat until tender. Add tomato and salt. Cook, uncovered, for 2 to 3 minutes or until most of the liquid is absorbed. Transfer beans to a serving platter or bowl. Top with onion mixture. Sprinkle bacon over the vegetables. Makes 4 servings.

*Note: Omit salt if using canned tomatoes.

Per serving: 132 cal., 9 g total fat (3 g sat. fat), 13 mg chol., 312 mg sodium, 10 g carbo., 3 g fiber, 4 g pro.

1 Place several beans at a time on a cutting board, lining up the stem ends. Cut off stems. Cut off pointed tips, if desired, or leave attached. Leave beans whole or cut or snap into pieces.

2 To test for crisp-tender, bite into a bean a minute or two before end of suggested timing. The bean should have a slight crunch to it. Or test by poking it with a fork.

Flavor Changes

Once you get the hang of cooking green beans (remember, just until crisp-tender), start experimenting with different flavors and textures. For a supersimple side dish, toss hot beans with butter and seasonings or sprinkle with lemon peel and chopped toasted almonds. For a special-occasion treat, top with crumbled feta cheese, chopped tomato, and toasted pine nuts.

Ask Mom How do I cut onion wedges? page 47 / How do I slice fresh mushrooms? page 45 / How do I chop a tomato? page 52 / What does crisp-tender mean? pages 79, 126

GREEN BEAN PERFECTION. Cook them correctly and green beans are anything but boring or bland. Keep them a little crunchy and brilliant green and you can sell these veggies to anyone—even kids.

Saucepan Baked Beans

1 16-ounce can pork and beans in tomato sauce
1 15-ounce can navy or Great Northern beans, rinsed and drained
¼ cup ketchup
2 tablespoons maple syrup or packed brown sugar
2 teaspoons dry mustard
¼ cup purchased cooked bacon pieces or 2 slices bacon, crisp-cooked and crumbled

1 In a 2- to 2½-quart saucepan combine pork and beans, navy beans, ketchup, maple syrup, and dry mustard. Bring mixture to boiling; reduce heat. Simmer, uncovered, about 10 minutes or until desired consistency, stirring frequently. Stir in bacon (below). Makes 6 servings.

Per serving: 211 cal., 3 g total fat (1 g sat. fat), 5 mg chol., 870 mg sodium, 39 g carbo., 8 g fiber, 11 g pro.

Good to Know What's a summer potluck or picnic without baked beans? Impress everyone with a big pot of the home-cooked kind. If you need to make more than the 6 servings this recipe dishes up, simply double the recipe for 12 servings or triple the recipe for 18 servings. To do this, just multiply each ingredient by 2 or 3, place everything in a larger saucepan, and complete the recipe as directed. These beans go great with burgers, hot dogs, ribs, and, well, everything!

Ask Mom How do I rinse and drain canned beans? page 390 / How do I pack brown sugar? page 58 / How do I cook bacon? page 172 / What does simmer mean? page 79

Thyme-Roasted Beets

3 ½ to 4 pounds baby beets (assorted colors) or small beets
6 cloves garlic, peeled
3 sprigs fresh thyme
5 tablespoons olive oil
½ teaspoon kosher salt or salt
¼ teaspoon freshly ground black pepper
2 tablespoons lemon juice
1 tablespoon snipped fresh thyme
  Snipped fresh thyme (optional)

Shopping Savvy
These days beets come in more colors than just the standard-issue red. Check out the local farmer's market to find an array of fun colors. Besides the common red beets, you can also find beets in rich tones of gold, as well as the whimsical new candy-cane stripe (the flesh is striped with magenta and white).

129
Satisfying Sides

1 Preheat oven to 400°F. Prepare beets (below). If using small beets, cut into 1- to 1½-inch wedges. Place beets in a 3-quart rectangular baking dish. Add garlic and thyme sprigs. In a small bowl stir together 3 tablespoons of the olive oil, the salt, and pepper. Drizzle over beets in dish (below); toss lightly to coat. Cover dish with foil.

2 To roast, place beets in the preheated oven for 40 to 45 minutes or until tender (below). Uncover and let beets cool in dish on a wire rack about 15 minutes. If using small beets, remove skins by wrapping the wedges, one at a time, in a paper towel and gently rubbing off the skins (below). (Baby beets do not need to be peeled.) Remove and discard thyme sprigs. Remove garlic from dish and finely chop.

3 In a small bowl combine the garlic, remaining 2 tablespoons olive oil, the lemon juice, and the 1 tablespoon snipped thyme. Drizzle oil mixture over beets; toss lightly to coat.

4 To serve, if desired, sprinkle servings with additional snipped thyme. Serve warm or at room temperature. Makes 8 servings.

Per serving: 165 cal., 9 g total fat (1 g sat. fat), 0 mg chol., 268 mg sodium, 20 g carbo., 6 g fiber, 3 g pro.

...t tops off the beets away the root ends. ...ets thoroughly under water.

2 Pour a little of the oil mixture at a time over the beet mixture and use a wooden spoon to toss together to coat the beets.

3 To test beets for doneness, stick with a paring knife. The knife should easily slide into beets when tender.

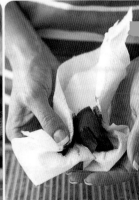
4 When rubbing off the skins of the cooled beet wedges, use new paper towels as needed.

Ask Mom What is a garlic clove? page 40 / What is kosher salt? page 79 / How do I freshly grind pepper? page 22 / How do I juice a lemon/lime? page 30 / How much juice does one lemon/lime yield? pages 30, 80 / How do I snip fresh herbs? pages 42, 328 / What does drizzle mean? page 79 / What does it mean to toss? page 77

② Skill Level

Nutty Broccoli

I pound broccoli, trimmed and cut into 2-inch pieces
3 tablespoons butter
½ teaspoon finely shredded orange peel (set aside)
2 tablespoons fresh orange juice
¼ teaspoon salt
3 tablespoons chopped walnuts, pine nuts, or pecans, toasted
Orange wedges (optional)

Flavor Changes
Pick your pleasure. Whether you go for the buttery richness of pecans, the meaty texture of walnuts, or the delicate flavor of pine nuts, this dish tastes great with each. Mix it up by trying cashews or sliced almonds another time. Or try a combination of pecans and walnuts.

1 If desired, cut broccoli stem pieces lengthwise in half. To steam, place a vegetable steamer basket in a 3-quart saucepan (below). Add water to reach just below the bottom of the basket (below). Bring water to boiling. Add broccoli to steamer basket (below). Cover and reduce heat (below). Steam for 8 to 10 minutes or just until broccoli stems are tender. Transfer broccoli to a serving dish.

2 Meanwhile, in an 8-inch skillet melt butter over medium-high heat; cook and stir butter for 3 to 4 minutes or until medium brown. Carefully add orange juice and cook for 10 seconds. Remove from heat; stir in orange peel and salt. Pour over broccoli. Sprinkle with walnuts. If desired, garnish with orange wedges. Makes 6 servings.

Per serving: 94 cal., 8 g total fat (4 g sat. fat), 15 mg chol., 153 mg sodium, 4 g carbo., 1 g fiber, 2 g pro.

1 A steamer basket generally has feet that sit on the bottom of the pan so that the food doesn't touch the water during steaming.

2 After the steamer basket is in place, add enough tap water to the saucepan so that the water level is below the bottom of the basket.

3 Bring the water to boiling. Add prepared broccoli to the steamer basket.

4 Cover the saucepan and reduce the heat so tha the water simmers and ste forms in the pan. Keep pa covered during steaming.

Ask Mom How do I trim and cut broccoli? page 36 / How do I measure butter? pages 58, 59 / How do I finely shred orange peel? page 30 / How do I juice an orange? page 30 / How much juice does one orange yield? page 30 / How do I toast nuts? page 65 / How do I cut orange wedges? page 30 / What does it mean to steam? page 69 / What does garnish mean? page 79

HOW DO I BUY THE BEST BROCCOLI? Look for bright green stalks that are fairly smooth that have an abundance of tightly closed florets—they'll be the most tender. The bigger and older the florets are, the tougher the broccoli will be.

Skill Level

Flavor Changes The sweetness of tarragon or basil is a natural complement to the sweetness of the carrot, but other herbs can be a nice contrast to it. Try thyme, dill, or rosemary. If you want to go the extra mile, use fresh herbs. To substitute fresh for dried, use 1 tablespoon chopped fresh herb for every 1 teaspoon dried.

Butter-Glazed **Carrots**

½ cup water
1 pound carrots, peeled and cut into ½-inch-thick diagonal slices
2 tablespoons butter or margarine, softened
1 to 2 teaspoons dried tarragon or basil, crushed
Salt
Ground black pepper

1 In a 2- to 2½-quart saucepan bring the water to boiling. Add the carrots and cook, covered, in the boiling water for 8 to 10 minutes or until carrots are just tender; drain off water.

2 Add butter and tarragon to the saucepan. Stir until combined; if necessary, heat over low heat to melt butter completely. Season to taste with salt and pepper. Makes 4 servings.

Microwave directions: In a microwave-safe baking dish or casserole combine carrots and ¼ cup water. Cover and microwave on 100 percent power (high) for 7 to 9 minutes or until carrots are just tender, stirring once. Drain off water. Add butter and tarragon to the baking dish. Stir until combined; if necessary, microwave for 10 to 20 seconds more to melt butter completely. Season to taste with salt and pepper.

Per serving: 98 cal., 6 g total fat (4 g sat. fat), 15 mg chol., 261 mg sodium, 11 g carbo., 3 g fiber, 1 g pro.

Maple-Glazed Carrots: Prepare as above, except use 1 tablespoon butter, omit the herb, and add 2 tablespoons maple syrup and 1 tablespoon sesame seeds, toasted.

For another variation on the Maple-Glazed Carrots, make as directed and toss with a teaspoon of finely grated orange peel instead of the sesame seeds.

Ask Mom How do I peel and cut carrots? pages 37, 64 / How do I measure butter? pages 58, 59 / How do I soften butter? page 59 / How do I crush dried herbs? page 78 / How do I toast sesame seeds? page 65

3 Skill Level

Cauliflower Cheese Bake

- 1 medium head cauliflower (about 2 pounds)
- ½ cup regular mayonnaise or light mayonnaise or salad dressing
- 1 tablespoon coarse-grain Dijon-style mustard
- 1 tablespoon milk
- ¼ teaspoon coarsely ground black pepper
- 1 cup dry firm-textured white or sourdough bread cubes
- 1 tablespoon butter or margarine, melted
- 1 cup shredded smoked Gruyère or cheddar cheese (4 ounces)

1 Preheat oven to 400°F. Remove leaves from cauliflower; trim core even with floret stems so the head will stand evenly. Place cauliflower in a 9-inch glass pie plate or a 2-quart microwave-safe baking dish. Add ½ cup water (below). Cover with vented plastic wrap (below). Microwave on 100 percent power (high) for 7 to 10 minutes or just until tender, turning dish after 4 minutes. Transfer cauliflower to cutting board; cool slightly.

2 Cut cauliflower head into 1-inch slices (below). Arrange slices in a 1½-quart shallow baking dish. For sauce, in a small bowl stir together mayonnaise, mustard, milk, and pepper. Spoon sauce over cauliflower (below). For topping, toss together bread cubes and melted butter; sprinkle over cauliflower and sauce. Top with cheese. Bake, uncovered, in the preheated oven about 10 minutes or until heated through and topping is golden brown. Makes 6 servings.

Make-ahead directions: Prepare and microwave cauliflower as above in Step 1, cut into slices, and place in baking dish. Cover; chill for up to 24 hours. Prepare sauce; cover and chill. To serve, bake cauliflower, covered, in a 400°F oven 20 minutes. Spoon on sauce, sprinkle with topping, and top with cheese. Bake about 10 minutes or until heated through and topping is golden brown.

Per serving: 265 cal., 23 g total fat (8 g sat. fat), 33 mg chol., 290 mg sodium, 7 g carbo., 1 g fiber, 7 g pro.

r tap water into
ve-safe dish to
am when the
r cooks.

2 Cover cauliflower and dish with plastic wrap. Turn back one corner of the wrap to create a vent so some steam can escape.

3 Use a chef's knife to cut across the cauliflower head into thick slices. Place slices in baking dish.

4 Spoon sauce over the cauliflower. Add crumb mixture, sprinkle with cheese, and bake.

Ask Mom How do I prepare cauliflower? page 38 / What is Dijon-style mustard? page 379 / How do I freshly grind pepper? page 22 / How do I make/toast bread cubes? page 79 / How do I measure butter? pages 58, 59 / How do I shred cheese? page 71

Corn on the Cob

8 fresh ears sweet corn

Butter, margarine, or I recipe Cajun Butter, Chipotle-Lime Butter, or Herb Butter

Salt

Ground black pepper

1 Remove husks and silks from ears of corn (below). Remove stems (below). Rinse thoroughly under cool tap water. In a large kettle cook corn, covered, in enough boiling lightly salted water to cover for 5 to 7 minutes or until tender. Serve with butter or desired flavored butter. Sprinkle corn with salt and pepper. Makes 8 servings.

Per ear with I tablespoon butter: I79 cal., I3 g total fat (7 g sat. fat), 3I mg chol., I68 mg sodium, I7 g carbo., 2 g fiber, 3 g pro.

Cajun Butter: In small mixing bowl beat $\frac{1}{2}$ cup softened butter, 1 teaspoon garlic salt, $\frac{1}{4}$ teaspoon ground black pepper, $\frac{1}{4}$ teaspoon cayenne pepper, $\frac{1}{8}$ teaspoon ground ginger, and $\frac{1}{8}$ teaspoon ground cloves with an electric mixer on low speed until combined. Cover; chill for 1 to 24 hours.

Chipotle-Lime Butter: In a small mixing bowl beat $\frac{1}{2}$ cup softened butter, 1 teaspoon finely shredded lime peel, $\frac{1}{2}$ teaspoon salt, $\frac{1}{8}$ to $\frac{1}{4}$ teaspoon ground chipotle chile pepper, and dash cayenne pepper with an electric mixer on low speed until combined. Cover; chill for 1 to 24 hours.

Herb Butter: In a small mixing bowl beat $\frac{1}{2}$ cup softened butter, 2 teaspoons snipped fresh thyme, and 2 teaspoons snipped fresh marjoram or oregano with an electric mixer on low speed until combined. Cover; chill for 1 to 24 hours.

1 Pull off the husks and silks section by section. Once husks are removed, use a stiff brush to remove the remaining silks.

2 Use a chef's knife to cut off the stems. Rinse the ears.

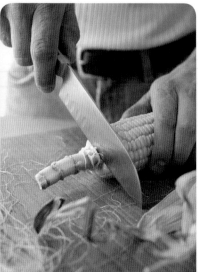

Ask Mom How do I measure butter? pages 58, 59 / How do I soften butter? page 59 / How do I shred lime peel? page 30 / How do I snip fresh herbs? pages 42, 328

Skillet Scalloped Corn

2 teaspoons butter
$\frac{1}{2}$ cup crushed rich round, wheat, or rye crackers
1 11-ounce can whole kernel corn with sweet peppers, drained
1 7- to 8.75-ounce can whole kernel corn with sweet peppers, whole kernel corn, or white (shoe peg) corn, drained
2 1-ounce slices process Swiss cheese, torn
$\frac{1}{3}$ cup milk
$\frac{1}{8}$ teaspoon onion powder
Dash ground black pepper

1 For topping, in a 10-inch skillet melt butter over medium heat. Add 2 tablespoons of the crushed crackers to the skillet. Cook and stir until light brown. Remove topping; set aside.

2 In same skillet combine remaining crushed crackers, corn, cheese, milk, onion powder, and pepper. Cook, stirring frequently, until cheese melts. Transfer to a serving dish; sprinkle with topping. Makes 4 servings.

Per serving: 183 cal., 9 g total fat (4 g sat. fat), 18 mg chol., 704 mg sodium, 19 g carbo., 2 g fiber, 6 g pro.

Good to Know You don't have to get your hands messy to crush crackers. Place a handful of crackers in a resealable plastic bag, let some of the air out, and seal the bag. Roll a rolling pin over the top of the bag several times. Flip the bag over and repeat until crackers are crumbled into small pieces. Pour the contents into a measuring cup and repeat the crushing process until you have $\frac{1}{2}$ cup of crumbs.

Ask Mom How do I make bread/cracker crumbs? page 76 / What is process cheese? page 408 / What does dash mean? page 79

Herbed Leek Gratin

  3 pounds slender leeks
$\frac{1}{2}$ cup whipping cream
$\frac{1}{2}$ cup chicken broth
  2 tablespoons snipped fresh marjoram or $1\frac{1}{2}$ teaspoons dried marjoram, crushed
$\frac{1}{2}$ teaspoon salt
$\frac{1}{2}$ teaspoon freshly ground black pepper
$1\frac{1}{2}$ cups soft French or Italian bread crumbs
  3 tablespoons grated Parmesan cheese
  3 tablespoons butter, melted
    Fresh marjoram sprigs (optional)

1 Preheat oven to 375°F. Prepare leeks, leaving pieces 4 to 5 inches long with white and pale green parts. Cut leeks in half lengthwise. Pat dry with paper towels. Arrange leeks, cut sides down, in a greased 2-quart rectangular baking dish or au gratin dish, overlapping leeks as necessary to fit (below).

2 For sauce, in a small bowl combine whipping cream and broth; pour sauce over leeks. Sprinkle with half of the marjoram, the salt, and pepper. Cover tightly with foil. Bake in the preheated oven for 20 minutes.

3 Meanwhile, in a small bowl combine bread crumbs, cheese, and remaining marjoram. Drizzle with butter; toss to coat crumbs. Sprinkle leeks with bread crumb mixture. Bake, uncovered, for 15 to 20 minutes more or until leeks are tender and crumbs are golden brown. If desired, garnish with fresh marjoram sprigs. Makes 6 servings.

Per serving: 224 cal., 15 g total fat (9 g sat. fat), 45 mg chol., 457 mg sodium, 21 g carbo., 2 g fiber, 4 g pro.

If you place the leeks in the baking dish so that they are all positioned crosswise in the dish, they will be easier to serve.

Ask Mom What is a leek? page 43 / How do I prepare leeks? page 43 / How do I snip fresh herbs? pages 42, 328 / How do I crush dried herbs? page 78 / How do I freshly grind pepper? page 22 / How do I make bread/cracker crumbs? page 76 / How do I grate cheese? page 71 / How do I measure butter? pages 58, 59 / What does garnish mean? page 79

WHAT'S A GRATIN? The word "gratin" may make the recipe sound fancy and difficult to make, but that's not the case at all. In fact, "gratin" just means any dish topped with cheese or a butter-bread crumb mixture and baked. Easy, right?

Garlic and
Pepper Stir-Fry

- 2 tablespoons soy sauce
- 1 teaspoon toasted sesame oil
- ¼ teaspoon cracked black pepper
- 1 tablespoon cooking oil or peanut oil
- 3 cloves garlic, minced
- 2 cups red, yellow, and/or green sweet peppers cut into bite-size strips; carrot slices; and/or fresh pea pods (stems and ends removed)
- 1 medium onion, sliced and separated into rings
- 2 cups sliced fresh mushrooms
- Sesame seeds, toasted

Ingredient Info Toasted sesame oil is the telltale flavor accent of many Asian dishes. Here just 1 teaspoon of the oil and a sprinkle of toasted seeds make this stir-fry sing with flavor. There are two kinds of sesame oil. One is light in color and has a delicate nutty taste. The other, which is perfect for this dish and other stir-fries, is darker and much stronger in flavor and aroma.

1 In a small bowl stir together soy sauce, sesame oil, and black pepper; set aside. In a 12-inch skillet or a wok heat cooking oil over high heat for 1 minute. Add garlic; cook and stir for 1 minute. Add sweet pepper and onion; cook and stir for 3 minutes. Add mushrooms; cook and stir for 2 to 3 minutes more or until vegetables are crisp-tender.

2 Add soy sauce mixture to skillet or wok. Cook and stir to coat vegetables. Transfer mixture to a serving dish. Sprinkle with sesame seeds. Makes 4 servings.

Per serving: 95 cal., 6 g total fat (1 g sat. fat), 0 mg chol., 464 mg sodium, 8 g carbo., 2 g fiber, 4 g pro.

Ask Mom How do I freshly grind pepper? page 22 / What is a garlic clove? page 40 / How do I mince garlic? page 40 / How do I seed sweet peppers and cut them into strips? page 49 / How do I slice an onion? page 47 / How do I slice fresh mushrooms? page 45 / What is a wok? page 267 / What does it mean to stir-fry? page 69 / What does crisp-tender mean? page 79 / How do I toast sesame seeds? page 65

Broiled Summer Squash
And Onions

¼ cup bottled olive oil vinaigrette or balsamic vinaigrette salad dressing

½ teaspoon dried basil or oregano, crushed

⅛ teaspoon ground black pepper

2 medium yellow summer squash or zucchini, quartered lengthwise

1 small onion, cut into thin wedges

1 Preheat broiler. In a small bowl whisk together salad dressing, basil, and pepper. Brush squash and onion with some of the salad dressing mixture.

2 Place squash and onion on the unheated rack of a broiler pan (below). Place pan in pre-heated broiler with food about 4 inches from the heat. Broil for 8 to 10 minutes or until crisp-tender, turning and brushing occasionally with salad dressing mixture (below).

3 Cut broiled vegetables into bite-size pieces (below); transfer to a serving bowl. Toss with any remaining salad dressing mixture. Makes 4 servings.

Per serving: 91 cal., 8 g total fat (1 g sat. fat), 0 mg chol., 77 mg sodium, 4 g carbo., 1 g fiber, 1 g pro.

...nge the brushed ...d onion pieces on ... the broiler pan.

2 Use tongs to turn vegetables during broiling for even cooking.

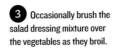
3 Occasionally brush the salad dressing mixture over the vegetables as they broil.

4 Transfer the cooked vegetables to a cutting board and cut into bite-size pieces.

Ask Mom How do I crush dried herbs? page 78 / What is summer squash? page 54 / How do I prepare summer squash/zucchini? page 54 / How do I cut onion wedges? page 47 / What does it mean to broil? page 68 / What does crisp-tender mean? page 79 / What does it mean to toss? page 77

Caramelized Acorn Squash

2 1- to 1 ½-pound acorn squash
¼ cup butter or margarine
¼ cup packed brown sugar
¼ cup apple cider or apple juice
½ teaspoon ground cinnamon
¼ teaspoon salt
¼ teaspoon ground nutmeg

1 Preheat oven to 350°F. Line a 15×10×1-inch baking pan with parchment paper or foil. Cut each squash in half; discard seeds and remove fibrous material. Place halves, cut sides down, in the prepared baking pan. Bake, uncovered, in the preheated oven for 40 to 45 minutes or until the squash is tender. Let stand until cool enough to handle; cut into 1-inch slices. Arrange squash slices in a 2-quart rectangular baking dish, overlapping as necessary.

2 For glaze, in a 10-inch skillet heat butter, brown sugar, cider, cinnamon, salt, and nutmeg to boiling, stirring to dissolve sugar. Reduce heat; boil gently, uncovered, about 5 minutes or until syrupy. Drizzle glaze over squash. Bake, uncovered, about 10 minutes more or until heated through. Spoon glaze over squash before serving. Don't eat squash skin. Makes 6 servings.

Make-ahead directions: Prepare as above through Step 1. Cover and chill for up to 24 hours. To prepare, let squash stand at room temperature for 30 minutes. Continue with Step 2.

Per serving: 154 cal., 8 g total fat (5 g sat. fat), 20 mg chol., 160 mg sodium, 22 g carbo., 2 g fiber, 1 g pro.

Good to Know Parchment paper is a heavy paper that stands up to grease, moisture, and heat. It's available at most grocery stores. It's perfect for lining pans—once baking is done, just pull the paper up and toss the mess. You can use foil for this recipe, too, but parchment paper and foil aren't always interchangeable. You can bake cookies and breads on parchment, for example, but not on foil.

Ask Mom How do I measure butter? pages 58, 59 / How do I pack brown sugar? page 58 / What is winter squash? page 56 / How do I prepare winter squash? page 56 / How do I line a pan with foil? page 60 / What does drizzle mean? page 79

Burst-of-Orange Butternut Squash

Nonstick cooking spray

1 pound butternut squash, peeled, seeded, and
cut into ½-inch pieces (below)

⅓ cup orange juice

1 tablespoon maple syrup

¼ teaspoon salt

⅛ teaspoon ground black pepper (optional)

Dash ground cinnamon

1 tablespoon butter or margarine

1 Preheat oven to 425°F. Lightly coat a 2-quart rectangular baking dish with cooking spray. Place squash pieces in prepared baking dish. In a small bowl combine orange juice, maple syrup, salt, pepper (if desired), and cinnamon. Drizzle over squash; toss to coat. Dot with butter.

2 Bake, uncovered, in the preheated oven about 25 minutes or until squash is tender, stirring twice. Makes 4 servings.

Per serving: 91 cal., 3 g total fat (2 g sat. fat), 8 mg chol., 182 mg sodium, 15 g carbo., 2 g fiber, 2 g pro.

GOOD TO KNOW When a recipe says to "dot" with something, it means to scatter small pieces over the mixture. In this recipe, butter is dotted over the squash.

To peel uncooked winter squash, such as a butternut squash, start with a seeded squash half placed on a cutting surface. Use a sturdy vegetable peeler to cut off long strips of the peel, cutting away from you. Cut the peeled squash into cubes for cooking.

Ask Mom What is winter squash? page 56 / How do I prepare winter squash? page 56 / How do I juice an orange? page 30 / How much juice does one orange yield? page 30 / How do I measure butter? pages 58, 59 / What does drizzle mean? page 79

Mashed Potatoes

1½ pounds potatoes, such as russet or Yukon gold, peeled and quartered
½ teaspoon salt
2 tablespoons butter or margarine
¼ teaspoon salt
⅛ teaspoon ground black pepper
3 to 5 tablespoons milk

1 In a 3-quart saucepan cook potatoes and the ½ teaspoon salt, covered, in enough boiling water to cover for 20 to 25 minutes or until tender; drain (below). Mash with a potato masher or beat with an electric mixer on low speed (below). Add butter, ¼ teaspoon salt, and pepper (page 143). Gradually mash in enough milk to make mixture light and fluffy (page 143). If desired, serve with additional butter or margarine. Makes 4 servings.

Per serving: 191 cal., 6 g total fat (4 g sat. fat), 16 mg chol., 346 mg sodium, 31 g carbo., 3 g fiber, 4 g pro.

Garlic Mashed Potatoes: Prepare as above, except add 4 peeled garlic cloves to the water while cooking potatoes and substitute 2 tablespoons olive oil for the butter.

Horseradish Mashed Potatoes: Prepare as above, except stir in 2 tablespoons creamy horseradish sauce along with the butter.

Italian Mashed Potatoes: Prepare as above, except stir in 1 teaspoon dried Italian seasoning, crushed, along with the salt and pepper and substitute 2 tablespoons olive oil for butter. Just before serving, stir in ¼ cup shredded Parmesan or Asiago cheese. If desired, drizzle with olive oil.

Ultimate Creamy Mashed Potatoes: Prepare as above, except stir in ¼ cup dairy sour cream and ¼ cup softened cream cheese along with the butter. Substitute half-and-half or light cream for the milk. Stir 2 tablespoons finely chopped green onion into the mashed potatoes. If desired, sprinkle with additional chopped green onion just before serving.

1 Potatoes should be covered with lightly salted water. Bring to boiling and cook, covered.

2 Pour the potatoes and water through a large colander or sieve to drain off the water.

3 Use a potato masher or electric mixer to mash potatoes before adding the butter, seasonings, and milk.

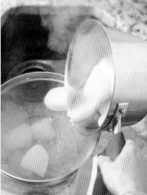

Ask Mom What are some potato varieties? page 50 / How do I prepare potatoes? page 51 / How do I measure butter? pages 58, 59 / What is a garlic clove? page 40 / How do I shred cheese? page 71 / What does drizzle mean? page 79 / How do I soften cream cheese? page 93

DO I HAVE TO PEEL MY POTATOES? It may be the norm for mashed, but no, you don't. For this quick version, use red new or Yukon gold potatoes and scrub them well. Quarter, cook, and mash as directed. An easy addition could include cooked bacon pieces.

4 After the potatoes have been mashed, mash in the butter and seasonings.

5 The last step is to add enough milk and beat potatoes with masher or mixer until light, fluffy, and desired consistency.

Mashed Sweet Potatoes

4 pounds sweet potatoes, peeled and cut into $\frac{1}{2}$-inch cubes (about 10 cups)

$\frac{1}{4}$ cup butter or margarine

$\frac{1}{3}$ cup dairy sour cream

$\frac{1}{4}$ cup milk

$\frac{1}{2}$ teaspoon salt

$\frac{1}{2}$ teaspoon freshly ground black pepper

Butter or margarine (optional)

1 In a 4-quart Dutch oven cook the potatoes, covered, in enough boiling lightly salted water to cover for 12 minutes or until tender; drain. Remove potatoes from pan.

2 Add the butter to the hot Dutch oven and let it melt. Add the potatoes to the Dutch oven; mash with a potato masher until smooth (see photo 3, page 142). Stir in the sour cream, milk, salt, and pepper. Cook and stir over low heat until heated through. Transfer to a serving dish. If desired, place a dot of butter on top. Makes 8 to 10 servings.

Make-ahead directions: Prepare potatoes through Step 2 but do not heat through. Transfer to a $2\frac{1}{2}$- to 3-quart casserole. Cover and chill for up to 24 hours. Before serving, preheat oven to 325°F. Bake, covered, in the preheated oven for 55 to 60 minutes or until heated through.

Per serving: 267 cal., 8 g total fat (5 g sat. fat), 19 mg chol., 312 mg sodium, 46 g carbo., 7 g fiber, 4 g pro.

Maple Mashed Sweet Potatoes (in photo): Prepare as above. Before serving, drizzle $\frac{1}{4}$ cup maple syrup over potatoes; sprinkle with $\frac{1}{4}$ cup chopped hazelnuts or almonds, toasted.

Mashed Sweet Potatoes with Caramelized Onions: Prepare as above, except add caramelized onions (see page 66) to the mashed potatoes in Step 2 after the salt and pepper.

Mashed White Potatoes: Prepare as above, except substitute peeled and cubed white potatoes for sweet potatoes.

Good to Know Here's a recipe that would be right at home on the holiday table (but is also great any time of year). And it couldn't be easier to make. The bonus is that sweet potatoes are one of nature's most healthful creations—they're jam-packed with vitamins A and C.

Ask Mom What are some potato varieties? page 50 / How do I prepare potatoes? page 51 / What does it mean to cube? page 64 / How do I measure butter? pages 58, 59 / How do I freshly grind pepper? page 22 / What does it mean to dot? page 141 / What's the best way to measure sticky liquids? pages 58, 81 / How do I chop nuts? page 65 / How do I toast nuts? page 65

Cheesy Garlic Potato Gratin

1 $\frac{1}{2}$ pounds Yukon gold or other yellow-flesh potatoes

$\frac{1}{3}$ cup sliced green onion

1 teaspoon salt

$\frac{1}{4}$ teaspoon ground black pepper

4 cloves garlic, minced

1 $\frac{1}{2}$ cups shredded Swiss cheese or 6 ounces Gruyère, provolone, or Jarslberg cheese, shredded

1 cup whipping cream

1 Preheat oven to 350°F. Grease a 2-quart square baking dish. Scrub potatoes thoroughly with a brush (see photo 1, page 147). Thinly slice potatoes; you should have about 5 cups potato slices (below). Layer half of the sliced potatoes and half of the green onion in the prepared dish. Sprinkle with half of the salt, pepper, garlic, and cheese. Repeat layers. Pour whipping cream over top.

2 Bake, covered, in the preheated oven for 1 hour and 10 minutes. Uncover and bake for 20 to 30 minutes more or until potatoes are tender when pierced with a fork and top is golden brown. Makes 6 servings.

Per serving: 349 cal., 24 g total fat (15 g sat. fat), 85 mg chol., 470 mg sodium, 21 g carbo., 2 g fiber, 13 g pro.

Yukon gold potatoes have rather thin skins, so there is no need to peel them before thinly slicing. Just scrub thoroughly with a brush. Use a chef's knife on a cutting board when slicing.

Ask Mom What are some potato varieties? page 50 / How do I slice green onions? page 43 / What is a garlic clove? page 40 / How do I mince garlic? page 40 / How do I shred cheese? page 71

3 Skill Level

Twice-Baked Potatoes

- 2 large Yukon gold potatoes (about I pound)
- 2 teaspoons olive oil
- ½ teaspoon salt
- 3 tablespoons milk
- 2 tablespoons butter or margarine
- 2 tablespoons dairy sour cream
- I tablespoon snipped fresh chives
- ¼ cup finely shredded Gruyère or Swiss cheese (I ounce)
  Salt
  Ground black pepper
  Snipped fresh chives (optional)

1 Preheat oven to 400°F. Scrub potatoes thoroughly with a brush (page 147); pat dry. Prick potatoes with a fork (page 147). Drizzle olive oil over each potato and sprinkle with salt. Wrap each potato in foil. Bake potatoes in the preheated oven about 1 hour or until tender. Remove and discard foil. Let potatoes stand for 15 minutes to cool slightly. Cut the potatoes in half lengthwise. Carefully scoop pulp out of each potato, leaving a ¼- to ½-inch shell (page 147); set potato shells aside. Place potato pulp in a large bowl. Mash potato pulp with a potato masher or an electric mixer on low speed until nearly smooth (page 147).

2 In a 1- to 1½-quart saucepan heat milk and butter over medium heat until butter is melted. Pour milk mixture over mashed potatoes; beat until smooth. Stir in sour cream, the 1 tablespoon snipped chives, and 2 tablespoons of the cheese. Season to taste with salt and pepper. Mound mixture into reserved potato shells (page 147). Sprinkle with remaining cheese. Place potatoes in a single layer in a 2-quart square baking dish.

3 Bake, uncovered, in the 400°F oven about 20 minutes or until golden brown and heated through. If desired, garnish with snipped chives. Makes 4 servings.

Make-ahead directions: Prepare as directed through Step 2. Place potatoes in a single layer in an airtight container. Cover and chill for up to 24 hours. Before serving, preheat oven to 325°F. Place potatoes in a 2-quart square baking dish. Bake, covered, in the preheated oven for 30 minutes. Uncover and bake about 15 minutes more or until potatoes are golden brown and heated through.

Per serving: 203 cal., 12 g total fat (6 g sat. fat), 27 mg chol., 517 mg sodium, 20 g carbo., 2 g fiber, 5 g pro.

Bacon-Cheddar Twice-Baked Potatoes (in photo): Prepare as above, except in Step 2 stir in ⅓ cup cooked, crumbled bacon along with the sour cream; substitute cheddar cheese for the Gruyère cheese (pictured above).

Southwestern Twice-Baked Potatoes: Prepare as above, except in Step 2 substitute snipped fresh cilantro for the chives; substitute Monterey Jack cheese with jalapeños for the Gruyère. Serve with purchased salsa. Omit the optional chive garnish.

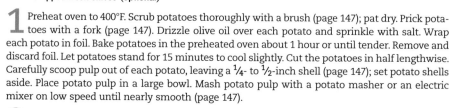

Ask Mom What are some potato varieties? page 50 / How do I measure butter? pages 58, 59 / How do I snip fresh herbs? pages 42, 328 / How do I shred cheese? page 71 / What does drizzle mean? page 79 / How do I cook bacon? page 172 / What does garnish mean? page 79

1 Scrub the potatoes with a brush and rinse thoroughly under cool tap water.

2 Use a fork to prick the potatoes all over. This lets steam escape so the potatoes don't explode during baking.

3 After letting potatoes cool slightly, hold each half with a paper towel or pot holder. Carefully scoop out pulp.

4 Mash or beat potatoes until nearly smooth, then mix in the other ingredients.

ONE POTATO, TWO. Once you work through all the variations on these yummy twice-baked potatoes, go back to the original and start experimenting with other fresh herbs and cheeses. Try Parmesan and basil or blue cheese and chives.

5 Use two spoons to scoop the mashed potato mixture into the potato shells. Mound the potato mixture slightly.

Herbed Potatoes

1 tablespoon butter or margarine
⅓ cup sliced green onion
½ teaspoon dried Italian seasoning, crushed
4½ cups frozen hash brown potatoes
¼ teaspoon salt
⅓ cup grated Parmesan cheese
1 tablespoon snipped fresh Italian (flat-leaf) parsley

1 In a 10-inch nonstick skillet melt butter over medium heat. Add green onion and Italian seasoning; cook about 2 minutes or until onion is tender. Stir in frozen potatoes and salt.

2 Cook about 15 minutes or until potatoes are tender and light brown, stirring twice. Stir in cheese and parsley. Makes 4 servings.

Per serving: 257 cal., 7 g total fat (4 g sat. fat), 13 mg chol., 354 mg sodium, 44 g carbo., 4 g fiber, 8 g pro.

Meal Maker Make a complete meal from a simple baked potato.
Here's how:
Scrub a russet potato thoroughly and pat dry. Prick all over with a fork; drizzle with olive oil and sprinkle with salt. Wrap potato in foil. Bake potato in a 450°F oven for 1 hour or until tender. Remove foil. Cool potato about 15 minutes. Split potato open. Now the fun part—top with one of these:
● warmed chili, shredded cheese, and sliced green onion
● crumbled blue cheese, sour cream, snipped chives, and crumbled cooked bacon
● chopped cooked ham, steamed broccoli, and shredded Gouda cheese
● sauteed sliced onion, sweet pepper strips, halved mushrooms, and sliced zucchini
● sour cream, salsa, and snipped cilantro

Ask Mom How do I measure butter? pages 58, 59 / How do I slice green onions? page 43 / How do I crush dried herbs? page 78 / How do I grate cheese? page 71 / How do I snip fresh herbs? pages 42, 328 / How do I chop an onion? page 47 / How do I shred cheese? page 71 / How do I crumble cheese? page 71 / How do I cook bacon? page 172 / What does it mean to saute? page 69 / What does it mean to steam? page 69

Savory Couscous

I cup chicken broth

¾ cup sliced fresh mushrooms

¼ cup shredded carrot

¼ cup thinly sliced green onion (2)

I tablespoon butter or margarine

2 teaspoons snipped fresh basil or thyme or
    ½ teaspoon dried basil or thyme, crushed

I cup quick-cooking couscous

1 In a 2- to 2½-quart saucepan bring chicken broth, mushrooms, carrot, green onions, butter, and dried basil (if using) to boiling. Stir in couscous and fresh basil (if using). Remove the saucepan from heat.

2 Cover saucepan and let stand about 5 minutes or until liquid is absorbed. Fluff couscous with a fork before serving (right). Makes 4 servings.

Per serving: 210 cal., 3 g total fat (2 g sat. fat), 8 mg chol., 271 mg sodium, 37 g carbo., 3 g fiber, 7 g pro.

After the couscous absorbs the liquid, it needs to be loosened (or fluffed). Use a fork for this task to lighten the mixture.

Ingredient Info For something with such an intimidating name, couscous couldn't be more basic. It is just granular semolina (ground durum wheat), the flour of which is used in many types of pasta. Couscous is a great substitute for rice, potatoes, and pasta. Look for it near the rice in your local supermarket.

Ask Mom How do I slice fresh mushrooms? page 45 / How do I shred vegetables? page 20 / How do I slice green onions? page 43 / How do I measure butter? pages 58, 59 / How do I snip fresh herbs? pages 42, 328 / How do I crush dried herbs? page 78

Autumn Vegetable Pilaf

1 6- to 7.2-ounce package rice pilaf mix

2 tablespoons olive oil

2 cloves garlic, minced

1 teaspoon dried thyme, crushed

1 large sweet potato or carrot, peeled and cut into ½-inch cubes

1 medium zucchini, halved lengthwise and cut into ½-inch pieces

1 small red onion, cut into wedges

⅓ cup chopped pecans or walnuts, toasted

1 tablespoon cider vinegar

1 Preheat oven to 400°F. In a saucepan cook rice pilaf mix according to package directions, except omit butter or oil.

2 Meanwhile, in a large bowl stir together the olive oil, garlic, and thyme. Add sweet potato, zucchini, and onion; stir to coat. Spread vegetables in a single layer in a 15×10×1-inch baking pan. Roast, uncovered, in the preheated oven for 15 to 20 minutes or until vegetables are light brown and tender, stirring occasionally. Stir roasted vegetables, nuts, and vinegar into hot rice pilaf. Makes 6 servings.

Per serving: 244 cal., 9 g total fat (1 g sat. fat), 0 mg chol., 349 mg sodium, 37 g carbo., 4 g fiber, 4 g pro.

Spring Vegetable Pilaf: Prepare as above, except substitute 1 medium red, yellow, or orange sweet pepper, seeded and cut into bite-size strips, and 1 pound asparagus, trimmed and cut into 1-inch pieces, for the sweet potato and zucchini.

Flavor Changes Rice pilaf is a tasty combo of rice and a variety of other ingredients— usually vegetables, but often cooked meat, poultry, and seafood as well. Because it is so versatile, you can easily swap ingredients, as with the spring vegetable variation. If you feel creative, try mixing equal amounts of your favorite cooked vegetables or meats into the basic rice mixture.

Ask Mom What is a garlic clove? page 40 / How do I mince garlic? page 40 / How do I crush dried herbs? page 78 / How do I prepare potatoes? page 51 / What does it mean to cube? page 64 / How do I peel and cut carrots? pages 37, 64 / How do I prepare zucchini? page 54 / How do I cut onion wedges? page 47 / How do I chop and toast nuts? page 65 / What is that vinegar? page 349 / How do I seed sweet peppers and cut them into strips? page 49 / How do I trim asparagus? page 34

Skill Level

Rice Vermicelli Pilaf

Ingredient Info
Vermicelli and angel hair pasta can be used interchangeably because they're similar in diameter—although you might be more familiar with the angel hair variety. Both pastas are long and need to be broken up for ease of eating.

   3 ounces dried vermicelli or angel hair pasta
   I cup uncooked long grain white rice
   $\frac{1}{3}$ cup finely chopped onion
   3 tablespoons butter
   I 14-ounce can chicken broth or beef broth
   $\frac{1}{4}$ cup water
   $\frac{1}{4}$ teaspoon salt
   $\frac{1}{4}$ teaspoon ground black pepper
   Snipped fresh basil, dill, and/or crumbled crisp-cooked bacon or pancetta

1 Break vermicelli into small pieces (below). In a 2- to $2\frac{1}{2}$-quart saucepan cook vermicelli, rice, and onion in hot butter over medium heat for 4 to 5 minutes or until pasta is light brown and onion is nearly tender.

2 Carefully add broth, water, salt, and pepper. Bring to boiling; reduce heat. Simmer, covered, for 15 to 20 minutes or until the rice is tender and broth is absorbed. Fluff mixture with a fork. Sprinkle with basil before serving. Makes 4 servings.

Per serving: 336 cal., 9 g total fat (6 g sat. fat), 24 mg chol., 607 mg sodium, 55 g carbo., I g fiber, 7 g pro.

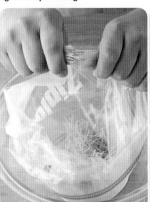

1 To finely break pasta, first use your hands to break the pasta into short lengths right into a plastic bag.

2 Hold the bag closed and use a can or other container to crush pasta into $\frac{1}{2}$- to $\frac{3}{4}$-inch-long pieces.

3 The pasta pieces will look like this when crushed.

Ask Mom What is that pasta shape? pages 308–309 / How do I chop an onion? page 47 / How do I measure butter? pages 58, 59 / How do I snip fresh herbs? pages 42, 328 / What does simmer mean? page 79 / How do I cook bacon? page I72

PATIENT STIRRING REQUIRED. This deliciously creamy—and utterly Italian—rice dish takes a little time to make, but it's not difficult. Just keep a watchful eye on the rice after each addition of broth, stir it often, and you're guaranteed fabulous results.

1 After sauteing the onion and garlic until tender, add the uncooked rice.

2 Use a wooden spoon to stir the rice during cooking until rice is golden brown.

3 Stir some of the hot broth into the saucepan. Add it carefully since the pan will be very hot and the contents will sizzle.

4 After adding the last of the broth and the vegetables, stir while cooking until rice is just tender but still creamy.

Many risotto recipes call for a tablespoon or two of butter to be added right at the end of cooking time. It adds flavor and silkiness to the finished dish.

(3) Skill Level

Classic Risotto
With Peas

½ cup chopped onion (1 medium)
2 cloves garlic, minced
2 tablespoons olive oil
1 cup uncooked Arborio rice
2 14-ounce cans vegetable broth or chicken broth (3½ cups)
1 cup frozen baby sweet peas or regular-size peas
¼ cup coarsely shredded carrot
1 tablespoon snipped fresh thyme or ½ teaspoon dried thyme, crushed
2 cups fresh spinach, shredded
¼ cup grated Parmesan cheese

Ingredient Info
Rice is rice is rice, right? Actually, not at all. To get the results you want for this recipe, you need to use Arborio rice. The shorter, fatter kernel has a high starch content that makes this dish so creamy (without cream). Most supermarkets carry Arborio rice; you'll likely find it in the aisle with the rest of the rice.

1 In a 3-quart saucepan cook onion and garlic in hot oil over medium heat about 5 minutes or until onion is tender, stirring occasionally. Add the rice (page 152). Cook about 5 minutes or until rice is golden brown, stirring frequently (page 152). Remove from heat.

2 Meanwhile, in a 1½-quart saucepan bring broth to boiling; reduce heat. Cover and keep broth simmering. Carefully stir 1 cup of the broth into rice mixture (page 152). Cook, stirring frequently, over medium heat until liquid is absorbed. Stir another 1 cup of the broth into rice mixture. Continue to cook, stirring frequently, until liquid is absorbed. Add another 1 cup broth, ½ cup at a time, stirring frequently until broth has been absorbed. (This should take 18 to 20 minutes total.)

3 Stir in remaining broth, the peas, carrot, and dried thyme (if using). Cook and stir until rice is just tender and creamy (page 152).

4 Stir in spinach, cheese, and fresh thyme (if using); heat through. Serve immediately. Makes 6 servings.

Per serving: 168 cal., 6 g total fat (1 g sat. fat), 3 mg chol., 608 mg sodium, 25 g carbo., 2 g fiber, 5 g pro.

Classic Risotto with Caramelized Onions: Prepare as above, except omit peas. While risotto is cooking, in a 10-inch skillet cook 2 cups sliced, halved onions in 1 tablespoon hot olive oil, covered, over medium-low heat for 15 minutes. Uncover and cook 10 to 15 minutes more or until onion is evenly golden brown; stir frequently. In Step 3 add caramelized onion with carrot.

Classic Risotto with Edamame: Prepare as above, except omit peas. Cook 1 cup frozen shelled sweet soybeans (edamame) according to package directions. In Step 3 add edamame with the carrot. Makes 4 main-dish or 6 side-dish servings.

Classic Risotto with Shrimp: Prepare as above, except omit peas. In Step 3 stir in 1½ cups cooked, peeled medium shrimp with the carrot. Makes 4 main-dish or 6 side-dish servings.

Shortcut Risotto with Peas: Prepare as above through Step 1. Carefully stir in all of the broth. Bring to boiling; reduce heat. Cover; simmer for 20 minutes (do not lift cover). Remove from heat. Stir in peas, carrot, and dried thyme (if using). Cover; let stand for 5 minutes. Rice should be just tender and mixture should be slightly creamy. (If necessary, stir in a little water to reach desired consistency.) Stir in spinach, cheese, and fresh thyme (if using); heat through. Serve at once.

Ask Mom How do I chop an onion? page 47 / What is a garlic clove? page 40 / How do I mince garlic? page 40 / How do I shred vegetables? page 20 / How do I crush dried herbs? page 78 / How do I snip fresh herbs? pages 42, 328 / How do I shred fresh herbs/spinach? page 42 / How do I grate cheese? page 71 / What does simmer mean? page 79

Corn Bread

1 cup all-purpose flour
¾ cup cornmeal
2 to 3 tablespoons sugar
2½ teaspoons baking powder
¾ teaspoon salt
1 tablespoon butter
2 eggs, beaten
1 cup milk
¼ cup cooking oil or melted butter
Honey (optional)

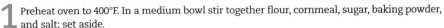

1 Preheat oven to 400°F. In a medium bowl stir together flour, cornmeal, sugar, baking powder, and salt; set aside.

2 Add the 1 tablespoon butter to a 10-inch cast-iron skillet, 9×1½-inch round baking pan, or 8×8×2-inch square baking pan. Place in the preheated oven about 3 minutes or until butter melts. Remove pan from oven; swirl butter in pan to coat bottom and sides of pan.

3 Meanwhile, in a small bowl combine eggs, milk, and oil. Add egg mixture all at once to flour mixture. Stir just until moistened. Pour batter into hot skillet or pan. Bake for 15 to 20 minutes or until a wooden toothpick inserted near center comes out clean (see photo, page 75). Cut into wedges or squares. Serve warm. If desired, drizzle with honey. Makes 8 to 10 servings.

Per serving: 219 cal., 10 g total fat (3 g sat. fat), 60 mg chol., 390 mg sodium, 26 g carbo., 1 g fiber, 5 g pro.

Double Corn Bread: Prepare as above, except fold ½ cup frozen whole kernel corn, thawed, into the batter.

Green Chile Corn Bread: Prepare as above, except fold 1 cup shredded cheddar cheese or Monterey Jack cheese (4 ounces) and one 4-ounce can diced green chile peppers, drained, into the batter.

Corn Muffins: Prepare as above, except omit the 1 tablespoon butter. Spoon the batter into 12 greased 2½-inch muffin cups, filling cups two-thirds full. Bake in the preheated oven about 15 minutes or until light brown and a wooden toothpick inserted near centers comes out clean (see photo, page 75). Makes 12 muffins.

Corn Sticks: Prepare as above, except omit the 1 tablespoon butter. Generously grease corn stick pans and heat in the preheated oven for 3 minutes. Carefully fill preheated pans two-thirds full. Bake in the preheated oven about 12 minutes or until a wooden toothpick inserted in centers comes out clean (see photo, page 75). Makes 18 to 26 corn sticks.

Meal Maker Slather it with honey or butter (or both) and corn bread is practically a meal in itself. But as a hearty serve-along, it has few peers. Dip chunks of it into thick chilies or meaty soups and stews or serve as a companion to fried chicken or barbecued ribs.

Ask Mom How do I measure flour? page 58 / How do I measure butter? pages 58, 59 / How do I beat eggs? page 62 / How do I combine wet and dry ingredients? page 63 / What does drizzle mean? page 79 / How do I shred cheese? page 71 / What does fold mean? page 79

② Skill Level

Focaccia Breadsticks

- ¼ cup oil-packed dried tomatoes
- ¼ cup grated Romano or Parmesan cheese
- 2 teaspoons water
- 1½ teaspoons snipped fresh rosemary or ½ teaspoon dried rosemary, crushed
- ⅛ teaspoon cracked black pepper
- 1 13.8-ounce package refrigerated pizza dough

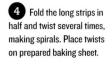

Ingredient Info
Since only ¼ cup dried tomatoes is used in this recipe, you'll probably have extra tomatoes left in the jar. Don't let them go to waste: Use snipped tomatoes on homemade pizzas, stir them into mayonnaise and spread on sandwiches, or stir into hot pasta with some purchased pesto.

1 Preheat oven to 350°F. Lightly grease a baking sheet; set aside.

2 Drain dried tomatoes, reserving oil; finely snip tomatoes with a kitchen scissors. In a small bowl combine tomatoes, 2 teaspoons of the reserved oil, the cheese, water, rosemary, and pepper. Set aside.

3 On a lightly floured surface, unroll the pizza dough. Roll the dough into a 10×8-inch rectangle. Spread the tomato mixture crosswise over half of the dough (below). Fold plain half of dough over filling (below); press lightly to seal edges. Cut the folded dough lengthwise into ten ½-inch strips (below). Fold each strip in half and twist two or three times (below). Place 1 inch apart on the prepared baking sheet.

4 Bake in the preheated oven for 12 to 18 minutes or until golden brown. Cool on a wire rack. Makes 10 breadsticks.

Per breadstick: 95 cal., 3 g total fat (1 g sat. fat), 2 mg chol., 157 mg sodium, 15 g carbo., 1 g fiber, 3 g pro.

1 ...ce pizza dough on ...urface. Spread half ...ed-out dough (along ...side) with the ...ixture.

2 Fold dough that isn't spread with tomato mixture over top of the filling. Press edges together lightly to seal in the filling.

3 On a lightly floured board, use a chef's knife to cut the filled pizza dough into 10 strips.

4 Fold the long strips in half and twist several times, making spirals. Place twists on prepared baking sheet.

Ask Mom What are dried tomatoes? page 53 / How do I grate cheese? page 71 / How do I snip fresh herbs? pages 42, 328 / How do I crush dried herbs? page 78 / How do I crack peppercorns? page 22 / How do I grease a baking pan/dish? page 61

CAN I USE WHOLE WHEAT ROLLS? Absolutely. And you can really use any combination of spices and/or seeds you like. Try dried dillweed and onion powder; cumin seeds, chili powder, and coarse salt; or flaxseeds and sesame seeds.

Not only are these rolls visually fun to serve from the pan, but they give you flavor options too. One kind is topped with a combination of poppy seeds, sesame seeds, and lemon pepper; the other with cornmeal and cheddar cheese.

Checkerboard Rolls (see recipe, page 158)

Menu Planning 101

It can be hard enough to figure out which entrée to make on any occasion—but what about what to serve with it? When planning a menu (and to keep it simple, that means an entrée and a side dish), there are a few things to keep in mind.

First you want balance. You want to have at least a protein and a vegetable (that can sometimes just be a mixed green salad) or fruit. Once you have that figured out, add a carbohydrate—pasta, rice, noodles, potato, bread, etc.

Then there are the tastes and textures to consider. You don't want to mix an Asian-style entrée with an Italian-style side dish. A rich entrée might call for a lighter, fresher side. A simple, relatively plain entrée such as a grilled chicken breast or steak becomes a veritable feast with a really great side dish.

Here are a few ideas for matchups from the recipe selection in this book:

Main Dish	Side Dish
Individual Sicilian Meat Loaves, page 244	Tomato Salad with Pickled Red Onions, page 354
Steak with Pan Sauce, page 246	Knife and Fork Caesar Salad, page 344
Jerk Pork Chops, page 252	Mashed Sweet Potatoes, page 144
Chicken with Skillet Gravy, page 260	Farm-Style Green Beans, page 126
Chicken Scaloppine, page 262	Classic Risotto with Peas, page 153
Ketchup-Glazed Meat Loaves, page 197	Twice-Baked Potatoes, page 146
Cheese-Topped Steaks, page 199	Herbed Leek Gratin, page 136
Braised Beef with Red Wine Sauce, page 205	Cauliflower Cheese Bake, page 133
Slow-Roasted Beef Tenderloin, page 206	Roasted Asparagus, page 125
Pork Chop and Rice Bake, page 209	Farm-Style Green Beans, page 126
Cranberry Pork Roast, page 210	Autumn Vegetable Pilaf, page 150
Blackberry-Glazed Pork Ribs, page 214	Red Potato Salad, page 353
Glazed Ham, page 216	Skillet Scalloped Corn, page 135
Oven-Fried Chicken, page 222	Cheesy Garlic Potato Gratin, page 145
Chicken with Pan Sauce, page 230	Mashed Potatoes, page 142
Roasted Chicken, page 234	Spring Greens with Sugared Nuts, page 341
BBQ Spice-Rubbed Turkey Breast, page 237	Saucepan Baked Beans, page 128
Crispy Pan-Fried Fish, page 278	Rice, Bean, and Corn Salad, page 355
Sesame-Crusted Salmon, page 281	Garlic and Pepper Stir-Fry, page 138
Halibut in Crazy Water, page 284	Bread Salad, page 342
Cold Roasted Salmon, page 285	Thyme-Roasted Beets, page 129
Baked Trout in Wine Sauce, page 289	Herbed Potatoes, page 148
Shrimp Scampi, page 299	Roasted Asparagus, page 125
Shrimp and Scallops en Papillote, page 301	Checkerboard Rolls, page 158
Broiled Lobster Tails, page 302	Classic Risotto with Peas, page 153
Spaghetti with Sauce and Meatballs, page 310	Greek Salad, page 343
Baked Cavatelli, page 305	Broiled Summer Squash and Onions, page 139
Roasted Red Pepper Lasagna, page 306	Bagged salad with "Best" vinaigrette, page 349
Baked Three-Cheese Macaroni, page 320	Butter-Glazed Carrots, page 132
Fettuccine Alfredo, page 322	Nutty Broccoli, page 130
Caribbean Rice and Beans, page 325	Corn Bread, page 154

Checkerboard Rolls

2 tablespoons poppy seeds

2 tablespoons sesame seeds

1 teaspoon lemon-pepper seasoning

2 tablespoons yellow cornmeal

2 tablespoons grated or finely shredded Parmesan cheese

3 tablespoons butter or margarine, melted

16 pieces (1.3 ounces each) frozen white roll dough

1 Grease a 9×9×2-inch square baking pan; set aside. In a shallow dish combine poppy seeds, sesame seeds, and lemon-pepper seasoning. In another shallow dish combine cornmeal and cheese. Place butter in a third dish. Working quickly, roll frozen dough pieces in butter, then in one of the seasoning mixtures to lightly coat, coating half of the rolls with the poppy seed-sesame seed mixture and the remaining rolls with the cornmeal-cheese seasoning mixture (below). Alternate rolls in the prepared pan (below). Cover rolls with greased plastic wrap. Let thaw in the refrigerator for at least 8 hours or up to 24 hours.

2 Remove pan from refrigerator; uncover and let stand at room temperature for 45 minutes. After 35 minutes, preheat oven to 375°F.

3 Bake rolls in the preheated oven for 20 to 25 minutes or until golden. Remove rolls from pan to wire rack. Cool slightly. Makes 16 rolls.

Per roll: 135 cal., 5 g total fat (2 g sat. fat), 6 mg chol., 189 mg sodium, 19 g carbo., 1 g fiber, 4 g pro.

Garlic-Herb Checkerboard Rolls: Prepare as above, except in Step 1 omit lemon-pepper seasoning. Substitute with 1 teaspoon dried Italian seasoning, crushed, and ½ teaspoon garlic powder.

1 Coat each roll of dough with melted butter so seasonings will stick.

2 Next dip the buttered ball of roll dough into the poppy seed-sesame seed or cornmeal-cheese mixture.

3 Place coated balls of roll dough in the greased baking pan, forming a checkerboard pattern.

Ask Mom How do I grate cheese? page 71 / How do I shred cheese? page 71 / How do I measure butter? pages 58, 59 / How do I grease a baking pan/dish? page 61 / How do I crush dried herbs? page 78

breakfast

ANYTIME

Start your day right with hotcakes or a cold smoothie. (It's the most important meal of the day, you know.)

1 Skill Level

Fried Eggs

2 teaspoons butter or margarine or nonstick cooking spray
4 eggs
Salt
Ground black pepper

1 In a 10-inch skillet melt butter over medium heat. (Or coat an unheated skillet with cooking spray.) Break eggs into skillet (below). If desired, sprinkle with salt and pepper. Reduce heat to low; cook for 3 to 4 minutes or until whites are completely set and yolks start to thicken.

2 For fried eggs over easy or over hard, turn eggs and cook about 30 seconds more (over easy) or about 1 minute more (over hard) (below). Makes 4 fried eggs.

Steam-Basted Fried Eggs: Prepare as above, except cook eggs until edges turn white; add 1 to 2 teaspoons water. Cook eggs, covered, for 3 to 4 minutes or until yolks begin to thicken but are not hard.

Per egg: 91 cal., 7 g total fat (3 g sat. fat), 217 mg chol., 84 mg sodium, 0 g carbo., 0 g fiber, 6 g pro.

Meal Maker As good as fried eggs taste on their own (with sides of bacon and hash browns, of course), they're even better in a breakfast sandwich. This is a great grab-and-go meal when you're running late. To make a sandwich, just toast two halves of an English muffin while you're making the egg. Place the egg on one muffin half. Top with your choice of cheese and cooked bacon or Canadian bacon. If you like, add mayo, sliced tomato, basil leaves, or anything else that sounds good. Top with the other muffin half and you're good to go.

1 Carefully break the eggs, one at a time, into the hot butter.

2 Use a wide spatula/turner to carefully lift and flip the eggs over so the yolks are down.

Ask Mom How do I work with eggs? page 62

Scrambled Eggs

  4 eggs
¼ cup milk, half-and-half, or light cream
⅛ teaspoon salt
  Dash ground black pepper
I tablespoon butter or margarine

1 In a medium bowl beat together eggs, milk, salt, and pepper with a wire whisk or fork. In a 10-inch skillet melt butter over medium heat; pour in egg mixture. Cook over medium heat, without stirring, until egg mixture begins to set on the bottom and around the edges.

2 With a spatula or a large spoon, lift and fold the partially cooked egg mixture so that the uncooked portion flows underneath (below). Continue cooking over medium heat for 2 to 3 minutes or until egg mixture is cooked through but is still glossy and moist (below). Remove from heat immediately. Makes 2 servings.

Per serving: 213 cal., 16 g total fat (7 g sat. fat), 441 mg chol., 339 mg sodium, 2 g carbo., 0 g fiber, 14 g pro.

Cheese-and-Onion Scrambled Eggs: Prepare as above, except cook 1 sliced green onion in the butter for 30 seconds; add egg mixture. Fold in ⅓ cup shredded cheddar or Swiss cheese after eggs begin to set.

Smoky Chicken Scrambled Eggs: Prepare as above, except cook ½ cup chopped deli-roasted chicken or smoked turkey and 2 tablespoons finely chopped red sweet pepper in the butter for 1 minute; add egg mixture. Fold in ⅓ cup shredded smoked mozzarella cheese after the eggs begin to set.

1 To cook the eggs evenly, lift and fold the partially cooked eggs toward the center of the skillet to allow the uncooked eggs to run to the edges.

2 The egg mixture is done when it is set but still looks glossy and moist. Overcooking makes the eggs dry and rubbery.

Ask Mom How do I work with eggs? page 62 / What does dash mean? page 79 / How do I measure butter? pages 58, 59 / What does fold mean? page 79 / How do I slice green onions? page 43 / How do I shred cheese? page 71 / How do I seed and chop sweet peppers? page 49 / How do I crumble cheese? pages 71, 96 / How do I cut onion wedges? page 47

SCRAMBLE YOUR STYLE. Change it up a little. Saute one or more of the following in olive oil or butter before adding the uncooked eggs—garlic, onions, sweet peppers, mushrooms, olives, and/or artichoke hearts. The finishing touch? Cheese, of course.

Greek-Style Scrambled Eggs
Prepare as on page 162, except cook and stir 2 cups fresh baby spinach in the butter until limp; add egg mixture. Fold in $\frac{1}{2}$ cup crumbled feta cheese with minced garlic and fresh oregano or dill after the eggs begin to set. Sprinkle very thin red onion wedges over the top.

Breakfast Burrito Wraps

4 eggs
¼ cup milk
¼ teaspoon salt
    Dash ground black pepper
I tablespoon snipped fresh cilantro (optional)
I tablespoon butter or margarine
4 strips bacon, crisp-cooked, drained, and crumbled
¼ cup sliced green onion (2)
4 8-inch flour tortillas
½ cup shredded Monterey Jack cheese or Monterey Jack cheese with jalapeño peppers (2 ounces)
    Salsa (optional)

1 In a medium bowl beat together eggs, milk, salt, and pepper with a wire whisk or fork. If desired, stir in cilantro. In a 10-inch skillet melt butter over medium heat; pour in egg mixture. Cook, without stirring, until mixture begins to set on the bottom and around the edges. With a spatula or large spoon, lift and fold the partially cooked egg mixture so that the uncooked portion flows underneath (see photo 1, page 162). Stir in bacon and green onion. Continue cooking over medium heat for 2 to 3 minutes or until egg mixture is cooked through but is still glossy and moist (see photo 2, page 162). Remove from heat immediately.

2 Meanwhile, warm the tortillas according to package directions. Divide egg mixture among tortillas (below). Sprinkle with cheese. If desired, top with salsa. Fold bottom edge of each tortilla over the egg mixture (below). Fold in the sides (below). Makes 4 burrito wraps.

Per wrap: 285 cal., 17 g total fat (8 g sat. fat), 240 mg chol., 585 mg sodium, 16 g carbo., 1 g fiber, 15 g pro.

1 Spoon the egg mixture down the center of each softened tortilla.

2 Fold the bottom edge of each tortilla up and over the egg mixture.

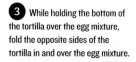
3 While holding the bottom of the tortilla over the egg mixture, fold the opposite sides of the tortilla in and over the egg mixture.

Ask Mom How do I work with eggs? page 62 / What does dash mean? page 79 / How do I snip fresh herbs? pages 42, 328 / How do I measure butter? pages 58, 59 / How do I cook bacon? page 172 / How do I shred cheese? page 71 / What does fold mean? page 79 / What is prosciutto? page 358 / How do I slice green onions? page 43

TRY A NEW TORTILLA. Flavored tortillas can add variety and flair to your morning routine. Try garlic-herb, spinach, dried tomato, whole wheat—even jalapeño. No matter how you wrap them up, eggs, meat, and cheese are a winning way to start your day.

2

1. **Ham and Artichoke Burrito Wraps:** Prepare as on page 164, except omit the salsa. Substitute I tablespoon snipped fresh Italian (flat-leaf) parsley for the cilantro; 2 ounces chopped cooked ham or prosciutto for the bacon; one 6-ounce jar marinated artichoke hearts, drained and chopped, for the green onions; and 2 ounces Havarti cheese, shredded, for the Monterey Jack cheese.

2. **Salami and Provolone Burrito Wraps:** Prepare as on page 164, except omit the salsa. Add I tablespoon snipped fresh basil in place of the cilantro. Add 2 ounces chopped salami in place of the bacon; ½ cup roasted red sweet peppers, drained and chopped, in place of the green onions; and 2 ounces provolone cheese, shredded, in place of the Monterey Jack cheese.

3. **Turkey and Smoked Cheddar Burrito Wraps:** Prepare as on page 164, except omit the green onion. Substitute I table-spoon snipped fresh parsley for the cilantro; 4 ounces shredded cooked turkey or chicken for the bacon; and 2 ounces smoked cheddar cheese, shredded, for the Monterey Jack cheese. To assemble, divide I cup fresh baby spinach among tortillas; add egg mixture. If desired, top with salsa.

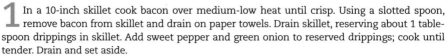

3 Skill Level

Breakfast Pizza

4 ounces plain or peppered bacon, finely chopped

½ cup chopped green sweet pepper

¼ cup sliced green onion (2)

I I2-inch packaged prebaked pizza crust

I 8-ounce tub cream cheese spread*

2 eggs

I cup cubed cooked ham

I cup shredded cheddar cheese (4 ounces)

1 In a 10-inch skillet cook bacon over medium-low heat until crisp. Using a slotted spoon, remove bacon from skillet and drain on paper towels. Drain skillet, reserving about 1 tablespoon drippings in skillet. Add sweet pepper and green onion to reserved drippings; cook until tender. Drain and set aside.

2 Preheat oven to 400°F. Place pizza crust on a large baking sheet; set aside. In a small bowl beat cream cheese spread with an electric mixer just until smooth. Add eggs, one at a time, beating until combined. Spread cream cheese mixture over pizza crust. Sprinkle with bacon, sweet pepper, and green onion. Top with ham.

3 Bake, uncovered, in the preheated oven for 15 to 20 minutes or until cream cheese layer is set. Sprinkle with cheddar cheese. Bake for 3 to 4 minutes more or until cheese melts. To serve, use a pizza cutter to cut into wedges. Makes 6 to 8 servings.

*Note: If desired, use an herb-flavored cream cheese spread.

Tip: For quicker preparation, used cooked bacon pieces and cook sweet pepper and green onion in 1 tablespoon olive oil.

Per serving: 4I0 cal., 27 g total fat (I3 g sat. fat), I26 mg chol., 635 mg sodium, 29 g carbo., I g fiber, I6 g pro.

Mushroom-Artichoke Breakfast Pizza: Prepare as above, except omit bacon, sweet pepper, and green onion. In a 10-inch skillet cook and stir 2 cups fresh mushrooms, sliced, in 1 tablespoon olive oil over medium-high heat until golden. Substitute cooked mushrooms for the ham and add ½ cup marinated artichoke hearts, drained and coarsely chopped, and ½ cup slivered roasted red sweet peppers. Substitute shredded Italian-blend cheese for the cheddar cheese.

Shrimp Breakfast Pizza: Prepare as above, except omit bacon. Substitute red sweet pepper for green sweet pepper. Cook sweet pepper and green onion in 1 tablespoon olive oil. Substitute 1 cup coarsely chopped cooked shrimp or two 4-ounce cans small shrimp, drained, for the ham. Substitute shredded Mexican-blend cheese for the cheddar cheese. (Or if desired, substitute one 6-ounce can crabmeat, drained, flaked, and cartilage removed, for the shrimp.)

Shopping Savvy Prebaked pizza shells are a dream come true for those who love homemade pizza. Forget the days of stirring, kneading, rising, and shaping pizza dough—now just open the package, top the prebaked shell, and you're ready to pop it in the oven to finish it off. Look for this superhandy product in supermarket aisles with other pizza-making ingredients (they're not refrigerated or frozen).

Ask Mom How do I work with eggs? page 62 / How do I seed and chop sweet peppers? page 49 / How do I slice green onions? page 43 / What does it mean to cube? page 64 / How do I shred cheese? page 7I / How do I slice fresh mushrooms? page 45

Poached Eggs

1 to 2 teaspoons instant chicken bouillon granules (optional)

4 eggs

Salt

Ground black pepper

1 If desired, lightly grease a 10-inch saute pan or skillet with *cooking oil* or *shortening*. Half-fill the skillet with *water*. If desired, stir in bouillon granules. Bring the water to boiling; reduce heat to simmering (bubbles should begin to break the surface of the water).

2 Break one of the eggs into a small dish or a measuring cup with a handle. Carefully slide egg into the simmering water, holding the lip of the cup as close to the water as possible (below). Add remaining eggs, one at a time.

3 Simmer eggs, uncovered, for 3 to 5 minutes or until the whites are completely set and the yolks begin to thicken but are not hard (below). Remove eggs with a slotted spoon. Season to taste with salt and pepper. Makes 4 poached eggs.

Poaching pan directions: Lightly grease each cup of an egg-poaching pan with cooking oil or shortening. Place poacher cups over the pan of boiling water (water should not touch bottoms of cups); reduce heat to simmering. Break an egg into a small dish or measuring cup with a handle. Carefully slide egg into a poacher cup. Repeat with remaining eggs. Cover and cook for 4 to 6 minutes or until the whites are completely set and yolks begin to thicken but are not hard. Run a knife around edges to loosen eggs. Invert poacher cups to remove eggs.

Per egg: 78 cal., 5 g total fat (2 g sat. fat), 212 mg chol., 62 mg sodium, 1 g carbo., 0 g fiber, 6 g pro.

1 Gently slide each egg into the simmering water, taking care not to break the eggs. Place eggs in the skillet so each one has an equal amount of space.

2 Do not let the water boil. Eggs cooked at high temperatures will have tough whites and mealy yolks.

Ask Mom What does poach mean? page 79 / How do I work with eggs? page 62 / How do I grease a baking pan/dish? page 61 / What does simmer mean? page 79

WHAT'S HOLLANDAISE? The original is a silky sauce made with eggs, butter, and lemon juice in a double boiler to avoid curdling. It's rich and delicious but tricky to pull off. This Mock Hollandaise Sauce tastes just as good, looks beautiful, and is surefire.

1

2

3

1. **Portobello Mushroom Benedict:** Prepare as on page 169, except before poaching eggs, in a skillet cook four 3½- to 4-inch-diameter stemmed portobello mushroom caps in I tablespoon hot olive oil about 6 minutes or until tender, turning once. Blot with a paper towel. Slice mushrooms; sprinkle with salt and ground black pepper. Cover with foil to keep warm. Continue as directed, except substitute the mushrooms for the Canadian-style bacon. Sprinkle with chopped tomato.

2. **Salmon Benedict:** Prepare as on page 169, except spread I tablespoon softened tub-style cream cheese spread with herbs on each toasted English muffin half. Substitute 4 ounces thinly sliced smoked salmon (lox-style) for the Canadian-style bacon. If desired, stir ½ teaspoon dried dillweed into the Mock Hollandaise Sauce. If desired, sprinkle with additional dillweed.

3. **Reuben Benedict:** Prepare as on page 169, except substitute 4 slices marble rye or rye bread for the English muffins and thinly sliced corned beef for the Canadian-style bacon. Divide ½ cup rinsed and drained sauerkraut evenly over the corned beef. Sprinkle with ½ cup shredded Swiss cheese.

3 Skill Level

Eggs Benedict

Ingredient Info
Although traditional English muffins are made with white flour, there are now several types of whole grain English muffins on the market—including whole wheat and multigrain, with crunchy millet and flaxseeds. You can use any kind in this recipe.

1 recipe Poached Eggs (page 167)
1 recipe Mock Hollandaise Sauce
2 English muffins, split
4 slices Canadian-style bacon
   Cracked black pepper (optional)

1 Prepare Poached Eggs. Remove eggs from skillet with a slotted spoon and place them in a large pan of warm water to keep them warm. Prepare Mock Hollandaise Sauce.

2 Place muffin halves, cut sides up, on a baking sheet. Broil 3 to 4 inches from the heat about 2 minutes or until toasted. Top muffin halves with Canadian-style bacon (below). Broil about 1 minute more or until bacon is heated.

3 To serve, top each bacon-topped muffin half with an egg (below). Spoon Mock Hollandaise Sauce over eggs (below). If desired, sprinkle with pepper. Makes 4 servings.

Mock Hollandaise Sauce: In a 1- to $1\frac{1}{2}$-quart saucepan combine $\frac{1}{3}$ cup dairy sour cream, $\frac{1}{3}$ cup mayonnaise or salad dressing, 2 teaspoons lemon juice, and 1 teaspoon yellow mustard. Cook and stir over medium-low heat until warm. If desired, stir in a little milk to thin. Makes about $\frac{2}{3}$ cup.

Make-ahead directions: Prepare Poached Eggs and toast English muffins as above. Place muffin halves in a greased 8×8×2-inch baking pan. Top each muffin half with a slice of Canadian-style bacon and 1 cooked egg. Cover and chill for up to 24 hours. To serve, prepare the Mock Hollandaise Sauce; spoon hot sauce over eggs. Bake, covered, in a 350°F oven about 30 minutes or until heated through.

Per serving: 352 cal., 25 g total fat (7 g sat. fat), 239 mg chol., 723 mg sodium, 15 g carbo., 1 g fiber, 15 g pro.

1 After toasting the muffins under the broiler, top each half with a slice of Canadian-style bacon.

2 Use a slotted spoon to remove an egg from the warm water. Set the spoon and egg briefly on a paper towel to drain. Place an egg on each bacon-topped muffin half.

3 Spoon some of the warm Mock Hollandaise Sauce over the top of each egg.

Ask Mom How do I work with eggs? page 62 / What does poach mean? page 79 / What does it mean to broil? page 68 / How do I juice a lemon/lime? pages 30, 80 / How much juice does one lemon/lime yield? page 30 / What are some mushroom varieties? page 44 / How do I seed tomatoes? page 52 / How do I chop a tomato? page 52 / What are capers? page 79 / How do I shred cheese? page 71

Frittata with Cheese

8 eggs, lightly beaten
$\frac{1}{2}$ cup milk
I tablespoon snipped fresh herb or I teaspoon dried herb, crushed*
$\frac{1}{4}$ teaspoon salt
$\frac{1}{8}$ teaspoon ground black pepper
I cup vegetables**
2 tablespoons olive oil
$\frac{1}{2}$ to I cup meat***
$\frac{1}{4}$ to $\frac{1}{2}$ cup shredded or crumbled cheese (I to 2 ounces)****

1 In a medium bowl combine eggs, milk, desired herb, salt, and pepper; set aside. In a 10-inch broilerproof skillet cook and stir desired vegetables in hot oil according to the time specified below or until vegetables are crisp-tender (page 171). Add desired meat to the skillet.

2 Pour egg mixture over vegetables and meat in the skillet (page 171). Cook over medium heat. As egg mixture sets, run a spatula around the skillet edge, lifting egg mixture so uncooked portion flows underneath (page 171). Continue cooking and lifting edges until egg mixture is almost set (surface will be moist). Sprinkle with desired cheese.

3 Preheat broiler. Broil 4 to 5 inches from heat for 1 to 2 minutes or until top is set and cheese melts (page 171). To serve, use a pizza cutter to cut into wedges. Makes 4 servings.

*Herbs: basil, chives, cilantro, parsley

**Vegetables: Cook 1 minute: cut-up marinated artichoke hearts. Cook 2 to 4 minutes: shredded carrot; chopped asparagus; cooked cubed potato; chopped red or green sweet pepper; chopped green or red onion. Cook 4 to 6 minutes: chopped zucchini or yellow summer squash, broccoli florets.

***Meats: $\frac{1}{2}$ cup: crisp-cooked, drained, and crumbled bacon; chopped cooked ham or prosciutto; flaked smoked salmon; chopped pepperoni. 1 cup: cooked and drained bulk sausage (pork, Italian, chorizo); chopped smoked turkey; shredded deli-roasted chicken (see photos, page 395).

****Cheeses: $\frac{1}{2}$ cup: shredded Swiss, shredded Gruyère, shredded cheddar (sharp or smoked), shredded American, shredded mozzarella (part-skim or smoked), shredded Gouda, shredded Edam, shredded Parmesan, shredded Colby-Jack. $\frac{1}{4}$ cup: crumbled feta, crumbled blue, shredded Monterey Jack with jalepeño peppers.

Per serving: 285 cal., 2I g total fat (6 g sat. fat), 443 mg chol., 563 mg sodium, 4 g carbo., I g fiber, I9 g pro.

Veggie Frittata with Cheese: Substitute vegetables for the meat in the ingredient list.

Ask Mom How do I beat eggs? page 62 / How do I snip fresh herbs? pages 42, 328 / How do I crush dried herbs? page 78 / How do I shred or crumble cheese? pages 7I, 96 / What does crisp-tender mean? page 79 / What does broil mean? page 68 / How do I shred vegetables? page 20 / How do I trim asparagus? page 34 / How do I chop sweet peppers? page 49 / How do I chop an onion? page 47 / How do I prepare summer squash/zucchini? page 54 / How do I cut broccoli? page 36

WHAT'S A FRITTATA? If you think this looks like a big omelet, you're basically right. Instead of folding the egg over the filling ingredients as the French do, this Italian version incorporates the ingredients into the egg mixture. Broiling the cheese on top as a final step makes it crisp and crusty. Yum!

1 Cook and stir your choice of vegetables with a wooden spoon over medium heat just until the vegetables are crisp-tender.

3 As the egg mixture begins to set, lift it with a spatula, allowing the uncooked mixture to flow underneath the cooked mixture.

4 Place the skillet under the preheated broiler 4 to 5 inches from the heat. If your skillet doesn't have a broilerproof handle, wrap the handle in a couple of layers of heavy-duty foil.

2 Carefully pour the egg mixture over the vegetables and meat in the skillet, taking care not to push all the ingredients away from the center of the skillet.

Cooking Bacon, Sausage, and Ham

Cooking pork bacon

Fry: Place bacon slices in an unheated skillet (if using an electric range, preheat the element for 2 to 4 minutes). Cook over medium heat for 8 to 10 minutes, turning occasionally. If bacon browns too quickly, reduce heat slightly. Drain well on paper towels.

Bake: Preheat oven to 400°F. Place bacon slices side by side on a rack in a foil-lined shallow baking pan with sides. Bake in preheated oven 18 to 21 minutes or until crisp-cooked. Drain well. To

Microwave: Place bacon slices on a microwave-safe rack or a plate lined with microwave-safe paper towels. Cover with a paper towel. Microwave on 100 percent power (high) to desired doneness, rearranging bacon once. Allow $1\frac{1}{2}$ to 2 minutes for two slices, $2\frac{1}{2}$ to 3 minutes for four slices, and $3\frac{1}{2}$ to 4 minutes for six slices.

Uncooked sausage patties

Fry: Place $\frac{1}{2}$-inch-thick uncooked sausage patties in an unheated skillet. Cook over medium-low heat about 12 minutes or until centers are no longer pink, turning once. Drain on paper towels.

Bake: Preheat oven to 400°F. Arrange $\frac{1}{2}$-inch-thick patties on a rack in a shallow baking pan. Bake in the preheated oven 18 to 20 minutes or until centers are no longer pink. Drain on paper towels.

Uncooked sausage links

Fry: Place uncooked sausage links in an unheated skillet. Cook over medium-low heat for 14 to 16 minutes or until centers are no longer pink, turning frequently to brown evenly. Drain on paper towels.

Bake: Preheat oven to 375°F. Place uncooked sausage links in a shallow baking pan. Bake in preheated oven for 16 to 18 minutes or until centers are no longer pink, turning once. Drain on paper towels.

Ham steaks and slices

Fry: Trim fat from a $\frac{1}{2}$-inch-thick cooked center-cut ham slice. Cut ham into serving-size pieces. In a 10-inch skillet heat 1 teaspoon cooking oil over medium-high heat until very hot. Add ham to skillet; reduce heat to medium. Cook, uncovered, for 6 to 8 minutes or until heated through (140°F), turning once.

Broil: Trim fat from a $\frac{1}{2}$-inch-thick cooked center-cut ham slice. Place on the unheated rack of a broiler pan. Broil 3 to 4 inches from heat for 6 to 9 minutes or until heated through (140°F), turning once.

Panfrying bacon, sausage, and ham is so easy—and it creates an irresistibly crispy texture and to-die-for flavor. If your stovetop is already covered with too many pans for cooking, just pop the meat in the oven.

HERE'S TO PORK! What would a leisurely Saturday-morning breakfast be without a hearty helping of bacon, sausage, or ham? And it's supereasy to make. Whether you fry it up crispy on the stovetop or tuck it away in the oven to bake, one of these meaty side dishes will keep you satisfied long into the day.

2 Skill Level

Ham-Asparagus Strata

- 4 English muffins, torn or cut into bite-size pieces (4 cups)
- 2 cups cubed cooked ham (10 ounces)
- 1 10-ounce package frozen cut asparagus, thawed and well drained, or 2 cups cut-up fresh cooked asparagus (see page 125)
- 4 ounces process Swiss cheese, torn, or process Gruyère cheese, cut up (1 cup)
- 2 tablespoons finely chopped onion
- 4 eggs, beaten
- ¼ cup dairy sour cream
- 1¼ cups milk

1 Spread half of the English muffin pieces in a greased 2-quart square baking dish. Add ham, asparagus, cheese, and onion (below). Top with the remaining English muffin pieces (below). Whisk together eggs and sour cream; stir in milk and ⅛ teaspoon *ground black pepper*; pour evenly over layers in dish (below). Press muffin pieces down (below). Cover and chill overnight.

2 Preheat oven to 325°F. Bake, uncovered, in the preheated oven for 65 to 75 minutes or until the internal temperature registers 170°F on an instant-read thermometer. Let stand for 10 minutes before serving. Makes 6 servings.

Per serving: 340 cal., 16 g total fat (7 g sat. fat), 192 mg chol., 1,211 mg sodium, 23 g carbo., 2 g fiber, 26 g pro.

Chicken-Broccoli Strata: Prepare as above, except substitute chopped cooked chicken for the ham, broccoli florets for the asparagus, and process cheddar cheese for the Swiss cheese. Add ¼ teaspoon salt to egg mixture.

Denver Strata: Prepare as above, except omit asparagus and onion. Sprinkle ¼ cup thinly sliced green onion, ¼ cup sliced, pitted ripe olives, and 1 cup slivered roasted red sweet peppers over English muffin pieces with ham. Substitute process American cheese for the Swiss cheese.

1 Layer the ham, asparagus, cheese, and onion over half of the torn English muffin pieces.

2 Add the rest of the torn English muffin pieces to the baking dish.

3 Combine the egg mixture in a large measuring cup so it's easy to pour over the layers in the baking dish.

4 Use the back of a wooden spoon to press English muffin pieces do into the egg mixture.

Ask Mom What does it mean to cube? page 64 / How do I trim asparagus? page 34 / What is process cheese? page 408 / How do I chop an onion? page 47 / How do I work with eggs? page 62 / How do I beat eggs? page 62 / How do I grease a baking pan/ dish? page 61 / How do I use a meat/instant-read thermometer? page 74 / How do I trim and cut broccoli? page 36 / How do I slice green onions? page 43 / What is process cheese? page 408

3 Skill Level

Spicy Sicilian Strata

Ingredient Info Frozen spinach is a superquick and convenient way to add flavor, texture, and healthfulness to a variety of dishes, but the extra water in it may drown your food. To avoid this, after the spinach has drained in a strainer, use the back of a spoon to press it firmly. You can accomplish the same thing by squeezing the spinach in your hands. Either way, the goal is to get as much liquid out as possible.

    5 cups cubed French bread (1-inch cubes)
    1 3.5-ounce package sliced pepperoni, coarsely chopped
  ¼ cup pepperoncini salad peppers, drained, stemmed, and chopped
  ½ of a 10-ounce package frozen chopped spinach, thawed and well drained
  ¼ cup oil-packed dried tomatoes, drained and chopped
    1 cup shredded Italian-blend cheese (4 ounces)
    3 eggs, lightly beaten
1½ cups milk
    1 teaspoon dried Italian seasoning, crushed
       Dash cayenne pepper
  ¼ cup grated Parmesan cheese

1 Preheat oven to 350°F. Place bread cubes in a 15×10×1-inch baking pan. Bake, uncovered, in the preheated oven for 10 minutes, stirring once.

2 Spread half of the bread cubes in a greased 2-quart square baking dish. Top with half of the pepperoni, half of the pepperoncini peppers, all of the spinach, and all of the tomatoes. Sprinkle with ½ cup of the Italian-blend cheese. Repeat layers with remaining bread, pepperoni, pepperoncini peppers, and Italian-blend cheese.

3 Whisk together eggs, milk, Italian seasoning, cayenne pepper, and ¼ teaspoon *salt;* pour evenly over layers in dish (see photo 3, page 174). Press bread cubes down with a wooden spoon (see photo 4, page 174). Sprinkle with Parmesan cheese. Cover and chill for 2 to 24 hours.

4 Preheat oven to 350°F. Bake, uncovered, in the preheated oven for 35 to 45 minutes or until the internal temperature registers 170°F on an instant-read thermometer. Let stand for 10 minutes before serving. Makes 6 servings.

Per serving: 316 cal., 18 g total fat (8 g sat. fat), 146 mg chol., 1,006 mg sodium, 22 g carbo., 2 g fiber, 18 g pro.

Spicy Mexican Strata: Prepare as above, except substitute 4 ounces chorizo sausage, cooked and crumbled, for the pepperoni; one 4.5-ounce can diced green chile peppers, drained, for the pepperoncini peppers; and Mexican-blend cheese for Italian-blend cheese. Omit Italian seasoning. Substitute crumbled queso fresco or additional Mexican-blend cheese for Parmesan cheese.

Ask Mom How do I make/toast bread cubes? pages 79, 334 / How do I drain spinach? page 321 / What are dried tomatoes? page 53 / How do I work with eggs? page 62 / How do I beat eggs? page 62 / How do I crush dried herbs? page 78 / How do I grate cheese? page 71 / How do I grease a baking pan/dish? page 61 / How do I use a meat/instant-read thermometer? page 74 / What is chorizo? page 312 / How do I crumble cheese? pages 71, 96

NOT JUST FOR BREAKFAST. Quiche—a specialty of Alsace-Lorraine in northeastern France—is essentially a custardy, sumptuous egg-cheese-bacon (or ham or vegetable) pie. It's fabulous for breakfast or brunch—or for dinner with crusty bread, a green salad, and a glass of white wine.

1 To prevent the pastry from shrinking during baking, line it with a double thickness of regular foil or one layer of heavy-duty foil.

2 Pour the egg mixture into the hot baked pastry shell. The pie shell should still be hot when the egg mixture is added.

3 To protect the edges of the pie from overbrowning, fold a 12-inch square of foil into quarters. Cut a 7-inch circle out of the center. Unfold and loosely mold the foil over the pie's edge.

4 To test for doneness, insert a knife near the center of the quiche. If it comes out clean, the quiche is done.

Classic Quiche

Pastry for Single-Crust Pie (page 471) or ½ of a 15-ounce package
rolled refrigerated unbaked piecrust (1 piecrust)*

- 8 slices bacon
- 1 medium onion, thinly sliced
- 4 eggs, beaten
- 1 cup half-and-half or light cream
- 1 cup milk
- ¼ teaspoon salt
  Dash ground nutmeg
- 1½ cups shredded Swiss cheese (6 ounces)
- 1 tablespoon all-purpose flour

1 Preheat oven to 450°F. Prepare and roll out Pastry for Single-Crust Pie. Line a 9-inch pie plate with pastry. Trim; crimp edges as desired. Line unpricked pastry with a double thickness of foil (page 176). Bake, uncovered, in the preheated oven for 8 minutes. Remove foil. Bake for 4 to 5 minutes more or until pastry is set and dry. Remove from oven. Reduce oven temperature to 325°F.

2 Meanwhile, in a 10-inch skillet cook bacon until crisp. Drain, reserving 2 tablespoons drippings in skillet. Crumble bacon; set aside. Cook onion in reserved drippings over medium heat until tender; drain.

3 In an 8-cup glass measuring cup or a medium bowl stir together eggs, half-and-half, milk, salt, and nutmeg; stir in crumbled bacon and onion. In a medium bowl toss together cheese and flour; add to egg mixture and mix well.

4 Pour egg mixture into the hot baked pastry shell (page 176). Bake in the 325°F oven for 50 to 60 minutes or until a knife inserted near the center comes out clean (page 176). If necessary, cover edge of crust with foil to prevent overbrowning (page 176). Let stand 10 minutes before serving. Cut into wedges. Makes 6 servings.

*Note: If using refrigerated unbaked piecrust, prepare and prebake as directed on package. Continue as directed in Step 2.

Per serving: 524 cal., 37 g total fat (16 g sat. fat), 198 mg chol., 501 mg sodium, 26 g carbo., 1 g fiber, 20 g pro.

Mushroom Quiche: Prepare as above, except omit bacon. Saute 8 ounces sliced fresh mushrooms in 1 tablespoon hot olive oil over medium-high heat until mushrooms are tender and slightly golden. Add mushrooms and 2 tablespoons snipped fresh Italian (flat-leaf) parsley or basil to egg mixture. Substitute shredded Italian-blend cheese for the Swiss cheese.

Ask Mom How do I cook bacon? page 172 / How do I slice an onion? page 47 / How do I work with eggs? page 62 / How do I beat eggs? page 62 / How do I shred cheese? page 71 / How do I slice fresh mushrooms? page 45 / How do I snip fresh herbs? pages 42, 328

Monkey Bread Rolls

½ of a 34.5-ounce package frozen cinnamon sweet roll dough or frozen orange sweet roll dough (6 rolls)

⅓ cup chopped pecans

¼ cup butter or margarine, melted

½ cup sugar

¼ cup caramel-flavored ice cream topping

1 tablespoon maple-flavored syrup

1 Place frozen rolls about 2 inches apart on a large greased baking sheet. (Discard frosting packets or reserve for another use.) Cover rolls with plastic wrap. Refrigerate overnight to let dough thaw and begin to rise.

2 Preheat oven to 350°F. Generously grease twelve 2½-inch muffin cups. Divide pecans evenly among muffin cups; set aside.

3 Cut each roll into four pieces (below). Dip each roll piece in melted butter, then roll in sugar. Place two dough pieces into each prepared muffin cup (below). Drizzle rolls with any remaining melted butter; sprinkle with any remaining sugar. In a small bowl stir together ice cream topping and syrup; drizzle over rolls (below).

4 Bake in the preheated oven about 20 minutes or until rolls are golden brown. Cool in muffin cups on a wire rack for 1 minute. Invert onto a large platter. Cool slightly. Serve warm. Makes 12 rolls.

Per roll: 252 cal., 12 g total fat (4 g sat. fat), 11 mg chol., 373 mg sodium, 36 g carbo., 0 g fiber, 2 g pro.

1 After the rolls have thawed overnight in the refrigerator, use kitchen scissors to cut each roll into 4 pieces.

2 Dip dough pieces in butter and roll in sugar. Place 2 dough pieces in each muffin cup on top of the chopped pecans.

3 Use a kitchen spoon to drizzle the ice cream topping and syrup mixture evenly over the dough.

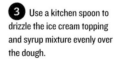

Ask Mom How do I chop nuts? page 65 / How do I measure butter? pages 58, 59 / What is maple-flavored syrup? page 457 / What's the best way to measure sticky liquids? pages 58, 81 / How do I grease a baking pan/dish? page 61

WHY MONKEY BREAD? Despite its name, this bread is banana free. This whimsical treat is made by arranging pieces of sweet roll dough in layers for each roll. Eating it requires a certain amount of "monkeying around" to pull the pieces apart by hand. If that seems too uncivilized, use silverware.

② Skill Level

Cinnamon Breakfast Muffins

$1\frac{1}{2}$ cups all-purpose flour
$\frac{1}{2}$ cup sugar
$1\frac{1}{2}$ teaspoons baking powder
$\frac{1}{4}$ teaspoon ground nutmeg
$\frac{1}{8}$ teaspoon salt
1 egg
$\frac{1}{2}$ cup milk
$\frac{1}{3}$ cup butter or margarine, melted
$\frac{1}{4}$ cup sugar
$\frac{1}{2}$ teaspoon ground cinnamon
$\frac{1}{4}$ cup butter or margarine, melted

Flavor Changes Cinnamon-sugar is the crowning glory on these breakfast bites, but a glaze does the trick too. To make a glaze, combine $\frac{3}{4}$ cup powdered sugar and 2 teaspoons milk. Stir in additional milk, $\frac{1}{2}$ teaspoon at a time, until the icing reaches drizzling consistency. For extra flavor, you can stir in $\frac{1}{2}$ teaspoon orange or lemon peel and $\frac{1}{8}$ teaspoon almond extract. Omit the cinnamon-sugar and drizzle the glaze over tops of muffins.

1 Preheat oven to 350°F. Grease twelve $2\frac{1}{2}$-inch muffin cups; set aside.

2 In a medium bowl stir together flour, the $\frac{1}{2}$ cup sugar, the baking powder, nutmeg, and salt. Make a well in the center of the flour mixture (page 181). In a small bowl beat egg with a fork; stir in milk and the $\frac{1}{3}$ cup melted butter. Add egg mixture to flour mixture all at once. Stir just until moistened (batter will be lumpy) (page 181).

3 Spoon batter into prepared muffin cups (page 181). Bake in the preheated oven for 20 to 25 minutes or until a wooden toothpick inserted in centers comes out clean (see photo, page 75).

4 Meanwhile, combine the $\frac{1}{4}$ cup sugar and the cinnamon. Cool muffins in muffin cups on a wire rack for 5 minutes. Remove from muffin cups. Dip muffins into the $\frac{1}{4}$ cup melted butter, then into sugar-cinnamon mixture (page 181). Serve warm. Makes 12 muffins.

Per muffin: 189 cal., 10 g total fat (6 g sat. fat), 42 mg chol., 128 mg sodium, 24 g carbo., 0 g fiber, 2 g pro.

Almond-Apricot Breakfast Muffins: Prepare as above, except fold $\frac{1}{2}$ cup chopped dried apricots; $\frac{1}{4}$ cup sliced almonds, toasted; and $\frac{1}{4}$ teaspoon almond extract into batter.

Banana-Coconut Breakfast Muffins: Prepare as above, except fold $\frac{3}{4}$ cup finely chopped banana and $\frac{1}{3}$ cup shredded coconut into batter.

Berry Breakfast Muffins: Prepare as above, except fold 1 cup fresh berries (raspberries, blackberries, blueberries) or chopped strawberries into batter.

Peanut Butter-Chocolate Breakfast Muffins: Prepare as above, except increase milk to $\frac{2}{3}$ cup and whisk $\frac{1}{2}$ cup creamy peanut butter into egg mixture. Fold $\frac{3}{4}$ cup miniature semisweet chocolate pieces into batter.

Toffee-Chocolate Breakfast Muffins: Prepare as above, except fold $\frac{1}{3}$ cup toffee pieces and $\frac{1}{3}$ cup semisweet chocolate pieces into batter.

Ask Mom How do I measure flour? page 58 / How do I measure butter? pages 58, 59 / How do I grease a baking pan/dish? page 61 / How do I combine wet and dry ingredients? page 63 / What does fold mean? page 79 / How do I toast nuts? page 65

A BUFFET OF MUFFINS.
This six-in-one recipe offers just about any flavor combo you could want. Whether you crave healthful favorites like berries and bananas or indulgent delights like chocolate and toffee, here's your new breakfast go-to.

1 Use a wooden spoon to gently push the flour mixture against the sides of the bowl to make a well.

2 Stir the batter just until the ingredients are moistened. Don't overmix or the muffins will be peaked and have tunnels and a tough texture.

3 Use a small spatula to push the batter off the wooden spoon into the greased muffin cups.

4 Immediately dip the tops of the hot muffins in the melted butter, then roll in the sugar-cinnamon mixture until well coated.

(3) Skill Level

Good to Know Coffee cake is one of those sweets that fills the bill for so many occasions. Not only is it a great stick-to-the-ribs breakfast, but you can also enjoy remaining nibbles with afternoon coffee, as a quick snack on the run, or even as that sweet something for after dinner. Wrap leftovers in plastic wrap, place in a freezerproof bag, and freeze for up to a month. Thaw at room temperature and enjoy—again.

Buttermilk
Coffee Cake

1 ½ cups all-purpose flour

1 cup packed brown sugar

⅓ cup butter or margarine

1 teaspoon baking powder

¼ teaspoon baking soda

¼ teaspoon ground cinnamon

¼ teaspoon ground nutmeg

½ cup buttermilk or sour milk (see page 445)

1 egg, beaten

⅓ cup chopped nuts (optional)

1 Preheat oven to 375°F. Grease an 8×8×2-inch baking pan; set aside. In a medium bowl stir together flour and brown sugar. Using a pastry blender, cut in butter until mixture resembles fine crumbs. Reserve ½ cup of the crumb mixture to sprinkle over batter. Stir baking powder, baking soda, cinnamon, and nutmeg into remaining crumb mixture. In a small bowl combine buttermilk and egg; add to crumb mixture, stirring just until moistened.

2 Spoon batter evenly into prepared baking pan. If desired, stir nuts into reserved crumb mixture; sprinkle over batter. Bake in the preheated oven about 25 minutes or until a wooden toothpick inserted near center comes out clean (see photo, page 75). Cool slightly. Serve warm. Makes 9 servings.

Per serving: 246 cal., 8 g total fat (5 g sat. fat), 43 mg chol., 184 mg sodium, 41 g carbo., 1 g fiber, 3 g pro.

Variations: Next time try folding one of the following into the batter: ¼ cup dried cherries and ¼ cup semisweet chocolate pieces; ½ cup raisins, dried cherries, or other chopped dried fruit; ¼ cup shredded coconut and ¼ cup chopped macadamia nuts; ½ cup toffee pieces; ¼ cup chopped peanuts and ¼ cup miniature semisweet chocolate pieces; 1 cup fresh blueberries, raspberries, or coarsely chopped strawberries.

Ask Mom How do I measure flour? page 58 / How do I pack brown sugar? page 58 / How do I measure butter? pages 58, 59 / How do I beat eggs? page 62 / How do I chop nuts? page 65 / How do I grease a baking pan/dish? page 61 / How do I cut in butter? page 63 / How do I combine wet and dry ingredients? page 63 / What does fold mean? page 79

(2) Skill Level

French Toast

4 eggs, beaten
1 cup milk
2 tablespoons sugar
2 teaspoons vanilla
8 ½-inch slices challah bread or brioche or
    8 slices dry white bread
2 tablespoons butter or margarine
    Maple syrup (optional)

Ingredient Info
Although you can use standard-issue white bread for this recipe—and it may be easier to find—try using challah, a traditional Jewish bread, or brioche, a buttery yeast bread. Both are light and airy yet rich with eggs and butter. Check out supermarket and specialty bakeries for these goodies.

1 In a medium bowl beat together eggs, milk, sugar, and vanilla. Dip bread slices into egg mixture, coating both sides (if using challah or brioche, let soak in egg mixture about 10 seconds on each side) (below).

2 In a 10-inch skillet or on a griddle melt 1 tablespoon of the butter over medium heat; add bread slices (below). Cook for 2 to 3 minutes on each side or until golden brown (below). Repeat with remaining butter and bread slices. Serve warm. If desired, serve with syrup. Makes 4 servings.

Per 2 slices: 291 cal., 13 g total fat (6 g sat. fat), 233 mg chol., 384 mg sodium, 29 g carbo., 1 g fiber, 12 g pro.

Choose-a-Bread French Toast: Prepare as above, except substitute cinnamon bread or banana bread for the challah.

Crispy-Coated French Toast: Prepare as above, except after dipping bread slices in egg mixture, coat both sides with shredded coconut, ground pecans, or crushed cornflakes.

Orange-Spiced French Toast: Prepare as above, except stir 2 teaspoons orange liqueur, ½ teaspoon ground cinnamon, and ¼ teaspoon ground nutmeg into egg mixture.

1 Use tongs to dip the bread slices into the egg mixture. Let the excess egg mixture drip off the bread before placing in the skillet.

2 Add half of the coated bread slices to the hot melted butter in the skillet.

3 Cook the bread slices until golden brown. Use a wide spatula to turn the bread over.

Ask Mom How do I work with eggs? page 62 / How do I beat eggs? page 62 / How do I slice bread? page 64 / How do I measure butter? pages 58, 59 / How do I crush cornflakes/chips? page 222

Stuffed Croissant French Toast

I 8-ounce package cream cheese, softened
¼ cup maple-flavored syrup
½ cup chopped fresh strawberries
4 large baked croissants (about 10 ounces total)
2 eggs
½ cup half-and-half or light cream
I tablespoon packed brown sugar
½ teaspoon ground cinnamon
½ teaspoon ground nutmeg
Fresh strawberries, halved
Maple-flavored syrup

1 For filling, in a medium mixing bowl beat cream cheese and the ¼ cup syrup with an electric mixer on medium speed until combined; stir in the ½ cup strawberries. Cut each croissant in half, leaving one side intact (below). Divide filling among croissants (below).

2 In a large bowl whisk together eggs, half-and-half, brown sugar, cinnamon, and nutmeg. Using your hands, carefully dip each side of the filled croissants into the egg mixture, being careful not to squeeze out the filling.

3 Lightly grease a 12-inch skillet or a griddle. Cook filled croissants, two at a time if necessary, over medium heat for 1 to 2 minutes on each side or until golden brown (below). If some of the filling leaks out into the skillet, wipe it off and lightly grease the skillet again before cooking remaining croissants. Serve warm. Top with additional strawberries and drizzle with additional syrup. Makes 4 servings.

Per serving: 856 cal., 45 g total fat (27 g sat. fat), 253 mg chol., 418 mg sodium, 105 g carbo., 2 g fiber, 14 g pro.

1 Use a serrated knife to carefully cut each croissant in half horizontally. Leave one side of each croissant intact.

2 Spoon some of the cream cheese and strawberry filling into each croissant.

3 If necessary, use a wide spatula and a fork to help turn the croissants over.

Ask Mom How do I soften cream cheese? page 93 / What is maple-flavored syrup? page 457 / What's the best way to measure sticky liquids? pages 58, 81 / How do I work with eggs? page 62 / How do I pack brown sugar? page 58

② Skill Level

Buttermilk Pancakes

1 ¾ cups all-purpose flour
2 tablespoons sugar
2 teaspoons baking powder
½ teaspoon baking soda
¼ teaspoon salt
1 egg, lightly beaten
1 ½ cups buttermilk or sour milk (see page 445)
3 tablespoons cooking oil
Desired fruit options (right)
Desired syrup (optional)

Flavor Changes
The next time you make pancakes, stir one of the following fruits into the batter: ½ cup chopped fresh apple, apricot, banana, peach, nectarine, or pear; ½ cup fresh or frozen blueberries; or ¼ cup chopped dried apple, pear, apricot, cranberries, blueberries, cherries, or mixed fruit.

1 In a large bowl stir together flour, sugar, baking powder, baking soda, and salt. Make a well in the center of the flour mixture (see photo 1, page 181). In another bowl use a fork to combine egg, buttermilk, and oil. Add egg mixture all at once to flour mixture. Stir just until moistened (batter should be slightly lumpy) (see photo 2, page 181). If desired, stir in fruit.

2 For standard-size pancakes, pour about ¼ cup batter onto a hot, lightly greased heavy skillet or griddle, spreading batter if necessary. (For dollar-size pancakes, use about 1 tablespoon batter.) Cook over medium heat for 1 to 2 minutes on each side or until pancakes are golden brown, turning to second side when pancakes have bubbly surfaces and edges are slightly dry (below). Serve warm. If desired, serve with syrup. Makes 12 standard-size pancakes or 40 dollar-size pancakes.

Per standard-size pancake: 117 cal., 4 g total fat (1 g sat. fat), 19 mg chol., 179 mg sodium, 16 g carbo., 0 g fiber, 3 g pro.

Cornmeal Pancakes: Prepare as above, except use 1¼ cups all-purpose flour and add ½ cup yellow cornmeal.

Pancakes: Prepare as above, except substitute milk for the buttermilk, increase the baking powder to 1 tablespoon, and omit the baking soda.

Whole Wheat Pancakes: Prepare as above, except substitute whole wheat flour for all-purpose flour and packed brown sugar for granulated sugar.

Pancakes are ready to turn when the tops are bubbly all over with a few broken bubbles. Edges will be slightly dry. Turn pancakes only once.

Ask Mom How do I measure flour? page 58 / How do I beat eggs? page 62 / How do I combine wet and dry ingredients? page 63 / How do I pack brown sugar? page 58

Skill Level

Waffles

1 ¾ cups all-purpose flour

2 tablespoons sugar

1 tablespoon baking powder

¼ teaspoon salt

2 eggs

1 ¾ cups milk

½ cup cooking oil or butter, melted

1 teaspoon vanilla

Gearing Up Unfortunately you just can't make a waffle without a waffle baker (otherwise it would be a pancake). When you set out to purchase this nifty device, look around a little first. The most common type makes square waffles, but others produce round, rectangular—or even heart-shape waffles.

1 In a medium bowl stir together flour, sugar, baking powder, and salt. Make a well in the center of the flour mixture; set aside (see photo 1, page 181).

2 In another medium bowl beat eggs lightly; stir in milk, oil, and vanilla. Add egg mixture all at once to the flour mixture. Stir just until moistened (batter should be slightly lumpy) (see photo 2, page 181).

3 Add batter to a preheated, lightly greased waffle baker according to manufacturer's directions (use a regular or Belgian waffle baker). Close lid quickly; do not open until done. Bake according to manufacturer's directions. When done, remove waffle from baker (below). Repeat with remaining batter. Serve warm. Makes twelve to sixteen 4-inch waffles or six 7-inch waffles.

Per 4-inch waffle: 180 cal., 11 g total fat (2 g sat. fat), 38 mg chol., 135 mg sodium, 17 g carbo., 0 g fiber, 4 g pro.

Variations: Next time try folding one of the following into the batter: ½ cup raisins or finely snipped dried fruit; ½ cup fresh or frozen blueberries, raspberries, or blackberries; ½ cup finely chopped nuts (toasted, if desired); ½ cup chopped banana; ½ cup crumbled cooked bacon; ½ cup shredded cheddar cheese; ¼ cup shredded coconut; ¼ cup miniature semisweet baking pieces.

Buttermilk Waffles: Prepare as above, except reduce baking powder to 1 teaspoon and add ½ teaspoon baking soda. Substitute 2 cups buttermilk or sour milk (see page 445) for the milk.

Waffles are done when steam stops escaping from the sides of the baker or when the indicator light comes on. Use a fork to lift the baked waffle off the grid.

Ask Mom How do I measure flour? page 58 / How do I work with eggs? page 62 / How do I measure butter? pages 58, 59 / How do I combine wet and dry ingredients? page 63 / What does fold mean? page 79 / How do I chop nuts? page 65 / How do I toast nuts? page 65 / How do I shred cheese? page 71

EVERYTHING ON A WAFFLE. You've done the maple syrup and butter thing—now it's time to think outside the bottle. Try topping waffles with fruit preserves, fresh fruit, whipped cream, or yogurt. For a real breakfast masterpiece, try this—scrambled eggs, salsa, and shredded cheese on Cornmeal Waffles.

Cornmeal Waffles
Prepare as on page 186, except decrease flour to 1 cup and add 1 cup cornmeal to the flour mixture.

Chocolate Waffles
Prepare as on page 186, except decrease flour to $1\frac{1}{2}$ cups, increase sugar to $\frac{1}{4}$ cup, and add $\frac{1}{3}$ cup unsweetened cocoa powder to the flour mixture. Fold $\frac{1}{4}$ cup miniature semisweet chocolate pieces into batter. (You may need to lightly coat waffle baker with nonstick cooking spray between each waffle to prevent sticking.)

Gingerbread Waffles
Prepare as on page 186, except increase flour to 2 cups, omit the sugar, and add $\frac{1}{2}$ teaspoon ground ginger, $\frac{1}{2}$ teaspoon ground cinnamon, and $\frac{1}{4}$ teaspoon ground cloves to the flour mixture. Add 2 tablespoons molasses to the egg mixture.

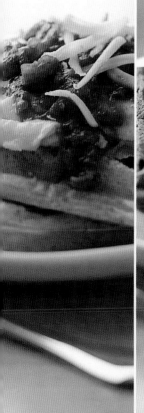

Real Oatmeal

2 cups water
¼ teaspoon salt
⅔ cup steel-cut oats

1 In a 2- to 2½-quart saucepan bring water and salt to boiling. Stir in oats. Simmer, covered, about 15 minutes or until the oats are just tender and the liquid is nearly absorbed. Makes 3 (⅔-cup) servings.

Per serving: 143 cal., 3 g total fat (0 g sat. fat), 0 mg chol., 197 mg sodium, 24 g carbo., 4 g fiber, 6 g pro.

Creamy Real Oatmeal: Prepare as above, except add ¼ cup milk to the water and salt (watch carefully as milk will foam when mixture comes to a boil). Simmer, covered, for 25 minutes. Remove from heat. Let stand 5 minutes before serving.

Toppers: Top your hot cooked oatmeal with dried fruit (cherries, raisins, tropical fruit bits, chopped dates), nuts (almonds, pecans, walnuts, hazelnuts, sunflower seeds), shredded coconut, brown sugar, maple syrup, and/or milk or half-and-half.

Steel-cut oats are a little different from the instant oatmeal you're used to. These whole-oat groats (the cleaned-up oat) are cut into pieces but aren't rolled flat like regular oatmeal. That's why they take longer to cook. They're chewier and have a nutty flavor.

Ask Mom What does simmer mean? page 79

② Skill Level

Granola

4 cups regular rolled oats
1 cup desired nuts*
½ cup packed brown sugar
¼ cup cooking oil
¼ cup honey or maple syrup
½ teaspoon salt
½ teaspoon ground cinnamon
1 teaspoon vanilla
1 cup desired dried fruit**
½ cup other desired ingredient***

Ingredient Info
The oats used in this recipe (as opposed to the steel-cut oats on page 188) are oat groats that have been steamed and flattened with big rollers. (Regular oats are also sometimes called old-fashioned oats.) Don't be tempted to substitute instant oats in either recipe. Instant oats have been precooked and dried, which softens them too much.

1 Preheat oven to 300°F. In a 15×10×1-inch baking pan combine oats and desired nuts; set aside. In a 1- to 1½-quart saucepan combine brown sugar, oil, honey, salt, and cinnamon. Heat and stir over medium heat until mixture is combined and smooth; stir in vanilla. Pour sugar mixture over oats mixture, stirring until well coated.

2 Bake in the preheated oven for 35 to 40 minutes or until mixture is golden brown, stirring carefully every 10 minutes. Stir in desired dried fruit. Spread granola onto buttered foil (see photo 3, page 117); cool completely. Stir in other desired ingredient (below). Store granola in an airtight container or large resealable plastic bag at room temperature for up to 1 week or freeze for up to 3 months. Makes 15 (½-cup) servings.

*Nuts (whole, chopped, or sliced): Almonds, walnuts, pecans, pistachios, cashews, hazelnuts (filberts), unsalted peanuts, sunflower seeds (use only ½ cup).

**Dried Fruit (whole or snipped): Raisins, currants, tropical fruit bits, mixed fruit bits, banana chips, pineapple, mango, cherries, blueberries, cranberries, dates, apples.

***Other ingredients: Flaked coconut (add with the nuts in Step 1), semisweet chocolate pieces, butterscotch-flavored pieces, peanut butter-flavored pieces, cinnamon-flavored pieces, roasted pumpkin seeds (pepitas).

Per serving: 250 cal., 11 g total fat (2 g sat. fat), 0 mg chol., 88 mg sodium, 37 g carbo., 4 g fiber, 5 g pro.

Sprinkle your choice of the "other ingredient" over the granola mixture after turning the mixture out onto buttered foil and cooling. Give the whole batch a gentle stir.

Ask Mom How do I pack brown sugar? page 58 / What's the best way to measure sticky liquids? pages 58, 81

Smoothies are so simple. Place all the ingredients into a blender and add ice cubes (or use frozen fruit) if you want a chilly crunch. Secure the blender top and whirl away.

1 Skill Level

Mix-and-Match
Smoothies

2 cups peeled and cut-up fruit of your choice*

I cup juice or low-fat milk*

I cup low-fat yogurt (plain, flavored, or frozen)*

1 Combine fruit, juice, and yogurt in a blender. Cover; blend until smooth. Makes 2 servings.

5 Fab Flavors: Not quite sure how to mix and match smoothie ingredients? Whip up these sure-to-please combos: strawberries, kiwifruit, apple juice, and plain low-fat yogurt; blueberries, blackberries, grape juice, and blueberry yogurt; peaches, raspberries, cranberry juice, and plain low-fat yogurt; nectarine, mango, orange juice, and plain low-fat yogurt; pineapple, strawberries, pineapple juice, and strawberry yogurt.

Per serving: 189 cal., 2 g total fat (I g sat. fat), 7 mg chol., 88 mg sodium, 36 g carbo., 3 g fiber, 8 g pro.

Ask Mom How do I peel and cut up some fresh fruits? pages 28–33 / How do I peel and cut up a mango? page 88 / How do I peel peaches? page 66

Mimosas

- 1 12-ounce can frozen orange juice concentrate, thawed
- 1 6-ounce can frozen limeade concentrate, thawed
- 2 cups cold water
- 6 cups pink Champagne and/or Champagne and/or sparkling apple juice, chilled
- 1 recipe Strawberry Ice Cubes or ice cubes

1 In a large container combine orange juice concentrate, limeade concentrate, and water. Cover and chill for 2 to 24 hours. Just before serving, carefully add the pink Champagne. To serve, transfer mixture to 2 large pitchers. Add Strawberry Ice Cubes to each glass before serving. Makes 12 servings.

Strawberry Ice Cubes: Fill two ice cube trays with small fresh strawberries; add white grape juice or water. Freeze until firm. For other variations, use fresh blueberries or raspberries.

Per serving: 164 cal., 0 g total fat (0 g sat. fat), 0 mg chol., 2 mg sodium, 23 g carbo., 0 g fiber, 1 g pro.

Cranberry Mimosas: Prepare as above, except substitute cranberry juice concentrate for the orange juice concentrate and apple juice concentrate for the limeade concentrate. Use whole cranberries in Strawberry Ice Cubes.

Pineapple Mimosas: Prepare as above, except substitute pineapple juice concentrate for the orange juice concentrate.

GOOD TO KNOW There's no time that's not right for Champagne—it's perfect at midnight and in the morning too. Mimosas have long been a favorite sipper with breakfast or brunch. (What kind of toast would you like?)

1 Skill Level

Flavor Changes
Change up the
garnishes: Swirl
your drink with
green olives on
picks, small pickles,
even a piece or two
of beef jerky.

Bloody Marys

2 cups tomato juice or vegetable juice cocktail, chilled
3 tablespoons lime juice
1 tablespoon Worcestershire sauce
1 teaspoon prepared horseradish
$\frac{1}{2}$ to $\frac{3}{4}$ teaspoon bottled hot pepper sauce
$\frac{1}{4}$ teaspoon celery salt or garlic salt
$\frac{1}{4}$ teaspoon ground black pepper
Ice cubes
Vodka (optional)
Celery stalks with leaves
Green onions

1 In a pitcher combine tomato juice, lime juice, Worcestershire sauce, horseradish, hot pepper sauce, celery salt, and pepper. Pour into ice-filled glasses. If desired, stir in vodka (1 jigger or 3 tablespoons per serving). Garnish each serving with a celery stalk and green onion. Makes 4 ($\frac{1}{2}$- to $\frac{2}{3}$ -cup) servings.

Per serving: 29 cal., 0 g total fat (0 g sat. fat), 0 mg chol., 484 mg sodium, 7 g carbo., 1 g fiber, 1 g pro.

Bloody Marias: Prepare as above, except add $\frac{1}{2}$ teaspoon ground cumin to tomato juice mixture and substitute tequila for the vodka.

Wasabi Marys: Prepare as above, except substitute 1 teaspoon wasabi paste for the hot pepper sauce.

Ask Mom How do I juice a lemon/lime? pages 30, 80 / How much juice does one lemon/lime yield? page 30 / What is prepared horseradish? page 429 / What is a jigger? page 119 / What does garnish mean? page 79 / What is wasabi paste? page 293

SKIP THE PAPER CUP. Instead of driving out of your way to drop $5 at the local coffee shop, brew up a pot of any-way-you-like-it java at home. You can calm your caffeine cravings in any number of stylish ways with the simple recipes below:

Coffee

For best results, look for an easy-to-use drip-style coffee maker, then follow these need-to-know tips to get a great cup of joe:

● Always use fresh, clean water—your coffee will only taste as good as the water you use.

● Use 1 to 2 tablespoons ground coffee for each 6-ounce cup (³⁄₄ cup). Use more or less depending on your preferred strength. Finely ground coffee is stronger than a coarse grind.

● Buy only a week's worth of coffee at a time; store coffee beans in an airtight container at room temperature.

● Clean your coffee pot regularly—most days you can just rinse it out, but occasionally you'll want to dunk it in soapy water.

Café au Lait

Café au Lait means coffee with milk—easy, right? All you do is add ¹⁄₃ cup milk to each cup of coffee. Sprinkle with ground cinnamon, nutmeg, or sweetened cocoa powder.

Iced Coffee

Iced Coffee is just as refreshing as iced tea. To make it, simply fill a glass with ice and pour in coffee. If you like, pour in ¹⁄₃ cup milk and sweeten to taste with sugar.

Mocha

Mocha means that chocolate has been added to the coffee. For this drink, add 2 tablespoons chocolate-flavored syrup and ¹⁄₃ cup milk to each cup of coffee. Or you can stir in 2 tablespoons of cocoa mix.

Hot Cocoa

⅓ cup sugar

⅓ cup unsweetened cocoa powder

4 cups half-and-half, light cream, or whole milk

1 teaspoon vanilla

Sweetened whipped cream (optional)

1 In a 2- to 2½-quart saucepan combine sugar and cocoa powder (below). Add 1 cup of the half-and-half (below). Cook and stir over medium-low heat until mixture just comes to boiling. Add the remaining half-and-half; heat through but *do not boil* (below).

2 Remove saucepan from heat; stir in vanilla. Serve in mugs. If desired, top each serving with whipped cream. Makes 4 servings.

Per serving: 406 cal., 29 g total fat (17 g sat. fat), 89 mg chol., 98 mg sodium, 29 g carbo., 0 g fiber, 9 g pro.

Irish Hot Cocoa: Prepare as above, except add 1 tablespoon Irish cream liqueur to each serving.

Mint Hot Cocoa: Prepare as above, except add 1 tablespoon peppermint schnapps or 2 to 3 drops peppermint extract to each serving. Garnish each serving with a peppermint stick.

Mocha Hot Cocoa: Prepare as above, except add 1 tablespoon instant espresso powder or instant coffee crystals to the sugar mixture.

Spiced Mexican Hot Cocoa: Prepare as above, except add ½ to 1 teaspoon ground cinnamon to the sugar mixture. Add ½ teaspoon almond extract with the vanilla. If desired, sprinkle each serving with additional ground cinnamon.

1 Use a whisk to thoroughly combine the sugar and the cocoa powder in the saucepan. This will help prevent lumps from forming when the liquid is added.

2 Slowly add 1 cup of the half-and-half to the saucepan and whisk until the dry ingredients are thoroughly combined.

3 When the mixture just comes to boiling (bubbles over the entire surface), gradually add the remaining half-and-half to the saucepan, whisking constantly.

Ask Mom How do I make sweetened whipped cream? page 59 / What does garnish mean? page 79

slow & savory
MEAT
main dishes

Have some time to putter away? Take a Sunday afternoon to simmer a comforting supper on the stove—or slow roast it in the oven.

5

Ketchup-Glazed Meat Loaves

2 eggs, lightly beaten
$2/3$ cup ketchup or hot-style ketchup
$1/3$ cup fine dry bread crumbs
1 envelope ($1/2$ of a 2-ounce package) dry onion soup mix
3 cloves garlic, minced
$11/2$ pounds lean ground beef or pork

1 Preheat oven to 350°F. Line a 15×10×1-inch baking pan with foil; set aside. Place a resealable plastic bag in a large bowl. Add eggs and $1/3$ cup of the ketchup to the bag. Stir in bread crumbs, soup mix, and garlic (below). Add ground beef; seal bag and knead with your hands to mix well (below). Form ground beef mixture into an 8-inch square; cut square into 6 portions. Form portions into six loaves that are 4 inches long and $21/2$ inches wide (below). Arrange loaves in the prepared pan so they aren't touching.

2 Bake, uncovered, in the preheated oven about 30 minutes or until internal temperature of loaves registers 160°F on an instant-read thermometer. Remove from oven. Spoon about 1 tablespoon of the remaining ketchup over each meat loaf (below). Let stand for 10 minutes before serving. Makes 6 servings.

Large loaf directions: Prepare as above, except lightly pat meat mixture into an 8×4×2-inch loaf pan. Bake, uncovered, for 1 to $11/4$ hours or until internal temperature registers 160°F on an instant-read thermometer. Remove from oven. Carefully drain excess fat. Spoon the remaining $1/3$ cup ketchup over loaf. Let stand for 10 minutes. Use 2 spatulas to carefully lift loaf from pan.

Per serving: 271 cal., 13 g total fat (5 g sat. fat), 142 mg chol., 928 mg sodium, 14 g carbo., 0 g fiber, 24 g pro.

a large resealable in a bowl. Roll op edges. Combine ⋯up, bread crumbs, ⋯nd garlic in bag.

2 Add ground beef to the bag; seal the bag, pressing out any air. Knead the bag to completely combine ingredients without the mess.

3 Dump the ground beef mixture onto the foil-lined pan and shape it into an 8-inch square. Cut the square into 6 equal portions.

4 After the loaves are done, spread ketchup on top of each. Let stand for 10 minutes so ketchup can warm up and glaze the loaves.

Ask Mom How do I beat eggs? page 62 / What are fine dry bread crumbs? page 76 / What is a garlic clove? page 40 / How do I mince garlic? page 40 / How do I line a pan with foil? page 60 / How do I use a meat/instant-read thermometer? page 74

2 Skill Level

Salsa Swiss Steak

Good to Know Round steak comes from the hindquarters of the beef animal. The good news is that it's lean and flavorful; the not-so-good news is that it can be tough unless cooked properly. It's sometimes machine tenderized before it's packaged and sold. Long, moist cooking— as in this recipe—makes it fork-knife tender.

2 pounds boneless beef top round steak, cut I inch thick
I to 2 large red and/or green sweet peppers,
  seeded and cut into bite-size strips
I medium onion, sliced
I 10.75-ounce can condensed cream of mushroom soup
I cup bottled salsa
2 tablespoons all-purpose flour
I teaspoon dry mustard
  Corn Bread (page 154) or Mashed Potatoes (page 142) (optional)

1 Trim fat from steak. Cut steak into 6 serving-size pieces. In a $3\frac{1}{2}$- or 4-quart slow cooker place steak, sweet pepper, and onion. In a medium bowl stir together soup, salsa, flour, and mustard. Pour over steak and vegetables in slow cooker.

2 Cover and cook on low-heat setting for 9 to 10 hours or on high-heat setting for $4\frac{1}{2}$ to 5 hours. If desired, serve with Corn Bread or Mashed Potatoes. Makes 6 servings.

Per serving: 251 cal., 6 g total fat (2 g sat. fat), 65 mg chol., 574 mg sodium, 10 g carbo., I g fiber, 37 g pro.

Ask Mom What is that cut of meat? pages 220–221 / How do I seed sweet peppers and cut them into strips? page 49 / How do I slice an onion? page 47 / What is a slow cooker? page 21

Ingredient Info
Blue cheese fans count Gorgonzola among their top picks. Named for the Italian town where it originated, Gorgonzola is a rich, creamy cow's milk cheese. It has an ivory interior streaked with blue-green veins— and a tangy, pungent, delicious flavor.

2 Skill Level

Cheese-Topped Steaks

½ cup crumbled Gorgonzola cheese or other blue cheese (2 ounces)
4 slices bacon, crisp-cooked and crumbled
¼ cup pine nuts or slivered almonds, toasted
4 teaspoons snipped fresh thyme
2 cloves garlic, minced
¼ teaspoon ground black pepper
4 boneless beef top loin steaks, cut ¾ inch thick (about 2 pounds total)
¼ teaspoon salt
  Nonstick cooking spray

1 In a small bowl stir together cheese, bacon, nuts, thyme, garlic, and pepper; set aside.

2 Trim fat from steaks. Sprinkle steaks with salt. Lightly coat a grill pan or 12-inch skillet with cooking spray (below). Heat pan over medium-high heat; reduce heat to medium. Add steaks, half at a time, if necessary; cook for 3 to 4 minutes per side or until steaks reach desired doneness (below).

3 To serve, spoon cheese mixture over steaks (below). Cover with foil and let stand for 5 minutes to soften cheese. Makes 4 servings.

Broiling directions: Preheat broiler. Place steaks on the unheated rack of a broiler pan. Broil 3 to 4 inches from heat until steaks reach desired doneness, turning once. Allow 10 to 12 minutes for medium rare and 12 to 15 minutes for medium. Top with cheese mixture as above.

Per serving: 440 cal., 22 g total fat (8 g sat. fat), 129 mg chol., 672 mg sodium, 2 g carbo., 1 g fiber, 56 g pro.

y coat the cold
h nonstick
ay. Heat the pan.

2 Add steaks to hot pan, being careful not to crowd the pan. You may need to cook half the steaks at a time.

3 Cook steaks for 3 to 4 minutes per side, turning them only once.

4 Spoon cheese mixture over the hot steaks. Cover with foil to let the cheese warm slightly before serving.

Ask Mom What is that cut of meat? pages 220–221 / How do I crumble cheese? pages 71, 96 / How do I cook bacon? page 172 / How do I toast pine nuts? pages 65, 245 / How do I toast nuts? page 65 / How do I snip fresh herbs? pages 42, 328 / What is a garlic clove? page 40 / How do I mince garlic? page 40 / What does it mean to broil? page 68

Honey-Balsamic Beef Stir-fry

12 ounces beef sirloin steak or beef top round steak

¾ cup beef broth

3 tablespoons reduced-sodium soy sauce

2 tablespoons balsamic vinegar

2 tablespoons honey

2 tablespoons cornstarch

¼ teaspoon crushed red pepper

2 tablespoons cooking oil or peanut oil

1 tablespoon finely chopped fresh ginger

2 medium red sweet peppers, seeded and cut into bite-size strips

1 medium red onion, cut into thin wedges

4 cups thin strips bok choy or baby bok choy

2 cups hot cooked rice or linguine

1 Trim fat from meat. If desired, partially freeze steak for easier slicing. Thinly slice steak across the grain into bite-size strips (below); set aside. In a small bowl whisk together broth, soy sauce, vinegar, honey, cornstarch, and crushed red pepper (below); set aside.

2 Add 1 tablespoon oil to a 12-inch skillet. Heat over medium-high heat. Add ginger; cook and stir for 15 seconds (below). Add sweet peppers and onion; cook and stir for 5 minutes (below). Add bok choy; cook and stir for 2 to 3 minutes (page 201). Remove vegetables from skillet.

3 Add remaining oil to skillet. Add steak; cook and stir for 2 to 3 minutes or until brown. Push the meat to the sides of the skillet. Stir broth mixture; add to center of the skillet (page 201). Cook and stir until thickened and bubbly. Return vegetables to the skillet (page 201). Stir to coat all with sauce. To serve, spoon beef mixture over rice. Serve immediately. Makes 4 servings.

Per serving: 424 cal., 15 g total fat (4 g sat. fat), 42 mg chol., 713 mg sodium, 51 g carbo., 3 g fiber, 21 g pro.

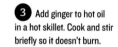
1 Partially frozen meat slices easily. Use a chef's knife to cut across the grain.

2 Combine sauce ingredients first; set aside so sauce is ready when you are.

3 Add ginger to hot oil in a hot skillet. Cook and stir briefly so it doesn't burn.

4 Add vegetables i[n] stages, starting with th[e] that need more cookin[g]

Ask Mom What is that cut of meat? pages 220–221 / What is that vinegar? page 349 / What is fresh ginger? page 41 / How do I seed sweet peppers and cut them into strips? page 49 / How do I cut onion wedges? page 47 / What is that pasta shape? pages 308–309 / What does it mean to stir-fry? page 69 / What does crisp-tender mean? pages 79, 126

WHAT'S BOK CHOY? That slightly sweet flavor you taste in so many Chinese stir-fries is a cabbage called bok choy. The stalks have the crunch of celery without the strings; the dark green leaves are mild tasting and packed with vitamins A and C and calcium.

Choose bok choy that has firm white stalks and crisp, upright leaves without brown spots and blemishes. Store it in a plastic bag in the refrigerator for 3 to 4 days.

5 Bok choy doesn't take long to cook, so it's added last. Remove all of the vegetables when crisp-tender.

6 After the meat is brown, push it to the sides of the pan. Add sauce to the middle; cook until bubbly.

7 Return the vegetables to the skillet. Cook and stir until all ingredients are coated with sauce.

1 Skill Level

Easy Shepherd's Pie

Good to Know
Created as a way to use leftovers from the Sunday roast, mashed potatoes, and vegetables— shepherd's pie is classic English pub food. Serve it with a cold pint and share it with friends.

Nonstick cooking spray
1 17-ounce package refrigerated cooked beef tips with gravy
2 cups frozen mixed vegetables
1 11-ounce can condensed tomato bisque soup
¼ cup finely chopped onion
1 tablespoon Worcestershire sauce
½ teaspoon dried thyme, crushed
⅛ teaspoon ground black pepper
1 24-ounce package refrigerated mashed potatoes
½ cup shredded cheddar cheese (2 ounces)

1 Preheat oven to 375°F. Lightly spray a 2-quart square baking dish or four 16-ounce casserole dishes with cooking spray; set aside. In a large saucepan stir together beef tips with gravy, vegetables, soup, onion, Worcestershire sauce, thyme, and pepper. Bring to boiling over medium heat, stirring occasionally. Transfer to the prepared baking dish or dishes (below).

2 Place potatoes in a large bowl; stir until nearly smooth. Spoon potatoes into 6 mounds on top of beef mixture (below).

3 Bake, uncovered, in the preheated oven for 20 to 25 minutes or until heated through and bubbly around edges. Sprinkle potatoes with cheese (below). Let stand for 10 minutes before serving. Makes 4 servings.

Per serving: 463 cal., 16 g total fat (6 g sat. fat), 65 mg chol., 1,624 mg sodium, 53 g carbo., 6 g fiber, 28 g pro.

1 Spoon meat mixture into prepared baking dish. Spread it and smooth the top so it cooks evenly.

2 Spoon potatoes into mounds on top of the meat mixture. This will make the dish easier to serve.

3 When the shepherd's pie is done, sprinkle cheese onto potato mounds. Let stand so cheese melts a bit.

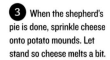

Ask Mom How do I chop an onion? page 47 / How do I crush dried herbs? page 78 / How do I shred cheese? page 71

Beef and Cheese Burritos

  8 8- to 10-inch flour tortillas
1½ cups shredded cooked beef, chicken, or pork
  1 cup bottled salsa
  1 9-ounce can jalapeño-flavored bean dip
  2 cups shredded cheddar or Monterey Jack cheese (8 ounces)
     Shredded lettuce (optional)
     Dairy sour cream (optional)
     Bottled salsa (optional)

1 Preheat oven to 400°F. Wrap tortillas in foil; heat in the preheated oven about 8 minutes or until heated through. Meanwhile, in a medium bowl stir together shredded beef and the 1 cup salsa.

2 To assemble, spread 2 tablespoons bean dip on each tortilla. Top bean dip with ¼ cup beef mixture near one edge. Top beef mixture with ¼ cup cheese. Fold in the sides of tortilla and roll up, starting from the edge with the filling. Place filled tortillas, seam sides down, in a greased 3-quart rectangular baking dish.

3 Bake, uncovered, in the preheated oven about 20 minutes or until heated through. If desired, serve with lettuce, sour cream, and additional salsa. Makes 8 servings.

Per serving: 311 cal., 16 g total fat (8 g sat. fat), 53 mg chol., 604 mg sodium, 21 g carbo., 2 g fiber, 19 g pro.

Spanish Rice Burritos: Prepare as above, except substitute one 8.8-ounce pouch cooked Spanish-style rice prepared according to package directions for the beef.

Bean dip

Shredded lettuce

Flour tortillas

Shredded beef

Shredded cheese

Ask Mom How do I shred cheese? page 71 / How do I shred lettuce? page 346

Oven Pot Roast

1   2½- to 3-pound boneless beef chuck pot roast
    Salt and ground black pepper
2   tablespoons olive oil or cooking oil
1   14-ounce can beef broth
1   cup chopped onion (1 large)
2   stalks celery, cut into 2-inch lengths
5   cups assorted vegetables, such as peeled Yukon gold or sweet potatoes, cut into 2-inch chunks;
        parsnips, peeled and cut into 2-inch chunks; whole shallots or garlic bulbs, halved horizontally;
        and/or medium carrots, peeled and cut into 1½-inch pieces
¼   cup cold water
3   tablespoons all-purpose flour

1 Preheat oven to 325°F. Trim fat from roast. Season roast with salt and pepper. In a 6-quart Dutch oven brown roast in hot oil over medium heat about 5 minutes per side (page 205). Drain fat from pan and discard (below). Add broth, onion, and celery to pan.

2 Roast, covered, in the preheated oven for 1¼ hours. Using a slotted spoon, remove celery from pan and discard. Add desired vegetables to pan (below), arranging them around the roast. Roast, uncovered, for 50 to 60 minutes more or until meat and vegetables are tender, spooning juices over roast and vegetables twice during roasting.

3 Using tongs and a slotted spoon, transfer roast and vegetables to a platter; keep warm. Pour pan juices into a 4-cup measure; skim off fat. Discard enough juices or add water to make 1½ cups; return to pan. Whisk together water and flour until smooth (below); whisk into pan. Cook and stir over medium heat until thickened and bubbly; cook and stir for 1 minute more (below). Season with salt and pepper. Serve with roast and vegetables. Makes 6 to 8 servings.

Per serving: 419 cal., 14 g total fat (4 g sat. fat), 112 mg chol., 584 mg sodium, 29 g carbo., 4 g fiber, 43 g pro.

1 Remove browned roast from pan and pour off any fat. Return roast to pan.

2 Add desired vegetables to the pan and arrange them around the roast.

3 Gradually whisk flour into cold water until smooth. You don't want any lumps.

4 Cook and stir the gravy over medium heat thickened and bubbly.

Ask Mom What is that cut of meat? pages 220–221 / How do I chop an onion? page 47 / How do I prepare celery? page 39 / What are some potato varieties? page 50 / How do I prepare potatoes? page 51 / What is a shallot? page 46 / What is a garlic bulb? page 40 / How do I peel and cut carrots? pages 37, 64 / What does it mean to sear? page 68 / What does it mean to braise? page 68 / What does skim mean? page 79

Braised Beef with Red Wine Sauce

4 ounces pancetta or bacon, diced
2 tablespoons olive oil
1 2½- to 3-pound boneless beef sirloin tip or round roast
1 cup chopped carrot (2 medium)
1 cup chopped onion (1 large)
¾ cup chopped red sweet pepper (1 medium)
½ cup chopped celery (1 stalk)
2 cloves garlic, minced

¾ cup dry red wine
1 28-ounce can Italian-style whole peeled tomatoes in puree, cut up
1 tablespoon tomato paste
1 teaspoon dried basil, crushed
¼ teaspoon dried oregano, crushed
1 bay leaf
¼ cup whipping cream

1 In a 4- to 6-quart Dutch oven cook and stir pancetta over medium heat until crisp. Using a slotted spoon, remove pancetta and set aside. Reserve any drippings in pot. Add olive oil to pan. Add roast and brown about 5 minutes per side (below). Sprinkle with ½ teaspoon *salt* and ¼ teaspoon *ground black pepper*. Transfer roast to a plate; reserve drippings in pot.

2 Add carrot, onion, sweet pepper, celery, and garlic to pot; cook and stir about 10 minutes or until vegetables are light brown. Add wine, scraping the bottom of the pan with a wooden spoon to loosen browned bits (below). Simmer for 1 minute. Stir in undrained tomatoes, tomato paste, basil, and oregano. Return roast to pot and add the bay leaf. Reduce heat to low. Simmer, covered, about 1½ hours or until the roast is tender. Discard bay leaf. Transfer roast to a serving platter (below); cover to keep warm.

3 For sauce, simmer pan juices, uncovered, about 12 minutes or until reduced to about 4½ cups. Stir in cream. Serve roast with sauce.* Sprinkle with pancetta. Makes 6 servings.

*Note: Leftover sauce can be covered and stored in the refrigerator for up to 3 days. Serve with cooked polenta or pasta.

Per serving: 483 cal., 24 g total fat (8 g sat. fat), 117 mg chol., 1,027 mg sodium, 13 g carbo., 2 g fiber, 47 g pro.

a utility knife or , dice pancetta eces.

2 Brown (sear) roast in hot oil for 5 minutes per side. Use tongs to turn roast just once.

3 Add wine to pan while you scrape the browned bits off the pan bottom. This is called deglazing the pan.

4 Using tongs, transfer roast to a serving platter. Be careful so it doesn't fall apart.

Ask Mom What does it mean to braise? page 68 / What is that cut of meat? pages 220–221 / How do I peel and cut carrots? pages 37, 64 / How do I chop onions? page 47 / How do I seed and chop sweet peppers? page 49 / How do I chop celery? page 39 / How do I mince garlic? page 40 / How do I cut up canned tomatoes? page 405 / How do I crush dried herbs? page 78 / What does it mean to sear? page 68 / What does simmer mean? page 79 / How do I deglaze? page 70

(3) Skill Level

Good to Know Here's a heads-up before you go to the grocery store to buy a tenderloin roast. Be prepared for a little sticker shock—it's the most expensive beef cut there is—but it is well worth it. If you're making a special meal for family or friends, they will be duly impressed.

Slow-Roasted Beef Tenderloin

1 2- to 2½-pound beef tenderloin
2 tablespoons cooking oil
1 to 2 cloves garlic, minced
1 teaspoon cracked black pepper
¼ teaspoon salt or ¼ teaspoon sea salt or kosher salt*
4 sprigs fresh rosemary
4 sprigs fresh oregano
4 sprigs fresh thyme
1 recipe Mushroom Tumble and/or Horseradish Cream
Snipped fresh thyme

1 Preheat oven to 250°F. Drizzle meat with oil. Rub garlic evenly over the surface of the tenderloin. Sprinkle with pepper and salt. Set aside.

2 Place rosemary, oregano, and thyme sprigs in the bottom of a 13×9×2-inch baking pan. Add a roasting rack. Place tenderloin on rack.

3 Roast tenderloin, uncovered, in the preheated oven for 20 minutes. Increase oven temperature to 425°F. Roast for 30 to 40 minutes or until the internal temperature registers 135°F. Remove from oven. Cover loosely with foil; let stand for 10 minutes.

4 Serve roast with Mushroom Tumble and/or Horseradish Cream. Garnish with snipped fresh thyme. Makes 8 to 10 servings.

*Note: Sea salt is derived from evaporated sea water. It has a bright, pure, clean flavor. Kosher salt is used in the preparation of meat according to Jewish dietary law. Kosher salt comes in flakes, not granules. Because it dissolves easily, its taste isn't as strong as regular salt.

Mushroom Tumble: In a very large bowl place 6 cups assorted fresh mushrooms, such as chanterelle, portobello, shiitake, and oyster (halve or slice any large mushrooms and remove any tough stems). Add 3 tablespoons olive oil, 2 tablespoons lemon juice, and 1 teaspoon reduced-sodium soy sauce; toss to combine. In a 12-inch skillet cook mushrooms over medium heat about 10 minutes or until tender, stirring occasionally. Sprinkle with salt and cracked black pepper.

Horseradish Cream: In a small bowl stir together one 8-ounce carton dairy sour cream, 2 tablespoons prepared horseradish, ⅛ teaspoon salt, and ⅛ teaspoon ground black pepper. Serve immediately or cover and chill for up to 3 days. If refrigerated, let stand for 30 minutes before serving.

Per serving: 316 cal., 20 g total fat (5 g sat. fat), 87 mg chol., 238 mg sodium, 3 g carbo., 1 g fiber, 32 g pro.

Ask Mom What does it mean to roast? page 68 / What is that cut of meat? pages 220–221 / How do I mince garlic? page 40 / How do I crack peppercorns? page 22 / How do I snip fresh herbs? pages 42, 328 / What does drizzle mean? page 79 / How do I use a meat thermometer? page 74 / What does garnish mean? page 79 / What are some mushroom varieties? page 44 / How do I slice fresh mushrooms? page 45 / How do I juice a lemon? pages 30, 80 / What is prepared horseradish? page 429

WHY LET THE COOKED ROAST STAND? It is essential to let cooked meat or poultry rest, lightly covered, out of the oven about 10 minutes before carving. Resting allows the juices to be absorbed back into the meat rather than spilling onto the cutting board.

You can plate up slices of this roast to serve to guests or arrange them on a platter and serve the Mushroom Tumble and Horseradish Cream on the side.

Italian-Style Pork Chops

4 pork rib chops, cut $\frac{3}{4}$ to I inch thick
$\frac{1}{2}$ teaspoon salt
$\frac{1}{2}$ teaspoon ground black pepper
2 tablespoons olive oil
3 cloves garlic, minced
$\frac{1}{4}$ teaspoon crushed red pepper
2 I4.5-ounce cans diced tomatoes with basil, garlic, and oregano, undrained
$\frac{1}{3}$ cup pitted kalamata olives, sliced
I teaspoon dried Italian seasoning, crushed
I6 ounces shelf-stable gnocchi or 8 ounces dried fettuccine, cooked according to package directions
$\frac{1}{4}$ cup finely shredded Parmesan cheese

1 Sprinkle both sides of chops with salt and black pepper. In a 12-inch skillet brown chops in hot oil over medium heat for 4 to 5 minutes, turning once (below). Remove chops from skillet; set aside.

2 Add garlic and crushed red pepper to skillet. Cook and stir for 1 minute. Stir in undrained tomatoes, olives, and Italian seasoning. Bring to boiling; reduce heat. Simmer, uncovered, about 6 minutes or until most of the liquid has evaporated (below).

3 Return chops to skillet (below). Simmer, covered, for 10 minutes or until internal temperature of chops registers 160°F on an instant-read thermometer. Uncover and remove chops from skillet; keep warm. Simmer tomato mixture, uncovered, about 5 minutes more or until tomato mixture reaches desired consistency. To serve, place chops on a platter on top of hot cooked gnocchi. Top with tomato sauce (below) and sprinkle with cheese. Makes 4 servings.

Per serving: 627 cal., 19 g total fat (5 g sat. fat), 102 mg chol., 2,199 mg sodium, 67 g carbo., 5 g fiber, 44 g pro.

1 Brown chops in the hot oil over medium heat. You need to turn them only once.

2 Simmer the tomato mixture uncovered so the liquid cooks off and the sauce thickens.

3 Nestle the browned chops into the sauce. They'll finish cooking as the sauce continues to simmer.

4 Serve the chops sauce over hot cooked gnocchi or fettuccine.

Ask Mom What is that cut of meat? pages 220–221 / What is a garlic clove? page 40 / How do I mince garlic? page 40 / How do I pit olives? page 75 / How do I crush dried herbs? page 78 / What is that pasta shape? pages 308–309 / How do I shred cheese? page 71 / What does it mean to sear? page 68 / What does simmer mean? page 79 / How do I use a meat/instant-read thermometer? page 74

Skill Level

Pork Chop and Rice Bake

4 pork rib chops, cut ¾ to I inch thick

I tablespoon cooking oil

Ground black pepper

I small onion, thinly sliced and separated into rings

I 10.75-ounce can condensed cream of mushroom with roasted garlic soup

¾ cup water

½ cup dry white wine

¾ cup uncooked long grain rice

I 4-ounce can sliced mushrooms, drained

I teaspoon Worcestershire sauce

¼ teaspoon dried thyme, crushed

2 tablespoons snipped fresh parsley

1 Preheat oven to 375°F. In a 12-inch skillet brown chops in hot oil over medium heat for 4 to 5 minutes, turning once. Remove chops from skillet, reserving drippings. Sprinkle chops with pepper; set aside.

2 In the same skillet cook onion in the drippings over medium heat until tender; set aside. In a large bowl stir together the soup, water, and wine; stir in rice, mushrooms, Worcestershire sauce, and thyme. Spoon soup mixture into an ungreased 3-quart rectangular baking dish. Top with pork chops; spoon cooked onion over top.

3 Bake, covered, in the preheated oven for 35 to 40 minutes or until rice is done and internal temperature of chops registers 160°F on an instant-read thermometer. Let stand, covered, for 10 minutes before serving. Sprinkle with parsley. Makes 4 servings.

Per serving: 602 cal., 22 g total fat (7 g sat. fat), 124 mg chol., 735 mg sodium, 36 g carbo., 2 g fiber, 55 g pro.

INGREDIENT INFO Any kind of dry white wine will do nicely in this nostalgic comfort-food dish—Chardonnay, Sauvignon Blanc, or Pinot Grigio. Serve it with steamed green beans on the side.

Ask Mom What is that cut of meat? pages 220–221 / How do I slice an onion? page 47 / How do I crush dried herbs? page 78 / How do I snip fresh herbs? pages 42, 328 / What does it mean to sear? page 68 / How do I use a meat/instant-read thermometer? page 74

Cranberry Pork Roast

| 3-pound boneless pork top loin roast (double loin, tied)
| tablespoon cooking oil
   Salt and ground black pepper
| 16-ounce can whole cranberry sauce
$\frac{1}{2}$ cup cranberry juice
$\frac{1}{4}$ cup sugar
| teaspoon dry mustard
$\frac{1}{4}$ teaspoon ground cloves
2 tablespoons cornstarch
2 tablespoons cold water
   Hot cooked rice pilaf, rice, or noodles (optional)

1 In a 10-inch skillet cook roast in hot oil over medium heat until browned on all sides. Place roast in a 4- or 5-quart slow cooker; sprinkle lightly with salt and pepper. In a medium bowl stir together cranberry sauce, cranberry juice, sugar, mustard, and cloves. Pour over roast. Cover and cook on low-heat setting for 6 to 7 hours or on high-heat setting for 3 to $3\frac{1}{2}$ hours.

2 Using tongs, transfer roast to a platter; keep warm. Skim fat from juices in slow cooker. Measure 2 cups of juices; transfer to a medium saucepan. In a small bowl stir together cornstarch and water; add to saucepan. Cook and stir over medium heat until thickened and bubbly; cook and stir 2 minutes more. Serve sauce with roast and, if desired, rice pilaf, rice, or noodles. Makes 8 to 10 servings.

Per serving: 404 cal., 11 g total fat (3 g sat. fat), 100 mg chol., 124 mg sodium, 38 g carbo., 1 g fiber, 37 g pro.

> Two boneless pork loins tied together into one roast is available at many supermarkets. If you can't find one, ask the butcher to prepare a tied roast for you.

Ask Mom What is that cut of meat? pages 220–221 / What does it mean to sear? page 68 / What is a slow cooker? page 21 / What does skim mean? page 79

(3) Skill Level

Pork Lo **Mein**

1¼ to 1½ pounds lean boneless pork*
10 ounces dried Chinese egg noodles, spaghetti, or angel hair pasta
¼ cup oyster sauce
¼ cup reduced-sodium soy sauce
2 tablespoons rice wine or sherry
1 tablespoon cooking oil
1 tablespoon toasted sesame oil
2 teaspoons finely chopped fresh ginger
1 medium red onion, halved lengthwise and thinly sliced (1 cup)
3 cups sliced fresh mushrooms (8 ounces)
2 cups sugar snap pea pods, halved

1 If desired, partially freeze meat for easier slicing. Thinly slice pork across the grain into bite-size strips (see photo 1, page 200); set aside. Cook noodles according to package directions until tender; drain. Rinse noodles with cold water (see photos, page 305); drain well. Set noodles aside. In a small bowl stir together oyster sauce, soy sauce, and rice wine. Set aside.

2 Pour cooking oil and sesame oil into a 12-inch skillet or wok. (If necessary, add more oil during cooking.) Heat over medium-high heat. Add ginger; cook and stir for 30 seconds. Add onion; cook and stir for 2 minutes. Add mushrooms; cook and stir for 2 minutes. Add pea pods; cook and stir for 1 minute. Remove vegetables from skillet.

3 Add half of the pork to skillet; cook and stir for 3 to 4 minutes or until no longer pink. Remove from skillet. Repeat with remaining pork. Return all meat to skillet. Add the noodles, vegetables, and oyster sauce mixture. Using two heat-resistant spatulas or wooden spoons, lightly toss mixture about 3 minutes or until heated through. Transfer to a platter. Makes 6 servings.

*Note: You may substitute skinless, boneless chicken breast halves; boneless beef sirloin steak; or fresh or frozen peeled and deveined medium shrimp for the pork.

Per serving: 408 cal., 11 g total fat (3 g sat. fat), 52 mg chol., 718 mg sodium, 44 g carbo., 3 g fiber, 30 g pro.

> **Ingredient Info** Asian cooking is popular enough that most supermarkets carry many Asian products—far beyond soy sauce. Oyster sauce, toasted sesame oil, rice wine, and Chinese noodles are usually stocked in the same aisle. If you can't find them, check out an Asian market.

Ask Mom What is that cut of meat? pages 220–221 / What is toasted sesame oil? page 138 / What is fresh ginger? page 41 / How do I slice an onion? page 47 / What are some mushroom varieties? page 44 / How do I slice fresh mushrooms? page 45 / What is a wok? page 267 / What does it mean to stir-fry? page 69 / What does it mean to toss? page 77

Pork Tenderloin with
Apples and Onions

2 tablespoons butter or margarine
1 medium onion, thinly sliced and separated into rings
2 medium cooking apples, cored and sliced (2 cups)
$\frac{1}{8}$ teaspoon salt
1 tablespoon cider vinegar
1 12- to 16-ounce pork tenderloin
Salt and ground black pepper
2 tablespoons olive oil

1 In a 10-inch skillet melt butter over medium heat. Add onion. Cook for 10 minutes, stirring occasionally. Add apple; cook for 15 to 20 minutes more or until apple and onion are tender and beginning to brown, stirring occasionally. Sprinkle with the $\frac{1}{8}$ teaspoon salt. Add vinegar; cook and stir for 30 seconds. Remove apple mixture from skillet; cover to keep warm.

2 While apple mixture is cooking, trim fat from tenderloin (see photos, page 362). Cut tenderloin crosswise into $\frac{1}{2}$-inch-thick slices (see photo 1, page 360). Sprinkle slices lightly with salt and pepper.

3 After removing apple mixture from skillet, in the same skillet heat oil over medium-high heat. Add pork; reduce heat to medium and cook for 6 to 8 minutes or until no longer pink, turning once.

4 To serve, spoon apple mixture onto the centers of dinner plates. Top each with one-fourth of the pork slices. Serve immediately. Makes 4 servings.

Per serving: 255 cal., 15 g total fat (5 g sat. fat), 70 mg chol., 222 mg sodium, 12 g carbo., 2 g fiber, 18 g pro.

Ingredient Info Every apple has a purpose, whether that's to be eaten out of hand or in a salad, baked into a pie, or made into applesauce. Certain varieties fare better as cooking apples because they hold their shape well. Here are some of the best cooking apples, by flavor: On the sweet side are Braeburn, Golden Delicious, and Jonagold; on the tart side are Cortland, Granny Smith, and Jonathan.

Ask Mom How do I measure butter? pages 58, 59 / How do I slice an onion? page 47 / How do I core and slice/chop apples? page 28 / What is that vinegar? page 349 / What is that cut of meat? pages 220–221

Maple-Glazed Pork Tenderloin

I tablespoon all-purpose flour
I 12- to 16-ounce pork tenderloin
I 16-ounce package crinkle-cut sliced carrots
⅓ cup pure maple syrup
4 tablespoons olive oil
2 teaspoons dried rosemary, crushed
¼ teaspoon ground black pepper
½ of a 22-ounce package (about 4 cups) frozen french-fried waffle-cut potatoes
   Salt and ground black pepper

1 Preheat oven to 350°F. Place flour in a large oven roasting bag; shake to coat inside of bag. Trim fat from tenderloin (see photos, page 362). Place tenderloin and carrots in bag. In a glass measuring cup stir together maple syrup, 2 tablespoons of the oil, 1 teaspoon of the rosemary, and the ¼ teaspoon pepper; pour into bag (below). Close bag using tie provided. Turn bag to coat meat and carrots with maple syrup mixture. Place filled bag on one end of a large roasting pan. Cut six ½-inch slits in top of bag (below).

2 In a large bowl toss potatoes with remaining 2 tablespoons olive oil and the remaining 1 teaspoon rosemary. Transfer potatoes to roasting pan beside oven bag (below).

3 Roast in the preheated oven for 30 minutes. Carefully cut open top of bag, being very careful to avoid any steam (below). Roast for 20 to 25 minutes more or until temperature in the thickest part of the meat registers 160°F on an instant-read thermometer and the potatoes are brown and crisp. Remove meat and carrots from oven bag. Cover meat with foil and let stand for 10 minutes before serving. Season to taste with salt and pepper. Makes 4 servings.

Per serving: 488 cal., 22 g total fat (4 g sat. fat), 50 mg chol., 97 mg sodium, 54 g carbo., 6 g fiber, 20 g pro.

e tenderloin and an oven roasting maple syrup to bag and seal bag.	**2** Use the tip of a knife to make 6 slits in the top of the bag to let steam escape. Don't cut on the sides of the bag or juices will leak out.	**3** Toss the potatoes with oil and rosemary, then place in roasting pan next to the bag. They will cook up crisp while the roast stays moist.	**4** Cut the bag top open with kitchen scissors. Hold the top away from you while you cut so steam escapes in the opposite direction.

Ask Mom What is that cut of meat? pages 220–221 / What is pure maple syrup? page 457 / What's the best way to measure sticky liquids? pages 58, 81 / How do I crush dried herbs? page 78 / What does it mean to toss? page 77 / How do I use a meat/instant-read thermometer? page 74

Blackberry-Glazed Pork Ribs

4 pounds pork baby back ribs

1 tablespoon herbes de Provence

½ teaspoon salt

¼ teaspoon ground black pepper

1 10-ounce jar blackberry spreadable fruit

2 tablespoons Dijon-style mustard

1 tablespoon red wine vinegar

1 tablespoon blackberry-flavored brandy (optional)

1 Preheat oven to 350°F. Cut ribs into 2- to 3-rib portions (below). In a small bowl combine herbes de Provence, salt, and pepper. Sprinkle evenly over both sides of ribs; rub in with your fingers (below). Place ribs, bone sides down, in a shallow roasting pan (below). Bake, uncovered, in the preheated oven for 1 hour. Drain off fat.

2 Meanwhile, for sauce, in a small bowl stir together spreadable fruit, mustard, vinegar, and, if desired, brandy. After draining fat off ribs, brush half of the sauce on ribs (below). Bake, uncovered, about 30 minutes more or until ribs are tender, basting once with the sauce.

3 To serve, transfer ribs to a platter. In a 1-quart saucepan heat any remaining sauce to boiling over medium-high heat. Serve heated sauce with ribs. Makes 4 to 6 servings.

Slow cooker directions: Lightly coat a 4- to 6-quart slow cooker with nonstick cooking spray; set aside. Prepare ribs as above in Step 1, except do not bake. Preheat broiler. Place ribs on the unheated rack of a broiler pan. Broil 6 inches from heat about 10 minutes or until browned, turning once. Transfer ribs to slow cooker. Prepare sauce as above in Step 2. Pour over ribs. Cover and cook on low-heat setting for 6 to 7 hours or on high-heat setting for 3 to 3½ hours. Transfer ribs to a platter. Pour cooking liquid into a bowl; skim off fat. Serve cooking liquid with ribs.

Per serving: 802 cal., 54 g total fat (20 g sat. fat), 184 mg chol., 641 mg sodium, 43 g carbo., 0 g fiber, 37 g pro.

1 Using a chef's knife, cut between rib bones to make 2- to 3-rib portions.

2 Sprinkle herb mixture all over ribs, rubbing it into the meat with your fingers.

3 Place the ribs in a shallow roasting pan with the bone sides down.

4 After baking the ri[bs] 1 hour, brush half of the [sauce] over the ribs.

Ask Mom What is that cut of meat? pages 220–221 / What is Dijon-style mustard? page 379 / What is that vinegar? page 349 / What is a slow cooker? page 21 / What does it mean to broil? page 68

WHAT IS HERBES DE PROVENCE? One way to travel to the south of France without an airline ticket! It's a blend of dried herbs common to that region's cooking. It includes basil, fennel seeds, lavender, marjoram, rosemary, sage, savory, and thyme.

It's not safe to eat sauce that has touched raw or partially-cooked meat. Heat any remaining sauce to boiling before serving it with the ribs.

Glazed Ham

1 5- to 6-pound cooked ham (rump half or shank portion)
24 whole cloves (optional)
1 recipe Orange Glaze or Chutney Glaze

1 Preheat oven to 325°F. Score ham by making diagonal cuts in a diamond pattern (below). If desired, stud ham with cloves (below). Place ham on a rack in a shallow roasting pan. Insert an oven-safe meat thermometer into center of ham. The thermometer should not touch the bone. Bake, uncovered, in the preheated oven for $1\frac{1}{2}$ to $2\frac{1}{4}$ hours or until thermometer registers 140°F. Brush ham with some of the desired glaze during the last 20 minutes of baking. Serve with remaining glaze. Makes 16 to 20 servings.

Orange Glaze: In a 2-quart saucepan stir together 2 teaspoons finely shredded orange peel, 1 cup orange juice, $\frac{1}{2}$ cup packed brown sugar, 4 teaspoons cornstarch, and $1\frac{1}{2}$ teaspoons dry mustard. Cook and stir over medium heat until thickened and bubbly. Cook and stir for 2 minutes more.

Chutney Glaze: In a food processor or blender combine one 9-ounce jar mango chutney, $\frac{1}{4}$ cup maple syrup, and 2 teaspoons stone-ground mustard. Cover and process until smooth.

Per serving with **Orange Glaze** or **Chutney Glaze:** 166 cal., 5 g total fat (2 g sat. fat), 47 mg chol., 1,078 mg sodium, 10 g carbo., 0 g fiber, 19 g pro.

1 Use a chef's knife to make diagonal cuts about I inch apart on the ham. Cut through the "skin" of the ham so the glaze can penetrate.

2 If desired, you can insert whole cloves into ham for looks and flavor. It's easiest to poke them in where the cuts intersect.

Good to Know If you get tapped (or you volunteer) to host the office holiday party— or any other large get-together—bake a big, gorgeous ham. You'll get rave reviews for entertaining with smarts and style. To serve the ham as finger food, slice it thinly and offer it with cocktail buns and several varieties of mustard.

Ask Mom What is that cut of meat? pages 220–221 / What does score mean? page 79 / How do I use a meat/instant-read thermometer? page 74 / How do I finely shred orange peel? page 30 / How do I juice an orange? page 30 / How much juice does one orange yield? page 30 / How do I pack brown sugar? page 58 / What's the best way to measure sticky liquids? pages 58, 81

Potatoes with Caramelized Onions and Ham Gratin

1 tablespoon olive oil

1 tablespoon butter

2 large yellow onions, cut into thin wedges

1½ cups whipping cream

½ cup milk

2 tablespoons snipped fresh sage or 1 teaspoon dried sage, crushed

3 cloves garlic, minced

1 teaspoon salt

¼ teaspoon ground black pepper

3 pounds Yukon gold or other yellow-fleshed potatoes, thinly sliced (about 8 cups)

8 ounces thinly sliced cooked ham, cut into bite-size strips (1½ cups)

2 cups shredded sharp white cheddar cheese (8 ounces)

1 Preheat oven to 350°F. In a 10-inch skillet heat oil and butter over medium heat. Add onion; cook about 20 minutes or until tender, stirring frequently. (If necessary, reduce heat to medium low to prevent overbrowning before onion is tender.) Increase heat to medium high; cook about 5 minutes more or until onion is golden (caramelized). Remove from heat; set onion aside. In a medium bowl stir together cream, milk, sage, garlic, salt, and pepper; set aside.

2 Lightly grease a 3-quart rectangular baking dish. Arrange half the potato in dish (below). Sprinkle with ham, onion, and half the cheese (below). Layer remaining potato on cheese. Pour cream mixture over potato; top with remaining cheese. Bake, uncovered, for 60 to 65 minutes or until golden and potato is tender. Cover; let stand for 15 minutes. Makes 6 servings.

Per serving: 631 cal., 43 g total fat (25 g sat. fat), 150 mg chol., 1,175 mg sodium, 41 g carbo., 4 g fiber, 22 g pro.

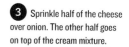 **1** Layer half of the potato in the baking dish, overlapping as necessary so they will fit.

 **2** Sprinkle ham and caramelized onion evenly over the potato.

3 Sprinkle half of the cheese over onion. The other half goes on top of the cream mixture.

Ask Mom How do I measure butter? pages 58, 59 / How do I cut onion wedges? page 47 / How do I snip fresh herbs? pages 42, 328 / How do I crush dried herbs? page 78 / What is a garlic clove? page 40 / How do I mince garlic? page 40 / What are some potato varieties? page 50 / How do I prepare potatoes? page 51 / How do I shred cheese? page 71 / How do I grease a baking pan/dish? page 61

Mediterranean Lamb Chops

- 6 lamb loin chops, cut 1 1/2 inches thick
- 2 teaspoons cooking oil
- 1 medium red onion, cut into thin wedges (1 cup)
- 1 26- to 28-ounce jar garlic and onion pasta sauce
- 1 19-ounce can cannellini beans (white kidney beans), rinsed and drained
- 1/2 cup pitted kalamata olives, halved
- 1/2 cup bottled roasted red sweet peppers, cut into strips
- 2 tablespoons balsamic vinegar
- 2 teaspoons snipped fresh rosemary
- Hot cooked orzo or rice (optional)

1 Trim fat from chops. In a 10-inch skillet cook chops in hot oil over medium heat for 9 to 11 minutes for medium (160°F), turning once halfway through cooking. Transfer chops to a large bowl or platter; cover with foil to keep warm. Reserve pan drippings.

2 In the same skillet cook and stir onion in pan drippings over medium heat about 5 minutes or until tender. Add pasta sauce, beans, olives, roasted pepper, vinegar, and rosemary. Cook and stir over medium heat until heated through. Return chops to skillet; cover and heat through about 3 minutes. If desired, serve lamb chops and sauce over orzo or rice. Makes 6 servings.

Per serving: 410 cal., 11 g total fat (3 g sat. fat), 40 mg chol., 798 mg sodium, 58 g carbo., 9 g fiber, 22 g pro.

Slow cooker directions: Place lamb chops in a 4- or 5-quart slow cooker. In a medium bowl stir together onion, pasta sauce, beans, olives, roasted pepper, vinegar, and rosemary. Pour over chops in slow cooker. Cover and cook on low-heat setting for 5 to 6 hours or on high-heat setting for 2 1/2 to 3 hours.

INGREDIENT INFO Despite what it may look like, orzo is not a type of rice. It's a rice-shape pasta. Orzo makes a quick-cooking side for all kinds of dishes and is often added to Italian-style soups.

Ask Mom What is that cut of meat? pages 220–221 / How do I cut onion wedges? page 47 / How do I rinse and drain canned beans? page 390 / How do I pit olives? page 75 / What is that vinegar? page 349 / How do I snip fresh herbs? pages 42, 328 / What is that pasta shape? pages 308–309 / What is a slow cooker? page 21

Moroccan Lamb

- 1 2-pound boneless lamb or pork shoulder roast
- 2 tablespoons olive oil
- $\frac{1}{2}$ cup chopped onion (1 medium)
- 2 cloves garlic, minced
- 1 tablespoon grated fresh ginger
- 2$\frac{1}{2}$ cups water
- 1 6-ounce package long grain and wild rice mix
- $\frac{1}{2}$ teaspoon coarsely ground black pepper
- $\frac{1}{4}$ teaspoon ground cinnamon
- $\frac{1}{8}$ to $\frac{1}{4}$ teaspoon cayenne pepper
- 2 medium yellow summer squash, cut into 1-inch pieces (2$\frac{1}{2}$ cups)
- 1 8-ounce package fresh mushrooms, halved or quartered (about 3 cups)
- $\frac{3}{4}$ cup dried apricots
- $\frac{1}{2}$ cup raisins
- $\frac{1}{2}$ cup dried tart cherries

Good to Know Dried fruit loses its chewy softness if it's not stored properly. Once you open a package of dried fruit, be sure to store it in an airtight container or tightly sealed plastic bag in the cupboard—or, for longer storage, in the refrigerator.

219

Slow Meat Dishes

1 Trim fat from roast; cut roast into 1-inch pieces (below). In a 12-inch skillet cook lamb, half at a time, in hot oil over medium heat until brown on all sides (below). Using a slotted spoon, remove lamb from skillet. Add remaining lamb, the onion, garlic, and ginger to skillet. Cook until lamb is brown and onion is tender, stirring occasionally. Return all lamb to skillet. Add the water. Bring lamb mixture to boiling; reduce heat. Simmer, covered, for 25 minutes.

2 Add rice mix, black pepper, cinnamon, and cayenne pepper to skillet. Return to boiling; reduce heat. Simmer, covered, for 20 minutes. Add squash, mushrooms, apricots, raisins, and cherries. Simmer, covered, about 10 minutes or until squash is tender. Makes 6 to 8 servings.

Per serving: 610 cal., 31 g total fat (12 g sat. fat), 102 mg chol., 490 mg sodium, 54 g carbo., 4 g fiber, 32 g pro.

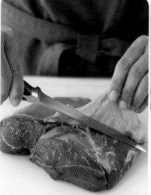
1 Carefully pull fat and silver skin away from roast as you cut under it with a knife.

2 Cut the roast into 1-inch pieces so it will cook quickly and evenly.

3 Brown lamb in batches. Crowding the skillet will make meat steam, not brown.

Ask Mom What is that cut of meat? pages 220–221 / How do I chop an onion? page 47 / What is a garlic clove? page 40 / How do I mince garlic? page 40 / What is fresh ginger? page 41 / How do I grate fresh ginger? page 41 / What is summer squash? page 54 / What are some mushroom varieties? page 44 / How do I clean fresh mushrooms? page 45 / What does simmer mean? page 79

Beef, Pork & Lamb

Meat of some kind is usually the centerpiece of the meal—the starting point. Different cuts are best prepared using specific cooking methods. Ask your butcher how to cook the cuts you buy.

First off, how much meat to buy? For boneless roasts and steaks, plan on three to four servings per pound. From bone-in roasts and steaks, you'll get two or three servings. For bony cuts, plan on one or two servings per pound.

Store meat in the coldest part of the refrigerator as soon as you get home from the supermarket. If you don't plan to use fresh ground and cubed meat within two days and steaks, chops, and roasts within three days, store the meat in the freezer.

For meat that's to be used within a week, freeze it in the film-wrapped supermarket packaging. For longer storage, put the meat in a food-safe freezer bag. See page 73 for safe thawing methods.

Beef

Flank steak

Top round steak

Ribeye steak

Top loin (strip) steak

Top round roast

Tri-tip roast

Chuck pot roast

Top sirloin steak (boneless)

Pork

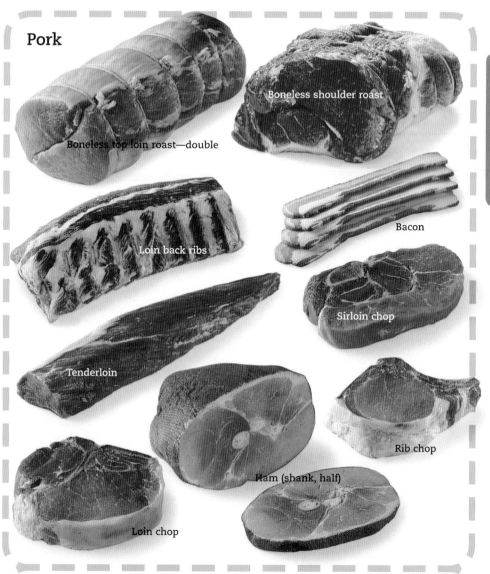

Boneless top loin roast—double

Boneless shoulder roast

Loin back ribs

Bacon

Sirloin chop

Tenderloin

Rib chop

Ham (shank, half)

Loin chop

Lamb

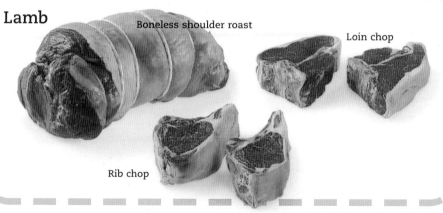

Boneless shoulder roast

Loin chop

Rib chop

Good to Know You can make chicken tenders yourself, if you'd like. Simply slice 1½ pounds of boneless, skinless chicken breast halves lengthwise into 1-inch-wide strips.

(2) Skill Level

Oven-Fried Chicken

1 egg, beaten

3 tablespoons milk

1¼ cups crushed cornflakes or finely crushed rich round crackers (about 35)

1 teaspoon dried thyme, crushed

½ teaspoon paprika

¼ teaspoon salt

⅛ teaspoon ground black pepper

2 tablespoons butter or margarine, melted

2½ to 3 pounds meaty chicken pieces (breast halves, thighs, and drumsticks)

1 Preheat oven to 375°F. In a small bowl combine egg and milk. In a shallow dish combine cornflakes, thyme, paprika, salt, and pepper; stir in butter. Set aside. Skin chicken (below). Dip chicken pieces, one at a time, into egg mixture; coat with cornflakes mixture (below).

2 In a greased 15×10×1-inch baking pan, arrange chicken pieces, bone sides down, so the pieces aren't touching (below). Sprinkle chicken with any remaining cornflakes mixture so the pieces are generously coated.

3 Bake, uncovered, in the preheated oven for 45 to 55 minutes or until chicken is tender and no longer pink (170°F for breasts; 180°F for thighs and drumsticks). Do not turn chicken pieces while baking. Makes 6 servings.

Per serving: 336 cal., 16 g total fat (5 g sat. fat), 133 mg chol., 351 mg sodium, 16 g carbo., 0 g fiber, 31 g pro.

Oven-Fried Parmesan Chicken: Prepare as above, except omit thyme and salt; reduce crushed cornflakes to ½ cup. For coating, combine cornflakes; ½ cup grated Parmesan cheese; 1 teaspoon dried oregano, crushed; the paprika; and pepper. Stir in melted butter. Continue as above.

1 To neatly crush cornflakes, place them in a resealable plastic bag; seal bag. Roll a can or rolling pin over cornflakes.

2 Use a paper towel to securely grip the skin of a chicken piece and pull it away from the meat.

3 After dipping in the egg mixture, press the chicken pieces into the cornflakes mixture to coat well.

4 Place pieces, bone sides down, in the baking pan. Leave space between pieces so they will get cri[...]

Ask Mom How do I beat eggs? page 62 / How do I make bread/cracker crumbs? page 76 / How do I crush dried herbs? page 78 / How do I measure butter? pages 58, 59 / How do I grease a baking pan/dish? page 61 / How do I use a meat/instant-read thermometer? page 74 / How do I grate cheese? page 71

Cheese-Stuffed Chicken

  4 chicken breast halves (2 to 2 ½ pounds total)
  ¾ cup shredded mozzarella cheese (3 ounces)
  ½ cup crumbled feta cheese (2 ounces)
  ¼ cup chopped cocktail peanuts
  2 slices bacon, crisp-cooked and crumbled, or ¼ cup cooked bacon pieces
    Salt and ground black pepper
    Paprika
    Bottled ranch salad dressing (optional)

1 Preheat oven to 350°F. If desired, skin chicken (see photo 2, page 222). Using a sharp knife, make a pocket in each breast half by cutting horizontally from side to side, cutting to but not through the opposite side and leaving edges intact (below).

2 In a medium bowl combine mozzarella, feta, peanuts, and bacon. Pack cheese mixture lightly into pockets in chicken (below) (pockets will be full). Place chicken, bone sides down, in a 3-quart rectangular baking dish. Lightly sprinkle chicken with salt, pepper, and paprika.

3 Bake, uncovered, in the preheated oven for 50 to 55 minutes or until internal temperature of chicken registers 170°F on an instant-read thermometer. If desired, drizzle dressing over chicken before serving. Makes 4 servings.

Per serving: 457 cal., 29 g total fat (10 g sat. fat), 136 mg chol., 587 mg sodium, 3 g carbo., 1 g fiber, 44 g pro.

Good to Know To skin a chicken breast, slip the point of a paring knife under the skin at either end of the breast. Once it is loosened, grasp it with a paper towel and slowly pull the skin away from the meat (see photo 2, page 222), keeping your fingers close to the meat to keep the skin from tearing. Cut the skin off, if necessary.

1 Using a boning knife, cut a pocket in the flat (not rounded) side of the chicken breast. Do not cut through.

2 Spoon the cheese filling into each pocket. Pack it in, but not too tightly, and pull edges of opening around it.

Ask Mom How do I shred cheese? page 71 / How do I crumble cheese? pages 71, 96 / How do I cook bacon? page 172 / How do I use a meat/instant-read thermometer? page 74 / What does drizzle mean? page 79

③ Skill Level

Chicken Potpie

- 1 recipe Pastry for Single-Crust Pie (see page 471) or half of a 15-ounce package of rolled refrigerated unbaked piecrust (1 crust)
- 1 10.75-ounce can condensed cream of onion or cream of chicken soup
- 1⅓ cups milk
- 1 3-ounce package cream cheese, cut up
- ½ teaspoon dried sage, crushed
- ¼ teaspoon ground black pepper
- 1½ cups chopped cooked chicken
- 1 10-ounce package frozen mixed vegetables
- ½ cup uncooked instant white rice

  Milk

Good to Know Think ahead: Next time you're broiling a chicken breast for dinner, put a couple extra on the broiler pan so you have cooked chicken for this homey dish. Wrap the leftovers tightly, put them in a resealable plastic bag, and store in the refrigerator for up to 3 days. (Or you can pick up a rotisserie chicken at the supermarket.)

1 Preheat oven to 400°F. Prepare pastry; set aside. For filling, in a 3-quart saucepan stir together soup, milk, cream cheese, sage, and pepper. Cook and stir over medium-high heat until cream cheese melts. Stir in chicken, vegetables, and uncooked rice. Pour chicken mixture into a 10-inch deep-dish pie plate.

2 On a lightly floured surface, roll pastry to an 11-inch circle. Place pastry over chicken mixture in dish (below). Turn edges of pastry under; use the tines of a fork to press to top edge of dish (below). Cut slits in crust to allow steam to escape (below). Use a pastry brush to lightly brush crust with milk.

3 Bake, uncovered, in the preheated oven for 20 to 25 minutes or until pastry is golden brown. Let stand for 10 minutes before serving. Makes 4 servings.

Per serving: 648 cal., 34 g total fat (12 g sat. fat), 83 mg chol., 863 mg sodium, 59 g carbo., 5 g fiber, 28 g pro.

① Transfer the pastry circle from the work surface to the pie plate. Completely cover the chicken mixture.

② Turn the edges of the pastry under. This looks nicer and seals the potpie.

③ Using the tines of a fork, press the edges of the pastry to the top edge of the pie plate.

④ Use a paring knife cut about 5 small slits in pastry. The slits let steam escape while the pie bake

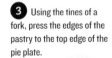

Ask Mom How do I crush dried herbs? page 78

Cheesy Chicken Enchiladas

6 6-inch corn tortillas
2 cups shredded cooked chicken, beef, or pork
1 10-ounce can enchilada sauce
1½ cups shredded Mexican cheese blend (6 ounces)
   Dairy sour cream (optional)
   Shredded lettuce (optional)

1 Preheat oven to 400°F. Wrap tortillas tightly in foil. Bake tortillas in the preheated oven about 8 minutes or until warm. Meanwhile, for filling, in a medium bowl stir together chicken, half of the enchilada sauce, and half of the cheese. Place ⅓ cup of the chicken mixture on one end of a tortilla; roll up. Place filled tortilla, seam side down, in a shallow 2-quart baking dish. Repeat with remaining chicken mixture and tortillas. Pour remaining enchilada sauce over filled tortillas. Sprinkle with the remaining cheese.

2 Bake, uncovered, in the preheated oven about 15 minutes or until cheese melts and enchiladas are heated through. If desired, top with sour cream and shredded lettuce. Makes 6 servings.

Per serving: 271 cal., 14 g total fat (6 g sat. fat), 67 mg chol., 603 mg sodium, 15 g carbo., 2 g fiber, 21 g pro.

Creamy Enchiladas: Prepare as above, except omit enchilada sauce. For sauce, stir together one 10.75-ounce can cream of chicken soup; one 8-ounce carton dairy sour cream; and one 4- to 4.25-ounce can diced green chile peppers, undrained. Stir together the chicken, ½ cup of the sauce, and half of the cheese. Assemble and bake as above.

Spicy Bean Enchiladas: Prepare as above, except omit meat. For filling, combine one 15-ounce can pinto beans or black beans, rinsed and drained; ¼ cup of the enchilada sauce; and ¼ cup of the cheese. Assemble and bake as above.

Ingredient Info There are several shredded Mexican cheese blends on the market. Though they may vary slightly, they are generally a combination of Monterey Jack, cheddar, queso quesadilla, asadero, Colby, and Cotija cheeses. With one bag you can get lots of cheesy flavors into a dish without the expense of buying different blocks of cheese—not to mention all of the shredding that would entail.

Ask Mom How do I shred chicken/beef/or pork? pages 395, 419 / How do I shred lettuce? page 346 / How do I rinse and drain canned beans? page 390

ONE DISH AND DINNER'S DONE. Skillet meals are supereasy on the cook. During the chopping, cooking, and stirring, you have only one pan to watch—and after you're full and happy, you have only one to wash.

Serve this saucy dish with lemon wedges. The yellow color accents the plate, while a squeeze of fresh lemon juice brightens the flavor.

Greek-Style Chicken Skillet

  4 skinless, boneless chicken breast halves (about 1¼ pounds total)
     Salt and ground black pepper
  1 tablespoon olive oil or cooking oil
1½ cups sliced zucchini (1 medium)
  ¾ cup chopped green sweet pepper (1 medium)
  1 medium onion, sliced and separated into rings
  2 cloves garlic, minced
  ⅛ teaspoon ground black pepper
  ¼ cup water
  1 10.75-ounce can condensed tomato soup
  2 cups hot cooked couscous*
  ½ cup crumbled feta cheese (2 ounces)
     Lemon wedges

1 Sprinkle chicken with salt and black pepper. In a 12-inch skillet cook chicken in hot oil over medium heat for 12 to 15 minutes or until internal temperature of chicken registers 170°F on an instant-read thermometer, turning once. Remove chicken from skillet; keep warm.

2 Add zucchini, sweet pepper, onion, garlic, and the ⅛ teaspoon black pepper to skillet. Add the water; reduce heat. Cover and cook for 5 minutes, stirring once or twice. Stir in soup. Bring to boiling; reduce heat. Cover and simmer for 5 minutes more, stirring once.

3 To serve, divide couscous among dinner plates. Place chicken on couscous. Spoon vegetable mixture over chicken and couscous. Sprinkle with feta cheese and serve with lemon wedges. Makes 4 servings.

*Note: For 2 cups cooked couscous, in a 1-quart saucepan bring 1 cup water and a dash of salt to boiling. Stir in ⅔ cup quick-cooking couscous. Remove from heat. Cover and let stand for 5 minutes. Fluff with a fork before serving.

Per serving: 401 cal., 10 g total fat (4 g sat. fat), 99 mg chol., 827 mg sodium, 36 g carbo., 4 g fiber, 41 g pro.

Ingredient Info Couscous, a specialty of North Africa and parts of the Mediterranean, is a great pinch-hitter side dish. These bits of semolina pasta require no cooking—only rehydration—so they can be ready, start to finish, in 5 to 6 minutes. Keep a box on hand for prepping those last-minute meals.

Ask Mom How do I slice summer squash/zucchini? page 54 / How do I seed and chop sweet peppers? page 49 / How do I slice an onion? page 47 / What is a garlic clove? page 40 / How do I mince garlic? page 40 / How do I crumble cheese? pages 71, 96 / What is couscous? pages 149, 227 / How do I cut lemon/lime wedges? page 30 / How do I use a meat/instant-read thermometer? page 74 / What does simmer mean? page 79

Ingredient Info
When a recipe calls for chicken drumsticks, it means the bottom part of the leg below the knee joint. A whole chicken leg consists of the drumstick and the thigh—the part of the leg above the knee joint that's connected to the rest of the bird.

2 Skill Level

Chicken and Noodles With Vegetables

2 10.75-ounce cans reduced-fat and reduced-sodium condensed cream of chicken soup

2 cups sliced carrot (4 medium)

1½ cups chopped onion (3 medium)

1 cup sliced celery (2 stalks)

1 cup water

2 tablespoons snipped fresh parsley

1 bay leaf

1 teaspoon dried thyme, crushed

½ teaspoon salt

¼ teaspoon ground black pepper

3 medium chicken legs (drumstick-thigh portion) (about 2 pounds total), skinned (see photo 2, page 222)

10 ounces dried wide noodles (about 5 cups)

1 cup frozen peas

Drumstick   Whole Chicken Leg

1 In a 4-quart Dutch oven stir together soup, carrot, onion, celery, water, parsley, bay leaf, thyme, salt, and pepper. Add chicken. Bring to boiling; reduce heat. Simmer, covered, for 25 to 30 minutes or until chicken is tender and no longer pink (180°F). Discard bay leaf.

2 Meanwhile, cook noodles according to package directions; drain (see photo, page 305) and return to pan to keep warm. Using tongs, transfer chicken to a cutting board; cool slightly. Remove chicken from bones; discard bones. Shred or chop chicken; return to the Dutch oven. Stir peas into chicken mixture; heat through. To serve, spoon chicken mixture over noodles. Makes 6 servings.

Per serving: 288 cal., 5 g total fat (2 g sat. fat), 69 mg chol., 680 mg sodium, 44 g carbo., 5 g fiber, 17 g pro.

Slow cooker directions: In a 3½- or 4-quart slow cooker stir together carrot, onion, celery, parsley, and bay leaf. Place chicken on top of vegetables. In a large bowl stir together soup, ½ cup water, the thyme, salt, and pepper. Pour over chicken in slow cooker. Cover and cook on low-heat setting for 8 to 9 hours or on high-heat setting for 4 to 4½ hours. Remove chicken from slow cooker; cool slightly. Discard bay leaf. Stir peas into soup mixture in slow cooker. Cook noodles according to package directions; drain (see photo, page 305). Remove chicken from bones; discard bones. Shred or chop chicken; stir into soup mixture in slow cooker. To serve, spoon chicken mixture over noodles.

Ask Mom How do I peel and cut carrots? pages 37, 64 / How do I chop an onion? page 47 / How do I prepare celery? page 39 / How do I snip fresh herbs? pages 42, 328 / How do I crush dried herbs? page 78 / What is that pasta shape? pages 308–309 / What does simmer mean? page 79 / How do I use a meat/instant-read thermometer? page 74 / What is a slow cooker? page 21

3 Skill Level

Chicken Thighs and Orzo

1 4-ounce package pancetta, chopped, or 4 slices bacon, chopped
  Olive oil (optional)
6 chicken thighs (about 2 ¼ pounds), skinned (see photo 2, page 222)
2 14.5-ounce cans diced tomatoes with garlic and onion
1 cup dried orzo
1 cup water
2 cloves garlic, minced
⅓ cup pitted kalamata olives
¼ cup snipped fresh basil
1 6-ounce bag (4 cups) baby spinach leaves
⅓ cup crumbled feta cheese with garlic and herb

1 In a 5- or 6-quart Dutch oven cook pancetta over medium heat until browned (below). Using a slotted spoon, transfer pancetta to paper towels to drain; set aside. Reserve 2 tablespoons drippings in Dutch oven (below). Add olive oil if necessary to equal 2 tablespoons.

2 Brown chicken in reserved drippings over medium heat about 10 minutes, turning to brown evenly; drain off fat. Add undrained tomatoes, orzo, water, and garlic. Bring to boiling; reduce heat. Simmer, covered, for 25 to 30 minutes or until chicken is tender and no longer pink (180°F) and orzo is tender. If necessary, uncover and cook for 2 to 3 minutes more or until sauce reaches desired consistency. Stir in pancetta, olives, and basil; heat through.

3 Divide spinach among serving plates. Top each with a chicken thigh and some of the orzo mixture. Top servings with feta. Makes 6 servings.

Per serving: 395 cal., 18 g total fat (5 g sat. fat), 77 mg chol., 1,229 mg sodium, 32 g carbo., 2 g fiber, 26 g pro.

...cetta is a round ...on. Use a utility ...ef's knife to chop it ...pieces.

2 Cook the pancetta over medium heat until brown and crisp, stirring frequently. Remove with a slotted spoon.

3 Drain off drippings from pan. Return 2 tablespoons drippings to the Dutch oven, adding oil, if necessary, to make 2 tablespoons.

4 Brown the chicken pieces in the reserved drippings. The drippings add flavor to the chicken.

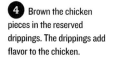

Ask Mom What is that pasta shape? pages 308–309 / What is a garlic clove? page 40 / How do I mince garlic? page 40 / How do I pit olives? page 75 / How do I snip fresh herbs? pages 42, 328 / How do I crumble cheese? pages 71, 96 / What does simmer mean? page 79 / How do I use a meat/instant-read thermometer? page 74

Chicken with Pan Sauce

Flavor Changes
Simple is always good, but you can "fancify" this sauce (and add flavor too) by adding snipped oil-packed dried tomatoes, capers, and/or fresh herbs such as basil or Italian (flat-leaf) parsley after the last of the butter is added at the end.

   4 skinless, boneless chicken breast halves (about 1¼ pounds total)
  ¼ teaspoon salt
  ¼ teaspoon ground black pepper
  5 tablespoons cold butter
  ⅔ cup dry white wine
  ½ cup chicken broth
  ¼ cup finely chopped shallot (2) or onion
  2 tablespoons whipping cream

1 Place each chicken breast half between two pieces of plastic wrap. Using the flat side of a meat mallet, pound the chicken lightly to about ¼ inch thick (below). Remove plastic wrap. Sprinkle with salt and pepper.

2 In a 10-inch skillet melt 1 tablespoon of the butter over medium-high heat. Reduce heat to medium. Cook chicken for 6 to 8 minutes or until no longer pink, turning once. Transfer chicken to a platter; cover with foil to keep warm.

3 Add wine, broth, and shallot to the hot skillet. To deglaze the skillet, stir and scrape brown bits from the bottom of the skillet (below). Bring to boiling. Boil gently for 10 to 15 minutes or until liquid is reduced to ¼ cup.* Reduce heat to medium low.

4 Stir in cream. Add the remaining 4 tablespoons butter, 1 tablespoon at a time, stirring after each addition until butter melts (below). Sauce should be slightly thickened. Season to taste with additional salt and pepper. To serve, spoon sauce over chicken. Makes 4 servings.

*Note: It is important to reduce the liquid to ¼ cup or the sauce will be too thin.

Per serving: 325 cal., 20 g total fat (10 g sat. fat), 117 mg chol., 444 mg sodium, 2 g carbo., 0 g fiber, 27 g pro.

① Starting in the middle and working to the edges, gently pound chicken pieces to an even thickness.

② Scrape the bottom of the skillet to loosen the flavorful browned bits. This technique is called deglazing.

③ Stir the butter in 1 tablespoon at a time to ensure a smooth, nicely thickened sauce.

Ask Mom How do I measure butter? pages 58, 59 / What is a shallot? page 46 / How do I chop an onion? page 47 / What is a meat mallet? page 19 / How do I use a meat mallet? pages 19, 74 / How do I deglaze a pan? page 70 / What is a reduction? page 70 / What is that vinegar? page 349 / What are capers? page 79 / How do I snip fresh herbs? pages 42, 328 / What is Dijon-style mustard? page 379 / How do I slice fresh mushrooms? page 45 / What are dried tomatoes? page 53

HOW MANY WAYS TO SAUCE A CHICKEN? Making a pan sauce is a quick, sure way to give a snoozer of a chicken breast real star power. Once you master this easy technique, you can change the flavoring elements to create limitless variations.

Try these other sauces

Balsamic-Caper Sauce Prepare as on page 230, except stir 2 teaspoons balsamic vinegar and 2 teaspoons drained capers into the finished sauce.

Mustard Sauce Prepare as on page 230, except stir I tablespoon snipped fresh Italian (flat-leaf) parsley and 2 teaspoons Dijon-style mustard into the finished sauce.

Mushroom-Tomato Sauce Prepare as on page 230 through Step I. In a large skillet cook I cup sliced fresh shiitake, porcini, or button mushrooms in I tablespoon of the butter over medium heat until tender. Remove mushrooms from skillet. Continue as directed in Step 2, using the same skillet. Add cooked mushrooms along with 2 tablespoons snipped, drained oil-packed dried tomatoes with the cream. There will be only 3 tablespoons of butter to add in Step 4. Stir 2 teaspoons snipped fresh basil or parsley into the finished sauce.

Cut into a boneless, skinless chicken breast to check its doneness. It should not have any pink and the juices that run out should be completely clear.

Smoky-Lime Chicken Succotash Skillet

1 16-ounce package frozen corn kernels

1 12-ounce package frozen sweet soybeans (edamame) or 16-ounce package frozen baby lima beans

1 3/4 cups water

1 1/2 teaspoons finely shredded lime peel

2 tablespoons fresh lime juice

1 2- to 2 1/2-pound deli-roasted chicken, cut into 6 to 8 pieces

1 16-ounce jar chipotle salsa

Lime wedges (optional)

1 In a 12-inch skillet combine corn and sweet soybeans; add water. Bring to boiling; reduce heat. Simmer, uncovered, for 5 to 6 minutes or until soybeans are just tender. Add lime peel and lime juice to skillet. Stir until combined. Place chicken pieces on top of corn mixture. Pour salsa over all. Cover and cook over medium heat about 10 minutes or until heated through. If desired, serve with lime wedges. Makes 4 to 6 servings.

Per serving: 621 cal., 28 g total fat (7 g sat. fat), 134 mg chol., 823 mg sodium, 41 g carbo., 8 g fiber, 58 g pro.

1 Skill Level

Easy Chicken and Dumplings

1 2- to 2 1/2-pound deli-roasted chicken

1 16-ounce package frozen mixed vegetables

1 1/4 cups reduced-sodium chicken broth or water

1 10.75-ounce can reduced-fat, reduced-sodium condensed cream of chicken soup

1/2 teaspoon dried Italian seasoning, crushed

1/8 teaspoon ground black pepper

1 11.5-ounce package refrigerated corn bread twists

1 Remove skin and bones from chicken; discard. Chop or shred chicken (you should have 3 1/2 to 4 cups chopped chicken) (see photos, page 395). In a 3-quart saucepan stir together chicken, vegetables, broth, soup, Italian seasoning, and pepper. Bring to boiling; reduce heat. Simmer, covered, about 15 minutes or until vegetables are tender.

2 Meanwhile, remove corn bread twists from package; cut along perforations. Lay twists on a baking sheet; roll 2 twists together to make a spiral. Repeat with remaining twists. Bake according to package directions.

3 To serve, spoon chicken mixture into bowls and top with corn bread spirals. Makes 4 to 6 servings.

Per serving: 650 cal., 30 g total fat (8 g sat. fat), 107 mg chol., 1,399 mg sodium, 57 g carbo., 5 g fiber, 42 g pro.

Ask Mom How do I shred lemon/lime peel? page 30 / How do I juice a lemon/lime? pages 30, 80 / How much juice does one lemon/lime yield? page 30 / How do I crush dried herbs? page 78 / What does simmer mean? page 79

Middle Eastern **Chicken Kabobs**

    I pound skinless, boneless chicken breast halves, cut into I-inch pieces
    ¼ cup plain low-fat yogurt
    I tablespoon lemon juice
    I teaspoon dry mustard
    I teaspoon ground cinnamon
    I teaspoon curry powder
    ½ teaspoon salt
    ¼ to ½ teaspoon crushed red pepper
    I large red sweet pepper, cut into I-inch pieces (I cup)
    I medium yellow summer squash, halved lengthwise and cut into ½-inch-thick slices
      Soft pita breads, warmed (optional)
      Tomato Relish (optional)

1 Place chicken in a resealable plastic bag set in a bowl (below). In a small bowl stir together yogurt, lemon juice, mustard, cinnamon, curry powder, salt, and crushed red pepper. Pour over chicken (below). Seal bag; turn to coat. Refrigerate for 1 to 4 hours, turning occasionally.

2 Preheat broiler. On 6 long metal skewers, thread chicken, sweet pepper, and squash, leaving ¼ inch between pieces (below). Broil 4 to 5 inches from heat for 8 to 10 minutes or until chicken is no longer pink, turning once. If desired, serve with pita bread and Tomato Relish. Makes 6 servings.

Per serving: I07 cal., 2 g total fat (0 g sat. fat), 44 mg chol., 254 mg sodium, 4 g carbo., I g fiber, I9 g pro.

Tomato Relish: Combine 2 roma tomatoes, chopped; ½ cup grape tomatoes, halved; 1 table-spoon balsamic vinegar; 1 teaspoon snipped fresh oregano; 1 teaspoon snipped fresh thyme; 1 teaspoon honey; and 1 clove garlic, minced. Add salt and ground black pepper to taste. Cover; chill up to 4 hours.

e the bag with the
a bowl in case the

2 Add yogurt marinade to the bag with the chicken. Seal bag; turn it to coat chicken.

3 Alternately thread chicken, pepper, and squash on skewers, leaving space between for even cooking.

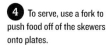

4 To serve, use a fork to push food off of the skewers onto plates.

Ask Mom How do I juice a lemon? pages 30, 80 / What is curry powder? page 4I0 / How do I seed and chop sweet peppers? page 49 / How do I slice summer squash? page 54 / What does it mean to marinate? page 73 / What is a skewer? page 79 / What does it mean to broil? page 68 / What is a roma/grape tomato? page 52 / How do I chop a tomato? page 52 / What is that vinegar? page 349 / How do I snip fresh herbs? pages 42, 328 / What is a garlic clove? page 40 / How do I mince garlic? page 40

Roasted Chicken

1 3- to 3½-pound broiler-fryer chicken
3 cloves garlic, thinly sliced lengthwise
2 tablespoons snipped assorted fresh herbs (such as Italian [flat-leaf] parsley, thyme, and sage)
2 tablespoons olive oil
1½ teaspoons finely shredded lemon peel
¼ teaspoon ground black pepper
½ to 1 teaspoon sea salt or coarse salt
1 small onion, quartered

1 Preheat oven to 375°F. Rinse the inside cavity of the chicken; pat dry with paper towels.

2 With a small knife, cut 8 to 10 small slits in the chicken skin, especially on the breast and hindquarters. Insert a slice of garlic into each slit, just under the skin (below). (You won't use all of the garlic.)

3 Chop remaining garlic. In a small bowl stir together chopped garlic, desired herbs, olive oil, lemon peel, and pepper. Rub chicken all over with herb mixture (below). Sprinkle salt all over chicken, including the cavity. Place onion in the cavity. Tie drumsticks to tail (below). Twist wing tips under the back (below). Place chicken, breast side up, on a rack in a shallow roasting pan.

4 Roast, uncovered, in the preheated oven for 1¼ to 1¾ hours or until drumsticks move easily in their sockets and chicken registers 180°F on an instant-read thermometer inserted in the thickest part of the thigh. (Thermometer should not touch bone.) Cut string from legs. Using tongs, remove the onion from the cavity and discard. Cover chicken loosely with foil and let stand for 10 minutes before carving. Makes 4 servings.

Per serving: 278 cal., 12 g total fat (2 g sat. fat), 119 mg chol., 375 mg sodium, 4 g carbo., 1 g fiber, 37 g pro.

1 Insert slices of garlic in slits in the skin of the chicken, pushing them just under the surface.

2 Using your fingers, rub the herb mixture all over the top and sides of the chicken.

3 Use 100-percent-cotton kitchen string to tie drumsticks to the tail.

4 Twist the wing tips behind the chicken to ke the neck skin in place ar wings tidy.

Ask Mom What is a garlic clove? page 40 / How do I slice garlic? page 40 / How do I snip fresh herbs? pages 42, 328 / How do I shred lemon/lime peel? page 30 / What is sea salt? page 79 / How do I prepare an onion? page 47 / What does it mean to roast? page 68 / How do I use a meat/instant-read thermometer? page 74

Roasted Chicken with Rosemary
And Garlic Herb Potatoes

- ½ cup kosher salt
- ¼ cup snipped fresh rosemary
- 2 3½- to 3¾-pound broiler-fryer chickens
- 8 sprigs fresh rosemary
- 1 small lemon
- ⅓ cup olive oil
- 4 cloves garlic, smashed
- 2 pounds red, white, or gold new potatoes (large ones, cut into ½-inch slices; small ones, halved)

1 In a 6-quart Dutch oven stir together 1 gallon *water*, the ½ cup salt, and the ¼ cup rosemary until salt dissolves. Rinse cavities of the chickens. Submerge chickens in brine (below). Tie 6 rosemary sprigs together to make a brush (below). Add to brine. Cover; chill for 6 to 8 hours.

2 Preheat oven to 425°F. Using a vegetable peeler, remove lemon peel, taking care not to remove any white pith. Halve lemon; set aside. In a 1-quart saucepan combine olive oil, 2 cloves garlic, and peel. Cook over low heat just until warm. Remove from heat; set aside.

3 Remove rosemary brush and chickens from brine; pat dry. Twist wing tips under backs (see photo 4, page 234). In each chicken cavity place a lemon half, a sprig of remaining rosemary, and a clove of remaining garlic. Tie drumsticks to tail (see photo 3, page 234). Place potatoes in a large roasting pan; sprinkle with *salt* and *ground black pepper*. Brush chickens with oil mixture. Place chickens, breast sides up, on potatoes (below); brush with oil mixture.

4 Roast, uncovered, for 30 minutes. Reduce oven temperature to 375°F. Roast for 45 to 60 minutes more or until drumsticks move easily in their sockets and each chicken registers 180°F on an instant-read thermometer inserted in the thickest part of the thigh, brushing twice. The thermometer should not touch bone. Cover; let stand for 10 minutes. Makes 8 servings.

Per serving: 767 cal., 53 g total fat (14 g sat. fat), 207 mg chol., 947 mg sodium, 20 g carbo., 2 g fiber, 52 g pro.

...merge chickens in brine.

2 Use 100-percent-cotton kitchen string to tie rosemary.

3 Use rosemary brush to brush oil mixture on potatoes.

4 Potatoes make a natural cooking rack for the chickens.

Ask Mom What is kosher salt? page 79 / How do I snip fresh herbs? pages 42, 328 / What is a garlic clove? page 40 / What are some potato varieties? page 50 / How do I prepare potatoes? page 51 / What is a brine? page 79 / What does it mean to roast? page 68 / How do I use a meat/instant-read thermometer? page 74

Cheesy Turkey and Spinach Pie

Nonstick cooking spray
4 ounces dried angel hair pasta
3 eggs
1 8-ounce package cream cheese, softened, or 8-ounce carton mascarpone cheese
⅓ cup dairy sour cream
⅓ cup mayonnaise
¼ cup snipped fresh basil or 1 tablespoon dried basil, crushed
½ teaspoon garlic salt
¼ teaspoon crushed red pepper
2 cups chopped cooked turkey or chicken
1 10-ounce package frozen chopped spinach, thawed and well drained (see photo 1, page 321)
1 cup shredded Monterey Jack cheese (4 ounces)
⅓ cup chopped bottled roasted red sweet peppers

1 Preheat oven to 350°F. Lightly coat a 9-inch deep-dish pie plate or a 2-quart square baking dish with cooking spray; set plate on a baking sheet. Set aside. Cook pasta according to package directions; drain well (see photo, page 305).

2 Meanwhile, in a large bowl stir together eggs, cream cheese, sour cream, mayonnaise, basil, garlic salt, and crushed red pepper until well combined. Stir in cooked pasta, turkey, spinach, cheese, and roasted red peppers. Spread mixture in prepared plate (if using pie plate, it will be very full).

3 Bake, uncovered, in the preheated oven for 45 to 50 minutes or until edges are slightly puffed and golden. Let stand on a wire rack for 10 minutes before serving. Makes 6 to 8 servings.

Per serving: 520 cal., 37 g total fat (17 g sat. fat), 225 mg chol., 481 mg sodium, 18 g carbo., 3 g fiber, 29 g pro.

Ask Mom What is that pasta shape? pages 308–309 / How do I soften cream cheese? page 93 / How do I snip fresh herbs? pages 42, 328 / How do I crush dried herbs? page 78 / How do I shred cheese? page 71

② Skill Level

BBQ Spice-Rubbed Turkey Breast

2 3- to 3½-pound fresh or frozen bone-in turkey breast halves
Nonstick cooking spray
2 tablespoons packed dark brown sugar
2 teaspoons paprika
2 teaspoons garlic powder
1½ teaspoons salt
1 teaspoon ground cumin
1 teaspoon chili powder
1 teaspoon ground black pepper

1 Thaw turkey, if frozen. Preheat oven to 400°F. Coat a large roasting pan and rack with cooking spray. In a small bowl stir together brown sugar, paprika, garlic powder, salt, cumin, chili powder, and pepper. Set aside.

2 Slip your fingers between the skin and meat of turkey breast halves to loosen skin, leaving skin partially attached at edges (below). Lift skin and spread brown sugar mixture evenly under skin over meat (below). Place turkey breast halves, bone sides down, on rack in prepared pan. Insert an ovensafe meat thermometer into the thickest part of a breast half (below). Thermometer should not touch bone.

3 Roast, uncovered, on the lower rack in the preheated oven for 20 minutes. Reduce oven temperature to 350°F. Roast for 1 to 1½ hours more or until thermometer registers 170°F and turkey is no longer pink, occasionally spooning pan juices over turkey. Cover loosely with foil and let stand for 10 minutes before slicing. Makes 10 to 12 servings.

Per serving: 311 cal., 6 g total fat (2 g sat. fat), 167 mg chol., 440 mg sodium, 4 g carbo., 0 g fiber, 57 g pro.

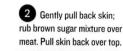
1 Starting at one side, slip your fingers between the skin and meat to loosen skin.

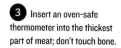
2 Gently pull back skin; rub brown sugar mixture over meat. Pull skin back over top.

3 Insert an oven-safe thermometer into the thickest part of meat; don't touch bone.

Ask Mom How do I thaw a turkey? page 73 / How do I pack brown sugar? page 58 / What does it mean to roast? page 68 / How do I use a meat/instant-read thermometer? page 74

Pan Gravy

1 After moving turkey to a cutting board, pour pan drippings into a large glass measure. Scrape browned bits from pan into cup. **2** Skim and reserve fat from drippings. Pour ¼ cup of fat into a 2-quart saucepan (discard any remaining fat). **3** Stir in ¼ cup all-purpose flour. Add enough reduced-sodium chicken broth to remaining drippings in measuring cup to equal 2 cups. **4** Add broth mixture to flour mixture in saucepan. Cook and stir over medium heat until bubbly. Cook and stir for 1 minute more. **5** Strain gravy into serving dish. Season with salt and black pepper.

1 With the turkey on a large cutting board, remove the leg portions by pulling the drumsticks away from the body and cutting the joints between the thighs and body.

Roast Turkey

I 8- to 10-pound fresh or frozen turkey
  Salt (optional)
I recipe uncooked Corn Bread-Sausage Stuffing (page 240) or
  Old-Fashioned Bread Stuffing (page 240) (optional)
  Cooking oil
I recipe Pan Gravy (page 238)

1 Thaw turkey, if frozen. Preheat oven to 325°F. Rinse the inside cavity of the turkey; pat dry with paper towels. If desired, season body cavity with salt. If desired, spoon stuffing loosely into neck and body cavities. Skewer the neck skin to the back.

2 Tuck the ends of the drumsticks under the band of skin across the tail, if available. If there is no band of skin, tie the drumsticks securely to the tail using 100-percent-cotton kitchen string (see photo 3, page 234). Twist wing tips under the back (see photo 4, page 234).

3 Place turkey, breast side up, on a rack in a shallow roasting pan. Brush with oil. If desired, insert an ovensafe meat thermometer into the center of an inside thigh muscle. The thermometer should not touch bone. Cover turkey loosely with foil.

4 Roast in the preheated oven for 2¼ hours. Remove foil; cut band of skin or string between drumsticks so thighs will cook evenly. Continue roasting for 30 to 45 minutes more (1 to 1¼ hours more if stuffed) or until the thermometer registers 180°F; if stuffed, the center of the stuffing should register 165°F. (The juices should run clear and drumsticks should move easily in their sockets.)

5 Remove turkey from oven; transfer to a cutting board. Cover with foil; let stand for 15 to 20 minutes. Carve turkey (page 238 and below). Serve with Pan Gravy. Makes 12 servings.

Per serving with Pan Gravy: 348 cal., 13 g total fat (4 g sat. fat), 187 mg chol., 194 mg sodium, 2 g carbo., 0 g fiber, 51 g pro.

2 Carve each entire breast half away from the breast bone and rib cage. Place whole breast halves on the cutting board.

3 Slice breast halves crosswise (across the grain). If desired, cut wings off turkey frame, cutting at the joints.

4 Hold leg portions on cutting board with fork; cut through joints to separate thighs and drumsticks. Cut meat slices away from bones.

Ask Mom How do I thaw a turkey? page 73 / What is a skewer? page 79 / What does it mean to roast? page 68 /
How do I use a meat/instant-read thermometer? page 74 / What does skim mean? page 79 / How do I measure flour? page 58

(1) Skill Level

Old-Fashioned Bread Stuffing

1 cup chopped celery (2 stalks)

½ cup chopped onion (1 medium)

⅓ cup butter or margarine

1 tablespoon snipped fresh parsley or 1 teaspoon ground sage

¼ teaspoon ground black pepper

8 cups purchased dry bread cubes

¾ to 1 cup chicken broth

1 Preheat oven to 325°F. In a 10-inch skillet cook celery and onion in hot butter over medium heat until vegetables are tender but not brown. Remove from heat. Stir in parsley and pepper. Place bread cubes in a large bowl; add onion mixture. Drizzle with enough broth to moisten, tossing lightly to combine. Spread stuffing evenly in a 2-quart casserole. Bake, covered, in the preheated oven for 30 to 45 minutes or until heated through. Makes 12 servings.

Per serving: 117 cal., 6 g total fat (3 g sat. fat), 14 mg chol., 274 mg sodium, 14 g carbo., 1 g fiber, 2 g pro.

(2) Skill Level

Corn Bread-Sausage Stuffing

8 cups 1-inch corn bread cubes (1 pound)

8 ounces mild bulk Italian sausage

1 cup chopped onion (1 large)

½ cup chopped celery (1 stalk)

¼ cup butter or margarine

1 cup shredded cheddar cheese (4 ounces) (optional)

1 cup chicken broth

4 eggs, lightly beaten

1 Preheat oven to 325°F. Spread corn bread cubes in a 15×10×1-inch baking pan. Bake, uncovered, in the preheated oven for 10 minutes, stirring once. Cool on a wire rack.

2 In a 10-inch skillet cook sausage until brown. Drain off fat; set aside. In the same skillet cook onion and celery in hot butter over medium heat until tender.

3 In a large bowl combine the corn bread, sausage, onion mixture, and, if desired, cheese. In a small bowl combine broth and eggs. Drizzle corn bread mixture with broth mixture, tossing lightly to combine. Spread stuffing evenly in a 2-quart rectangular baking dish.

4 Bake, covered, in the preheated oven for 40 minutes. Uncover and bake for 5 to 10 minutes more or until an instant-read thermometer inserted near the center reaches 165°F. Makes 12 servings.

Per serving: 232 cal., 14 g total fat (6 g sat. fat), 110 mg chol., 22 mg sodium, 18 g carbo., 1 g fiber, 8 g pro.

Ask Mom How do I chop celery? page 39 / How do I chop an onion? page 47 / How do I measure butter? pages 58, 59 / How do I snip fresh herbs? pages 42, 328 / What does drizzle mean? page 79 / What does it mean to toss? page 77 / How do I make/toast bread cubes? page 77 / How do I shred cheese? page 71 / How do I beat eggs? page 62 / How do I use a meat/instant-read thermometer? page 74

quick-to-fix
MEAT
meals

Here's the fast answer to what's for dinner: Bypass the drive-through, even on the busiest weeknights.

6

Skillet Tostadas

    8 ounces ground beef, ground pork, ground chicken, or ground turkey
    ½ cup chopped onion (I medium)
    I I5-ounce can light red kidney beans, black beans, or pinto beans, rinsed and drained
    I II-ounce can condensed nacho cheese soup
    ⅓ cup bottled salsa
    8 tostada shells
    I cup shredded taco cheese (4 ounces)
       Shredded lettuce
       Chopped or wedged tomatoes
       Dairy sour cream or refrigerated avocado dip (guacamole) (optional)

1 In a 10-inch skillet cook ground beef and onion until meat is brown and onion is tender. Drain fat; discard. Stir beans, soup, and salsa into beef mixture. Heat through.

2 Divide beef-bean mixture among tostada shells. Top with cheese, lettuce, and tomatoes. If desired, serve with sour cream or avocado dip. Makes 4 servings.

Per serving: 576 cal., 33 g total fat (15 g sat. fat), 81 mg chol., 1,277 mg sodium, 42 g carbo., 11 g fiber, 26 g pro.

Skillet Tacos: Prepare as above, except omit tostada shells. Warm 8 corn taco shells according to package directions. Divide beef-bean mixture among taco shells.

Top the beef-bean mixture with favorites such as lettuce, tomatoes, cheese, sour cream, and guacamole. Or try something traditional but more unusual, such as shredded cabbage or chopped radishes.

Ask Mom How do I chop an onion? page 47 / How do I rinse and drain canned beans? page 390 / How do I shred lettuce? page 346 / How do I chop a tomato? page 52

Individual Sicilian Meat Loaves

- 1 egg, lightly beaten
- 1 14-ounce jar garlic and onion pasta sauce (1¾ cups)
- ¼ cup seasoned fine dry bread crumbs
- ¼ teaspoon salt
- ¼ teaspoon ground black pepper
- 12 ounces ground beef
- 2 ounces mozzarella cheese (2¼ x 1½ x 1-inch block) or 2 sticks mozzarella string cheese
- 4 thin slices prosciutto or cooked ham (about 2 ounces)
- 1 9-ounce package refrigerated plain or spinach fettuccine

1 Preheat oven to 400°F. In a medium bowl combine egg, ¼ cup of the pasta sauce, the bread crumbs, salt, and pepper. Add ground beef; mix well (below).

2 Cut mozzarella cheese block into four 2¼ × ¾ × ½-inch logs (below) or cut each string cheese stick in half crosswise. Wrap a slice of prosciutto around each cheese log (below). Shape one-fourth of the ground beef mixture around each cheese log to form a loaf (below). Flatten the four meat loaves to 1½ inches thick and place in a shallow baking pan.

3 Bake loaves, uncovered, in the preheated oven about 20 minutes or until internal temperature registers 160°F on an instant-read thermometer. Meanwhile, prepare fettuccine according to package directions; drain well (see photo, page 305) and keep warm. In a small saucepan heat remaining pasta sauce over medium heat until bubbly.

4 Arrange meat loaves over hot fettuccine. Spoon sauce over top and, if desired, sprinkle with finely shredded *Parmesan cheese*. Makes 4 servings.

Per serving: 618 cal., 29 g total fat (11 g sat. fat), 171 mg chol., 1,150 mg sodium, 55 g carbo., 3 g fiber, 31 g pro.

1 Using your hands, gently mix the ground beef with the other ingredients. Don't overwork the beef or it will become tough when cooked.

2 For the filling, either cut a block of mozzarella cheese into four logs or cut two sticks of mozzarella string cheese in half.

3 Lay a slice of prosciutto on a flat surface and place mozzarella cheese at one end. Wrap the mozzarella cheese log in the prosciutto.

4 Use one-fourth of meat to completely enca prosciutto-wrapped moz log, forming a small loaf

Ask Mom How do I beat eggs? page 62 / What are fine dry bread crumbs? page 76 / What is prosciutto? page 358 / How do I use a meat/instant-read thermometer? page 74

Quick Italian Pepper Steak

  I 9-ounce package refrigerated fettuccine
  I 16-ounce package frozen sweet pepper and onion stir-fry vegetables, thawed and drained
  2 tablespoons olive oil
  2 tablespoons balsamic vinegar
 12 ounces boneless beef top sirloin steak, cut into thin bite-size strips
 ¼ teaspoon crushed red pepper
  I 15-ounce can tomato sauce with Italian seasonings
  2 tablespoons pine nuts, toasted (optional)

1 Prepare fettuccine according to package directions; drain well (see photo, page 305) and keep warm. Meanwhile, in a 10-inch skillet cook sweet pepper blend in 1 tablespoon of hot oil over medium-high heat for 2 to 3 minutes or until crisp-tender, stirring occasionally. Carefully add balsamic vinegar; toss to coat. Remove sweet pepper mixture from skillet. Cover; keep warm.

2 In the same skillet cook beef and crushed red pepper in the remaining 1 tablespoon hot oil for 2 to 3 minutes or until meat is slightly pink in the center, stirring occasionally. Add tomato sauce; heat through.

3 Add sweet pepper mixture back to skillet and heat through. Serve over hot fettuccine. If desired, sprinkle with pine nuts and additional crushed red pepper. Makes 4 servings.

Per serving: 457 cal., 14 g total fat (3 g sat. fat), 55 mg chol., 761 mg sodium, 54 g carbo., 5 g fiber, 29 g pro.

Toasting pine nuts brings out their rich flavor, but be careful. Toast these nuts like any other (page 65) but keep a very close eye on them. They burn fast and once they do, you have to toss them. Ouch!

Ask Mom What is that vinegar? page 349 / What is that cut of meat? pages 220–221 / What does crisp-tender mean? page 79 / What does it mean to toss? page 77

Skill Level

Steak with Pan Sauce

Ingredient Info Unsalted butter versus salted—which is better? It's up to you, but unsalted butter allows you to control how much salt you put in your food, especially when you're using other high-sodium ingredients. A bonus with unsalted: The rich, creamy flavor of butter really shines through—not just that of the salt.

5 tablespoons cold unsalted butter

2 beef steaks, such as top loin, ribeye, or tenderloin, cut about ³⁄₄ inch thick

¹⁄₃ cup dry red wine or apple juice

¹⁄₄ cup reduced-sodium beef broth

2 tablespoons finely chopped shallot or I clove garlic, minced

I tablespoon whipping cream (no substitutes)

Salt and white pepper

1 Heat a 10-inch skillet over medium-high heat (do not use a nonstick skillet). Add 1 tablespoon of the butter; reduce heat to medium. Cook steaks about 3 minutes per side or until medium rare (145°F) (below). Transfer steaks to a platter; cover with foil to keep warm (steaks will continue to cook as they stand). Drain fat from skillet.

2 Add wine, broth, and shallot to the hot skillet. To deglaze the skillet, stir and scrape the bottom of the skillet with a wire whisk to loosen the brown bits (below). Cook over medium heat for 3 to 4 minutes or until liquid is reduced to about 2 tablespoons (below). Reduce heat to medium low.

3 Stir in cream. Stir in remaining butter, 1 tablespoon at a time (below), whisking until butter is incorporated and sauce has thickened slightly. Season to taste with salt and white pepper. Spoon sauce over steaks. Serve immediately. Makes 2 servings.

Per serving: 651 cal., 45 g total fat (25 g sat. fat), 211 mg chol., 338 mg sodium, 3 g carbo., 0 g fiber, 53 g pro.

1 Make sure the skillet is hot before adding the butter and the steaks. A hot skillet will give the steaks a rich brown color.

2 After quickly draining the fat from the skillet, immediately add the liquid while the skillet is hot. Use a whisk to scrape the brown bits on the bottom.

3 Continue to cook the wine and broth to evaporate some of the liquid. This concentrates the flavors of the broth and wine.

4 After stirring cream the reduced sauce, whis butter in, I tablespoon at time, until incorporated.

Ask Mom How do I measure butter? pages 58, 59 / What is that cut of meat? pages 220–221 / What is a shallot? page 46 / How do I chop an onion? page 47 / What is a garlic clove? page 40 / How do I mince garlic? page 40 / How do I deglaze a pan? page 70 / What is a reduction? page 70 / What are capers? page 79 / What does it mean to saute? page 69 / How do I slice green onions? page 43 / How do I snip fresh herbs? pages 42, 328

WHY ADD THE BUTTER SO SLOWLY? Whisking the butter in the pan 1 tablespoon at a time allows the cream and butter to become completely incorporated and prevents separating. The end result is an irresistible supersilky sauce.

Flavor Changes For extra flavor, try stirring one of the following into the finished sauce: $\frac{1}{2}$ cup sauteed mushrooms; $\frac{1}{2}$ teaspoon balsamic or white wine vinegar; 2 tablespoons sliced green onion; or 1 teaspoon capers. Or with the shallot stir in $\frac{1}{2}$ teaspoon dill-flavored mustard.

Beef and Broccoli Stroganoff

3 cups dried wide egg noodles

3 cups broccoli spears (12 ounces)

$\frac{1}{2}$ cup dairy sour cream

$1\frac{1}{2}$ teaspoons prepared horseradish

$\frac{1}{2}$ teaspoon snipped fresh dill or $\frac{1}{2}$ teaspoon dried dillweed

1 pound beef top sirloin steak

1 small onion, cut into $\frac{1}{2}$-inch slices

1 clove garlic, minced

1 tablespoon cooking oil

4 teaspoons all-purpose flour

1 14-ounce can beef broth

3 tablespoons tomato paste

1 teaspoon Worcestershire sauce

1 Cook noodles according to package directions, adding broccoli the last 5 minutes of cooking. Drain; keep warm (below). Stir together the sour cream, horseradish, and dill. Cover; chill.

2 Trim fat from beef. Cut into bite-size strips. In a 10-inch skillet cook and stir onion, garlic, and half of the beef in hot oil until onion is tender and beef is slightly pink in center (below). Remove from skillet. Repeat with remaining beef. Return rest of meat mixture to the skillet; sprinkle flour and $\frac{1}{2}$ teaspoon *ground black pepper* over meat (below). Stir to coat.

3 Stir in broth, tomato paste, and Worcestershire sauce (below). Cook and stir until thickened and bubbly. Cook and stir for 1 minute more. Divide noodle-broccoli mixture among 4 serving bowls. Spoon beef mixture over noodles. Top with sour cream mixture. Makes 4 servings.

Per serving: 431 cal., 19 g total fat (7 g sat. fat), 101 mg chol., 587 mg sodium, 34 g carbo., 4 g fiber, 31 g pro.

1 After cooking the broccoli with the noodles for the last 5 minutes, drain the mixture well in a colander.

2 Cook only half the beef at a time so the skillet doesn't become overcrowded and cool off too much.

3 Place the entire beef mixture in the skillet and sprinkle with flour and pepper. Stir to coat well.

4 Add the beef broth Worcestershire sauce, a tomato paste to the beef Cook and stir until it thic

Ask Mom What is that pasta shape? pages 308–309 / How do I drain pasta? page 305 / How do I trim and cut broccoli? page 36 / What is prepared horseradish? page 429 / How do I snip fresh herbs? pages 42, 328 / What is that cut of meat? pages 220–221 / How do I slice an onion? page 47 / What is a garlic clove? page 40 / How do I mince garlic? page 40

Simple Beef and Noodles

I 17-ounce package refrigerated cooked beef tips with gravy

½ teaspoon dried basil, crushed

¼ teaspoon ground black pepper

I 10.75-ounce can condensed golden mushroom soup

½ cup beef broth

I½ cups sliced fresh mushrooms

I cup packaged peeled baby carrots, halved lengthwise

I small onion, halved and thinly sliced (⅓ cup)

I 12-ounce package frozen egg noodles

1 In a 3-quart saucepan combine beef tips with gravy, basil, and pepper. Stir in soup and broth. Bring to boiling. Add mushrooms, carrots, and onion. Return to boiling; reduce heat to low. Simmer, covered, for 20 to 25 minutes or until vegetables are tender, stirring frequently.

2 Meanwhile, cook noodles according to package directions; drain (see photo, page 305). Serve meat mixture over noodles. Makes 4 to 6 servings.

Per serving: 458 cal., 12 g total fat (4 g sat. fat), 150 mg chol., 1,349 mg sodium, 61 g carbo., 4 g fiber, 27 g pro.

Meal Maker Starting with precooked beef tips is a great way to speed up a traditionally slow-cooking dish. All you need is 20 to 25 minutes—it's so easy you can even make it on a weeknight. Complete the meal by serving this dish with a crisp green salad and some crusty rolls.

Ask Mom How do I crush dried herbs? page 78 / What are some mushroom varieties? page 44 / How do I slice fresh mushrooms? page 45 / How do I slice an onion? page 47 / What does simmer mean? page 79

CHERRIES—WITH POT ROAST? You bet! The combination of meat and fruit is very French—you'll feel so sophisticated when you serve this little number to your friends. The dark cherries, along with the balsamic vinegar, add body and a little sweetness to the sauce.

Skillet Pot Roast with Cherries

I 12-ounce package frozen unsweetened pitted dark sweet cherries

8 ounces fresh mushrooms, halved (3 cups)

¾ cup bite-size strips red sweet pepper (I medium)

I cup chopped onion (I large)

2 tablespoons snipped fresh sage or thyme or 2 teaspoons dried sage or thyme, crushed

I tablespoon olive oil or cooking oil

2 16- to 17-ounce packages refrigerated cooked beef pot roast with juices

2 tablespoons balsamic vinegar

I 24-ounce package refrigerated mashed potatoes or Mashed Potatoes (see page 142)

1 Place cherries in a colander. Run cold water over cherries to partially thaw; drain well. Set aside.

2 In a 12-inch skillet cook mushrooms, sweet pepper, onion, and 1 tablespoon of the sage in hot oil about 7 minutes or until tender, stirring occasionally. Add pot roasts and juices, cherries, and balsamic vinegar to the skillet. Bring to boiling; reduce heat. Simmer, uncovered, for about 10 minutes or until heated through and juices thicken slightly, stirring occasionally. Sprinkle with remaining sage; stir to combine.

3 Meanwhile, prepare potatoes according to package directions. Serve with pot roast. Makes 4 to 6 servings.

Per serving: 571 cal., 21 g total fat (7 g sat. fat), 120 mg chol., 982 mg sodium, 47 g carbo., 4 g fiber, 52 g pro.

Ingredient Info Like other produce, fresh mushrooms always have little bits of soil clinging to them (after all, they are grown in soil!), so they'll need some cleanup before they can be cooked or eaten. However, mushrooms are like little sponges and will soak up water when they are rinsed off, so the best way to clean fresh mushrooms is to simply wipe them with a slightly damp paper towel. Trim the stems and cut or slice as needed.

Ask Mom What are some mushroom varieties? page 44 / How do I clean fresh mushrooms? page 45 / How do I seed sweet peppers and cut them into strips? page 49 / How do I chop an onion? page 47 / How do I snip fresh herbs? pages 42, 328 / How do I crush dried herbs? page 78 / What is that vinegar? page 349 / What does simmer mean? page 79

Jerk Pork Chops

4 boneless pork loin chops, cut ¾ inch thick (about 1½ pounds total)
3 tablespoons orange juice or grapefruit juice
2 teaspoons Jamaican jerk or steak seasoning
1 tablespoon cooking oil
2 tablespoons Dijon-style mustard
⅓ cup orange marmalade
   Mashed Sweet Potatoes (page 144) (optional)

Ingredient Info "Jerk" refers to a Jamaican method of spicing and cooking meats (usually over a smoky fire). Jerk seasoning can be a dry rub, paste, or marinade. It includes chiles, allspice, thyme, cinnamon, ginger, garlic, cloves, and green onions. The result is spicy-sweet (and best enjoyed on a beach).

1 Brush both sides of pork chops with 1 tablespoon of the orange juice. Sprinkle both sides with seasoning. In a 10-inch skillet cook chops in hot oil over medium heat for 8 to 12 minutes or until internal temperature of chops registers 160°F on an instant-read thermometer, turning once halfway through cooking. Remove skillet from heat. Transfer chops to a serving platter.

2 For sauce, stir mustard into skillet drippings. Whisk in marmalade and remaining 2 tablespoons orange juice. Return to heat. Cook and stir just until boiling. Pour sauce over chops. If desired, serve pork chops with Mashed Sweet Potatoes. Makes 4 servings.

Per serving: 342 cal., 11 g total fat (3 g sat. fat), 107 mg chol., 435 mg sodium, 20 g carbo., 0 g fiber, 39 g pro.

Jerk Chicken: Prepare as above, except substitute 4 medium skinless, boneless chicken breast halves for the pork. Cook chicken breasts for 12 to 15 minutes or until no longer pink (170°F), turning once halfway through cooking.

To check the doneness of the pork without an instant-read thermometer, cut into the center of each pork chop. The inside should be just slightly pink and the juices should run clear.

Ask Mom What is that cut of meat? pages 220–221 / How do I juice an orange? page 30 / How much juice does one orange yield? page 30 / What is Dijon-style mustard? page 379 / How do I use a meat/instant-read thermometer? page 74

Asian-Apricot Glazed Chops

$\frac{1}{3}$ cup apricot preserves

2 to 3 teaspoons Asian chili-garlic sauce

2 teaspoons soy sauce

$\frac{1}{4}$ teaspoon ground ginger

4 boneless pork sirloin chops, cut $\frac{3}{4}$ inch thick

   Salt and ground black pepper

1 tablespoon cooking oil

1 recipe Tri-Color Slaw (optional)

1 For glaze, place apricot preserves in a small bowl. Using clean kitchen scissors, snip any large pieces of fruit. Stir in chili-garlic sauce, soy sauce, and ginger. Set glaze aside. Sprinkle both sides of chops with salt and pepper.

2 In a 10-inch skillet cook chops in hot oil over medium heat for 8 to 12 minutes or until internal temperature of chops registers 160°F on an instant-read thermometer, turning once halfway through cooking and brushing with glaze.

3 Spoon any glaze remaining in skillet on top of chops before serving. If desired, serve chops with Tri-Color Slaw. Makes 4 servings.

Per serving: 253 cal., 8 g total fat (2 g sat. fat), 71 mg chol., 320 mg sodium, 20 g carbo., 0 g fiber, 24 g pro.

Tri-Color Slaw: In a large glass bowl stir together 2 tablespoons rice vinegar or cider vinegar, 1 tablespoon fresh lime juice, 1 tablespoon toasted sesame oil, and $\frac{1}{2}$ teaspoon sugar; whisk until sugar is dissolved. Add 4 cups packaged shredded cabbage with carrot (coleslaw mix), $\frac{3}{4}$ cup chopped yellow sweet pepper, $\frac{1}{4}$ cup snipped fresh cilantro, $\frac{1}{8}$ teaspoon salt, and $\frac{1}{8}$ teaspoon ground black pepper. Toss together just until combined. Before serving, cover and chill in the refrigerator for at least 20 minutes or up to 24 hours.

Ingredient Info Chili-garlic sauce is a really versatile Asian condiment that adds lots of zing to sauces, stir-fries, and soups. But a word to the wise—it's pretty darn hot. Your best bet is to taste a dab of it on your tongue before adding it to whatever you're cooking so you know how much to use (especially if you're cooking for guests who can't take the heat). You can always add more at the table. Check out the Asian section of your supermarket for chili-garlic sauce. If you don't find it there, you'll find it at any Asian market.

Ask Mom What is that cut of meat? pages 220–221 / How do I use a meat/instant-read thermometer? page 74 / What is that vinegar? page 349 / How do I juice a lemon/lime? pages 30, 80 / How much juice does one lemon/lime yield? page 30 / What is toasted sesame oil? page 138 / How do I seed and chop sweet peppers? page 49 / How do I snip fresh herbs? pages 42, 328

Thai Pork Roll-Ups

  6 8- to 10-inch spinach, tomato, and/or plain flour tortillas
  $\frac{1}{2}$ teaspoon garlic salt
  $\frac{1}{4}$ to $\frac{1}{2}$ teaspoon ground black pepper
 12 ounces pork tenderloin, cut into $\frac{1}{4}$-inch-thick strips
  1 tablespoon cooking oil
  4 cups packaged shredded broccoli (broccoli slaw mix)
  1 medium red onion, cut into thin wedges
  1 teaspoon grated fresh ginger
  1 recipe Peanut Sauce

1 Preheat oven to 350°F. Wrap tortillas in foil. Bake in the preheated oven about 10 minutes or until warm. Meanwhile, in a medium bowl combine garlic salt and pepper. Add pork strips, tossing to coat evenly.

2 In a 10-inch skillet cook and stir seasoned pork in hot oil over medium-high heat for 4 to 6 minutes or until no longer pink, turning to brown evenly (see photo 3, page 255). Turn heat down if pork gets too brown. Remove pork from skillet; keep warm. Add shredded broccoli, onion, and ginger to skillet. Cook and stir for 4 to 6 minutes or until vegetables are crisp-tender. Remove from heat.

3 To assemble, spread one side of each tortilla with Peanut Sauce. Top with pork strips and broccoli mixture. Roll up each tortilla, securing with a wooden toothpick if necessary. Serve immediately. Makes 6 roll-ups.

Peanut Sauce: In a 1- to 1$\frac{1}{2}$-quart saucepan combine $\frac{1}{4}$ cup creamy peanut butter; 3 tablespoons water; 1 tablespoon sugar; 2 teaspoons soy sauce; and 1 clove garlic, minced. Heat over medium-low heat, whisking constantly, until peanut butter mixture is smooth and warm. Use immediately or keep warm over very low heat, stirring occasionally.

Per roll-up: 389 cal., 13 g total fat (3 g sat. fat), 33 mg chol., 649 mg sodium, 44 g carbo., 5 g fiber, 22 g pro.

Thai Chicken Roll-Ups: Prepare as above, except substitute 12 ounces skinless, boneless chicken breast halves, cut into $\frac{1}{4}$-inch-thick strips, for the pork tenderloin.

Ingredient Info Most of the time you'll find pork tenderloin vacuum-packed in packages of two tenderloins (each tenderloin usually weighs between 12 and 16 ounces). If your recipe calls for only one—as this one does—tightly wrap the other tenderloin in plastic wrap and freeze it in a resealable freezer bag for up to 6 months.

Ask Mom What is that cut of meat? pages 220–221 / How do I cut onion wedges? page 47 / What is fresh ginger? page 41 / How do I grate fresh ginger? page 41 / What does crisp-tender mean? page 79 / How do I mince garlic? page 40 / What is a garlic clove? page 40

1 Skill Level

Oriental Pork and Vegetables

6 ounces rice stick noodles or two 3-ounce packages ramen noodles (any flavor), broken if desired

2 teaspoons toasted sesame oil or olive oil

1 16-ounce package frozen stir-fry vegetables

12 ounces pork tenderloin, cut into $\frac{1}{4}$-inch-thick strips

$\frac{1}{4}$ cup teriyaki sauce*

2 tablespoons plum sauce*

1 If using ramen noodles, discard seasoning packet from the package. Prepare noodles as directed on package (below); drain (see photo, page 305). Set aside and keep warm.

2 In a 12-inch skillet heat 1 teaspoon of the hot sesame oil over medium-high heat. Add vegetables; cook and stir for 4 to 6 minutes or until crisp-tender. Remove from skillet (below). Set aside and keep warm.

3 Add remaining oil to skillet. Add pork strips and cook over medium-high heat for 4 to 6 minutes or until no longer pink, turning to brown evenly (below). Stir in vegetables (drained, if necessary), teriyaki sauce, and plum sauce; heat through. Add noodles; toss to coat (below). Makes 4 servings.

*Note: Find bottled teriyaki and plum sauces in the ethnic foods aisle of your supermarket.

Per serving: 341 cal., 5 g total fat (1 g sat. fat), 55 mg chol., 820 mg sodium, 48 g carbo., 3 g fiber, 22 g pro.

Oriental Beef and Vegetables: Prepare as above, except substitute 12 ounces boneless beef top round or sirloin, cut into $\frac{1}{4}$-inch-thick slices, for the pork tenderloin.

2 After cooking the vegetables in the skillet, place them in a bowl. Before adding them to the cooked pork, you can drain the excess liquid from the bowl if necessary.

3 Add the remaining oil to the same skillet. Cook the pork until it is no longer pink on the inside, turning pieces with tongs to brown evenly.

4 Once the vegetables and teriyaki and plum sauces have been added to the pork and heated, toss the noodles into the pork mixture to coat.

e rice stick or ⸝dles in boiling ⸝cook as directed ⸝kage.

Ask Mom What is toasted sesame oil? page 138 / What is that cut of meat? pages 220–221 / What does it mean to stir-fry? page 69 / What does crisp-tender mean? page 79

Balsamic Pork Medallions

- 2 tablespoons butter
- 2 cups sliced fresh mushrooms
- 2 cups chopped broccoli rabe, small broccoli florets, or chopped broccolini
- 12 ounces pork tenderloin
- 2 ounces prosciutto or thinly sliced ham, cut into bite-size strips
- ¼ cup balsamic vinegar
- 1 tablespoon packed brown sugar
- 1 recipe Cheesy Polenta (optional)

1 In a 10-inch skillet heat 1 tablespoon of the butter over medium-high heat. Add mushrooms and broccoli; cook about 3 minutes or until crisp-tender, stirring occasionally. Remove vegetables from the skillet; set aside.

2 Meanwhile, trim fat from pork; cut into ½-inch-thick slices (see photos, pages 362 and 360). Sprinkle slices with *salt* and *ground black pepper*. Add to skillet; cook in remaining 1 tablespoon butter for 4 to 6 minutes or until juices run clear, turning once halfway through cooking.

3 Return vegetables to skillet; add prosciutto, balsamic vinegar, and brown sugar. Heat through. If desired, serve with Cheesy Polenta. Makes 4 servings.

Cheesy Polenta: Prepare Polenta and Black Beans (page 338) as directed, except after cooking polenta for 5 to 10 minutes at the end of Step 1, stir in ½ cup shredded fontina cheese until melted. Omit black beans, tomatoes, salsa, and Mexican cheese blend.

Per serving: 238 cal., 10 g total fat (5 g sat. fat), 80 mg chol., 559 mg sodium, 10 g carbo., 4 g fiber, 25 g pro.

A Broccoli rabe or rapini

B Broccolini

Ingredient Info A Broccoli rabe, also called rapini, is a slightly bitter Italian vegetable similar to broccoli, but leafier. **B** Broccolini is a hybrid cross between broccoli and Chinese kale. It has slimmer stems than broccoli, is slightly more tender, and—when young—is somewhat sweeter. Both green vegetables are nutritional powerhouses.

Ask Mom How do I measure butter? pages 58, 59 / What are some mushroom varieties? page 44 / How do I slice fresh mushrooms? page 45 / How do I trim and cut broccoli? page 36 / What is that cut of meat? pages 220–221 / What is prosciutto? page 358 / What is that vinegar? page 349 / How do I pack brown sugar? page 58 / What does crisp-tender mean? page 79

Monterey Shredded Pork Tacos

1 17-ounce package refrigerated cooked pork roast or beef roast au jus
³⁄₄ cup bottled salsa
8 taco shells or four 8-inch flour tortillas
1¹⁄₂ cups shredded romaine or leaf lettuce
³⁄₄ cup finely shredded Monterey Jack cheese or cheddar cheese (3 ounces)
Dairy sour cream (optional)
1 recipe Fruit Salsa (optional)
1 recipe Guacamole (page 89) or refrigerated avocado dip (guacamole) (optional)

1 Place pork and juices in a 2-quart square microwave-safe baking dish. Cover loosely with waxed paper and microwave on 100 percent power (high) for 2 minutes. Using two forks, shred the pork by pulling the meat in opposite directions (see photos, page 419). Drain pork and return to baking dish. Stir in bottled salsa. Cover loosely and microwave on high for 2 minutes more or until hot. Keep warm.

2 To warm taco shells, place them on a baking sheet and heat according to package directions. (Or to warm flour tortillas, wrap tortillas tightly in foil. Heat in a 350°F oven for about 10 minutes or until heated through.)

3 To assemble tacos, place pork mixture in warm taco shells. Top with lettuce and cheese. (If using flour tortillas, place pork mixture in center of warm tortillas and top with lettuce and cheese; fold tortillas in half.) If desired, serve with sour cream, Fruit Salsa, and/or Guacamole. Makes 8 tacos.

Per taco: 367 cal., 19 g total fat (7 g sat. fat), 91 mg chol., 842 mg sodium, 19 g carbo., 3 g fiber, 32 g pro.

Fruit Salsa: In a medium bowl combine one 15.25-ounce can tropical fruit salad, drained; 2 tablespoons chopped red onion; 1 tablespoon white balsamic vinegar; 1 tablespoon lime juice; 1 tablespoon snipped fresh cilantro; and ¹⁄₄ teaspoon salt. Cover and chill in the refrigerator for at least 1 hour before serving or up to 24 hours.

MEAL MAKER Create a complete menu out of this Mexican specialty by serving it with something fresh—thick slices of fresh pineapple, maybe, or a simple salad of orange sections drizzled with honey and sprinkled with shredded coconut.

Ask Mom How do I shred lettuce? page 346 / How do I shred cheese? page 71 / How do I chop an onion? page 47 / What is that vinegar? page 349 / How do I juice a lemon/lime? pages 30, 80 / How much juice does one lemon/lime yield? page 30 / How do I snip fresh herbs? pages 42, 328

Shredded Potatoes
With Sausage and Apple

2 tablespoons olive oil

2 tablespoons butter

5 cups frozen shredded hash brown potatoes (about half of a 26-ounce package)

1 tablespoon snipped fresh thyme or 1 teaspoon dried thyme, crushed

¼ teaspoon ground black pepper

6 ounces cooked smoked sausage, coarsely chopped

1 medium apple (such as Golden Delicious), cored and cut into thin wedges

Salt (optional)

1 In a 10-inch skillet heat oil and 1 tablespoon of the butter over medium heat. Add potatoes in an even layer. Cook about 8 minutes or until light brown, stirring occasionally. Stir in half of the thyme and pepper. With a wide spatula press down firmly. Cook for about 8 minutes more or until potatoes are tender.

2 Meanwhile, in an 8-inch skillet melt remaining 1 tablespoon butter over medium heat. Add sausage and apple. Cook about 10 minutes or until apple is tender, stirring occasionally. Stir in remaining thyme.

3 Slide potatoes onto a cool plate; cover with another plate and flip the plates over (below). Remove the top plate (below). Spoon sausage-apple mixture over the potatoes. If desired, season to taste with salt. Makes 4 servings.

Per serving: 376 cal., 27 g total fat (10 g sat. fat), 45 mg chol., 866 mg sodium, 23 g carbo., 2 g fiber, 12 g pro.

1 Tilt the skillet to slide the potatoes onto a large clean plate or platter.

2 Cover the potatoes on the plate with another large plate or platter.

3 Invert the two plates so that the bottom plate is now on the top.

4 Now the delicious brown side of the potato facing up on the plate. F the top plate and spoon sausage-apple mixture c

Ask Mom How do I measure butter? pages 58, 59 / How do I snip fresh herbs? pages 42, 328 / How do I crush dried herbs? page 78 / How do I core and slice/chop apples? page 28

Fruited Lamb Chops With Nutty Couscous

1 teaspoon dried thyme, crushed

8 lamb rib or loin chops, cut ¾ to 1 inch thick (1½ to 2 pounds total)

1 tablespoon cooking oil

2 tablespoons finely chopped shallot or onion

2 tablespoons balsamic vinegar

2 tablespoons honey

2 small pears or apples, cored and thickly sliced

2 to 3 tablespoons dried cranberries, golden raisins, or raisins

1 recipe Nutty Couscous

1 In a small bowl combine thyme, ½ teaspoon *coarsely ground black pepper,* and ¼ teaspoon *salt.* Trim fat from meat. Rub thyme mixture over both sides of lamb chops (below).

2 In a 12-inch skillet heat oil over medium-high heat until very hot. Add lamb chops; reduce heat to medium and cook for 7 to 9 minutes for medium (160°F) (below), turning once. Remove from skillet; set aside. Add shallot to drippings in skillet; cook and stir until tender.

3 Combine vinegar and honey. Add to the skillet. Bring to boiling; add pears and cranberries to the skillet. Return to boiling; reduce heat. Simmer, covered, for 3 minutes, stirring once (below). Return lamb to the skillet. Cook, covered, for 3 minutes or until fruit is tender and lamb is heated through (below). Serve pear-cranberry mixture with lamb and Nutty Couscous. Makes 4 servings.

Nutty Couscous: In a 2- to 2½-quart saucepan bring one 14-ounce can chicken broth to boiling. Stir in 1½ cups quick-cooking couscous. Cover; remove from heat. Let stand for 5 minutes. Fluff with a fork. Stir in ⅓ cup chopped pistachios and season with salt and ground black pepper.

Per serving: 739 cal., 25 g total fat (7 g sat. fat), 113 mg chol., 676 mg sodium, 82 g carbo., 7 g fiber, 46 g pro.

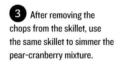

...ake the seasoning ...o the chops, ...over the meat, then ...th your hands.

2 To check the doneness, insert an instant-read thermometer into the center of the meat.

3 After removing the chops from the skillet, use the same skillet to simmer the pear-cranberry mixture.

4 Return the lamb to the skillet and continue cooking to heat the lamb and soften the pears.

Ask Mom How do I crush dried herbs? page 78 / What is that cut of meat? pages 220–221 / What is a shallot? page 46 / How do I chop an onion? page 47 / What is that vinegar? page 349 / How do I core and slice pears? page 32 / How do I core and slice/chop apples? page 28 / How do I freshly grind pepper? page 22 / How do I use a meat/instant-read thermometer? page 74 / What does simmer mean? page 79 / What is couscous? page 149 / How do I chop nuts? page 65

Chicken with Skillet Gravy

⅓ cup fine dry seasoned bread crumbs

2 tablespoons grated Parmesan cheese

½ teaspoon paprika

1 egg, lightly beaten

2 tablespoons milk

4 skinless, boneless chicken breast halves (about 1¼ pounds total)

2 tablespoons cooking oil

3 tablespoons all-purpose flour

¼ teaspoon dried sage, crushed

3 tablespoons butter

1 14-ounce can chicken broth

1 16-ounce package refrigerated mashed potatoes, heated according to package directions

1 In a shallow dish combine bread crumbs, cheese, and paprika; set aside. In another shallow dish combine egg and milk. Sprinkle chicken pieces with *salt* and *ground black pepper*. Dip chicken pieces into egg mixture (below); dredge through crumb mixture to coat (below).

2 In a 12-inch heavy skillet heat oil over medium-high heat until a few of the remaining bread crumbs sizzle when added to the skillet (below). Add chicken pieces to the skillet; reduce heat to medium. Cook, uncovered, for 12 to 15 minutes or until chicken is no longer pink (170°F), turning once to brown evenly. Transfer chicken to a serving platter; keep warm.

3 Stir flour and sage into melted butter in skillet (page 261). Add broth. Cook and stir over medium heat until thickened and bubbly; cook and stir for 1 minute (page 261). Season with salt and pepper. Serve gravy with chicken and potatoes. Makes 4 servings.

Per serving: 528 cal., 27 g total fat (12 g sat. fat), 180 mg chol., 988 mg sodium, 28 g carbo., 2 g fiber, 42 g pro.

1 Place egg mixture in a shallow dish, such as a pie plate, for easy dipping. Coat both sides of the chicken.

2 Dredge the egg-coated chicken pieces in the bread crumbs, coating both sides.

3 To check if the skillet is hot, sprinkle a few crumbs in the oil. When they sizzle and bubble, add the chicken.

Ask Mom What are fine dry bread crumbs? page 76 / How do I grate cheese? page 71 / How do I beat eggs? page 62 / How do I crush dried herbs? page 78 / How do I measure butter? pages 58, 59 / What does it mean to dredge? page 72 / How do I use a meat/instant-read thermometer? page 74

SUNDAY DINNER AT YOUR HOUSE! Few foods bring back childhood memories like fried chicken and gravy. But there's no reason to deal with the mess of the deep-fried variety. This panfried version made with boneless chicken breasts is easy, soulful, and so good.

For flipping and turning meat (and just about anything else), long-handled tongs are a must-have around high heat—perfect because they keep your hands at a safe distance from the hot pan.

Pan Sauce

1 After removing the chicken, melt the butter in the skillet. Stir the flour into the butter to create a paste.

2 Add the broth to the butter-flour paste. Cook and stir the mixture until it is smooth and thickened.

Chicken Scaloppine

4 skinless, boneless chicken breast halves (about 1 ¼ pounds total)

½ teaspoon salt

¼ teaspoon ground black pepper

2 eggs, lightly beaten

2 tablespoons milk

1 cup seasoned fine dry bread crumbs

¾ cup finely shredded Romano or Parmesan cheese

⅓ cup all-purpose flour

2 tablespoons butter

2 tablespoons olive oil

4 lemon wedges

1 Place each chicken breast half between two pieces of plastic wrap. Using the flat side of a meat mallet, pound chicken lightly to about ¼ inch thick. Remove plastic wrap. Sprinkle chicken pieces with salt and pepper.

2 In a shallow dish combine eggs and milk. In a second shallow dish combine bread crumbs and cheese. Lightly dredge chicken pieces on both sides through flour; shake off excess. Dip both sides in egg mixture (see photo 1, page 260). Dredge in crumb mixture to coat (see photo 2, page 260). If necessary, press crumbs onto chicken with your hands to make crumbs stick.

3 In a 12-inch skillet melt butter over medium-high heat; add oil. Cook half the chicken breasts in melted butter and oil, uncovered, for 8 to 10 minutes or until chicken is no longer pink (170°F), turning once. Remove from skillet; keep warm. Add more oil if needed. Cook remaining chicken. Serve immediately with lemon wedges. Makes 4 servings.

Per serving: 523 cal., 23 g total fat (8 g sat. fat), 215 mg chol., 1,442 mg sodium, 29 g carbo., 0 g fiber, 47 g pro.

Pork Scaloppine: Prepare as above, except substitute 1¼ to 1½ pounds pork tenderloin for the chicken. Slice tenderloin into 8 portions. Continue as directed above.

Good to Know "Scaloppine" (skah-luh-PEE-nee) refers, in Italian, to a scallop-shape piece of meat—usually veal, pork, or chicken—that's given its characteristic tenderness and quick-cooking quality by pounding it thin with a meat mallet before being panfried. Scaloppine meats are usually dredged in flour and/or bread crumbs before cooking and are served with fresh lemon wedges or a wine- or tomato-based sauce.

Ask Mom How do I beat eggs? page 62 / What are fine dry bread crumbs? page 76 / How do I shred cheese? page 71 / How do I measure butter? pages 58, 59 / How do I cut lemon/lime wedges? page 30 / What is a meat mallet? page 19 / How do I use a meat mallet? page 74 / What does it mean to dredge? page 72

② Skill Level

Coconut **Curry Chicken**

1½ teaspoons red curry paste

½ teaspoon salt

¼ teaspoon ground black pepper

6 skinless, boneless chicken breast halves (about 2 pounds total)

1 tablespoon cooking oil

½ cup unsweetened coconut milk

1 10.75-ounce can condensed cream of potato soup

1 9- to 10-ounce package frozen mixed vegetables (about 2 cups)

¼ cup coconut, toasted (optional)

Shopping Savvy

Traditional Thai cooks take great pride in their homemade curry pastes—red, yellow, and green—and use the freshest ingredients available. But for the rest of the cooks out there, high-quality prepared curry pastes are easy to find in the Asian section of your supermarket.

1 In a small bowl combine ½ teaspoon of the curry paste, the salt, and pepper. Use your fingers to rub chicken breasts with curry paste mixture. In a 12-inch skillet cook chicken in hot oil for about 4 minutes or until brown, turning once; remove chicken from skillet.

2 In a small bowl use a wire whisk to mix a small amount of the coconut milk into the remaining curry paste until smooth (below). Whisk in remaining coconut milk (below).

3 In the skillet combine coconut milk mixture, potato soup, and vegetables. Bring to boiling, stirring occasionally. Add chicken breasts to the skillet. Cover and simmer for 15 to 20 minutes or until chicken is tender and no longer pink (170°F). If desired, sprinkle with toasted coconut before serving. Makes 6 servings.

Per serving: 379 cal., 21 g total fat (13 g sat. fat), 123 mg chol., 760 mg sodium, 13 g carbo., 2 g fiber, 34 g pro.

1 Place 1 teaspoon curry paste in a bowl with about 1 to 2 tablespoons of the coconut milk. Use a wire whisk to stir the mixture until lumps are gone.

2 Whisk more of the coconut milk into the curry paste mixture to combine. Once all of the lumps are out, pour in the remaining coconut milk and stir well.

Ask Mom What is coconut milk? page 272 / How do I toast coconut? page 65 / What does simmer mean? page 79 / How do I use a meat/instant-read thermometer? page 74

Rosemary Chicken
With Vegetables

1 5.8-ounce package quick-cooking couscous

4 skinless, boneless chicken breast halves (1 to 1$\frac{1}{4}$ pounds total)

$\frac{1}{2}$ teaspoon lemon-pepper seasoning

1 tablespoon olive oil

2 cloves garlic, minced

2 medium zucchini and/or yellow summer squash, halved lengthwise
   and cut crosswise into $\frac{1}{4}$-inch-thick slices (2$\frac{1}{2}$ cups)

$\frac{1}{2}$ cup apple juice

2 teaspoons snipped fresh rosemary or $\frac{1}{2}$ teaspoon dried rosemary, crushed

$\frac{1}{4}$ teaspoon salt

2 tablespoons dry white wine or apple juice

2 teaspoons cornstarch

12 cherry tomatoes, halved (1 cup)

   Fresh rosemary sprigs (optional)

1 Prepare couscous according to package directions; keep warm. Sprinkle chicken with lemon-pepper seasoning. In a 10-inch skillet cook chicken in hot oil over medium heat for 12 to 15 minutes or until chicken is no longer pink, turning twice. (Reduce heat to medium low if chicken gets too brown.) Remove chicken from the skillet; cover and keep warm.

2 Add garlic to the skillet; cook and stir for 15 seconds. Add zucchini, apple juice, rosemary, and salt. Bring to boiling; reduce heat. Simmer, covered, for 2 minutes.

3 In a small bowl stir together wine and cornstarch until smooth; add to zucchini mixture in skillet. Cook and stir until thickened and bubbly; cook and stir for 2 minutes more. Stir in tomatoes. Serve vegetables and couscous with chicken. If desired, garnish with rosemary sprigs. Makes 4 servings.

Per serving: 377 cal., 6 g total fat (1 g sat. fat), 82 mg chol., 378 mg sodium, 38 g carbo., 3 g fiber, 39 g pro.

Ask Mom What is couscous? page 149 / What is a garlic clove? page 40 / How do I mince garlic? page 40 / How do I crush dried herbs? page 78 / What is summer squash? page 54 / How do I slice summer squash/zucchini? page 54 / How do I snip fresh herbs? pages 42, 328 / What is a cherry tomato? page 52 / What does simmer mean? page 79 / What does garnish mean? page 79

HOW DO I USE FRESH ROSEMARY? The best way to get the aromatic leaves off the woody stem is to hold the stem at the top and, moving down the stem, strip the leaves off with your fingers. Then snip them into smaller pieces in a cup with kitchen scissors.

WHAT'S THE BEST OIL TO USE FOR STIR-FRY? Use any kind of cooking oil, but peanut oil is ideal. It can reach a higher temperature than other oils before it starts smoking. Flash frying is the key to a good stir-fry—vegetables stay flavorful and crisp-tender.

Ginger Chicken Stir-Fry (see recipe, page 268)

Pass a bottle of soy sauce at the table—and maybe a shaker of crushed red pepper flakes, so people can sprinkle a little fire on their stir-fry, if they'd like. Chopped cashews or peanuts add crunch and flavor to the finished dish.

Wok This Way

If you do a lot of stir-frying, you might want to invest in a wok—the traditionally round-bottomed pan used in Chinese cooking. Woks sold in this country have flat bottoms (or rings to sit over a gas burner). The gentle, sloping sides of the pan allow you to cook in stages. The sides serve as a resting place to get ingredients up and out of the hot spot—the oil in the bottom of the pan—so that nothing gets overcooked.

Ginger Chicken Stir-Fry

1¼ cups sliced zucchini (1 medium)

½ cup sliced carrot (1 medium)

½ cup sliced onion (1 medium)

1 small red sweet pepper, cut into strips (¾ cup)

2½ cups shredded green cabbage (about half of a small cabbage head)

1 tablespoon cooking oil or peanut oil

12 ounces skinless, boneless chicken breast halves or turkey tenderloins, cut into 1-inch pieces

½ cup bottled stir-fry sauce

½ teaspoon ground ginger

3 to 4 cups hot cooked white or brown rice

¾ cup chopped cocktail peanuts or cashews

1 In a 12-inch skillet or wok cook and stir half of the zucchini, carrot, onion, pepper, and cabbage in hot oil over medium-high heat for about 2 minutes or until crisp-tender. Remove vegetables from the skillet. Repeat with remaining vegetables; remove from the skillet.

2 If necessary, add more oil to the hot skillet. Add chicken to the skillet. Cook and stir for 3 to 5 minutes or until chicken is no longer pink. Push chicken from center of the skillet. Add stir-fry sauce and ginger to center of the skillet. Cook and stir until bubbly.

3 Return the vegetables to the skillet. Cook and stir about 1 minute more or until chicken-vegetable mixture is coated and heated through. Serve over rice. Sprinkle servings with chopped peanuts. Makes 6 servings.

Per serving: 355 cal., 14 g total fat (2 g sat. fat), 33 mg chol., 816 mg sodium, 37 g carbo., 5 g fiber, 22 g pro.

Good to Know For the best, fluffiest white rice, combine one part rice to two parts water in a covered saucepan (1 cup of rice and 2 cups of water makes about 3 cups of cooked rice). Bring the water to a boil, then turn the heat to low and let the rice cook until all of the water is absorbed (no peeking—or you'll let out the valuable steam!), usually about 14 or 15 minutes. Let the rice sit off the heat, covered, to absorb the last of the liquid and fluff it with a fork before serving.

Ask Mom How do I prepare summer squash/zucchini? page 54 / How do I peel and cut carrots? pages 37, 64 / How do I slice an onion? page 47 / How do I seed sweet peppers and cut them into strips? page 49 / What is a wok? page 267 / What does it mean to stir-fry? page 69

Chicken and Spinach on Phyllo

Nonstick cooking spray

10 sheets frozen phyllo dough (14×9-inch rectangles), thawed according to package directions

8 medium green onions, cut into 2-inch pieces (1 cup)

1 tablespoon olive oil

12 ounces refrigerated grilled chicken breast strips (3 cups)

1 package (6-ounce) fresh baby spinach or 4 to 5 cups fresh spinach leaves

¾ cup halved or quartered cherry tomatoes (optional)

1 tablespoon snipped fresh tarragon

¼ teaspoon ground black pepper

½ cup bottled balsamic vinaigrette

1 Preheat oven to 425°F. Lightly coat a 15×10×1-inch baking pan with nonstick cooking spray; set aside. Roll stack of phyllo sheets into a cylinder shape (below). With a sharp knife cut phyllo roll crosswise into ¼- to ½-inch strips (below). Gently separate phyllo into strips and spread evenly in the prepared baking pan. Coat phyllo generously with additional nonstick cooking spray (below). Bake, uncovered, in the preheated for 6 to 8 minutes or until phyllo strips are golden brown, gently tossing twice during baking.

2 Meanwhile, in a 12-inch skillet cook green onion in hot oil over medium-high heat about 1 minute or just until tender. Add chicken strips; cook and stir until heated through. Remove skillet from heat. Add spinach, tomatoes (if desired), tarragon, and pepper. Toss to combine.

3 Divide phyllo strips among 6 bowls. Spoon chicken mixture over phyllo. Drizzle with balsamic vinaigrette. Serve immediately. Makes 6 servings.

Per serving: 197 cal., 10 g total fat (2 g sat. fat), 40 mg chol., 760 mg sodium, 14 g carbo., 1 g fiber, 14 g pro.

ove thawed phyllo n the package. stack onto a flat ghtly roll the sheets der shape.

2 Working quickly so the phyllo dough doesn't dry out, use a sharp knife to cut the roll into slices.

3 Carefully separate the phyllo slices into individual strips. Spread phyllo strips onto the sprayed pan; coat with additional cooking spray.

4 Toss the phyllo strips occasionally during baking to obtain an even color and prevent burning.

Ask Mom How do I slice green onions? page 43 / What is a cherry tomato? page 52 / How do I snip fresh herbs? pages 42, 328 / What does it mean to toss? page 77 / What does drizzle mean? page 79

WAY BEYOND MEXICAN. Quesadillas are incredibly versatile—you can fill them with almost anything and have them for breakfast, lunch, dinner, or a snack. Consider combos like Brie and dried cherries or mozzarella, arugula, and sliced kalamata olives.

Crown your quesadillas with spoonfuls of salsa, sour cream, and sliced green onions. Or serve the toppings on the side.

1 Skill Level

Barbecue Quesadillas

Nonstick cooking spray
4 7- or 8-inch flour tortillas
1 cup shredded extra-sharp cheddar cheese or Mexican cheese blend (4 ounces)
1 4-ounce can diced green chiles, drained
1 18-ounce tub refrigerated barbecue sauce with shredded chicken (2 cups)
1 cup bottled salsa
¼ cup dairy sour cream
¼ cup sliced green onion (2)

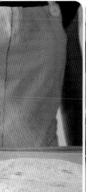

Good to Know
Spraying the tortillas with cooking spray serves two functions here—it keeps them from sticking to the hot pan and gives them nice crispy exteriors that give way to the gooey centers after they are cooked. Yum!

271

Quick Meat Meals

1 Coat one side of each tortilla with cooking spray. Place, coated sides down, on cutting board or waxed paper. Sprinkle ¼ cup of the cheese over half of each tortilla. Top with green chiles and barbecue sauce with chicken. Fold tortillas in half, pressing gently.

2 Preheat oven to 350°F. In a hot 10-inch skillet cook quesadillas, two at a time, over medium heat for 6 to 8 minutes or until golden brown, turning once. Place quesadillas on a baking sheet. Keep warm in preheated oven for up to 30 minutes. Repeat with remaining quesadillas. Cut each quesadilla into 3 wedges. Serve with salsa, sour cream, and green onion. Makes 4 servings.

Per serving: 469 cal., 21 g total fat (10 g sat. fat), 86 mg chol., 1,606 mg sodium, 44 g carbo., 2 g fiber, 25 g pro.

Turkey-Havarti Quesadillas: Prepare as above, except coat the unsprayed side of each tortilla with 2 teaspoons stone-ground mustard. Substitute Havarti cheese for the cheddar and 16 ounces cooked sliced turkey for the chicken. Omit green chiles, salsa, sour cream, and green onion.

Bacon, Tomato, and Avocado Quesadillas: Prepare as above, except substitute Monterey Jack cheese for the cheddar; use 8 crisp-cooked and crumbled bacon slices, 2 small seeded and coarsely chopped tomatoes, and 1 seeded, peeled, and chopped avocado for the filling. Omit green chiles, barbecue sauce with chicken, salsa, sour cream, and green onion.

e tortillas on waxed spray one side of nonstick spray. rtillas over.

2 Top half of the uncoated side of each tortilla with cheese, green chiles, and barbecue sauce with chicken.

3 Fold each tortilla in half and press down gently. Cook quesadillas until golden brown.

4 Place quesadillas on a cutting board. Using a sharp knife, cut each into three wedges.

Ask Mom How do I shred cheese? page 71 / How do I slice green onions? page 43 / How do I seed tomatoes? page 52 / How do I chop a tomato? page 52 / How do I cook bacon? page 172 / How do I seed and peel an avocado? page 36

Oriental Chicken
And Noodle Bowl

- I 2- to 2.25-pound deli-roasted chicken or 2 cups chopped cooked turkey
- I 14-ounce can chicken broth
- I cup unsweetened coconut milk
- I cup chopped broccoli
- I cup red sweet pepper strips (I medium)
- I cup sliced bok choy
- I 3-ounce package ramen noodles (any flavor), broken apart slightly
- I cup halved snow pea pods (cut crosswise)
- I teaspoon grated fresh ginger
- ½ teaspoon toasted sesame oil

1 Remove the meat from chicken (discard skin and bones) (see photos 1 and 2, page 395). Chop meat; reserve 2 cups. Cover remaining chicken and chill or freeze for another use.

2 In a 3-quart saucepan stir together broth, coconut milk, broccoli, sweet pepper, and bok choy. Bring to boiling. Stir in ramen noodles (discard seasoning packet); reduce heat. Simmer, covered, for 3 minutes. Stir in chicken, pea pods, ginger, and sesame oil; heat through. To serve, divide noodle mixture and broth among 4 shallow bowls. Makes 4 servings.

Per serving: 480 cal., 25 g total fat (13 g sat. fat), 110 mg chol., 539 mg sodium, 21 g carbo., 2 g fiber, 41 g pro.

Oriental Pork and Noodle Bowl: Prepare as above, except substitute 2 cups chopped cooked pork for the chicken.

SHOPPING SAVVY Be sure you buy unsweetened coconut milk for this recipe. Look for it in the baking aisle of your supermarket or in the Asian section. You can use the light coconut milk—your sauce will be slightly less thick than if you use the regular kind.

Ask Mom How do I seed sweet peppers and cut them into strips? page 49 / How do I trim and cut broccoli? page 36 / What is bok choy? page 201 / What is fresh ginger? page 41 / How do I grate fresh ginger? page 41 / What does simmer mean? page 79 / What is toasted sesame oil? page 138

(2) Skill Level

Mediterranean Pizza Skillet

3 medium skinless, boneless chicken breast halves, cut into ¾-inch pieces

2 cloves garlic, minced

2 tablespoons olive oil

4 roma tomatoes, chopped

1 14-ounce can quartered artichoke hearts, drained

1 2.25-ounce can sliced, pitted ripe olives, drained

½ teaspoon dried Italian seasoning, crushed

¼ teaspoon ground black pepper

2 cups romaine lettuce or mesclun mix, chopped

1 cup crumbled feta cheese (4 ounces)

⅓ cup fresh basil leaves, shredded or torn

Sliced crusty Italian or French bread, toasted

Ingredient Info
Mesclun—from the French "mescla," or "to mix"—is a blend of young lettuces and baby greens that might include arugula, spinach, frisée, Swiss chard, mustard greens, endive, and dandelion. It is fabulously flavorful and incredibly good for you. You can buy it prebagged or in bulk.

1 In a 10-inch skillet cook and stir chicken and garlic in hot oil over medium heat for 3 to 5 minutes or until chicken is brown. Stir in tomato, artichoke hearts, olives, Italian seasoning, and pepper. Bring to boiling; reduce heat. Simmer, covered, about 10 minutes or until chicken is no longer pink. Top with lettuce and cheese. Cook, covered, for 1 to 2 minutes more or until lettuce starts to wilt. Sprinkle with basil and serve on or with bread. Makes 4 servings.

Per serving: 395 cal., 17 g total fat (6 g sat. fat), 82 mg chol., 1,003 mg sodium, 27 g carbo., 6 g fiber, 33 g pro.

Ask Mom What is a garlic clove? page 40 / How do I mince garlic? page 40 / What is a roma tomato? page 52 / How do I chop a tomato? page 52 / How do I crumble cheese? pages 71, 96 / How do I crush dried herbs? page 78 / How do I shred fresh herbs/spinach? page 42 / What does simmer mean? page 79

German-Style Turkey Sausage Skillet

Good to Know
Celebrate Oktoberfest in style. Invite a few friends over for this sweet-sour dish, some dark rye bread, and cold beer—and have some rousing polka music playing in the background. "Prost!" (Or for you non-German speakers, "Cheers!")

½ cup sliced onion (1 medium)
1 tablespoon cooking oil
2 tablespoons all-purpose flour
1 cup apple cider or apple juice
½ cup chicken broth
2 tablespoons stone-ground mustard
1 20-ounce package refrigerated red potato wedges
1 pound cooked smoked turkey sausage, cut into bite-size slices
1 14-ounce can Bavarian-style sauerkraut*
¼ cup dried cranberries (optional)

1 In a 12-inch skillet cook and stir onion in hot oil over medium-high heat for about 8 minutes or until tender. Sprinkle with flour. Cook and stir for 2 minutes.

2 Stir in apple cider, broth, and mustard. Add potato wedges, sausage pieces, and sauerkraut. Bring to boiling; reduce heat. Simmer, covered, about 20 minutes or until thickened and bubbly and potatoes are tender. If desired, stir cranberries into the sausage mixture. Spoon sausage mixture into dishes; serve immediately. Makes 6 servings.

*Note: If Bavarian-style sauerkraut is unavailable, substitute one 14.5-ounce can sauerkraut plus 2 tablespoons packed brown sugar and ½ teaspoon caraway seeds.

Per serving: 269 cal., 10 g total fat (2 g sat. fat), 50 mg chol., 2,552 mg sodium, 30 g carbo., 3 g fiber, 14 g pro.

market-fresh
FISH
& SHELLFISH

The catch of the day is whatever you want. Be fearless and cook some fish. It's simple, delicious, and good for you.

7

2 Skill Level

Tilapia Fillets with Lemon-Tarragon Sauce

Shopping Savvy
Fish—like most other foods—is best fresh rather than frozen. To get the very best fresh fillets, look for those that are firm and moist and that smell like the ocean (they shouldn't smell fishy). If you can, get center-cut fish, not tail pieces. They're thicker and meatier than the tail and won't dry out when cooked.

1½ pounds fresh or frozen tilapia fillets or other lean white fish fillets, ½ to ¾ inch thick

1 teaspoon seasoned salt

1 tablespoon olive oil

1 tablespoon butter or margarine

¼ cup dry white wine or chicken broth

1 tablespoon lemon juice

1 teaspoon Dijon-style mustard

1 teaspoon snipped fresh tarragon or ¼ teaspoon dried tarragon, crushed

1 recipe Spinach Orzo

1 Thaw fish, if frozen. Rinse fish; pat dry with paper towels (below). Cut into four serving-size pieces, if necessary (see photo 1, page 278). Sprinkle both sides of fish with seasoned salt. In a 12-inch skillet heat oil and butter over medium heat. Add fish in a single layer, frying on one side until golden. Turn carefully; fry until second side is golden and fish flakes easily when tested with a fork (see photo, page 75). Allow 3 to 4 minutes per side. Transfer fish to a serving platter; keep warm.

2 For sauce, add wine and lemon juice to the skillet. To deglaze the skillet, use a whisk to scrape up any bits in the bottom of the skillet. Whisk in mustard and tarragon; heat through. Pour sauce over fish. Serve with Spinach Orzo. Makes 4 servings.

Spinach Orzo: Prepare 8 ounces dried orzo pasta according to package directions; drain. Return to pan; toss orzo with 5 or 6 cups baby spinach, 2 tablespoons olive oil, 2 teaspoons finely shredded lemon or orange peel, ¼ teaspoon salt, and freshly ground black pepper to taste.

Per serving: 512 cal., 17 g total fat (4 g sat. fat), 93 mg chol., 695 mg sodium, 45 g carbo., 3 g fiber, 43 g pro.

Tilapia Fillets with Orange-Basil Sauce: Prepare as above, except substitute orange juice for lemon juice and snipped fresh basil for tarragon.

1 Rinse fish briefly under cold running water.

2 Lay fish on paper towels and gently pat dry.

Ask Mom What other kinds of fish can I use? page 295 / How do I measure butter? pages 58, 59 / How do I juice a lemon? pages 30, 80 / What is Dijon-style mustard? page 379 / How do I snip fresh herbs? pages 42, 328 / How do I crush dried herbs? page 78 / How do I thaw fish? page 73 / What does panfry mean? page 68 / How do I deglaze a pan? page 70 / What is that pasta shape? pages 308–309 / How do I shred lemon peel? page 30 / How do I grind pepper? page 22

(2) Skill Level

Pan-Fried Fish

I pound fresh or frozen skinless white-fleshed fish fillets, $\frac{1}{2}$ to $\frac{3}{4}$ inch thick

I egg, lightly beaten

$\frac{2}{3}$ cup cornmeal or fine dry bread crumbs

$\frac{1}{2}$ teaspoon salt

Dash ground black pepper

Cooking oil for frying

1 Thaw fish, if frozen. Rinse fish; pat dry with paper towels (see photos, page 277). Cut into four serving-size pieces (below). In a shallow dish combine egg and 2 tablespoons *water*. In another shallow dish stir together cornmeal, salt, and pepper. Dip fish into egg mixture; coat fish with cornmeal mixture (below).

2 In a 10-inch skillet heat $\frac{1}{4}$ inch oil over medium heat for 10 minutes. Add half of the fish in a single layer (below), frying on one side until golden. Turn carefully; fry until second side is golden (page 279) and fish flakes easily when tested with a fork (see photo, page 75). Allow 3 to 4 minutes per side. Drain on paper towels. Keep warm in a 300°F oven while frying remaining fish. Makes 4 servings.

Per serving: 355 cal., 20 g total fat (3 g sat. fat), 102 mg chol., 370 mg sodium, 18 g carbo., 2 g fiber, 24 g pro.

Crispy Pecan Pan-Fried Fish: Prepare as above, except substitute $1\frac{1}{4}$ cups finely crushed corn-flakes (about 4 cups cornflakes) or cheese-flavored crackers (about $2\frac{1}{2}$ cups crackers) and $\frac{1}{4}$ cup finely chopped pecans (about $\frac{1}{3}$ cup pecans) for the cornmeal.

Potato Chip Pan-Fried Fish: Prepare as above, except substitute $1\frac{1}{3}$ cups finely crushed potato chips (about 4 cups chips) for the cornmeal and omit salt.

Pretzel-Coated Pan-Fried Fish: Prepare as above, except substitute $1\frac{1}{3}$ cups finely crushed pretzel sticks (about 4 cups pretzels) for the cornmeal and omit the salt.

1 If necessary, cut large fillets into serving-size pieces—about 4 ounces each.

2 Dip fish in egg mixture, turning to coat both sides.

3 After dipping in the egg mixture, press both sides of fish into cornmeal mixture.

4 Place fish in hot oil single layer. Don't crowd pan or fish won't be crisp

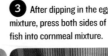
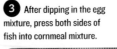

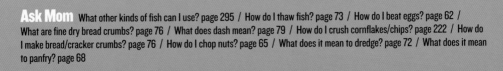

Ask Mom What other kinds of fish can I use? page 295 / How do I thaw fish? page 73 / How do I beat eggs? page 62 / What are fine dry bread crumbs? page 76 / What does dash mean? page 79 / How do I crush cornflakes/chips? page 222 / How do I make bread/cracker crumbs? page 76 / How do I chop nuts? page 65 / What does it mean to dredge? page 72 / What does it mean to panfry? page 68

WHAT KIND OF OIL SHOULD I USE? You can use any kind of cooking oil for panfrying—vegetable, corn, canola, sunflower, or safflower. Or try peanut oil. It can reach higher temperatures without burning than other oils. Hotter oil means crispier fish.

5 When the fish is golden brown on the bottom, use tongs to carefully turn it to brown the other side. Fish fillets get very flaky and delicate when cooked. Only turn them once so they do not fall apart.

IT'S FRESH AND LIGHT, ALL RIGHT. There are too many good reasons to eat fish to list them all. But here's a start: It's simple and quick to cook. It's good for you (you've heard about those heart-healthy oils). Best of all, it's absolutely delicious.

Skill Level

Sesame-Crusted
Salmon

1 pound fresh or frozen skinless salmon or halibut fillets

½ cup mayonnaise

⅓ cup chopped roasted red sweet pepper

2 teaspoons lemon juice

1 teaspoon snipped fresh chives

   Salt and ground black pepper

⅓ cup all-purpose flour

1 tablespoon white sesame seeds

1 tablespoon black sesame seeds

¼ teaspoon salt

¼ cup milk

2 tablespoons cooking oil

   Lemon or lime wedges (optional)

   Fresh watercress (optional)

Ingredient Info Sesame seeds can be natural, hulled, or black. The hulled white seeds are the most common. Light brown sesame seeds have their outer bran layer still intact. They can be found at natural food stores. Black sesame seeds are frequently used in Chinese and Indian cooking—look for them in ethnic markets. If you can't find black, use all white seeds in this recipe.

1 Thaw fish, if frozen. Rinse fish; pat dry with paper towels (see photos, page 277). Cut into four serving-size pieces, if necessary (see photo 1, page 278). Set aside.

2 For sauce, in a small bowl stir together mayonnaise, red sweet pepper, lemon juice, and chives. Season with salt and black pepper. Cover and chill until serving time.

3 In a shallow dish bowl stir together the flour, white sesame seeds, black sesame seeds, and ¼ teaspoon salt. Place milk in a second shallow dish. Dip salmon in milk. Firmly press both sides of fish in flour mixture.

4 In a 10-inch skillet cook fish in hot oil over medium-high heat for 4 to 5 minutes per side or until fish flakes easily when tested with a fork (see photo, page 75). Serve sauce with fish. If desired, garnish with lemon wedges and fresh watercress. Makes 4 servings.

Make-ahead directions: Prepare sauce; cover and chill for up to 24 hours. Prepare fish as directed above. Stir sauce before serving; if necessary, stir in a little extra water.

Per serving: 539 cal., 44 g total fat (8 g sat. fat), 78 mg chol., 404 mg sodium, 10 g carbo., 1 g fiber, 25 g pro.

Ask Mom What other kinds of fish can I use? page 295 / How do I thaw fish? page 73 / How do I roast sweet peppers? page 67 / How do I juice a lemon/lime? pages 30, 80 / How much juice does one lemon/lime yield? page 30 / How do I snip fresh herbs? page 42 / How do I cut lemon/lime wedges? page 30 / What does it mean to dredge? page 72 / What does it mean to panfry? page 68 / What does garnish mean? page 79

Fish with Roma Relish

1 pound fresh or frozen skinless fish fillets (orange roughy, cod, flounder, catfish, or trout)
　Salt and freshly ground black pepper
3 tablespoons lemon juice
　Olive oil
2 medium roma tomatoes, halved lengthwise
1 19-ounce can cannellini beans (white kidney beans), rinsed and drained
2 thin slices prosciutto or cooked ham, cut into thin strips
1 tablespoon olive oil
1 clove garlic, minced
1 teaspoon snipped fresh rosemary or $\frac{1}{4}$ teaspoon dried rosemary, crushed
　Lemon wedges

1 Thaw fish, if frozen. Rinse fish; pat dry with paper towels (see photos, page 277). Cut into four serving-size pieces, if necessary (see photo 1, page 278). Measure thickness of fish. Sprinkle fish with salt and pepper; drizzle with 1 tablespoon of the lemon juice. Set aside.

2 Heat a 12-inch nonstick grill pan or skillet over medium heat. Brush tomatoes lightly with olive oil. Add tomato halves to grill pan, cut sides down (below). Cook for 6 to 8 minutes or until tomatoes are very tender, turning once. Remove from pan; set aside.

3 Add fish to grill pan. Cook until fish flakes easily when tested with a fork (see photo, page 75), turning once halfway through cooking. (Allow 4 to 6 minutes per $\frac{1}{2}$-inch thickness.)

4 Coarsely chop tomatoes (below). In a serving bowl gently toss together tomatoes, remaining 2 tablespoons lemon juice, the beans, prosciutto, the 1 tablespoon olive oil, the garlic, rosemary, and $\frac{1}{8}$ teaspoon *salt*. Serve fish with bean mixture and lemon wedges. Makes 4 servings.

Per serving: 221 cal., 5 g total fat (1 g sat. fat), 74 mg chol., 684 mg sodium, 21 g carbo., 7 g fiber, 29 g pro.

1 Using a pastry brush, brush both sides of tomatoes with oil. Start grilling with cut sides down.

2 While the fish cooks, coarsely chop the tomatoes. Combine them with remaining relish ingredients.

3 Serve the fish alongside or right on top of the roma relish. Add a lemon wedge to squeeze over top of the fish.

Ask Mom What other kinds of fish can I use? page 295 / How do I thaw fish? page 73 / How do I grind pepper? page 22 / How do I juice a lemon? pages 30, 80 / How do I rinse and drain canned beans? page 390 / What is prosciutto? page 358 / What is a garlic clove? page 40 / How do I mince garlic? page 40 / How do I snip fresh herbs? pages 42, 328 / How do I crush dried herbs? page 78 / How do I cut lemon wedges? page 30 / What does drizzle mean? page 79 / What does it mean to toss? page 77

Margarita Fish Tacos
With Mango Salsa

- 1 pound fresh or frozen swordfish, halibut, or mahi mahi steaks, cut 1 inch thick
- ½ cup margarita drink mix (no alcohol)
- 1 teaspoon Jamaican jerk seasoning
- 1 15-ounce can black beans, rinsed and drained
- 1 large mango, seeded, peeled, and chopped (1 cup)
- ¾ cup chopped seeded tomato (1 large)
- 2 to 4 tablespoons snipped fresh cilantro
- 2 tablespoons thinly sliced green onion (1)
- 1 fresh jalapeño chile pepper, seeded and chopped
- 1 tablespoon lime juice
- ½ teaspoon ancho chile powder* or regular chili powder
- ¼ teaspoon salt
- 1 tablespoon cooking oil
- 8 6-inch flour or corn tortillas
- 2 cups shredded fresh leaf lettuce or spinach

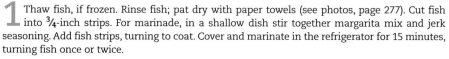

1 Thaw fish, if frozen. Rinse fish; pat dry with paper towels (see photos, page 277). Cut fish into ¾-inch strips. For marinade, in a shallow dish stir together margarita mix and jerk seasoning. Add fish strips, turning to coat. Cover and marinate in the refrigerator for 15 minutes, turning fish once or twice.

2 Meanwhile, for salsa, in a large bowl stir together the beans, mango, tomato, cilantro, green onion, jalapeño pepper, lime juice, ancho chile powder, and salt. Set aside.

3 Drain fish, discarding marinade. In a 10-inch skillet cook fish in hot oil over medium heat for 2 to 4 minutes or until fish flakes easily when tested with a fork (see photo, page 75), turning fish occasionally. Meanwhile, heat tortillas according to package directions. Fill tortillas with lettuce, fish strips, and mango salsa. Serve immediately. Makes 4 servings.

*Note: Ancho chile powder is made from ground ancho chiles (dried poblanos). It has a darker color and spicier flavor than regular chili powder. Find it with the spices in your supermarket.

Make-ahead directions: The salsa can be made ahead and chilled for up to 2 hours. If chilled, it should be allowed to stand at room temperature for 30 minutes before serving for best flavor and so it doesn't chill the fish when you add it to the tacos.

Per serving: 522 cal., 16 g total fat (2 g sat. fat), 43 mg chol., 580 mg sodium, 58 g carbo., 7 g fiber, 36 g pro.

Fish Tostadas: Prepare as above, except substitute 8 corn tostada shells for the flour tortillas. Top tostada shells with lettuce, fish strips, and salsa.

Ask Mom What other kinds of fish can I use? page 295 / How do I thaw fish? page 73 / How do I rinse and drain canned beans? page 390 / How do I prepare a mango? page 88 / How do I seed and chop tomatoes? page 52 / How do I snip fresh herbs? pages 42, 328 / How do I slice green onions? page 43 / How do I handle hot chile peppers? page 48 / How do I juice a lime? pages 30, 80 / How do I shred spinach? page 42 / What does it mean to marinate? page 73 / What does it mean to panfry? page 68

② Skill Level

Good to Know
Neapolitan fishermen
used to poach the catch
of the day in "acqua
pazza," or "crazy water,"
a concoction of salty
seawater, tomatoes, and
olive oil. This modern
version calls for white
wine and sweet peppers.
How much crushed red
pepper you use depends
on how "crazy" you like
your food!

Halibut in Crazy Water

    4 fresh or frozen halibut steaks (1½ to 1¾ pounds)
      or 4 cod or other whitefish fillets
      Salt and freshly ground black pepper
 1½ cups dry white wine or chicken broth
    1 cup water
 1½ cups chopped yellow sweet pepper (2 medium)
    3 tablespoons capers, drained
    4 cloves garlic, minced
   ¼ to ½ teaspoon crushed red pepper
    2 tablespoons olive oil
      Coarsely snipped fresh parsley

1 Thaw fish, if frozen. Rinse fish; pat dry with paper towels (see photos, page 277). Measure thickness of fish. Season fish with salt and black pepper; set aside.

2 For crazy water, in a 12-inch skillet stir together wine, water, sweet pepper, capers, garlic, and crushed red pepper. Bring to boiling; reduce heat. Simmer, uncovered, for 7 minutes, stirring occasionally.

3 Add fish to the crazy water in a single layer. Spoon liquid over fish (below). Return to a simmer. Cook, covered, for 4 to 6 minutes per ½-inch thickness or until fish flakes easily when tested with a fork (see photo, page 75).

4 Using a slotted spatula, transfer fish to a platter; spoon sweet peppers and capers over fish. Pour crazy water into a serving pitcher. Drizzle cooked fish with the olive oil and a little of the crazy water. Sprinkle with parsley. Serve with remaining crazy water. Makes 4 servings.

Per serving: 338 cal., 11 g total fat (1 g sat. fat), 54 mg chol., 437 mg sodium, 8 g carbo., 1 g fiber, 37 g pro.

1 After adding fish to the skillet, spoon crazy water, peppers, and capers over the fish.

2 Bring the water back to a simmer, then cover the pan. The fish will poach in the water and won't need turning.

3 Spoon sweet peppers and capers over the fish on a serving platter. Drizzle with additional crazy water.

Ask Mom What other kinds of fish can I use? page 295 / How do I thaw fish? page 73 / How do I freshly grind pepper? page 22 / How do I seed and chop sweet peppers? page 49 / What are capers? page 79 / What is a garlic clove? page 40 / How do I mince garlic? page 40 / How do I snip fresh herbs? pages 42, 328 / What does poach mean? page 79 / What does simmer mean? page 79

Cold Roasted Salmon

Olive oil

6 6-ounce center-cut salmon fillets, skinned

2 tablespoons peppercorn or tarragon mustard

6 slices bacon, crisp-cooked, drained, and coarsely crumbled

3 ounces goat cheese (chèvre), crumbled

Snipped fresh chives (optional)

1 Preheat oven to 475°F. Lightly oil a 15×10×1-inch baking pan with olive oil. Arrange salmon fillets in prepared pan. Turn under any thin portions of fillets to make uniform thickness. Spread mustard over tops of fillets.

2 Roast in the preheated oven for 15 to 18 minutes or until fish flakes easily when tested with a fork (see photo, page 75). Transfer to a plate; cover and chill for at least 4 hours or up to 24 hours.

3 To serve, arrange salmon in a serving dish. Sprinkle salmon with bacon, goat cheese, and, if desired, chives. Makes 4 servings.

Per serving: 407 cal., 26 g total fat (8 g sat. fat), 118 mg chol., 387 mg sodium, 1 g carbo., 0 g fiber, 40 g pro.

Roasted Salmon Sandwiches: Prepare as above, except divide salmon among 4 French rolls that have been spread with mayonnaise and mustard. Top with bacon, goat cheese, and chives.

Good to Know Salmon is one of those foods that is every bit as good cold as it is hot (ever had gravlax or smoked salmon?). This makes a terrific main course on a warm summer night. Chill the serving dish for an hour or so in the refrigerator before you put the salmon on it to keep the fish cool as a cucumber.

Ask Mom What does it mean to roast? page 68 / How do I cook bacon? page 172 / How do I crumble cheese? pages 71, 96 / How do I snip fresh herbs? pages 42, 328 / How do I grease a baking pan/dish? page 61

Asian Salmon with Oven-Roasted Sweet Potatoes

1 1¾-pound fresh or frozen salmon fillet, skinned
2 pounds sweet potatoes (4 medium)
1 tablespoon cooking oil
2 tablespoons toasted sesame oil
   Salt and ground black pepper
⅓ cup reduced-sodium bottled teriyaki sauce
2 cloves garlic, minced
2 tablespoons apricot or peach preserves
2 tablespoons dry sherry or orange juice
2 teaspoons grated fresh ginger
1 teaspoon Dijon-style mustard
¼ teaspoon freshly ground black pepper
¼ cup sliced green onion (2)
1 tablespoon sesame seeds, toasted

1 Thaw fish, if frozen. Rinse fish; pat dry with paper towels (see photos, page 277). Set aside.

2 Preheat oven to 425°F. Peel sweet potatoes. Cut into 1½-inch chunks. In a large bowl combine potatoes, cooking oil, and 1 tablespoon of the sesame oil. Sprinkle lightly with salt and pepper. Toss to coat. Place sweet potatoes in a large roasting pan. Roast, uncovered, in the preheated oven for 15 minutes.

3 Meanwhile, in a 1-quart saucepan stir together the remaining 1 tablespoon sesame oil, the teriyaki sauce, garlic, apricot preserves, dry sherry, ginger, mustard, and the ¼ teaspoon pepper. Bring to boiling; reduce heat. Simmer, uncovered, about 5 minutes or until slightly thickened, stirring occasionally. Reserve ¼ cup sauce.

4 Push sweet potatoes to the edges of the roasting pan; place salmon fillet in center. Spoon remaining sauce over salmon and potatoes.

5 Roast, uncovered, for 20 to 25 minutes or until fish flakes easily when tested with a fork (see photo, page 75). Carefully transfer fish and potatoes to a serving platter. Drizzle with reserved sauce. Sprinkle with green onion and sesame seeds. Makes 4 servings.

Per serving: 470 cal., 22 g total fat (4 g sat. fat), 77 mg chol., 500 mg sodium, 35 g carbo., 5 g fiber, 30 g pro.

Ask Mom What does it mean to roast? page 68 / What other kinds of fish can I use? page 295 / How do I thaw fish? page 73 / How do I prepare potatoes? page 51 / What is toasted sesame oil? page 138 / How do I mince garlic? page 40 / How do I grate fresh ginger? page 41 / What is Dijon-style mustard? page 379 / How do I freshly grind pepper? page 22 / How do I slice green onions? page 43 / How do I toast sesame seeds? page 65 / What does it mean to toss? page 77 / What do simmer/drizzle mean? page 79

HOW DO I SKIN A SALMON FILLET? Lay the fillet, skin side down, on a flat surface. Using a long thin knife, make a small cut at one end of the fillet to separate the skin from the flesh. Grasp the flap of skin and slide the knife under the fillet all the way to the end.

Sure, the sliced green onions and sesame seeds look pretty. But garnishes like this go more than skin deep: The cool, fresh crunch of the green onions and the nutty flavor of the sesame seeds provide a palate-tickling contrast to the warm, slightly sweet salmon.

Crispy Fish and Vegetables

4 6-ounce fresh or frozen skinless white sea bass, catfish, or tilapia fillets, about $\frac{1}{2}$ inch thick

4 ounces fresh haricots verts (young green beans)

1 small zucchini or yellow summer squash, cut in bite-size sticks (1 cup)

8 ounces cipolline onions, peeled and quartered, or 1 cup thinly sliced red onion

1 cup cherry or grape tomatoes, halved

2 tablespoons olive oil

$\frac{1}{4}$ teaspoon salt

$\frac{1}{4}$ teaspoon ground black pepper

$\frac{1}{3}$ cup fine dry bread crumbs

$\frac{1}{3}$ cup crushed plain potato chips

$\frac{1}{4}$ cup grated Parmesan cheese

$\frac{1}{2}$ teaspoon paprika

$\frac{1}{8}$ teaspoon cayenne pepper

2 tablespoons butter or margarine, melted

1 Thaw fish, if frozen. Rinse fish; pat dry with paper towels (see photos, page 277); set aside. If desired, trim haricots verts (see photo 1, page 126). In a small saucepan cook haricots verts in a small amount of boiling salted water for 5 minutes; drain.

2 Preheat oven to 450°F. In a 3-quart rectangular baking dish combine haricots verts, zucchini, onions, and tomatoes. Drizzle with olive oil and sprinkle with salt and black pepper; toss to coat. Spread vegetables in an even layer. Place fillets on top of vegetables.

3 In a small bowl stir together bread crumbs, potato chips, cheese, paprika, and cayenne pepper. Add melted butter; stir to combine. Top fillets evenly with crumb mixture, pressing it into fillets.

4 Bake, uncovered, in the preheated oven for 25 to 30 minutes or until fish flakes easily when tested with a fork (see photo, page 75). Makes 4 servings.

Per serving: 491 cal., 26 g total fat (9 g sat. fat), 89 mg chol., 736 mg sodium, 27 g carbo., 4 g fiber, 38 g pro.

Ingredient Info Cipolline (chee-poh-LEE-neh) onions are small, flat Italian onions that are about 2 inches in diameter. Technically they're not onions at all, rather the bulbs of the grape hyacinth. They have a rich, sweet flavor and are a fun seasonal thing to try—fresh cipolline onions are available in the supermarket in late summer and fall. They're sometimes labeled in the plural Italian as "cipollini."

Ask Mom What other kinds of fish can I use? page 295 / How do I thaw fish? page 73 / How do I prepare summer squash/zucchini? page 54 / How do I prepare an onion? page 47 / How do I slice an onion? page 47 / What is a cherry/grape tomato? page 52 / What are fine dry bread crumbs? page 76 / How do I crush cornflakes/chips? page 222 / How do I grate cheese? page 71 / How do I measure butter? pages 58, 59 / What does drizzle mean? page 79 / What does it mean to toss? page 77

Baked Trout in Wine Sauce

2   8- to 10-ounce fresh or frozen whole pan-dressed rainbow trout
2   cups sliced fresh button, shiitake (remove tough stems), or cremini mushrooms
½   cup finely chopped red sweet pepper
¼   cup chopped shallot or sliced green onion (2)
4   tablespoons butter or margarine
1   cup herb-seasoned stuffing mix
2   tablespoons snipped fresh parsley
½   teaspoon dried thyme, crushed
¼   teaspoon salt
¼   teaspoon ground black pepper
¾   cup dry white wine
¼   cup lemon juice

1 Preheat oven to 400°F. Thaw fish, if frozen. Rinse fish; pat dry with paper towels (see photos, page 277). Set aside. In a 10-inch skillet heat 3 tablespoons butter over medium heat. Cook and stir mushrooms, sweet pepper, and shallot in the hot butter about 5 minutes or until tender. Remove from heat. Stir in stuffing mix, parsley, thyme, salt, and pepper.

2 To stuff fish, sprinkle fish cavities lightly with additional salt. Spoon stuffing mixture into fish cavities (below). Loosely tie fish closed with 100-percent-cotton kitchen string (below). Place fish in a greased 2-quart rectangular baking dish. In the same skillet bring the remaining 1 tablespoon butter, the wine, and lemon juice to boiling. Pour over the fish.

3 Bake, uncovered, in the preheated oven about 35 minutes or until fish flakes easily when tested with a fork (see photo, page 75) and stuffing temperature reaches 160°F, spooning wine mixture over fish halfway through cooking. Makes 4 servings.

Per serving: 377 cal., 18 g total fat (9 g sat. fat), 97 mg chol., 472 mg sodium, 18 g carbo., 2 g fiber, 27 g pro.

1 Open pan-dressed fish and spoon stuffing down one side of cavity. Close fish.

2 Loosely tie fish with two or three pieces of kitchen string to keep the stuffing in.

Ask Mom What other fish can I use? page 295 / How do I thaw fish? page 73 / How do I slice mushrooms? page 45 / How do I seed/chop sweet peppers? page 49 / What is a shallot? page 46 / How do I chop onion? page 47 / How do I slice green onions? page 43 / How do I measure butter? pages 58, 59 / How do I snip fresh herbs? pages 42, 328 / How do I crush dried herbs? page 78 / How do I juice a lemon? pages 30, 80 / How do I grease a baking dish? page 61 / How do I use a thermometer? page 74

Glazed Fish

I pound fresh or frozen skinless fish steaks or fillets, I inch thick (salmon, halibut, sea bass, swordfish, tuna)

I recipe Asian Glaze, Maple-Balsamic Glaze, or Orange-Horseradish Glaze

I recipe Spinach Saute

1 Thaw fish, if frozen. Rinse fish; pat dry with paper towels (see photos, page 277). Cut fish into four serving-size pieces, if necessary (see photo 1, page 278). Set aside.

2 Preheat broiler. Prepare desired glaze. Place fish on the greased unheated rack of a broiler pan. Broil 4 to 5 inches from the heat (below) for 8 to 12 minutes or until fish flakes easily when tested with a fork (see photo, page 75), carefully turning once halfway through broiling time and brushing with glaze during the last 2 to 3 minutes of broiling time (below). While fish broils, prepare Spinach Saute. Serve fish with spinach. Makes 4 servings.

Asian Glaze: In a small bowl stir together 2 tablespoons bottled hoisin sauce, 1 tablespoon soy sauce, 1 teaspoon toasted sesame oil, 1 teaspoon grated fresh ginger, and 1 clove garlic, minced.

Maple-Balsamic Glaze: In a small bowl whisk together 3 tablespoons maple syrup, 1 tablespoon balsamic vinegar, and 1 to 2 teaspoons Dijon-style mustard.

Orange-Horseradish Glaze: In a small bowl stir together 3 tablespoons orange marmalade, 1 tablespoon fresh lime juice, and 1 teaspoon prepared horseradish.

Spinach Saute: In a 4-quart Dutch oven cook and stir 3 tablespoons pine nuts or chopped walnuts in 2 tablespoons hot olive oil over medium heat until golden. Using a slotted spoon, remove nuts from pan; set aside. Increase heat to medium high. To the Dutch oven, add 1 pound fresh spinach leaves, trimmed; saute for 1 to 2 minutes or just until wilted. Remove from heat. Add nuts, a dash of Worcestershire sauce or soy sauce, and salt and ground black pepper to taste.

Per serving with Asian Glaze: 369 cal., 25 g total fat (4 g sat. fat), 67 mg chol., 552 mg sodium, 9 g carbo., 3 g fiber, 28 g pro.

1 To grease a broiler pan, dip a brush in softened butter or shortening. Lightly brush the cold rack in the pan.

2 In a cold oven, place pan with fish on top oven rack. Adjust rack until surface of fish is 4 to 5 inches from the heat.

3 Pull the oven rack out of the oven before turning or brushing fish. The heating element is very hot, and it's easy to get burned if you try to reach in.

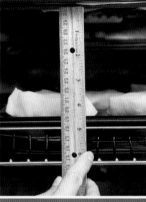
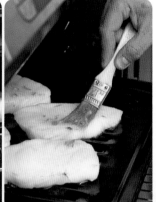

Ask Mom What other kinds of fish can I use? page 295 / How do I thaw fish? page 73 / What does broil mean? page 68 / What is toasted sesame oil? page 138 / How do I grate fresh ginger? page 41 / What is a garlic clove? page 40 / How do I mince garlic? page 40 / What is that vinegar? page 349 / What is Dijon-style mustard? page 379 / How do I juice a lemon/lime? pages 30, 80 / What is prepared horseradish? page 429 / What does it mean to saute? page 69 / What does dash mean? page 79

HOW DO I BROIL FISH?
The general rule for broiling fish is to cook it for about 10 minutes per inch of thickness. Measure fish at the thickest part and turn under any very thin edges to ensure even cooking. Watch carefully—it's easy to overcook.

This is the ultimate in flexible recipes. You can use salmon, halibut, sea bass, swordfish, or tuna and flavor it any way you like—with Asian, Maple-Balsamic, or Orange-Horseradish Glaze.

Broiled Fish Steaks
With Flavored Butter

  4 5- to 6-ounce fresh or frozen halibut, tuna, or salmon steaks, cut 1 inch thick
$\frac{1}{4}$ teaspoon salt
$\frac{1}{4}$ teaspoon ground black pepper
$\frac{1}{2}$ cup dry white wine or chicken broth
  1 recipe Tarragon Butter, Jalapeño-Lime Butter, or Lemon-Parsley-Caper Butter

1 Thaw fish, if frozen. Rinse fish; pat dry with paper towels (see photos, page 277). Sprinkle both sides of fish with salt and pepper. Place fish in a shallow baking dish. Add wine; cover and marinate in the refrigerator for 30 minutes, turning fish occasionally.

2 Preheat broiler. Remove fish from dish; discard wine. Arrange fish on the lightly greased unheated rack of a broiler pan. Broil 4 to 5 inches from heat for 8 to 12 minutes or until fish flakes easily when tested with a fork (see photo, page 75), turning once (see photos, page 290). Serve fish with flavored butter. Makes 4 servings.

Per serving (without butter): 180 cal., 3 g total fat (0 g sat. fat), 45 mg chol., 222 mg sodium, 1 g carbo., 0 g fiber, 30 g pro.

Tarragon Butter: In a small bowl stir together $\frac{1}{2}$ cup butter, softened, with 3 tablespoons snipped fresh tarragon. Place butter mixture on a piece of plastic wrap. Shape butter mixture into a 4×1$\frac{1}{2}$-inch log, lifting plastic wrap to help shape; twist ends of wrap to seal. Freeze for 30 minutes. Unwrap and slice to serve. Chill any leftover Tarragon Butter for up to 1 week or freeze for up to 3 months.

Jalapeño-Lime Butter: In a small bowl stir together $\frac{1}{2}$ cup butter, softened, with 3 tablespoons snipped fresh cilantro, 1 tablespoon finely chopped jalapeño chile pepper, and $\frac{1}{2}$ teaspoon finely shredded lime peel. Place butter mixture on a piece of plastic wrap. Shape butter mixture into a 4×1$\frac{1}{2}$-inch log, lifting plastic wrap to help shape; twist ends of wrap to seal. Freeze for 30 minutes. Unwrap and slice to serve. Chill any leftover Jalapeño-Lime Butter for up to 1 week or freeze for up to 3 months.

Lemon-Parsley-Caper Butter: In a small bowl stir together $\frac{1}{2}$ cup butter, softened, with 3 tablespoons snipped fresh parsley, 2 teaspoons drained capers, and $\frac{1}{2}$ teaspoon finely shredded lemon peel. Place butter mixture on a piece of plastic wrap. Shape butter mixture into a 4×1$\frac{1}{2}$-inch log, lifting plastic wrap to help shape; twist ends of wrap to seal. Freeze for 30 minutes. Unwrap and slice to serve. Chill any leftover Lemon-Parsley-Caper Butter for up to 1 week or freeze for up to 3 months.

Good to Know Flavored butters are a supereasy way to add an elegant touch to simple broiled fish. Obviously you don't have to use the whole recipe at any one meal—leftovers freeze beautifully. (Use it the next time you have fish—or on baked potatoes or warm bread.) Just slice off the desired amount and place on the hot fish. It melts to create its own sauce. Fabulous!

Ask Mom What other kinds of fish can I use? page 295 / How do I thaw fish? page 73 / What does it mean to marinate? page 73 / What does it mean to broil? page 68 / How do I measure butter? pages 58, 59 / How do I soften butter? page 59 / How do I snip fresh herbs? pages 42, 328 / How do I handle hot chile peppers? page 48 / How do I shred lemon/lime peel? page 30 / What are capers? page 79

Ingredient Info
Wasabi powder is a dried, pulverized, nose-tingling, head-clearing green horseradish used widely in Japanese cooking. (If you've ever had sushi, you've had it in paste form, accompanied by pink pickled ginger called "gari.") If you can't find it in the Asian section of your supermarket, look for it at Asian markets.

② Skill Level

Tuna Skewers with Vegetable Rice

  I pound fresh or frozen tuna or salmon steaks, bones and skin removed
 ½ cup bottled teriyaki sauce or other Asian marinade sauce
  2 tablespoons thinly sliced green onion (I)
I½ to 2 teaspoons wasabi powder
  2 cups water
  I cup uncooked brown rice
 ½ cup thinly sliced carrot (I medium)
  I medium red sweet pepper, cut into thin strips (I cup)
 ¼ teaspoon salt
  I cup broccoli florets

1 Thaw fish, if frozen. Rinse fish; pat dry with paper towels (see photos, page 277). Cut fish into ¼-inch-thick strips (below). In a small bowl combine teriyaki sauce, green onion, and wasabi powder. Place fish in a shallow dish; add half of the teriyaki mixture, stirring to coat fish. Set remaining teriyaki mixture aside. Cover fish and marinate in the refrigerator for 30 minutes, stirring once. If using bamboo skewers, soak them in water for 30 minutes; drain.

2 Meanwhile, in a 2-quart saucepan combine water, rice, carrot, sweet pepper, and salt. Bring to boiling; reduce heat. Simmer, covered, for 40 minutes. Stir in broccoli. Cook, covered, for 5 minutes more or until rice is tender. Remove from heat. Let stand, covered, for 5 minutes. Stir in reserved teriyaki mixture.

3 Preheat broiler. Thread fish strips accordion-style on four 12-inch skewers (below). Place skewers on the unheated rack of a broiler pan. Broil 4 to 5 inches from heat for 5 to 7 minutes or until fish flakes easily when tested with a fork (see photo, page 75), turning once halfway through broiling (see photos, page 290). Serve with rice. Makes 4 servings.

Per serving: 194 cal., 4 g total fat (I g sat. fat), 22 mg chol., 805 mg sodium, 23 g carbo., 2 g fiber, I7 g pro.

1 Cut tuna across the grain into ¼-inch-thick strips.

2 Loosely thread fish on skewers in an accordian fold.

Ask Mom What other kinds of fish can I use? page 295 / How do I thaw fish? page 73 / How do I slice green onions? page 43 / How do I peel and cut carrots? pages 37, 64 / How do I seed sweet peppers and cut them into strips? page 49 / How do I trim and cut broccoli? page 36 / What does it mean to marinate? page 73 / What is a skewer? page 79 / What does simmer mean? page 79 / What does it mean to broil? page 68

WON'T THE SKEWERS BURN IN THE BROILER?

They could. If you use bamboo skewers (instead of metal) under the broiler or on the grill, soak them in water for 30 minutes before loading them up with food to keep them from scorching.

This dish is efficient to make and delicious to eat—one batch of wasabi-spiked teriyaki sauce, divided in half, flavors both the fish and the rice. Pile everything on a platter to serve it with style.

Tuna Skewers with Vegetable Rice (*see recipe, page 293*)

What if I can't get a certain kind of fish?

Fish is not only categorized by whether it's a freshwater or saltwater fish but also loosely by whether it is lean and white fleshed (such as cod or mahi mahi) or meatier, oilier, and darker fleshed (such as tuna, salmon, or trout). You might not always be able to get the kind of fish a recipe calls for, but fish is easily substituted, one kind for another. See the chart below for recommendations. There are a few things you want to look for when buying fish, whether it's fillets (thin, boneless pieces) or steaks (½- to 1-inch thick pieces): firm, elastic, moist, and cleanly cut pieces that smell fresh, not fishy.

Type of Fish	Substitution
Freshwater Fish	
Catfish	Grouper, rockfish, sea bass, tilapia
Lake trout (North American char)	Pike, sea trout, whitefish
Rainbow trout	Salmon, sea trout
Tilapia	Catfish, flounder, orange roughy
Whitefish	Cod, lake trout, salmon, sea bass
Saltwater Fish	
Atlantic ocean perch (redfish)	Orange roughy, rockfish, snapper
Cod	Flounder, haddock, pollack
Flounder	Cod, orange roughy, sea trout, sole, whitefish, whiting
Grouper	Mahi mahi, sea bass
Haddock	Cod, grouper, halibut, lake trout, sole, whitefish, whiting
Halibut*	Cod, grouper, red snapper, sea bass
Mackerel*	Mahi mahi, swordfish, tuna
Mahi mahi (dolphin fish)	Grouper, orange roughy, red snapper
Orange roughy	Cod, flounder, haddock, ocean perch, sea bass, sole
Red snapper	Grouper, lake trout, ocean perch, rockfish, whitefish
Rockfish	Cod, grouper, ocean perch, red snapper
Salmon*	Rainbow trout, swordfish, tuna
Shark (mako)	Swordfish, tuna
Sole	Flounder, haddock, halibut, pollack
Swordfish*	Halibut, shark, tuna
Tuna*	Mackerel, salmon, shark, swordfish

* Good source of omega-3 fatty acids

(3) Skill Level

Broiled Tuna
Fajitas

- 2 5- to 6-ounce fresh or frozen tuna steaks, cut I inch thick
- ¼ cup fresh lime juice
- 2 tablespoons snipped fresh cilantro or parsley
- I tablespoon olive oil
- 2 cloves garlic, minced
- ¼ teaspoon coarsely ground black pepper
- ⅛ teaspoon cayenne pepper
- 8 6-inch flour tortillas
- Nonstick cooking spray
- 2 medium red and/or yellow sweet peppers, quartered
- I recipe Tomatillo Salsa

Ingredient Info Salsa verde wouldn't be green without tomatillos (also called husk tomatoes since they're covered in a papery skin). Tomatillos have a tart, citrusy flavor. They should be firm, bright green, and unblemished. If they're yellow, they're overripe.

1 Thaw fish, if frozen. Rinse fish; pat dry with paper towels (see photos, page 277). Place fish in a large resealable plastic bag set in a shallow dish.

2 For marinade, in a small bowl stir together lime juice, cilantro, olive oil, garlic, black pepper, and cayenne pepper. Pour over fish in bag. Seal bag; turn to coat fish. Marinate in the refrigerator for 30 minutes, turning bag occasionally.

3 Preheat broiler. Wrap tortillas tightly in foil. Drain fish, reserving marinade. Lightly coat the unheated rack of a broiler pan with nonstick cooking spray. Place fish on prepared broiler pan. Place sweet pepper quarters beside fish. Broil 4 to 5 inches from heat for 8 to 12 minutes or just until fish flakes easily when tested with a fork (see photo, page 75) and peppers are tender, turning fish and peppers once. Brush fish with reserved marinade halfway through broiling (see photos, page 290). Discard any remaining marinade. Place wrapped tortillas alongside the broiler pan; broil about 8 minutes or until heated through, turning once.

4 Flake fish into large chunks with a fork. Cut sweet peppers into ½-inch-wide strips. Immediately fill warm tortillas with fish and sweet pepper strips. Serve with Tomatillo Salsa. Makes 4 servings.

Tomatillo Salsa: Halve 2 fresh serrano or jalapeño chile peppers; remove seeds, stems, and veins. Finely chop peppers. Remove husks from 3 fresh tomatillos. Finely chop tomatillos (you should have about 1½ cups). In a medium bowl stir together chopped serrano peppers; tomatillos; 3 green onions, thinly sliced; 2 tablespoons finely chopped onion; 1 tablespoon lemon juice; 1 tablespoon snipped fresh cilantro or parsley; ¼ teaspoon salt; and 1 clove garlic, minced.

Make-ahead directions: The salsa can be made ahead and chilled until ready to serve. If chilled, let it stand at room temperature for 30 minutes before serving.

Per serving: 305 cal., II g total fat (2 g sat. fat), 27 mg chol., 360 mg sodium, 3I g carbo., 3 g fiber, 2I g pro.

Ask Mom What other fish can I use? page 295 / How do I thaw fish? page 73 / How do I juice a lemon/lime? pages 30, 80 / How do I snip fresh herbs? pages 42, 328 / What is a garlic clove? page 40 / How do I mince garlic? page 40 / How do I grind pepper? page 22 / How do I quarter sweet peppers? page 49 / What does it mean to marinate? page 73 / What does it mean to broil? page 68 / How do I handle hot chile peppers? page 48 / How do I slice green onions? page 43 / How do I chop an onion? page 47

2 Skill Level

Shrimp and Rice Jambalaya

12 ounces fresh or frozen medium peeled and deveined shrimp (below)

1 cup sliced celery (2 stalks)

¾ cup chopped green sweet pepper (1 medium)

½ cup chopped onion (1 medium)

½ teaspoon Cajun seasoning

¼ teaspoon dried oregano, crushed

2 tablespoons cooking oil

1 14-ounce can chicken broth

¾ cup uncooked long grain white rice

½ cup chopped tomato (1 medium)

Bottled hot pepper sauce (optional)

Lemon wedges (optional)

Shopping Savvy
The number of shrimp per pound increases as their size decreases. For instance, "16/20" shrimp are considered extra large, meaning there are 16 to 20 shrimp per pound. With medium shrimp, you'll get 41 to 50 per pound. When buying fresh shrimp, look for firm meat, translucent and moist shells with no black spots, and a fresh scent.

1 Thaw shrimp, if frozen. Rinse shrimp; pat dry with paper towels. Set aside. In a 12-inch skillet cook and stir celery, sweet pepper, onion, Cajun seasoning, and oregano in hot oil over medium-high heat until vegetables are tender. Carefully add broth. Stir in rice; bring to boiling. Simmer, covered, about 20 minutes or until rice is tender.

2 Stir in the shrimp and tomato. Cook, covered, about 5 minutes or until shrimp turn opaque. To serve, fluff mixture with a fork. Transfer mixture to a shallow serving bowl. If desired, serve with hot pepper sauce and lemon wedges. Makes 4 servings.

Per serving: 307 cal., 9 g total fat (1 g sat. fat), 130 mg chol., 574 mg sodium, 34 g carbo., 2 g fiber, 21 g pro.

eel shrimp, open engthwise down the s belly side.

2 Starting at the head end, peel back the shell. Gently pull on the tail to remove it or, if you prefer, leave it intact.

3 To devein shrimp, use a sharp knife to make a shallow slit along the back from the head to the tail end. Locate the black vein.

4 Place the tip of your knife under the vein and lift it out, then rinse the shrimp with cold water.

Ask Mom How do I prepare celery? page 39 / How do I seed and chop sweet peppers? page 49 / How do I chop an onion? page 47 / How do I crush dried herbs? page 78 / How do I chop a tomato? page 52 / How do I cut lemon/lime wedges? page 30 / What does simmer mean? page 79

Shrimp and Ramen
Noodle Stir-Fry

- 12 ounces fresh or frozen peeled and deveined cooked shrimp or tub-style firm tofu, drained and cubed
- 2 3-ounce packages shrimp- or mushroom-flavor ramen noodles
- 2 teaspoons toasted sesame oil or cooking oil
- 1 tablespoon cooking oil
- 1 medium red or yellow sweet pepper, cut into thin strips
- ¾ cup fresh pea pods, strings and tips removed, or ½ of a 6-ounce package frozen pea pods, thawed
- 2 cups chopped bok choy
- ⅓ cup sliced green onions (4)
- ¼ cup bottled hoisin or stir-fry sauce
- ¼ cup orange juice
- ¼ teaspoon crushed red pepper (optional)
- 2 teaspoons sesame seeds, toasted

1 Thaw shrimp, if frozen, removing tails. Rinse shrimp; pat dry with paper towels. Set aside. In a 3-quart saucepan cook noodles with seasoning packet according to package directions. Drain noodles. Return noodles to pan and toss with toasted sesame oil. Snip noodles several times with kitchen scissors. Set aside.

2 Meanwhile, in a 12-inch skillet heat 1 tablespoon oil over medium-high heat. Add sweet pepper strips; cook and stir for 2 minutes. Add pea pods and bok choy; cook and stir for 2 minutes. Add shrimp or tofu, green onions, hoisin sauce, orange juice, and crushed pepper, if using; cook and stir for 1 minute more.

3 To serve, place noodles on serving plates. Spoon the shrimp mixture over noodles and sprinkle with toasted sesame seeds. Makes 4 servings.

Per serving: 406 cal., 17 g total fat (1 g sat. fat), 130 mg chol., 1,233 mg sodium, 41 g carbo., 3 g fiber, 25 g pro.

Ask Mom What does it mean to stir-fry? page 69 / What is toasted sesame oil? page 138 / How do I seed sweet peppers and cut them into strips? page 49 / What is bok choy? page 201 / How do I slice green onions? page 43 / How do I juice an orange? page 30 / How much juice does one orange yield? page 30 / How do I toast sesame seeds? page 65

Shrimp Scampi

12 ounces fresh or frozen peeled and deveined medium shrimp

1 ounce prosciutto, cut into thin strips

1 tablespoon butter or margarine

1 tablespoon olive oil

6 cloves garlic, minced

1/4 cup finely chopped shallot (2 medium)

1 1/2 cups dry white wine

2 tablespoons lemon juice

1/4 teaspoon salt

1 roma tomato, seeded and finely chopped (1/3 cup)

1 tablespoon snipped fresh Italian (flat-leaf) parsley

1 teaspoon snipped fresh thyme

8 ounces dried angel hair pasta (optional)

1 Thaw shrimp, if frozen. Rinse shrimp; pat dry with paper towels. Set aside. In a 10-inch skillet saute prosciutto over medium heat until crisp. Remove from pan and drain on paper towels; set aside.

2 To the same skillet add butter and olive oil. Heat over medium heat. Add garlic; cook and stir for 30 seconds. Add shallot; cook and stir about 1 minute or until tender. Add shrimp, wine, lemon juice, and salt. Bring to boiling; reduce heat. Simmer, uncovered, for 2 to 3 minutes or until shrimp turn opaque, stirring occasionally. Using a slotted spoon, remove shrimp from pan. Cover shrimp and keep warm.

3 Continue to gently boil liquid in skillet, uncovered, about 10 minutes or until liquid is slightly thickened and reduced to about 1 cup. Stir in tomato, parsley, and thyme; heat through. Return shrimp to skillet and toss gently to coat.

4 Meanwhile, if desired, cook pasta according to package directions; drain (see photo, page 305). Place pasta on a serving platter or four plates. Top with shrimp mixture; sprinkle with prosciutto. Makes 4 servings.

Per serving: 247 cal., 8 g total fat (3 g sat. fat), 142 mg chol., 486 mg sodium, 8 g carbo., 0 g fiber, 20 g pro.

Scallop Scampi: Prepare as above, except substitute 12 ounces sea scallops for the shrimp.

GOOD TO KNOW Though there are lots of variations on shrimp scampi, what makes the dish is garlic—and lots of it. So don't be afraid of the number of garlic cloves used here. It wouldn't be scampi without it.

Ask Mom What is prosciutto? page 358 / How do I measure butter? pages 58, 59 / What is a garlic clove? page 40 / How do I mince garlic? page 40 / What is a shallot? page 46 / How do I chop an onion? page 47 / How do I juice a lemon/lime? pages 30, 80 / What is a roma tomato? page 52 / How do I seed tomatoes? page 52 / How do I chop a tomato? page 52 / How do I snip fresh herbs? pages 42, 328 / What is that pasta shape? pages 308–309 / What does simmer mean? page 79 / What does it mean to toss? page 77

WHAT'S EN PAPILLOTE MEAN? Quite simply, it means "in a paper casing" in French. It refers to the method of oven-steaming food—usually fish and vegetables—in a package of parchment paper. It is an extremely light and healthful way to cook.

As the fish and vegetables cook, the lemon bastes everything with juice and citrus oil. So it not only looks pretty when the packet is cut open, it tastes great too!

③ Skill Level

Shrimp and Scallops En Papillote

- 2 cups sliced leek (2 large)
- 4 large sprigs fresh thyme
- ¼ cup Dijon-style mustard
- 2 tablespoons dry white wine
- ⅛ teaspoon ground white pepper
- 12 sea scallops
- 8 fresh peeled and deveined jumbo shrimp
- 1 cup julienned carrot (2 medium)
- 1 cup julienned zucchini or sweet pepper strips (1 small)
- 4 tablespoons butter, melted
- 4 slices lemon

Flavor Changes One of the coolest things about cooking "en papillote" is its versatility. You can use any combination of fish or shellfish, vegetables, herbs, and liquid. Try mushrooms, leeks, and trout with white wine and lemon; salmon with leeks, green beans, dill, and white wine; or sole with asparagus, white wine, capers, and green peppercorns (find them packed in brine in jars or cans).

1 Preheat oven to 450°F. Cut four 12×16-inch sheets of parchment paper. Fold in half; crease fold and unfold.

2 On half of each sheet of parchment, place ½ cup leek and top with a sprig of thyme. In a bowl stir together mustard, wine, and white pepper. Add scallops and shrimp; toss to coat. Spoon one-fourth of seafood mixture over leek. Top with ¼ cup carrot and ¼ cup zucchini. Drizzle with 1 tablespoon butter and top with a lemon slice. Seal parchment (below). Repeat to make three more packets. Place packets on a very large baking sheet. Bake in the preheated oven for 10 to 12 minutes or until scallops and shrimp are opaque. To serve, cut an "X" in the top of the parchment; serve immediately. Makes 4 servings.

Per serving: 254 cal., 14 g total fat (8 g sat. fat), 163 mg chol., 752 mg sodium, 18 g carbo., 2 g fiber, 40 g pro.

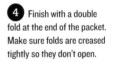

parchment over ...ack like a book. ...ng at the edge of

2 Working in 2-inch sections, fold about ¼ inch of the open edges over and crease tightly. Fold again.

3 Continue working around the open edges of the parchment, overlapping folded sections slightly.

4 Finish with a double fold at the end of the packet. Make sure folds are creased tightly so they don't open.

Ask Mom What is a leek? page 43 / How do I slice a leek? page 43 / What is Dijon-style mustard? page 379 / How do I peel and cut carrots? page 37 / How do I prepare summer squash/zucchini? page 54 / How do I seed sweet peppers and cut them into strips? page 49 / How do I measure butter? pages 58, 59 / How do I slice lemons/limes? page 30 / What does drizzle mean? page 79

Broiled Lobster Tails

4 8-ounce fresh or frozen lobster tails
¼ cup butter
1 teaspoon finely shredded orange peel
½ teaspoon chili powder
1 clove garlic, minced
1 recipe Clarified Butter (optional)

1 Thaw lobster tails, if frozen. Preheat broiler. Using kitchen scissors, butterfly the lobster tails by cutting through the center of the hard top shells and meat, cutting to, but not through, bottoms of shells (below). Spread the tail halves apart (below). Place lobster tails, meat sides up, on the unheated rack of a broiler pan.

2 In a 6-inch skillet or 1-quart saucepan melt butter over medium heat. Add orange peel, chili powder, and garlic; cook and stir about 30 seconds or until garlic is tender. Brush mixture evenly over lobster tails.

3 Broil 4 inches from heat for 12 to 14 minutes or until lobster meat is opaque. If desired, serve with Clarified Butter for dipping. Makes 4 servings.

Per serving: 243 cal., 12 g total fat (7 g sat. fat), 133 mg chol., 624 mg sodium, 2 g carbo., 0 g fiber, 29 g pro.

Clarified Butter: In a 1-quart saucepan melt ½ cup butter over low heat without stirring; cool slightly, about 10 minutes. Using a spoon, skim off milky top layer, if present, and discard. Pour off clear top layer and save; discard milky bottom layer. The clear top layer is the Clarified Butter.

Lemon-Chive Lobster Tails: Prepare as above, except substitute lemon peel for the orange peel. Omit chili powder and garlic. Stir in 2 tablespoons snipped fresh chives after butter is melted.

Basil Lobster Tails: Prepare as above, except omit orange peel and chili powder. Stir in 2 tablespoons snipped fresh basil after cooking the garlic.

1 Use sturdy kitchen scissors to cut through tops of the shells and the meat. Don't cut all the way through.

2 Spread the shells apart and loosen from the meat with your thumbs and fingers.

3 Separate the meat with your thumbs to allow melted butter to penetrate.

Ask Mom How do I measure butter? pages 58, 59 / How do I finely shred orange peel? page 30 / What is a garlic clove? page 40 / How do I mince garlic? page 40 / What does it mean to broil? page 68 / How do I shred lemon/lime peel? page 30 / How do I snip fresh herbs? pages 42, 328

PLATEFULS OF
pasta, rice
& GRAINS

Asian, Cajun, Caribbean, Italian, and more: These go-with-the-grain main dishes cover a world of flavors.

8

Baked Cavatelli

2 ⅓ cups dried cavatelli or wagon wheel macaroni (7 ounces)

12 ounces bulk Italian sausage or lean ground beef

¾ cup chopped onion

½ cup chopped green sweet pepper (1 small) (optional)

2 cloves garlic, minced

1 26-ounce jar tomato and basil pasta sauce

1 ¼ cups shredded mozzarella cheese (5 ounces)

¼ cup sliced, pitted ripe olives (optional)

¼ teaspoon ground black pepper

Good to Know If you plan to fill the cooked pasta or use it in a salad, rinse it with cold water to remove the light coating of starch that covers each piece of pasta. Drain again.

1 Preheat oven to 375°F. Cook cavatelli according to package directions; drain and set aside (below).

2 Meanwhile, in a 10-inch skillet cook and stir sausage, onion, sweet pepper (if using), and garlic until sausage is brown; drain off fat.

3 In a large bowl stir together pasta sauce, 1 cup of the mozzarella cheese, olives (if using), and black pepper. Add cavatelli and sausage mixture to bowl, stirring gently to combine. Transfer cavatelli mixture to a 2-quart casserole.

4 Bake, covered, in the preheated oven for 35 to 40 minutes or until heated through. Uncover; sprinkle with the remaining ¼ cup mozzarella cheese. Bake, uncovered, about 5 minutes more or until cheese melts. Makes 6 main-dish servings.

Per serving: 432 cal., 21 g total fat (8 g sat. fat), 51 mg chol., 1,237 mg sodium, 36 g carbo., 3 g fiber, 20 g pro.

Meal Maker Everybody loves Baked Cavatelli. Make it a casual company meal: Start with an appetizer of ripe cantaloupe wedges wrapped in prosciutto and serve a peppery all-arugula salad (see pages 346–349) topped with shredded Parmesan alongside. Finish it with a dessert of make-ahead Chocolaty Tiramisu Parfaits (see page 456).

Drain the cooked pasta in a colander and shake it well to get rid of any excess water. Never let cooked pasta stand in the hot cooking water; the pasta will continue to cook and become too soft.

Ask Mom What is that pasta shape? pages 308–309 / How do I chop an onion? page 47 / How do I seed and chop sweet peppers? page 49 / What is a garlic clove? page 40 / How do I mince garlic? page 40 / How do I shred cheese? page 71

Roasted Red Pepper Lasagna

Nonstick cooking spray

2 cups purchased tomato-based pasta sauce (such as portobello mushroom, garden vegetable, or tomato and basil)

6 no-boil lasagna noodles

½ of a 15-ounce carton ricotta cheese (about 1 cup)

1½ cups shredded mozzarella cheese (6 ounces)

¼ cup finely shredded Parmesan cheese

1 cup bottled roasted red sweet peppers, drained and cut into strips, or 2 cups torn fresh spinach

8 ounces lean ground beef or bulk pork sausage, cooked and drained

1. Preheat oven to 350°F. Lightly coat a 2-quart square baking dish with cooking spray. Spread ⅓ cup of the pasta sauce into the prepared dish. Top with 2 of the lasagna noodles (below). Combine ricotta cheese and 1 cup of the mozzarella cheese; spread half of the cheese mixture over the noodles. Sprinkle with half of the Parmesan cheese. Top with half of the sweet pepper strips (below) and ground beef. Pour half the remaining pasta sauce over ground beef (below).

2. Top with 2 more noodles, the remaining cheese mixture, and the remaining sweet pepper strips. Add the last 2 noodles. Spoon the remaining pasta sauce over the noodles (below). Sprinkle with the remaining ½ cup mozzarella cheese and the remaining Parmesan cheese.

3. Lightly coat a sheet of foil with cooking spray. Cover lasagna with foil, coated side down. Bake in the preheated oven for 50 minutes. Let stand, covered, for 20 minutes before serving. Makes 4 to 6 main-dish servings.

Per serving: 518 cal., 21 g total fat (10 g sat. fat), 86 mg chol., 946 mg sodium, 44 g carbo., 3 g fiber, 36 g pro.

Spicy Sausage Lasagna: Prepare as above, except substitute Monterey Jack cheese with jalapeño peppers for the mozzarella cheese and bulk Italian sausage for the ground beef.

1 Place 2 of the no-boil lasagna noodles on top of the pasta sauce in the prepared baking dish.

2 Arrange half of the roasted sweet pepper strips on top of the cheese mixture.

3 Pour half of the remaining pasta sauce evenly over the cooked and drained ground beef.

4 Spoon the remain[ing] pasta sauce evenly over remaining 2 lasagna no[odles]

Ask Mom What is that pasta shape? pages 308–309 / How do I shred cheese? page 71 / How do I drain bottled roasted sweet peppers? page 416

Skill Level

Ravioli Skillet Lasagna

2 cups purchased pasta sauce

⅓ cup water

1 9-ounce package refrigerated or frozen cheese- or meat-filled ravioli

1 egg, lightly beaten

1 15-ounce carton ricotta cheese

¼ cup grated Romano or Parmesan cheese

1 10-ounce package frozen chopped spinach, thawed and well drained

Grated Romano or Parmesan cheese

1 In a 10-inch skillet combine pasta sauce and the water. Bring to boiling; stir in ravioli. Reduce heat. Cook, covered, over medium heat about 5 minutes or until ravioli are nearly tender, stirring once to prevent sticking.

2 Meanwhile, in a medium bowl stir together egg, ricotta cheese, and the ¼ cup Romano cheese. Top ravioli with spinach. Spoon ricotta mixture on top of spinach. Cook, covered, over low heat about 10 minutes or until ricotta layer is set and ravioli are tender. Sprinkle each serving with additional Romano cheese. Makes 4 main-dish servings.

Per serving: 433 cal., 14 g total fat (3 g sat. fat), 131 mg chol., 501 mg sodium, 49 g carbo., 3 g fiber, 36 g pro.

GOOD TO KNOW Make this with cheese ravioli and both vegetarians and nonvegetarians will be supremely happy and well fed.

Ask Mom What is that pasta shape? pages 308–309 / How do I beat eggs? page 62 / How do I grate cheese? page 71 / How do I drain spinach? page 321

Pasta

In the mood for noodles? Whether you cook up long and thin spaghetti or fat, tubular, ridged rigatoni depends on what kind of sauce you're serving. The mind-boggling variety of pasta is all about the sauce.

In general, light, thin sauces are best paired with thin, delicate pastas, such as angel hair (capellini) or thin spaghetti (vermicelli). Chunky sauces are best partnered with pastas that have holes or ridges, such as mostaccioli, ziti, rotini, and radiatore. Heavy sauces go best with sturdier pastas such as fettuccine, linguine, bucatini, and lasagna.

How many people does a pound of pasta feed? Unless they're carbing up to run a marathon, figure the average eater will down about 1 cup of cooked pasta when it's combined with meat, vegetables, and/or sauce. Half of a

1-pound box of uncooked small to medium pasta such as bow ties, penne, ziti, and elbow macaroni or spaghetti, angel hair, linguine, or fettuccine will yield about 4 cups cooked pasta.

After the pasta is cooked, drain it in a colander in the sink and shake it well to get rid of excess water. And don't rinse it unless you're making pasta salad. Rinsing removes the light coating of starch that covers each piece of pasta. That coating helps the sauce and seasonings cling. Serve it immediately though; it keeps cooking even after draining, and you want it to be "al dente" (see page 321), not soft and mushy.

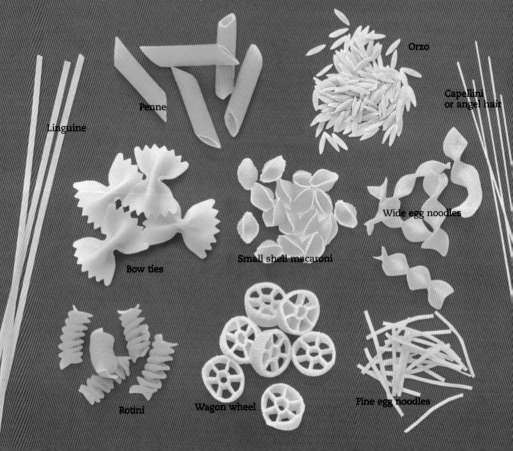

Orzo

Capellini or angel hair

Penne

Linguine

Wide egg noodles

Bow ties

Small shell macaroni

Rotini

Wagon wheel

Fine egg noodles

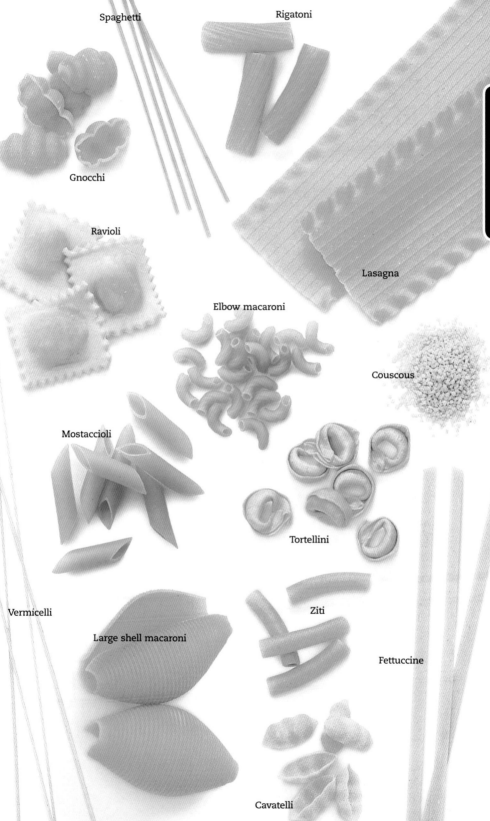

Spaghetti

Rigatoni

Gnocchi

Ravioli

Lasagna

Elbow macaroni

Couscous

Mostaccioli

Tortellini

Vermicelli

Large shell macaroni

Ziti

Fettuccine

Cavatelli

Spaghetti with Sauce And Meatballs

1 recipe Meatballs
8 ounces dried spaghetti or fettuccine
1 medium fennel bulb, trimmed and cut into thin bite-size strips
1 medium onion, quartered and thinly sliced
1 cup thinly bias-sliced carrot (1 medium)
2 cloves garlic, minced
1 tablespoon olive oil or cooking oil
1 26-ounce jar marinara, mushroom, or ripe olive pasta sauce
1 cup shredded fontina or mozzarella cheese (4 ounces)
½ cup finely shredded Parmesan or Romano cheese (2 ounces)

1 Prepare Meatballs. In a 4-quart Dutch oven cook spaghetti according to package directions; drain (see photo, page 305) and return spaghetti to Dutch oven.

2 Meanwhile, in a 10-inch skillet cook and stir fennel, onion, carrot, and garlic in hot oil over medium heat about 7 minutes or until vegetables are tender. Add Meatballs, vegetable mixture, and pasta sauce to Dutch oven; toss to coat. Heat through. Season to taste with *salt* and *ground black pepper*. Transfer to a warm serving dish. Sprinkle with fontina and Parmesan cheeses. Makes 6 main-dish servings.

Meatballs: Preheat oven to 400°F. Combine 1 egg, lightly beaten; ½ cup soft bread crumbs; ¼ cup finely chopped onion; 1 teaspoon dried oregano, crushed; ½ teaspoon salt; ⅛ teaspoon cayenne pepper or ¼ teaspoon ground black pepper; and 2 cloves garlic, minced. Add 1 pound lean ground beef; mix well. Shape into a 6×4-inch rectangle; cut into 24 squares (below). Shape into meatballs (see photo, page 311). Arrange meatballs in a 15×10×1-inch baking pan. Bake, uncovered, in preheated oven about 15 minutes or until done; drain off fat. Makes 24 meatballs.

Per serving including meatballs: 515 cal., 22 g total fat (9 g sat. fat), 112 mg chol., 935 mg sodium, 47 g carbo., 5 g fiber, 31 g pro.

For 24 meatballs of equal size, shape the meat mixture into a 6×4-inch rectangle on a cutting board. Cut into twenty-four 1-inch squares.

Ingredient Info Fontina cheese originated in northern Italy. There it is a pungent, aromatic aged cheese. Here it is milder in flavor—buttery and nutty tasting—but it still has a stronger flavor than supermild mozzarella. It has the meltability of mozzarella though, so if you like brawny cheeses, seek it out.

Ask Mom What is that pasta shape? pages 308–309 / How do I chop an onion? page 47 / How do I slice an onion? page 47 / What does bias-slice mean? page 79 / How do I peel and cut carrots? pages 37, 64 / What is a garlic clove? page 40 / How do I mince garlic? page 40 / How do I shred cheese? page 71 / What does it mean to toss? page 77 / How do I warm a serving dish/plate? page 316 / How do I beat eggs? page 62 / How do I make bread crumbs? page 76 / How do I crush dried herbs? page 78

WHAT'S FENNEL? This licorice-flavor plant is an important ingredient in Italian cooking. The crunchy bulb is roasted, chopped, and added to sauce. It's also eaten raw in salads. The seeds flavor Italian sausage, and the feathery fronds are used like a fresh herb.

How do I cut fennel?

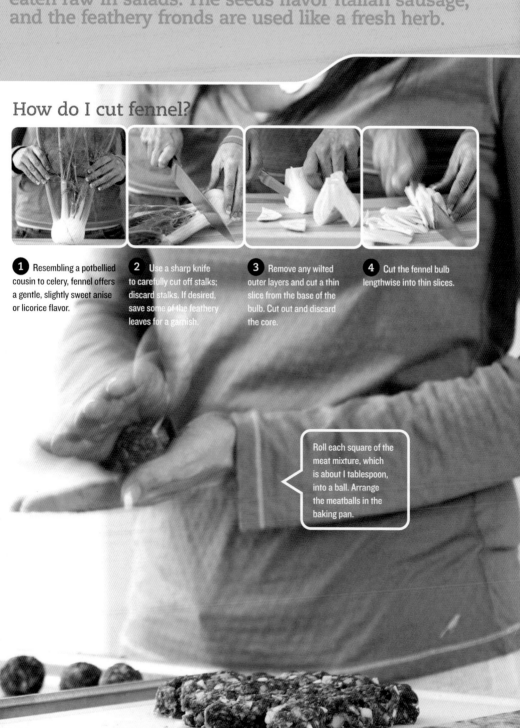

1 Resembling a potbellied cousin to celery, fennel offers a gentle, slightly sweet anise or licorice flavor.

2 Use a sharp knife to carefully cut off stalks; discard stalks. If desired, save some of the feathery leaves for a garnish.

3 Remove any wilted outer layers and cut a thin slice from the base of the bulb. Cut out and discard the core.

4 Cut the fennel bulb lengthwise into thin slices.

Roll each square of the meat mixture, which is about 1 tablespoon, into a ball. Arrange the meatballs in the baking pan.

WHAT'S CHORIZO? Almost every culture has its favorite sausage. In Mexico it's highly spiced chorizo, made with pork, dried chiles (which give it a distinctive red color), and spices such as oregano, garlic, cumin, paprika, and black pepper.

Buy a little extra chorizo and start your day in a spicy way. In Mexico chorizo is a popular breakfast food. Crumble and cook it with scrambled eggs and eat as is or bundle everything up in a tortilla with salsa.

Mexican Chorizo Noodle Bowl

1 pound uncooked chorizo sausage or hot Italian sausage
2 cloves garlic, minced
3 14-ounce cans chicken broth or vegetable broth
2 cups bottled salsa
1 to 2 canned chipotle peppers in adobo sauce, drained and finely chopped (see photo, page 373)
1 teaspoon dried oregano, crushed
1 teaspoon ground cumin
10 ounces dried vermicelli or angel hair pasta
1 cup chopped zucchini (1 small)
⅔ cup shredded mozzarella or asadero cheese
¼ cup snipped fresh cilantro or Italian (flat-leaf) parsley
   Fresh cilantro (optional)

1 Remove casing from chorizo, if present (below). Crumble chorizo (below). In a 4-quart Dutch oven cook chorizo and garlic until chorizo is brown; drain off fat.

2 Stir broth, salsa, chipotle pepper, oregano, and cumin into Dutch oven. Bring to boiling; reduce heat. Simmer, covered, for 15 minutes. Stir in vermicelli and zucchini. Simmer, uncovered, for 2 to 3 minutes more or until vermicelli is tender but still firm, stirring occasionally. Remove Dutch oven from heat; stir in ⅓ cup of the mozzarella cheese and the cilantro.

3 Transfer to a warm serving dish. Sprinkle with the remaining ⅓ cup mozzarella cheese. If desired, garnish with additional cilantro. Makes 6 main-dish servings.

Per serving: 621 cal., 36 g total fat (14 g sat. fat), 82 mg chol., 2,129 mg sodium, 43 g carbo., 3 g fiber, 30 g pro.

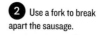

1 Use a sharp knife to cut through the thin casings on the sausage.

2 Use a fork to break apart the sausage.

Ask Mom What is a garlic clove? page 40 / How do I mince garlic? page 40 / How do I crush dried herbs? page 78 / What is that pasta shape? pages 308–309 / How do I prepare summer squash/zucchini? page 54 / How do I shred cheese? page 71 / How do I snip fresh herbs? pages 42, 329 / What does simmer mean? page 79 / How do I warm a serving dish/plate? page 316

Meal Maker This rich dish calls for something refreshing and light as a side. How about a salad of torn romaine lettuce, grapefruit sections, and red onion slices tossed with balsamic vinaigrette?

Gorgonzola-Sauced
Tortellini with Artichokes

- 1 9-ounce package refrigerated cheese-filled spinach tortellini or three-cheese tortellini
- 8 ounces bulk sweet or hot Italian sausage
- 1½ cups sliced fresh cremini, stemmed shiitake, or button mushrooms
- 1 small onion, cut into thin wedges
- ½ cup crumbled Gorgonzola cheese (2 ounces)
- 1 14.5-ounce can diced tomatoes with basil, garlic, and oregano, drained
- 1 6-ounce jar marinated artichoke hearts, drained and quartered
- 2 tablespoons snipped fresh basil
- 1 tablespoon finely shredded Parmesan cheese

1 Cook tortellini according to package directions; drain (see photo, page 305) and set aside.

2 Meanwhile, in a 3-quart saucepan cook and stir sausage, mushrooms, and onion until sausage is brown and onion is tender; drain off fat.

3 Add Gorgonzola cheese to saucepan. Cook and stir over low heat until cheese melts. Gently stir in tortellini, drained tomatoes, and artichokes; heat through. Transfer to a warm serving dish. Sprinkle with basil and Parmesan cheese. Makes 4 main-dish servings.

Per serving: 624 cal., 36 g total fat (13 g sat. fat), 96 mg chol., 1,695 mg sodium, 52 g carbo., 3 g fiber, 26 g pro.

To avoid getting your hands messy while crumbling the Gorgonzola, hold the wedge over the measuring cup and chunk the cheese off into it with a fork. The veining helps the cheese crumble easily.

Ask Mom What is that pasta shape? pages 308–309 / What are some mushroom varieties? page 44 / How do I slice fresh mushrooms? page 45 / How do I cut onion wedges? page 47 / How do I snip fresh herbs? pages 42, 328 / How do I shred cheese? page 71 / How do I warm a serving dish/plate? page 316

(2) Skill Level

White Bean and Sausage Rigatoni

6 cups dried rigatoni (1 pound)
8 ounces cooked kielbasa
$\frac{1}{2}$ of a 6-ounce can ($\frac{1}{3}$ cup) Italian-style tomato paste
$\frac{1}{4}$ cup dry red wine or reduced-sodium chicken broth
2 10-ounce packages frozen chopped spinach, thawed and well drained
2 14.5-ounce cans diced tomatoes with basil, oregano, and garlic, undrained
1 15-ounce can Great Northern beans, rinsed and drained
$\frac{1}{3}$ cup grated or finely shredded Parmesan cheese (1 $\frac{1}{2}$ ounces)

1 Preheat oven to 375°F. Cook rigatoni according to package directions; drain (see photo, page 305) and transfer to a large bowl.

2 Cut kielbasa in half lengthwise; cut into thin slices (below). In a small bowl combine tomato paste and wine (below).

3 Add the kielbasa, tomato paste mixture, spinach, undrained tomatoes, and beans to the rigatoni; stir to combine (below). Transfer rigatoni mixture to an ungreased 3-quart rectangular baking dish.

4 Bake, covered, in the preheated oven about 25 minutes or until heated through. Uncover; sprinkle with Parmesan cheese (below). Bake, uncovered, about 5 minutes more or until cheese melts. Makes 6 to 8 main-dish servings.

Per serving: 564 cal., 20 g total fat (11 g sat. fat), 48 mg chol., 1,706 mg sodium, 62 g carbo., 7 g fiber, 30 g pro.

Shopping Savvy
Kielbasa is a smoked Polish link sausage that is usually sold cooked. Traditionally made with pork, it's highly flavored with garlic and marjoram. Look for it in the grocery store near other precooked and/ or cured meats such as cold cuts, hot dogs, and bacon.

a cutting board, use a e to halve the kielbasa e. Thinly bias-slice asa half.

2 Use a wire whisk to combine the tomato paste and the red wine.

3 Add all of the ingredients except the Parmesan cheese to the cooked rigatoni.

4 After baking, sprinkle the Parmesan cheese over the top. Return dish to oven until cheese melts.

Ask Mom What is that pasta shape? pages 308–309 / How do I drain spinach? page 321 / How do I rinse and drain canned beans? page 390 / How do I grate cheese? page 71 / How do I shred cheese? page 71

(2) Skill Level

Good to Know
Pasta always tastes
better warm—and it
stays warm longer if
it's served in a warm
dish. To warm the
serving dishes, preheat
your oven to 200°F,
then turn it off. Put the
dishes in for just a few
minutes before you fill
them up.

Fettuccine with Creamy Tomato-Mushroom Sauce

    3 ounces pancetta or 4 slices bacon, chopped
    2 cups sliced fresh cremini or stemmed shiitake mushrooms
  ½ cup pine nuts
1½ cups whipping cream
1¾ cups chopped, seeded tomato (2 medium)
    8 ounces dried spinach fettuccine
      Finely shredded Parmesan cheese (optional)

1 For sauce, in a 10-inch skillet cook pancetta over medium heat just until crisp. Remove pancetta from skillet, reserving 1 tablespoon drippings in skillet (below). Drain pancetta on paper towels; set aside.

2 Add mushrooms and pine nuts to drippings in skillet. Cook over medium heat for 3 to 5 minutes or until mushrooms are tender and pine nuts are golden brown, stirring frequently (below). Add pancetta, whipping cream, ¼ teaspoon *salt*, and ¼ teaspoon *ground black pepper* to skillet. Bring to boiling; reduce heat. Boil gently, uncovered, for 8 to 10 minutes or until mixture is slightly thickened, stirring occasionally. Stir in tomato (below).

3 Meanwhile, in a 4-quart Dutch oven cook fettuccine according to package directions; drain (see photo, page 305) and return to Dutch oven. Pour sauce over fettuccine; toss to coat (below). Transfer to a warm serving dish. If desired, sprinkle with Parmesan cheese. Makes 4 main-dish servings.

Per serving: 733 cal., 53 g total fat (24 g sat. fat), 138 mg chol., 601 mg sodium, 51 g carbo., 4 g fiber, 16 g pro.

1 Remove the cooked pancetta from the skillet with a slotted spoon.

2 Use a wooden spoon to cook and stir the mushrooms and pine nuts in the reserved pancetta drippings.

3 After the sauce is slightly thickened, stir in the chopped tomatoes.

4 Pour the sauce ove the cooked fettuccine in Dutch oven. Toss gently coat the fettuccine.

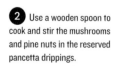
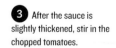

Ask Mom What is pancetta? page 229 / What are some mushroom varieties? page 44 / How do I slice fresh mushrooms? page 45 / How do I seed tomatoes? page 52 / How do I chop a tomato? page 52 / What is that pasta shape? pages 308–309 / How do I shred cheese? page 71 / What does it mean to toss? page 77

Skill Level

Penne with Broccoli Rabe and Pancetta

12 ounces broccoli rabe (see photo, page 256) or 1 ½ cups broccoli florets

3 cups dried whole wheat or multigrain penne (8 ounces)

½ cup chopped onion (1 medium)

2 ounces pancetta or 3 slices bacon, chopped

2 cloves garlic, minced

1 ⅓ cups chopped, seeded roma tomato (4 medium)

⅓ cup dry white wine or chicken broth

¼ cup finely shredded Asiago cheese (1 ounce)

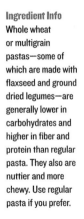

Ingredient Info
Whole wheat or multigrain pastas—some of which are made with flaxseed and ground dried legumes—are generally lower in carbohydrates and higher in fiber and protein than regular pasta. They also are nuttier and more chewy. Use regular pasta if you prefer.

1 Wash broccoli rabe; drain well. Remove and discard large leaves; cut into 4-inch lengths. Set broccoli rabe aside.

2 In a 3-quart saucepan cook penne in a large amount of lightly salted boiling water for 9 minutes; add broccoli rabe. Cook about 3 minutes more or until penne is tender; drain (see photo, page 305). Return pasta mixture to saucepan; cover and keep warm.

3 Meanwhile, in a 2- to 2½-quart saucepan cook onion, pancetta, and garlic over medium heat until pancetta is crisp and onion is tender, stirring occasionally. Reduce heat to low; add tomato and wine. Cook and stir for 2 minutes.

4 Add tomato mixture to penne mixture in saucepan; toss to combine. Season to taste with *salt* and *ground black pepper*. Transfer to a warm serving dish. Sprinkle with cheese. Makes 4 to 6 main-dish servings.

Per serving: 348 cal., 8 g total fat (3 g sat. fat), 18 mg chol., 462 mg sodium, 51 g carbo., 8 g fiber, 16 g pro.

Ask Mom How do I trim and cut broccoli? page 36 / What is that pasta shape? pages 308–309 / How do I chop an onion? page 47 / What is pancetta? page 229 / What is a garlic clove? page 40 / How do I mince garlic? page 40 / What is a roma tomato? page 52 / How do I seed tomatoes? page 52 / How do I chop a tomato? page 52 / How do I shred cheese? page 71 / How do I warm a serving dish/plate? page 316 / What does it mean to toss? page 77

1 Skill Level

Pesto Pasta with
Roasted Chicken

  3 cups dried bow ties, penne, or mostaccioli (8 ounces)
  2 cups broccoli florets
  1 7-ounce container purchased basil pesto
2 ½ cups bite-size strips purchased deli-roasted chicken
  1 cup bottled roasted red sweet peppers, drained and cut into strips
  ¼ cup finely shredded Parmesan cheese
  ½ teaspoon coarsely ground black pepper
    Finely shredded Parmesan cheese (optional)

1 In a 4-quart Dutch oven cook bow ties according to package directions, adding broccoli the last 2 minutes of cooking. Drain well, reserving ½ cup of the pasta water. Return drained bow ties and broccoli to Dutch oven; set aside.

2 In a small bowl combine the reserved pasta water and pesto. Add pesto mixture, chicken, and roasted sweet peppers to Dutch oven; toss to combine. Heat through. Remove Dutch oven from heat; add the ¼ cup Parmesan cheese and black pepper; toss to combine.

3 Transfer to a warm serving dish. If desired, sprinkle with additional Parmesan cheese. Makes 4 main-dish servings.

Per serving: 648 cal., 28 g total fat (7 g sat. fat), 96 mg chol., 598 mg sodium, 55 g carbo., 5 g fiber, 41 g pro.

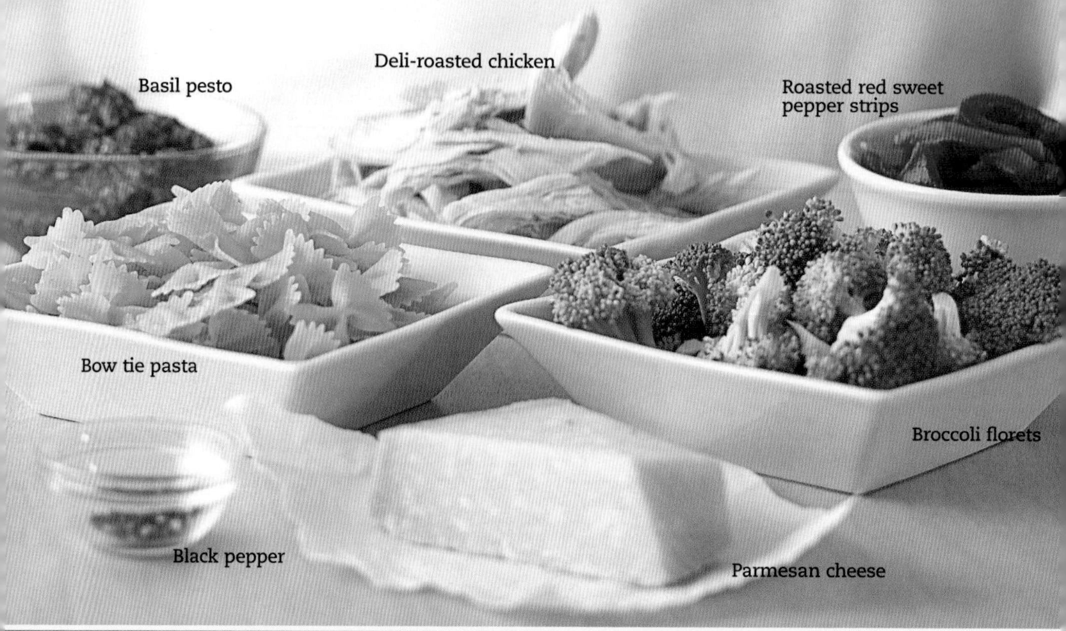

Basil pesto

Deli-roasted chicken

Roasted red sweet pepper strips

Bow tie pasta

Broccoli florets

Black pepper

Parmesan cheese

Ask Mom What is that pasta shape? pages 308–309 / How do I trim and cut broccoli? page 36 / How do I drain bottled roasted sweet peppers? page 416 / How do I shred cheese? page 71 / How do I freshly grind pepper? page 22 / What does it mean to toss? page 77 / How do I warm a serving dish/plate? page 316

② Skill Level

Salmon and Soba Noodle Bowl

1¼ pounds fresh or frozen skinless salmon fillet, 1 inch thick

¼ cup olive oil

¼ cup balsamic vinegar

8 ounces dried soba (buckwheat noodles) or whole wheat noodles

⅓ cup orange juice

2 oranges, peeled, sectioned, and halved

½ of a small red onion or 2 green onions, thinly sliced

2 teaspoons anise seeds, crushed (below)

1 clove garlic, minced

Ingredient Info The Japanese love their noodles, and one of the most popular types is soba—made with intensely flavored buckwheat and whole wheat flours. At the supermarket look for soba noodles in the pasta aisle or in the Asian section, if there is one. Or check out an Asian market. (Sometimes you can find them fresh too.)

1 Thaw fish, if frozen. Rinse fish; pat dry with paper towels (see photos, page 277). Cut into four serving-size pieces (see photo 1, page 278). Preheat broiler. In a small bowl combine 1 tablespoon of the olive oil, 1 tablespoon of the vinegar, and 1½ teaspoons *cracked black pepper*. Place fish on the unheated rack of a broiler pan. Brush both sides of salmon with oil mixture. Broil 4 to 5 inches from the heat for 8 to 12 minutes or until fish flakes easily when tested with a fork (see photo, page 75), turning once (see photos, page 290).

2 Meanwhile, in a 3-quart saucepan cook soba in boiling water about 4 minutes (or 8 to 10 minutes for whole wheat noodles) or until just slightly chewy; drain (see photo, page 305). Transfer to a large bowl. Add the remaining 3 tablespoons oil, the remaining 3 tablespoons vinegar, the orange juice, oranges, onion, anise seeds, and garlic; toss to coat (below).

3 Divide noodle mixture among four warm pasta bowls. Top each serving with a piece of salmon (below). Makes 4 main-dish servings.

Per serving: 548 cal., 19 g total fat (3 g sat. fat), 74 mg chol., 549 mg sodium, 59 g carbo., 5 g fiber, 38 g pro.

...anese soba ...buckwheat flour, ...es the noodles a ...nish gray color.

② Crush the anise seeds with a mortar and pestle. Or crush them with a spoon against the inside of a bowl.

③ Use a couple of kitchen forks to toss the soba mixture until the noodles are coated.

④ To serve, place salmon on top of the noodle mixture.

Ask Mom How do I thaw fish? page 73 / What is that vinegar? page 349 / How do I juice an orange? page 30 / How much juice does one orange yield? page 30 / How do I peel and section an orange? page 31 / How do I slice an onion? page 47 / How do I slice green onions? page 43 / What is a garlic clove? page 40 / How do I mince garlic? page 40 / What does it mean to broil? page 68 / What does it mean to toss? page 77 / How do I warm a serving dish/plate? page 316

Baked Three-Cheese Macaroni

1⅓ cups dried elbow macaroni or penne (6 ounces)

¾ cup milk

2 tablespoons butter or margarine

¼ teaspoon ground white pepper

⅛ teaspoon salt

4 ounces American cheese, cut into ½-inch cubes

1 cup shredded sharp cheddar cheese (4 ounces)

¼ cup shredded mozzarella cheese (1 ounce)

1 Preheat oven to 350°F. In a 3-quart saucepan cook macaroni according to package directions; drain (see photo, page 305) and return to saucepan. Add milk, butter, pepper, and salt to saucepan; stir in American cheese, cheddar cheese, and mozzarella cheese. Transfer the macaroni mixture to a greased 1½-quart casserole.

2 Bake, uncovered, in the preheated oven for 15 minutes; stir gently. Bake about 5 minutes more or until just heated through (don't overheat or mixture will curdle). Let stand for 10 minutes before serving. Makes 4 main-dish servings.

Per serving: 474 cal., 27 g total fat (17 g sat. fat), 81 mg chol., 776 mg sodium, 35 g carbo., 1 g fiber, 22 g pro.

Baked Blue Cheese Macaroni: Prepare as above, except substitute shredded process Swiss cheese for the American cheese and crumbled blue cheese for the cheddar cheese.

Baked Three-Cheese Macaroni with Smoked Chicken: Prepare as above, except omit American cheese, cheddar cheese, and mozzarella cheese. Stir in 1 cup chopped smoked chicken or purchased deli-roasted chicken, 1 cup shredded Asiago cheese, ½ cup shredded fontina cheese, ¼ cup crumbled blue cheese, and 1 clove garlic, minced, with the milk.

Good to Know Mac 'n' cheese is so beloved, most American children are made—at least partly—of the yummy stuff. Comforting childhood memories and great taste make the homemade variety a hit at any potluck. Take Baked Three-Cheese Macaroni next time you're asked to bring something to share—simply double the ingredients and increase the size of the baking dish.

Ask Mom What is that pasta shape? pages 308–309 / How do I measure butter? pages 58, 59 / What is process cheese? page 408 / What does it mean to cube? page 64 / How do I shred cheese? page 71 / How do I crumble cheese? pages 71, 96 / What is a garlic clove? page 40 / How do I mince garlic? page 40

(2) Skill Level

Good to Know For al dente (tender but slightly firm), cook the shells no longer than the package instructs—maybe even a minute or two less. (They're going to bake in the oven for 40 minutes, after all.) Overcooking the shells can make them fall apart as you're trying to stuff them.

Spinach-Stuffed Pasta Shells

- 12 dried jumbo shell macaroni
- 1 10-ounce package frozen chopped spinach, thawed
- 2 eggs, lightly beaten
- 2 cups shredded Italian cheese blend (8 ounces)
- 1 cup ricotta cheese
- 1 26- to 32-ounce jar pasta sauce

1 Cook jumbo shells according to package directions; drain. Rinse with cold water; drain again (see photo, page 305). Set shells aside. Meanwhile, drain thawed spinach well (below).

2 Preheat oven to 350°F. For filling, in a medium bowl stir together spinach, eggs, 1½ cups of the Italian cheese blend, and the ricotta cheese (below). Spoon a generous 2 rounded tablespoons of the filling into each jumbo shell (below). Arrange shells in a 2-quart square baking dish. Pour pasta sauce over shells (below).

3 Bake, covered, in the preheated oven about 40 minutes or until heated through. Sprinkle with the remaining ½ cup Italian cheese blend. Let stand 5 minutes before serving. Makes 4 main-dish servings.

Make-ahead directions: Prepare as above through Step 2. Cover with plastic wrap, then foil. Chill for up to 24 hours. To bake, remove plastic wrap and replace the foil. Bake in a preheated 375°F oven for 50 to 55 minutes or until heated through. Continue as directed.

Per serving: 592 cal., 31 g total fat (14 g sat. fat), 117 mg chol., 2,049 mg sodium, 52 g carbo., 12 g fiber, 34 g pro.

emove as much
uid from the thawed
s possible, place
a sieve and press
den spoon.

2 In a medium bowl stir together all filling ingredients, but use only 1½ cups of the shredded cheese.

3 Use a flatware tablespoon to fill each of the cooked jumbo shells with the spinach mixture.

4 Pour the jar of pasta sauce evenly over the filled jumbo shells.

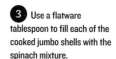
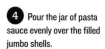

Ask Mom What is that pasta shape? pages 308–309 / How do I beat eggs? page 62

Gearing Up You will go hungry trying to serve long noodles such as fettuccine or spaghetti with a spoon. They just drop off and slide back into the pot. Use a pasta server or tongs—either works well at grabbing the long, slippery strands.

2 Skill Level

Fettuccine Alfredo

- 8 ounces dried fettuccine
- 2 tablespoons butter
- 1 cup whipping cream
- ½ teaspoon salt
- ⅛ teaspoon freshly ground black pepper
- ½ cup freshly grated Parmesan cheese
- Grated or finely shredded Parmesan cheese (optional)

1 Cook fettuccine according to package directions.

2 Meanwhile, for sauce, in a 3-quart saucepan melt butter (below). Add cream, salt, and pepper to saucepan (below). Bring to boiling; reduce heat. Boil gently, uncovered, for 3 to 5 minutes or until mixture begins to thicken, stirring frequently (below). Remove saucepan from heat; stir in the ½ cup Parmesan cheese (below). Drain fettuccine (see photo, page 305); add to hot sauce. Toss to coat (page 323). Transfer to a warm serving dish. Serve immediately. If desired, sprinkle with additional Parmesan cheese. Makes 4 main-dish servings.

Per serving: 515 cal., 32 g total fat (19 g sat. fat), 107 mg chol., 512 mg sodium, 45 g carbo., 1 g fiber, 12 g pro.

Chicken and Tomato Fettuccine Alfredo: Prepare as above, except stir 1½ cups chopped cooked chicken and ¼ cup drained oil-packed snipped dried tomatoes into the thickened sauce and heat through before adding the Parmesan cheese.

Shrimp Fettuccine Alfredo: Prepare as above, except stir 12 ounces cooked medium shrimp and 1 tablespoon fresh snipped basil or 1 teaspoon dried basil, crushed, into the thickened sauce and heat through before adding the Parmesan cheese.

1 Begin making the sauce while the fettuccine is cooking. Melt the butter in a 3-quart saucepan over medium heat.

2 Carefully pour the whipping cream into the saucepan with the melted butter; add salt and pepper.

3 Boil the sauce gently until it begins to thicken, stirring frequently with a wooden spoon.

4 Once the sauce is thickened, remove the saucepan from heat and in the Parmesan cheese.

Ask Mom What is that pasta shape? pages 308–309 / How do I measure butter? pages 58, 59 / How do I freshly grind pepper? page 22 / How do I grate cheese? page 71 / How do I shred cheese? page 71 / What does it mean to toss? page 77 / What are dried tomatoes? page 53 / How do I warm a serving dish/plate? page 316 / How do I snip fresh herbs? pages 42, 328 / How do I crush dried herbs? page 78

5 Add the cooked noodles to the pan of warm sauce and work quickly to toss the two together. Use the wooden spoon and scrape around edge of the pan bottom, where sauce tends to collect. Then serve it, pronto!

(3) Skill Level

Cajun Rice Patties On Portobellos

- 4 4- to 5-inch fresh portobello mushroom caps
- ¼ cup bulgur
- 2 eggs, lightly beaten
- 1½ cups cooked brown rice, chilled
- ¼ cup sliced green onion (2)
- ¼ cup chopped pecans, toasted
- ¼ cup seasoned fine dry bread crumbs
- 1½ teaspoons Cajun seasoning
- 3 tablespoons mayonnaise or salad dressing
- 1 tablespoon Creole mustard
- 2 teaspoons milk

Ingredient Info
Brown rice—which still has its bran coating—has more fiber and nutrients than white rice. It does, though, require a longer cooking time. White rice takes about 15 minutes, while brown rice takes about 45 minutes. Cook brown rice according to the package directions.

1 Remove stems and gills from mushroom caps (below). Set mushroom caps aside. Preheat oven to 350°F. In a 1-quart saucepan combine bulgur and enough water to cover. Bring to boiling; reduce heat. Simmer, covered, for 5 minutes. Drain well.

2 In a medium bowl combine drained bulgur, eggs, brown rice, green onion, pecans, bread crumbs, and Cajun seasoning; shape into four 3½-inch-diameter patties (below). Place a rice patty in each mushroom cap (below). Arrange mushroom caps in a greased 3-quart rectangular baking dish. Bake, covered, in the preheated oven for 15 minutes. Bake, uncovered, for 5 to 10 minutes more or until heated through. Meanwhile, in a small bowl stir together mayonnaise, mustard, and milk; drizzle over patties (below). Makes 4 main-dish servings.

Per serving: 325 cal., 17 g total fat (3 g sat. fat), 110 mg chol., 408 mg sodium, 35 g carbo., 5 g fiber, 10 g pro.

1 Snap off the mushroom stems and discard. Remove the gills (black portion under the caps) by gently scraping with a spoon.

2 On a sheet of waxed paper, use your fingers to shape the rice mixture into patties of equal size.

3 Use the waxed paper to invert one rice patty into each mushroom cap.

4 To serve, drizzle so of the mayonnaise mixtu over each baked rice pat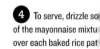

Ask Mom What are some mushroom varieties? page 44 / How do I clean fresh mushrooms? page 45 / How do I beat eggs? page 62 / How do I slice green onions? page 43 / How do I chop nuts? page 65 / How do I toast nuts? page 65 / What are fine dry bread crumbs? page 76 / What does simmer mean? page 79 / What does drizzle mean? page 79

Caribbean Rice and Beans

½ cup finely chopped onion (1 medium)

2 cloves garlic, minced

1 tablespoon butter or margarine

¾ cup uncooked Arborio rice or short grain rice

1 15.5-ounce can small red beans or light red kidney beans, rinsed and drained

1 14-ounce can vegetable broth or chicken broth

1 cup unsweetened coconut milk

1 fresh jalapeño chile pepper, chopped

1 tablespoon snipped fresh thyme or 1 teaspoon dried thyme, crushed

¼ teaspoon salt

¼ teaspoon ground allspice

¼ cup thinly sliced green onion (2)

1 In a 2- to 2½-quart saucepan cook onion and garlic in hot butter until tender; add rice. Cook and stir constantly over medium heat about 5 minutes or until rice is golden.

2 Stir beans, broth, coconut milk, jalapeño pepper, dried thyme (if using), salt, and allspice into saucepan. Bring to boiling; reduce heat. Simmer, covered, over medium heat for 15 to 20 minutes or until rice is tender and mixture is creamy. Stir in fresh thyme (if using). Sprinkle with green onion. Makes 4 to 5 main-dish servings.

Per serving: 380 cal., 15 g total fat (11 g sat. fat), 8 mg chol., 913 mg sodium, 52 g carbo., 7 g fiber, 10 g pro.

Good to Know There are several ingredients that—when used in concert—earmark a dish as Caribbean. A few of them appear in this recipe: coconut milk (of course), hot chile in the form of a jalapeño, thyme, and ground allspice. The allspice tree is native to the West Indies and is an integral part of Jamaican jerk seasoning.

325

Pasta, Rice & Grains

Vegetable broth

Arborio rice

Jalapeño chile pepper

Onion

d beans

Ask Mom How do I chop an onion? page 47 / What is a garlic clove? page 40 / How do I mince garlic? page 40 / How do I measure butter? pages 58, 59 / What is Arborio rice? page 153 / How do I rinse and drain canned beans? page 390 / What is coconut milk? page 272 / How do I handle hot chile peppers? page 48 / How do I snip fresh herbs? pages 42, 328 / How do I crush dried herbs? page 78 / How do I slice green onions? page 43 / What does simmer mean? page 79

Savory Stuffed Portobellos

½ cup chopped onion (1 medium)

4 cloves garlic, minced

1 tablespoon olive oil

1 6.75- to 8-ounce package rice pilaf mix with lentils

1 6-ounce jar marinated artichoke hearts

6 4- to 5-inch fresh portobello mushroom caps

¼ cup finely shredded Parmesan cheese

1 Preheat oven to 350°F. In a 2- to 2½-quart saucepan cook onion and garlic in hot oil until tender. Add the rice pilaf mix to the onion mixture in saucepan and prepare according to the package directions.

2 Meanwhile, drain artichoke hearts, reserving marinade. Coarsely chop artichokes; set aside. Remove stems and gills from mushroom caps (see photo 1, page 324). Brush mushroom caps with some of the reserved marinade; discard any remaining marinade. Arrange mushroom caps, stemmed sides up, in an ungreased shallow baking pan.

3 Bake, uncovered, in the preheated oven for 15 to 20 minutes or until tender. Transfer mushroom caps to serving plates, stemmed sides up. Stir the artichoke hearts and Parmesan cheese into hot rice pilaf mixture; spoon into the mushroom caps. Makes 6 main-dish servings.

Per serving: 288 cal., 14 g total fat (5 g sat. fat), 16 mg chol., 817 mg sodium, 31 g carbo., 4 g fiber, 20 g pro.

Chicken-Stuffed Portobellos: Prepare as above, except substitute 1 cup chopped cooked chicken for the artichokes.

Ingredient Info With their saucer-size proportions and dense, meaty texture, portobello mushrooms are favorites for stuffing and grilling. They are the mature form of the small brown mushrooms called cremini—which are a variation on standard white button mushrooms. Don't use the stems—they're extremely woody and tough.

Ask Mom How do I chop an onion? page 47 / What is a garlic clove? page 40 / How do I mince garlic? page 40 / What are some mushroom varieties? page 44 / How do I clean fresh mushrooms? page 45 / How do I shred cheese? page 71

2 Skill Level

French Lentils with Rice and Vegetables

Ingredient Info There are three main types of lentils. Shown below, they include common brown lentils, French lentils (also called du Puy or green lentils), and red lentils. French lentils are prized for their peppery flavor and delicate texture and the fact that they hold their shape well when cooked. If you can't find them at your supermarket, look at a whole foods or specialty market.

3 cups water

½ teaspoon salt

½ cup dry French lentils, rinsed and drained

½ cup uncooked basmati rice or long grain rice

1 recipe Dijon Dressing

⅔ cup coarsely chopped yellow, red, or green sweet pepper (1 medium)

½ cup chopped carrot (1 medium)

½ cup chopped yellow summer squash

½ cup chopped seedless cucumber

2 roma tomatoes, seeded and finely chopped

2 tablespoons chopped shallot

½ cup crumbled feta cheese (2 ounces) (optional)

1 In a 2- to 2½-quart saucepan bring water and salt to boiling; stir in lentils. Return to boiling; reduce heat. Simmer, covered, for 15 minutes. Add rice. Simmer, covered, about 15 minutes more or until rice and lentils are tender. Let stand, covered, for 5 minutes. If necessary, drain well. Spoon into a large bowl; set aside to cool about 1 hour.

2 Meanwhile, prepare Dijon Dressing; set aside. Stir sweet pepper, carrot, summer squash, cucumber, tomato, and shallot into rice mixture. Add dressing; toss gently to coat. Serve at room temperature or chilled. If desired, just before serving sprinkle with feta cheese. Makes 6 side-dish servings or 4 main-dish servings.

Dijon Dressing: In a blender container combine ¼ cup olive oil, 2 tablespoons lemon juice, 2 tablespoons Dijon-style mustard, ¼ teaspoon salt, ¼ teaspoon ground black pepper, and 1 clove garlic, minced. Cover and blend until smooth.

Per serving: 216 cal., 9 g total fat (1 g sat. fat), 0 mg chol., 423 mg sodium, 28 g carbo., 6 g fiber, 7 g pro.

Dry brown lentils   Dry French lentils   Dry red lentils

Ask Mom How do I seed/chop sweet peppers? page 49 / How do I peel and cut carrots? page 37 / What is summer squash? page 54 / What does it mean to chop? page 64 / What is a roma tomato? page 52 / How do I seed and chop tomatoes? page 52 / What is a shallot? page 46 / How do I chop an onion? page 47 / How do I crumble cheese? pages 71, 96 / How do I juice a lemon? pages 30, 80 / What is Dijon-style mustard? page 379 / What is a garlic clove? page 40 / How do I mince garlic? page 40

Red Lentil Rice

½ cup chopped onion (I medium)

I teaspoon cumin seeds, crushed

½ teaspoon salt

⅛ teaspoon cayenne pepper

2 cloves garlic, minced

I tablespoon olive oil

1⅓ cups uncooked basmati rice or long grain rice

2 14-ounce cans chicken broth

½ cup water

I cup frozen peas

½ cup dry red lentils (see photo, page 327), rinsed and drained

¼ cup snipped fresh mint

I teaspoon garam masala

I recipe Yogurt Raita

Ingredient Info Indian cuisine is known for its sophisticated spice blends—one of them is curry. Another is garam masala. "Garam" means warm or hot; "masala" means spice blend. While garam masala is not fiery hot, it does add a sense of warmth to a dish. It can include black pepper, cinnamon, mace, cloves, coriander, cumin, cardamom, chiles, fennel, and nutmeg. Look for it at Indian markets, spice shops, or import food shops.

1 In a 4-quart Dutch oven cook and stir onion, cumin seeds, salt, cayenne pepper, and garlic in hot oil over medium heat for 2 minutes; add rice. Cook and stir for 1 minute more. Carefully add broth and water. Bring to boiling; reduce heat. Simmer, covered, for 10 minutes.

2 Stir peas and lentils into onion mixture. Return to boiling; reduce heat. Simmer, covered, for 8 to 10 minutes more or until lentils are just tender. Remove Dutch oven from heat; stir in mint and garam masala. Let stand, covered, for 5 minutes before serving. Serve with Yogurt Raita. Makes 6 main-dish servings.

Yogurt Raita: In a medium bowl stir together one 6-ounce carton plain yogurt; ¾ cup chopped, seeded cucumber (1 small); ½ cup chopped, seeded tomato (1 medium); 1 tablespoon snipped fresh mint; ⅛ teaspoon salt; and dash ground black pepper.

Per serving: 274 cal., 3 g total fat (I g sat. fat), 3 mg chol., 827 mg sodium, 50 g carbo., 4 g fiber, IO g pro.

Kitchen scissors are an ideal tool for snipping fresh herbs for cooking. Just put the herbs in a glass measuring cup or small bowl and snip away. If you don't have kitchen scissors, pile the herbs on a cutting board and chop them with a chef's knife by rocking the knife back and forth over them.

Ask Mom How do I chop an onion? page 47 / How do I crush seeds? page 78 / What is a garlic clove? page 40 / How do I mince garlic? page 40 / What does simmer mean? page 79 / How do I seed tomatoes? page 52 / How do I chop a tomato? page 52 / What does dash mean? page 79

WHAT'S RAITA? Raita (RI-tah) is a yogurt salad eaten in India as a cooling counterpoint to the cuisine's more fiery foods. Raita usually contains cucumber and tomato, but it can include other vegetables—even fruits—as well.

DOES IT MATTER WHAT KIND OF TOFU I USE?

Actually, yes. Tofu comes in different textures: silken (good for smoothies), soft, firm, and extra-firm. For a stir-fry, use the extra-firm style so it doesn't disintegrate as you cook it.

1 As the egg mixture cooks, use a heat-resistant plastic spatula to stir gently but continuously until set.

2 Slide the egg mixture from the skillet onto a cutting board. Roll up the sheet of egg. Use a large knife to cut the roll into ½-inch slices.

3 After adding the rice, carrot, and peas to the skillet, pour the 2 tablespoons soy sauce over all.

4 Cook and stir the rice mixture about I minute or until it's completely heated through.

2 Skill Level

Fried Rice

- 2 eggs, lightly beaten
- 1 teaspoon soy sauce
- 1 teaspoon sesame oil or vegetable oil
- 1 clove garlic, minced
- 1 tablespoon cooking oil
- ½ cup thinly bias-sliced celery (1 stalk)
- 1 cup sliced fresh mushrooms
- 1 8.8-ounce pouch cooked white rice (2 cups)*
- ½ cup shredded carrot (1 medium)
- ½ cup frozen peas, thawed
- 2 tablespoons soy sauce
- ¼ cup sliced green onion (2)

Ingredient Info Tofu is a supernutritious food made from soymilk. It's low in fat and high in protein. It comes in several types—soft, firm, extra-firm, and silken (sort of like custard). Look for it in the refrigerated section.

1 In a small bowl combine eggs and the 1 teaspoon soy sauce. Set aside.

2 Pour the sesame oil into an 8-inch nonstick skillet with flared sides. Preheat over medium heat. Add egg mixture and garlic to skillet. Stir egg mixture gently but continuously until mixture resembles small pieces of cooked egg surrounded by liquid egg (page 330). Stop stirring. Cook for 30 to 60 seconds more or until egg mixture is set and shiny. Slide egg mixture onto a cutting board; roll up. Cut into ½-inch slices; set aside (page 330).

3 Pour the cooking oil into the same skillet. (Add more oil if necessary during cooking.) Preheat over medium-high heat. Add celery to skillet; cook and stir for 1 minute. Add mushrooms; cook and stir for 1 to 2 minutes more or until vegetables are crisp-tender.

4 Add rice, carrot, and peas to skillet. Add the 2 tablespoons soy sauce (page 330). Cook and stir 4 to 6 minutes or until heated through. Add egg strips and green onion; cook and stir until heated through (page 330). Makes 6 side-dish servings.

*Note: You can substitute 2 cups of leftover cooked white rice for the pouch of white rice.

Per serving: 141 cal., 6 g total fat (1 g sat. fat), 71 mg chol., 418 mg sodium, 18 g carbo., 2 g fiber, 5 g pro.

Shrimp Fried Rice: Prepare as above, except add 12 ounces peeled and deveined fully cooked shrimp when adding the rice. Makes 4 main-dish servings.

Tofu Fried Rice: Prepare as above, except add 8 ounces extra-firm tofu (fresh bean curd), drained and cut into ¾-inch cubes, when adding the rice. Makes 4 main-dish servings.

Ask Mom How do I beat eggs? page 62 / What is a garlic clove? page 40 / How do I mince garlic? page 40 / What does bias-slice mean? page 79 / How do I prepare celery? page 39 / What are some mushroom varieties? page 44 / How do I slice fresh mushrooms? page 45 / How do I shred vegetables? page 20 / How do I slice green onions? page 43 / What does it mean to stir-fry? page 69 / What does crisp-tender mean? page 79

Barley and Green Bean Skillet

I 14-ounce can low-sodium chicken broth or vegetable broth

⅓ cup water

1¼ cups quick-cooking barley

1½ cups frozen cut green beans

I 10.75-ounce can condensed cream of onion soup

I cup cubed cooked ham, chicken, or turkey

½ cup shredded carrot (I medium)

½ cup milk

½ teaspoon dried thyme, crushed

I cup shredded sharp cheddar cheese (4 ounces)

1 In a 10-inch nonstick skillet bring broth and the water to boiling; stir in barley. Return to boiling; reduce heat. Simmer, covered, for 5 minutes.

2 Stir green beans, soup, ham, carrot, milk, and thyme into skillet. Bring to boiling; reduce heat. Simmer, covered, for 12 to 15 minutes or until barley is tender and most of the liquid is absorbed, stirring occasionally. Stir in ½ cup of the cheese.

3 Sprinkle with the remaining ½ cup cheese. Let stand for 2 to 3 minutes or until cheese melts. Makes 4 main-dish servings.

Per serving: 434 cal., 16 g total fat (8 g sat. fat), 59 mg chol., 1,099 mg sodium, 50 g carbo., 7 g fiber, 22 g pro.

Quick-cooking barley

Pearl barley

Good to Know

Barley is most commonly sold in two forms: pearl, in which the grain has been steamed and polished, and quick-cooking pearl, in which the whole grain has been further processed by being sliced and rolled into flakes. Pearl barley takes 45 minutes to cook; quick-cooking is ready in 10 to 12 minutes.

Ask Mom What does it mean to cube? page 64 / How do I shred vegetables? page 20 / How do I crush dried herbs? page 78 / How do I shred cheese? page 71 / What does simmer mean? page 79

Good to Know
Creamy classic Italian risotto is made by slowly cooking Arborio rice with hot broth, a ladleful at a time, and stirring almost constantly. This dish uses the same technique—only with chewy barley rather than rice.

Risotto-Style Barley And Vegetables

- 2 tablespoons butter or margarine
- 1 tablespoon olive oil
- 1 cup quick-cooking barley
- ½ cup finely chopped onion (1 medium)
- 1 clove garlic, minced
- 2½ cups chicken broth or vegetable broth
- 8 ounces fresh asparagus spears, trimmed and cut into 1-inch pieces
- 1 cup shredded carrot (2 medium)
- 1 15- to 16-ounce can cannellini beans (white kidney beans) or pinto beans, rinsed and drained
- ½ cup finely shredded Asiago or Parmesan cheese (2 ounces)
- ¼ cup snipped fresh basil

1 In a 3-quart saucepan heat butter and oil. Add barley, onion, and garlic. Cook and stir over medium heat for 3 to 5 minutes or until onion is tender and barley is golden (below).

2 Meanwhile, in a 1½-quart saucepan bring broth to simmering. Slowly add ¾ cup of the broth to the barley mixture, stirring constantly (below). Continue to cook and stir over medium heat until liquid is absorbed. Add another ½ cup of the broth, stirring constantly. Continue to cook and stir until the liquid is absorbed. Add remaining broth, about ½ cup at a time, stirring constantly until liquid is almost all absorbed but is still creamy (below). (This should take about 12 minutes.) Add asparagus and carrot to saucepan (below). Reduce heat and cook, covered, about 5 minutes or until barley and vegetables are tender. Stir in beans, cheese, and basil; heat through. If desired, season to taste with *ground black pepper*. Makes 4 main-dish servings.

Per serving: 371 cal., 15 g total fat (8 g sat. fat), 32 mg chol., 981 mg sodium, 49 g carbo., 10 g fiber, 15 g pro.

...a wooden spoon barley and onion ...y until the barley

2 Add the hot broth to the barley mixture in small amounts, adding more only after the previous broth has been absorbed.

3 Stirring constantly keeps the barley from sticking and helps the barley absorb the hot broth evenly.

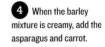
4 When the barley mixture is creamy, add the asparagus and carrot.

Ask Mom How do I measure butter? pages 58, 59 / How do I chop an onion? page 47 / What is a garlic clove? page 40 / How do I mince garlic? page 40 / How do I trim asparagus? page 34 / How do I shred vegetables? page 20 / How do I rinse and drain canned beans? page 390 / How do I shred cheese? page 71 / How do I snip fresh herbs? pages 42, 328 / What does simmer mean? page 79

Vegetable Two-Grain Casserole

Nonstick cooking spray

1 19-ounce can ready-to-serve lentil soup

1 15- to 16-ounce can red kidney beans or black beans, rinsed and drained

1 cup shredded smoked cheddar cheese or Gouda cheese (4 ounces)

1 cup fresh shiitake or cremini mushrooms, stemmed and halved

1 cup frozen whole kernel corn

$\frac{1}{2}$ cup shredded carrot (1 medium)

$\frac{1}{2}$ cup pearl barley (see photo, page 332)

$\frac{1}{3}$ cup bulgur

$\frac{1}{4}$ cup chopped onion

$\frac{1}{2}$ teaspoon dried thyme, crushed

$\frac{1}{2}$ teaspoon ground black pepper

$\frac{1}{4}$ teaspoon salt

1 cup chicken broth or vegetable broth

Pita wedges (optional)

1 Preheat oven to 350°F. Lightly coat a 2-quart casserole with cooking spray. In prepared casserole combine soup, beans, $\frac{1}{2}$ cup of the cheese, mushrooms, corn, carrot, barley, bulgur, onion, thyme, pepper, and salt. Stir in the broth.

2 Bake, covered, in the preheated oven about 60 minutes or until barley and bulgur are tender, stirring twice. Sprinkle with the remaining $\frac{1}{2}$ cup cheese. Let stand, covered, about 3 minutes or until cheese melts. If desired, serve with pita wedges. Makes 4 to 6 main-dish servings.

Per serving: 498 cal., 12 g total fat (6 g sat. fat), 32 mg chol., 1,489 mg sodium, 77 g carbo., 19 g fiber, 25 g pro.

Ask Mom How do I rinse and drain canned beans? page 390 / How do I shred cheese? page 71 / What are some mushroom varieties? page 44 / How do I clean fresh mushrooms? page 45 / How do I shred vegetables? page 20 / How do I chop an onion? page 47 / How do I crush dried herbs? page 78

Good to Know Rich, buttery Muenster is a semisoft cheese. To make it easier to grate, wrap it tightly and stick it in the freezer for a few minutes.

Peppers Stuffed with Cranberry Bulgur

    1 cup vegetable broth or chicken broth
    1/3 cup shredded carrot
    1/4 cup chopped onion
    1/2 cup bulgur
    1/4 cup dried cranberries, cherries, or raisins
    1/2 cup shredded Muenster, brick, or mozzarella cheese (2 ounces)
    2 large yellow, green, or red sweet peppers
    1/2 cup water
    2 tablespoons sliced almonds or chopped pecans, toasted

1 In a 10-inch skillet stir together broth, carrot, and onion. Bring to boiling; reduce heat. Simmer, covered, for 5 minutes. Stir in bulgur and cranberries (below). Remove from heat. Let stand, covered, for 5 minutes. Drain off any excess liquid. Stir cheese into bulgur mixture.

2 Meanwhile, halve the sweet peppers lengthwise, removing the seeds and membranes (below). Divide bulgur mixture among sweet pepper halves (below). Arrange sweet pepper halves in skillet; add water (below). Bring to boiling; reduce heat. Simmer, covered, for 5 to 10 minutes or until sweet peppers are crisp-tender and bulgur mixture is heated through. Sprinkle with almonds. Makes 4 main-dish servings.

Per serving: 199 cal., 7 g total fat (3 g sat. fat), 14 mg chol., 338 mg sodium, 30 g carbo., 6 g fiber, 8 g pro.

2 Use a sharp knife to halve the sweet peppers lengthwise, leaving the stems attached. Remove the seeds and membranes.

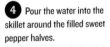
3 Spoon some of the bulgur mixture into each sweet pepper half.

4 Pour the water into the skillet around the filled sweet pepper halves.

...bulgur and dried ...s to the simmering ...ure.

Ask Mom How do I shred vegetables? page 20 / How do I chop an onion? page 47 / How do I shred cheese? page 71 / How do I toast nuts? page 65 / What does simmer mean? page 79 / What does crisp-tender mean? page 79

Greek Quinoa
And Avocado Salad

½ cup uncooked quinoa, rinsed and drained*

1 cup water

2 roma tomatoes, seeded and finely chopped

½ cup shredded fresh spinach

⅓ cup finely chopped red onion (1 small)

2 tablespoons lemon juice

2 tablespoons olive oil

½ teaspoon salt

Spinach leaves

2 ripe avocados, halved, seeded, peeled, and sliced**

⅓ cup crumbled feta cheese

1 In a 1½-quart saucepan combine quinoa and water. Bring to boiling; reduce heat. Simmer, covered, about 15 minutes or until liquid is absorbed.

2 Transfer quinoa to a bowl. Add tomato, shredded spinach, and onion; stir to combine. In a small bowl whisk together lemon juice, oil, and salt. Add to quinoa mixture; toss to coat.

3 Place spinach leaves on 4 salad plates. Arrange avocado slices on spinach leaves. Spoon quinoa mixture over avocado slices. Sprinkle with some of the feta. Makes 4 main-dish servings.

*Note: Rinse quinoa thoroughly before cooking to remove a bitter substance called saponin that coats the seeds.

**Note: Brush avocado slices with additional lemon juice to prevent browning.

Per serving: 332 cal., 24 g total fat (5 g sat. fat), 11 mg chol., 457 mg sodium, 27 g carbo., 8 g fiber, 7 g pro.

MEAL MAKER This Mediterranean-inspired grain salad is great on a plate—or stuffed into a pita as a portable lunch.

Ask Mom What is a roma tomato? page 52 / How do I seed tomatoes? page 52 / How do I chop a tomato? page 52 / How do I shred fresh herbs/spinach? page 42 / How do I chop an onion? page 47 / How do I juice a lemon/lime? pages 30, 80 / How much juice does one lemon/lime yield? page 30 / How do I seed and peel an avocado? page 36 / What does simmer mean? page 79 / How do I crumble cheese? pages 71, 96

Quinoa Chicken Ragout

2 tablespoons all-purpose flour

1 teaspoon chili powder

½ teaspoon salt

½ teaspoon ground black pepper

1 pound skinless, boneless chicken thighs, cut into 1-inch pieces

½ cup chopped onion (1 medium)

1 clove garlic, minced

1 tablespoon cooking oil

1 28-ounce can diced tomatoes, undrained

1 14-ounce can chicken broth

1 cup finely chopped, peeled potato (1 medium)

1 cup frozen whole kernel corn

¾ cup uncooked quinoa, rinsed and drained (see note, page 336)

2 cups packed fresh spinach leaves

2 teaspoons finely shredded lemon peel

2 tablespoons lemon juice

1 Place flour, chili powder, salt, and pepper in a large resealable plastic bag. Add chicken to bag, shaking to coat.

2 In a 4- to 6-quart Dutch oven cook and stir chicken, onion, and garlic in hot oil over medium heat for 3 to 4 minutes or until chicken is no longer pink. Add undrained tomatoes, broth, potato, corn, and quinoa to Dutch oven. Bring to boiling; reduce heat. Simmer, covered, for 15 to 20 minutes or until potatoes and quinoa are tender.

3 Stir in spinach and lemon juice; cook just until spinach wilts. Transfer to a serving dish. Sprinkle with lemon peel. Makes 6 main-dish servings.

Per serving: 286 cal., 7 g total fat (1 g sat. fat), 63 mg chol., 752 mg sodium, 35 g carbo., 4 g fiber, 21 g pro.

Ingredient Info Tiny, beadlike quinoa (pronounced KEEN-wah) was a staple of the ancient Incas. It is still important in South American cuisine and is considered a "supergrain" because it has more protein than any other grain, contains all eight essential amino acids, and is lower in carbohydrates than most grains.

Ask Mom How do I chop an onion? page 47 / What is a garlic clove? page 40 / How do I mince garlic? page 40 / What are some potato varieties? page 50 / How do I prepare potatoes? page 51 / How do I shred lemon/lime peel? page 30 / How do I juice a lemon/lime? pages 30, 80 / How much juice does one lemon/lime yield? page 30 / What does simmer mean? page 79

2 Skill Level

Polenta and
Black Beans

Ingredient Info
Cornmeal comes
in many different
textures. The best kind
to use for polenta is
coarse ground; it has
a more toothsome
texture than more
finely ground
cornmeal. Although
you can use regular
yellow cornmeal,
try to look for that
specifically labeled
"polenta."

4 cups water
1 cup yellow cornmeal
½ teaspoon salt
¾ cup shredded Mexican cheese blend (3 ounces)
1 15-ounce can black beans, rinsed and drained
1 14.5-ounce can diced tomatoes, undrained
1 cup bottled salsa with cilantro or regular salsa

1 For polenta, in a 3-quart saucepan bring 3 cups of the water to boiling. Meanwhile, in a medium bowl or large glass measuring cup combine cornmeal and salt. Stir in the remaining 1 cup water (below). Stir cornmeal mixture slowly into the boiling water (below). Cook and stir until mixture returns to boiling. Reduce heat to low. Cook for 5 to 10 minutes or until mixture is thick, stirring frequently (below). (If mixture is too thick, stir in additional water.) Stir ½ cup of the cheese into the polenta.

2 Meanwhile, in a 10-inch skillet stir together beans, undrained tomatoes, and salsa. Bring to boiling; reduce heat. Simmer, uncovered, for 10 minutes, stirring frequently.

3 Divide polenta among 4 serving bowls (below). Top each serving with some of the bean mixture; sprinkle with the remaining ¼ cup cheese. Makes 4 main-dish servings.

Per serving: 311 cal., 8 g total fat (4 g sat. fat), 19 mg chol., 751 mg sodium, 49 g carbo., 8 g fiber, 15 g pro.

1 In a medium bowl combine the cornmeal and salt. Use a wire whisk to stir in 1 cup water.

2 Slowly add the cornmeal mixture to the boiling water, stirring constantly.

3 Return the cornmeal mixture to boiling; reduce to low heat. Stir often with the wire whisk until the cornmeal mixture is thick.

4 Spoon the polenta shallow serving bowls.

Ask Mom How do I rinse and drain canned beans? page 390 / What does simmer mean? page 79

make-it-a-meal
SALADS

Mom always said to eat your veggies. Here are 20-plus delicious ways to get them—and the rest of dinner too.

9

3 Skill Level

Spring Greens With Sugared Nuts

Nonstick cooking spray
½ cup coarsely chopped walnuts or pecans
2 tablespoons sugar
⅛ teaspoon salt
1 teaspoon butter
5 cups packaged spring mix salad greens or torn romaine lettuce
⅓ cup thin red onion wedges or sliced green onion
¼ cup dried cherries or dried cranberries
⅓ cup bottled reduced-calorie raspberry vinaigrette or raspberry-walnut vinaigrette salad dressing
2 ounces Asiago cheese, shredded, or blue cheese, crumbled (½ cup)

Good to Know If you're running short on time, you can skip making the sugared nuts and simply sprinkle the six salads with a total of ½ cup purchased glazed walnuts or almonds.

341

Salads

1 Preheat oven to 325°F. Line a baking sheet with foil. Lightly coat the foil with cooking spray; set aside. Spread nuts evenly in a shallow baking pan. Bake nuts, uncovered, in the preheated oven about 10 minutes or until toasted, stirring once.

2 Meanwhile, for sugared nuts, place sugar and salt in a heavy 6-inch skillet. Heat over medium-high heat, shaking skillet several times to heat sugar evenly (do not stir). Heat until some of the sugar is melted and looks syrupy (below). Begin to stir only the melted sugar to keep it from overbrowning, stirring in remaining sugar as it melts (below). Reduce heat to low. Continue to cook and stir until all the sugar is melted and golden; stir in butter. Add the warm nuts to the skillet, stirring to coat (below). Pour nut mixture onto the prepared baking sheet. While the nut mixture is still warm, use two forks to separate it into clusters (below). Cool completely.

3 In a large bowl combine greens, onion, and cherries; drizzle with dressing and toss to coat. Divide among six salad plates. Top with nuts and cheese. Makes 6 side-dish servings.

Per serving: 182 cal., 13 g total fat (3 g sat. fat), 12 mg chol., 283 mg sodium, 14 g carbo., 2 g fiber, 5 g pro.

en sugar starts to only the melted part n't overbrown.

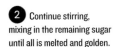
2 Continue stirring, mixing in the remaining sugar until all is melted and golden.

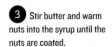
3 Stir butter and warm nuts into the syrup until the nuts are coated.

4 Spread nuts on coated baking sheet and separate the nuts into small clusters.

Ask Mom How do I chop nuts? page 65 / What is that salad green? page 347 / How do I cut onion wedges? page 47 / How do I slice green onions? page 43 / How do I shred cheese? page 71 / How do I crumble cheese? pages 71, 96 / How do I line a pan with foil? page 60 / What does it mean to toss? page 77

Bread Salad

3 cups Italian bread torn into bite-size pieces or cut into
l-inch cubes, dried*

1½ cups coarsely chopped, seeded tomato (3 medium)

½ of a medium red onion, cut into thin wedges
and separated

¼ cup snipped fresh basil or fresh Italian (flat-leaf)
parsley

2 tablespoons red wine vinegar or white wine vinegar

2 tablespoons olive oil

2 cloves garlic, minced

¼ teaspoon salt

¼ teaspoon ground black pepper

4 cups torn or chopped romaine lettuce

1 In a large bowl toss together dried bread pieces, tomato, onion, and basil; set aside.

2 For dressing, in a screw-top jar combine vinegar, olive oil, garlic, salt, and pepper. Cover and shake well (see photos, page 357). Pour the dressing over the bread mixture; toss to coat. Let stand for 15 minutes to allow the flavors to blend. Place romaine on four salad plates. Spoon bread mixture over romaine. Makes 4 side-dish servings.

*Note: To dry bread, spread bread pieces or cubes in a shallow baking pan. Let stand overnight at room temperature, stirring once or twice. Or preheat oven to 300°F. Bake, uncovered, in the preheated oven for 8 to 10 minutes, stirring once or twice until dry but not toasted.

Per serving: 213 cal., 9 g total fat (1 g sat. fat), 0 mg chol., 417 mg sodium, 29 g carbo., 4 g fiber, 6 g pro.

Quick Bread Salad: Prepare as above, except omit vinegar, olive oil, garlic, salt, and pepper for the dressing. Substitute ¼ to ⅓ cup bottled Italian salad dressing and let stand as above.

Shopping Savvy You can buy romaine lettuce any one of three ways for this salad: a whole head, hearts of romaine (the extra-crunchy, densely packed center leaves of the head), or a bag of pretorn hearts of romaine. Buying hearts of romaine is going to cost you a little more, but they are particularly crisp and delicious.

Ask Mom How do I make/toast bread cubes? pages 79, 334 / How do I seed tomatoes? page 52 / How do I chop a tomato? page 52 / How do I cut onion wedges? page 47 / How do I snip fresh herbs? pages 42, 328 / What is that vinegar? page 349 / What is that oil? page 348 / What is a garlic clove? page 40 / How do I mince garlic? page 40 / What is that salad green? page 347 / What does it mean to toss? page 77

Greek Salad

6 cups torn mixed salad greens or romaine lettuce

2 medium tomatoes, cut into wedges, or 8 cherry tomatoes, halved

1 small cucumber, peeled, halved lengthwise, and thinly sliced (below)

1 small red onion, cut into thin wedges

½ cup pitted kalamata olives

½ cup crumbled feta cheese (2 ounces)

1 recipe Greek Vinaigrette

2 small pita bread rounds, cut into wedges (see photos, page 87) (optional)

Ingredient Info To get the best cucumbers, choose those that have firm, smooth flesh with no soft spots or wrinkles. Also look for smaller cucumbers. The larger they are, the more bitter the seeds. Peeling cucumbers is not necessary. Just make sure to wash them thoroughly.

1 In a salad bowl combine salad greens, tomato, cucumber, onion, olives, and cheese. Add Greek Vinaigrette; toss to coat. If desired, serve with pita bread. Makes 6 side-dish servings.

Greek Vinaigrette: In a screw-top jar combine 2 tablespoons olive oil or salad oil; 2 tablespoons lemon juice; 2 teaspoons snipped fresh oregano or ½ teaspoon dried oregano, crushed; ⅛ teaspoon salt; and ⅛ teaspoon ground black pepper. Cover and shake well (see photos, page 357). Makes about ¼ cup.

Per serving: 105 cal., 8 g total fat (2 g sat. fat), 8 mg chol., 286 mg sodium, 7 g carbo., 2 g fiber, 2 g pro.

Greek Chicken Salad: Prepare as above, except add 2 cups shredded deli-roasted or cooked chicken or turkey (see photo 3, page 395) to salad. Makes 4 main-dish servings.

Greek Lamb Salad: Preheat the broiler. Trim the fat from eight 1-inch-thick lamb rib or loin chops. Place chops on the unheated rack of a broiler pan. Broil chops 3 to 4 inches from heat for 10 to 15 minutes for medium (160°F), turning chops once halfway through broiling. Season with lemon-pepper seasoning or salt and ground black pepper. Prepare salad as above, except serve two chops on top of each salad. Makes 4 main-dish servings.

2 Place both halves on a board, cut sides down and side by side. Cut across both halves at once, making slices about ⅛ to ¼ inch thick.

1 Peel the cucumber. For easier slicing, use a chef's knife to cut cucumber in half.

Ask Mom What is that salad green? page 347 / How do I cut tomato wedges? page 52 / What is a cherry tomato? page 52 / How do I cut onion wedges? page 47 / How do I pit olives? page 75 / How do I crumble cheese? pages 71, 96 / What does it mean to toss? page 77 / What is that oil? page 348 / How do I juice a lemon? pages 30, 80 / How do I snip fresh herbs? pages 42, 328 / How do I crush dried herbs? page 78 / What does broil mean? page 68

Knife and Fork Caesar Salad

1 recipe Caesar Dressing
1 recipe Parmesan Croutons
3 hearts of romaine lettuce, trimmed and quartered lengthwise
6 canned anchovy fillets, halved lengthwise
1 ounce Parmesan cheese, shaved (optional)

1 Chill six salad plates. Prepare Caesar Dressing and Parmesan Croutons. To serve, place 2 romaine wedges on each chilled plate. Drizzle with dressing; top each salad with 2 anchovy strips, Parmesan Croutons, and, if desired, Parmesan cheese. Makes 6 side-dish servings.

Caesar Dressing: In a blender or food processor combine 3 cloves garlic, 3 canned anchovy fillets, and 2 tablespoons fresh lemon juice. Cover and blend or process until mixture is smooth, scraping sides of container as necessary. Add ¼ cup olive oil, 1 hard-cooked egg yolk (see page 436), 1 teaspoon Dijon-style mustard, and ½ teaspoon sugar. Cover and blend or process until smooth. Use immediately or cover and chill for up to 24 hours. Stir before using.

Parmesan Croutons: Preheat oven to 300°F. Cut four ¾-inch-thick slices Italian or French bread into 1-inch cubes (about 3½ cups) (below); set aside. In a large microwave-safe bowl microwave ¼ cup butter on 50 percent power (medium) about 1 minute or until melted.* Stir in 3 tablespoons grated Parmesan cheese and 2 cloves garlic, minced (below). Add bread cubes, stirring until bread cubes are coated with butter mixture (below). Spread cubes in a single layer on a baking sheet or in a shallow baking pan. Bake, uncovered, in the preheated oven for 10 minutes; stir. Bake about 10 minutes more or until cubes are crisp and golden (page 345). Cool completely; store in an airtight container for up to 24 hours.

*Note: If you don't have a microwave, melt the butter in a small saucepan, remove from heat, and transfer butter to a large bowl.

Per serving: 262 cal., 21 g total fat (8 g sat. fat), 65 mg chol., 521 mg sodium, 13 g carbo., 2 g fiber, 8 g pro.

1 To cut bread into cubes for the croutons, stack bread slices and slice in both directions, making cubes.

2 To season the bread cubes, combine melted butter, Parmesan cheese, and garlic in a large bowl.

3 Toss the cubes in the butter mixture until coated. A spatula or spoon is a good tool to use for this task.

Ask Mom What is a garlic clove? page 40 / How do I mince garlic? page 40 / How do I juice a lemon/lime? pages 30, 80 / How much juice does one lemon/lime yield? page 30 / What is that oil? page 348? / What is Dijon-style mustard? page 379 / How do I make/toast bread cubes? pages 79, 334 / What is that salad green? page 347 / What does drizzle mean? page 79

HOW DO I MAKE THIS A MAIN-DISH SALAD? For four main-dish servings: Make salad as shown but use 3 wedges of romaine lettuce per serving. Divide 1 pound of cooked, peeled shrimp or 2 cups of shredded cooked chicken among the four salads.

As long as you're making one batch of homemade croutons, you might as well make two—or more. They freeze beautifully and are terrific not only on salads but also on soups (and as a crunchy snack).

Salad Greens

Mom always said to eat your greens. Crisp, satisfying salads are a versatile source of what's good for you. A small tossed salad makes a great side; a main-dish salad is a simple, healthful meal.

To pick the best greens of any kind, choose those that are crisp looking with no brown or slimy spots and eat them as soon as you can.

When you get them home, discard wilted outer leaves.

For leafy lettuces such as green or red-tip leaf, butterhead, and romaine, separate leaves and hold them under cold running water to remove any dirt.

For smaller greens such as spinach and arugula, swirl them in a bowl filled with cold water or a clean sink about 30 seconds. Remove the leaves and shake gently to let dirt and other debris fall into the water. Repeat the process if necessary. Drain in colander.

For iceberg lettuce, remove the core by hitting the stem end on the countertop; twist and lift out the core. Hold the head, core side up, under cold running water, pulling leaves apart slightly. Invert the head and drain thoroughly.

Dry loose greens on clean paper towels or in a salad spinner to remove excess water. Get them as dry as you can; wet greens rot faster—and dressing clings better to dry greens. Once the greens are dry, don't cut or tear them until you use them. (When you're ready to use salad greens, tear or cut the greens into bite-size pieces with a stainless-steel knife.)

Shopping Savvy Look for prepackaged salad greens combinations in the supermarket's produce section. They're a real timesaver and add variety to a salad. They're packaged in specially designed bags that allow the greens to "breathe," so store leftovers in the original bag. Even if the package label says the greens have been prewashed, it's a good idea to wash them again.

Storing Greens

Store freshly washed-and-dried greens in a resealable plastic bag lined with paper towels following these suggested storage times:

Iceberg lettuce Remove core. Rinse; invert to drain; refrigerate for up to 5 days.

Romaine lettuce Cut off bottom core. Rinse; pat dry; refrigerate for up to 5 days. Before using, remove fibrous rib from each leaf.

Leaf lettuce Cut off bottom core. Rinse; pat dry; refrigerate for up to 5 days.

Mesclun A mixture of young, small salad greens that may be available packaged or in bulk. The mixture varies but usually includes arugula, dandelion, frisée, mâche, mizuna, oak leaf lettuce, radicchio, and sorrel. Rinse; pat dry; refrigerate for up to 5 days.

Belgian endive Cut off bottom core. Rinse; pat dry; refrigerate and use within 1 day.

Arugula Rinse; pat dry; refrigerate for up to 2 days.

Spinach and baby spinach Rinse; pat dry; refrigerate for up to 3 days.

How do I shred lettuce?

To shred iceberg lettuce for salads and dishes such as tacos and tostadas, core and clean the head of lettuce as instructed above. Cut the head into quarters, then lay each quarter on a cutting board. With a sharp stainless-steel chef's knife, cut the lettuce into $\frac{1}{4}$-inch slices, holding the lettuce firm but keeping your fingers safely out of the way.

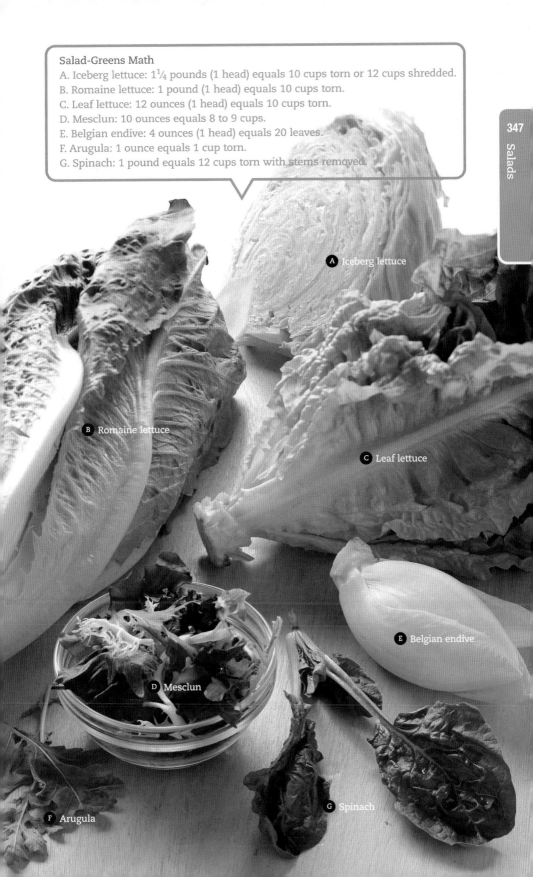

Salad-Greens Math

A. Iceberg lettuce: 1¼ pounds (1 head) equals 10 cups torn or 12 cups shredded.
B. Romaine lettuce: 1 pound (1 head) equals 10 cups torn.
C. Leaf lettuce: 12 ounces (1 head) equals 10 cups torn.
D. Mesclun: 10 ounces equals 8 to 9 cups.
E. Belgian endive: 4 ounces (1 head) equals 20 leaves.
F. Arugula: 1 ounce equals 1 cup torn.
G. Spinach: 1 pound equals 12 cups torn with stems removed.

A Iceberg lettuce

B Romaine lettuce

C Leaf lettuce

E Belgian endive

D Mesclun

F Arugula

G Spinach

Salad Dressings

While a plate of fresh greens is a beautiful thing, it's not ready for dinner until it gets dressed. Homemade salad dressing is a breeze to make and tastes so fresh on crisp greens.

There are two basic types of salad dressings: vinaigrettes, made with oil and vinegar (or other acidic liquid, such as citrus juice) and sometimes other flavorings such as garlic and herbs, and creamy dressings, often with a mayonnaise base. Both types involve making an emulsion, a thorough blending of two ingredients that are resistant to mixing (like the oil and vinegar), and require some vigorous action (like shaking or whisking) to make a smooth dressing. When making a vinaigrette, adding an emulsifier—such as mustard—helps hold all the ingredients together.

Salad dressings are easy to make from scratch, though when time is at a premium, off-the-shelf dressing varieties are handy. You don't need any fancy equipment to make a salad dressing—just a glass jar with a screw-top lid. For most vinaigrettes, pour the ingredients in the jar, tighten the lid, shake, and serve. Vinaigrette can be stored in the jar in the refrigerator for up to two weeks, depending on the recipe. Creamy dressings come together best when the ingredients are blended in a bowl with a whisk.

If vinaigrette has been stored in the refrigerator, bring it to room temperature before shaking and serving. Oils, especially olive oil, thicken and get cloudy when cold but clear up and come back to normal consistency as they warm up.

Don't toss your salad too early. Toss the greens with dressing just before serving so they don't wilt. And go light on the dressing for starters; you can always add more. Overdressing a salad makes for limp, gloppy greens.

Oils

The kind of oil you use in a dressing has a big impact on its flavor. The most mildly flavored oils are salad or vegetable oils such as soybean, sunflower, safflower, canola, and corn. They are also the lightest in color. Use them when you want a neutral background so other flavors can dominate your dressing. At the opposite end of the spectrum are nut oils like walnut, sesame, peanut, or hazelnut. Each has a distinct flavor.

(Nut oils are highly perishable and should be stored in the refrigerator.) You can use a blend of different types of oils to get the flavor you like best.

Olive oil ranges greatly in color, flavor, and body. It also comes in several grades (and price ranges). Extra virgin olive oil, from the first pressing of the olives, is the fruitiest and most flavorful—and usually the most expensive. It also makes the best vinaigrette. Olive oil that is labeled "light" is not lower in fat or calories but is milder in flavor than extra virgin. Sample different brands (and grades and origins) until you find an olive oil that suits your palate and your pocketbook.

Vinegars

Vinegar cuts through the fat—literally—of the oil in dressing. Vinegar adds acidity and balance, as well as a world of flavors and colors. If the oil is the foundation of the dressing, the vinegar is the flourish. Here are the main types of vinegar you'll find at your supermarket:

Balsamic Made from the juice of white Trebbiano grapes; gets its color and intense, sweet flavor from aging in barrels.

Cider Made from apple cider; has a crisp bite and a subtle apple flavor.

Fruit or herb Made by steeping fruit (such as raspberries) or fresh herbs (such as tarragon) in cider or white wine vinegar.

Rice Made from rice wine or sake; has tang and sweetness; available plain or seasoned.

White or distilled Made from grain alcohol; colorless; has the strongest and sharpest flavor of any vinegar; not often used in dressings.

Wine Made from red or white wine, sherry, or Champagne; reflects the color and flavors of its source.

Given all of the combinations of vinegars, citrus juices, oils, and flavorings out there, the salad dressing possibilities are nearly endless. Experiment until you find a salad dressing combination you love.

How do I make a basic vinaigrette?

Basic vinaigrette is usually 1 to 2 parts oil to 1 part vinegar, plus salt and pepper. You can also add mustard (Dijon-style is a good choice) to help bind the dressing and add flavor. Fresh herbs, garlic, and other seasonings add yet more flavor. If you like your vinaigrette a little thicker and creamier than the consistency you can get by shaking it in a glass jar, put all of the ingredients except for the oil in a bowl, then slowly drizzle in the oil while whisking vigorously. (A quick-thick trick is to put an ice cube in the glass jar with vinaigrette ingredients; shake well until mixed, then discard the ice cube.) For a flavor twist, substitute lemon or lime juice for vinegar.

Good

1 to 2 parts oil + 1 part vinegar + salt & pepper to taste

Better

1 to 2 parts oil + 1 part vinegar + salt & pepper to taste + a smidge of Dijon-style mustard

Best

1 to 2 parts oil + 1 part vinegar + salt & pepper to taste + a smidge of Dijon-style mustard + garlic & herbs to taste

Penne Salad with Beans and Gorgonzola

1¾ cups dried penne or ziti pasta (6 ounces)

8 ounces fresh green beans, trimmed and bias-sliced into 1-inch pieces (2 cups), or one 9-ounce package frozen cut green beans, thawed

⅓ cup bottled Italian salad dressing

1 tablespoon snipped fresh tarragon or ½ teaspoon dried tarragon, crushed

¼ teaspoon ground black pepper

1 cup shredded radicchio or red cabbage (below)

1 6-ounce package fresh baby spinach

½ cup crumbled Gorgonzola cheese or blue cheese (2 ounces)

Ingredient Info Radicchio looks like a small head of burgundy-color lettuce. It adds a slightly bitter flavor to salads. To store it, rinse in cold water. Pat dry and refrigerate dry leaves in a plastic bag lined with paper towels up to 1 week. One 8-ounce head yields about 5½ cups torn radicchio.

1 Cook pasta according to package directions, adding fresh green beans to pasta the last 5 to 7 minutes of cooking. (Or add thawed beans the last 3 to 4 minutes.) Drain. Rinse pasta and beans under cold running water; drain again (see photos, page 305).

2 In a large bowl combine dressing, tarragon, and pepper. Add pasta mixture and radicchio; toss gently to coat. Place spinach on a serving platter and spoon pasta mixture over spinach. Top with cheese. Makes 8 side-dish servings.

Per serving: 147 cal., 5 g total fat (2 g sat. fat), 5 mg chol., 280 mg sodium, 20 g carbo., 2 g fiber, 6 g pro.

Cheese and Herb Options: Substitute 3 ounces mozzarella cheese cubes or fresh mozzarella cheese cubes for the Gorgonzola cheese. Or substitute 1 ounce shaved Parmesan cheese for the Gorgonzola. Substitute snipped fresh basil or oregano for the fresh tarragon.

Main-Dish Options: Prepare as above, except add 8 ounces coarsely chopped pastrami or cooked chicken or cooked turkey to dressing mixture along with pasta mixture. Makes 4 main-dish servings.

To shred radicchio or cabbage, work on a cutting board. Use a chef's knife to cut into shreds that are about ¼ inch wide. Hold onto the head, keeping your fingers out of the way.

Ask Mom What is that pasta shape? pages 308–309 / How do I trim green beans? page 126 / What does bias-slice mean? page 79 / How do I snip fresh herbs? pages 42, 328 / How do I crush dried herbs? page 78 / How do I crumble cheese? pages 71, 90 / What does it mean to toss? page 77 / What does it mean to cube? page 64

Vegetable Pasta Salad

2 cups dried short pasta, such as mostaccioli, penne, or rotini
6 ounces provolone cheese, cut into $\frac{3}{4}$-inch cubes
1 small zucchini, halved lengthwise and thinly sliced (1 cup)
1 cup halved cherry tomatoes
1 small red onion, thinly sliced and separated into rings
$\frac{3}{4}$ cup chopped red or green sweet pepper (1 medium)
1 2.25-ounce can sliced, pitted ripe olives, drained
2 ounces Parmesan cheese, shaved ($\frac{1}{2}$ cup)
$\frac{1}{4}$ cup snipped fresh parsley
$\frac{3}{4}$ cup bottled balsamic vinaigrette salad dressing or Italian salad dressing

1 Cook pasta according to package directions; drain. Rinse pasta under cold running water; drain again (see photos, page 305).

2 In a very large bowl combine the pasta, provolone, zucchini, tomato, onion, sweet pepper, olives, Parmesan, and parsley. Add salad dressing and toss to coat. Cover and chill for 4 to 24 hours. Stir before serving to coat again with dressing. Makes 16 side-dish servings.

Per serving: 132 cal., 8 g total fat (3 g sat. fat), 10 mg chol., 316 mg sodium, 10 g carbo., 1 g fiber, 6 g pro.

Clean-Out-the-Fridge Pasta Salad: Use ingredients you have handy in the refrigerator to combine with pasta for an inviting salad. For example, broccoli or cauliflower florets; artichoke heart quarters; sliced, pitted green olives; sliced or shredded carrot; sliced green onion; cubed mozzarella or cheddar cheese; and/or bottled ranch salad dressing are all possibilities. For amounts: Use 2 cups dried pasta, cooked according to package directions, rinsed with cold water, and drained; up to 4 cups cut-up vegetables; 6 ounces cubed cheese; and $\frac{3}{4}$ cup bottled salad dressing. If desired, add $\frac{1}{4}$ cup snipped fresh parsley for color.

Good to Know Pasta salad is incredibly versatile and great to have waiting in your refrigerator as a one-dish meal on a warm summer night. You can turn the Clean-Out-the-Fridge variation, above, into a main-dish salad by substituting 1 cup of cubed cooked chicken or turkey, sliced pepperoni, or slivered cooked ham for 1 cup of the vegetables.

Ask Mom What is that pasta shape? pages 308–309 / What does it mean to cube? page 64 / How do I prepare zucchini? page 54 / What is a cherry tomato? page 52 / How do I slice an onion? page 47 / How do I chop sweet peppers? page 49 / How do I snip fresh herbs? pages 42, 328 / How do I cut broccoli? page 36 / How do I prepare cauliflower? page 38 / How do I peel and cut carrots? pages 37, 64 / How do I shred vegetables? page 20 / How do I slice green onions? page 43

CAN I USE ANY KIND OF POTATO? You could use a yellow-fleshed potato, such as Yukon gold or Finnish yellow, and certainly a round white potato—perfect for making potato salad—but don't use baking potatoes. They turn to mush when boiled.

Give your finished salad extra flavor and crunch by stirring in I to 2 tablespoons snipped fresh parsley, dill, or basil and $\frac{1}{2}$ cup chopped radishes and/or celery.

(2) Skill Level

Red Potato Salad

1 ½ pounds new round red potatoes

1 cup light mayonnaise or salad dressing or
  regular mayonnaise or salad dressing

1 tablespoon yellow mustard

1 tablespoon white wine vinegar

2 teaspoons sugar

½ teaspoon ground black pepper

¼ teaspoon salt

⅓ cup sweet or dill pickle relish

⅓ cup sliced green onion

3 hard-cooked eggs (see page 436), coarsely chopped

Flavor Changes If you like your potato salad on the sweet side, use salad dressing instead of mayonnaise and sweet pickle relish instead of dill. If you like it on the savory side, use mayonnaise and dill pickle relish.

1 Scrub potatoes thoroughly; cut into bite-size pieces. In a large saucepan place potatoes and enough lightly salted water to cover potatoes. Bring to boiling; reduce heat. Simmer, covered, for 8 to 10 minutes or just until tender; drain. Cool slightly.

2 In a very large bowl stir together the mayonnaise, mustard, vinegar, sugar, pepper, and salt. Stir in the pickle relish and onion. Add the potatoes and eggs (below). Toss lightly to coat. Cover and chill for 2 to 24 hours. Makes 10 side-dish servings.

Per serving: 162 cal., 8 g total fat (1 g sat. fat), 72 mg chol., 307 mg sodium, 19 g carbo., 1 g fiber, 4 g pro.

Bacon-Avocado Potato Salad: Prepare as above, except before serving stir in 1 avocado, seeded, peeled, and chopped, and 3 slices bacon, crisp-cooked, drained, and crumbled.

Place hard-cooked eggs on a cutting board. Cut each in half, then into quarters. Use a chef's knife to coarsely chop into pieces about the size of a small olive. If eggs are chopped too finely, the pieces will break up.

Ask Mom What are some potato varieties? page 50 / How do I prepare potatoes? page 51 / What is that vinegar? page 349 / How do I slice green onions? page 43 / What does simmer mean? page 79 / What does it mean to toss? page 77 / How do I seed and peel an avocado? page 36 / How do I cook bacon? page 172

(2) Skill Level

Tomato Salad with Pickled Red Onions

Shopping Savvy An heirloom tomato is simply a type of tomato that is not a commercial hybrid and, by some definitions, one that was grown by home gardeners at least 50 years ago. Heirloom tomatoes come in a dizzying array of colors and shapes and are generally more flavorful than hybrid tomatoes. Check out local farmers' markets for what's available to you.

    1 recipe Pickled Red Onions
    1 cup balsamic vinegar
    4 to 6 assorted heirloom tomatoes or other tomatoes, sliced
       Salt
       Ground black pepper
 $\frac{1}{2}$ cup olive oil
    1 cup cubed mozzarella cheese* (4 ounces)
 $\frac{1}{4}$ cup loosely packed small fresh basil leaves

1 Prepare Pickled Red Onions; cover and chill. In a small saucepan bring vinegar to boiling. Reduce heat to medium. Simmer, uncovered, about 20 minutes or until vinegar is reduced to $\frac{1}{3}$ cup. Let cool.

2 Arrange the sliced tomato on four salad plates (below). Sprinkle with salt and pepper. Drizzle with olive oil. Sprinkle tomato with Pickled Red Onions and mozzarella. Top with basil leaves. Drizzle the reduced balsamic vinegar over salads (below). Serve immediately. Makes 4 side-dish servings.

Pickled Red Onions: In a medium saucepan cook 1 cup thin wedges red onion in boiling lightly salted water for 45 seconds; drain. In a medium bowl combine the onion; 1 cup cold water; 1 cup rice vinegar; 2 cloves garlic, halved; and 2 teaspoons cumin seeds. Cover and chill for 3 to 24 hours. Drain before using.

*Note: If desired, substitute 4 ounces bocconcini (small balls of fresh mozzarella) or sliced fresh mozzarella for cubed mozzarella. Arrange bocconcini or slices on salad plates with tomatoes.

Per serving: 487 cal., 34 g total fat (4 g sat. fat), 25 mg chol., 656 mg sodium, 31 g carbo., 4 g fiber, 8 g pro.

1 For added color use different tomato varieties, such as red and yellow, on the salad plates.

2 After ingredients are arranged on salad plates, use a spoon to drizzle with the reduced balsamic to finish the salad.

Ask Mom How do I cut onion wedges? page 47 / What is a garlic clove? page 40 / What is that vinegar? page 349 / How do I slice tomatoes? page 52 / What does it mean to cube? page 64 / What is that oil? page 348 / What does simmer mean? page 79 / What is a reduction? page 70 / What does drizzle mean? page 79

Rice, Bean, and Corn Salad

1½ cups cooked rice (see page 268), chilled
1 15-ounce can black beans or pinto beans, rinsed and drained
1 cup chopped, seeded tomato (1 large)
1 cup frozen whole kernel corn, thawed
1 4-ounce can diced green chile peppers, drained
¼ cup chopped red onion or sliced green onion (2)
2 tablespoons snipped fresh cilantro or parsley
1 recipe Garlic Dressing or ⅓ cup bottled Italian salad dressing
1 recipe Tortilla Strips or crushed tortilla chips

1 In a large bowl stir together rice, beans, tomato, corn, chile peppers, onion, and cilantro. Pour Garlic Dressing over rice mixture; toss to coat. Spoon into salad bowls or onto plates; top servings with Tortilla Strips (below). Makes 6 side-dish servings.

Garlic Dressing: In a screw-top jar combine 3 tablespoons white wine vinegar, 2 tablespoons olive oil or salad oil, 1 tablespoon water, ¼ teaspoon salt, ¼ teaspoon garlic powder, and ¼ teaspoon ground black pepper. Cover and shake well (see photos, page 357).

Tortilla Strips: Preheat oven to 350°F. Roll up 2 flour tortillas and slice into strips (below). Lightly coat the strips with nonstick cooking spray and spread out on a baking sheet. Bake in the preheated oven for 10 to 15 minutes or until golden. Remove from oven and set aside to cool.

Per serving: 205 cal., 6 g total fat (1 g sat. fat), 0 mg chol., 369 mg sodium, 34 g carbo., 5 g fiber, 8 g pro.

Shrimp or Scallop Rice Salad: For a main dish, toss 1 pound medium peeled and deveined shrimp or sea scallops with 1 teaspoon chili powder and ¼ teaspoon salt. In a large skillet cook shrimp or scallops in 1 tablespoon hot olive oil over medium-high heat for 2 to 3 minutes or until opaque. Spoon over rice salad. Makes 6 main-dish servings.

1 To cut strips, roll up tortillas together. Use a serrated knife to cut roll into ¼- to ½-inch-wide strips.

2 To keep the Tortilla Strips crisp, sprinkle them over the plated salads just before serving.

Ask Mom How do I rinse and drain canned beans? page 390 / How do I seed tomatoes? page 52 / How do I chop a tomato? page 52 / How do I chop an onion? page 47 / How do I slice green onions? page 43 / How do I snip fresh herbs? pages 42, 328 / What is that vinegar? page 349 / What is that oil? page 348 / What does it mean to toss? page 77

Wheat Berry Tabbouleh

2 ⅔ cups cooked wheat berries*
 ¾ cup coarsely chopped tomato
 ¾ cup cut-up cucumber
 ½ cup snipped fresh parsley
 ¼ cup thinly sliced green onion (2)
 1 tablespoon snipped fresh mint
 3 tablespoons salad oil
 3 tablespoons lemon juice
 ¼ teaspoon salt
 5 lettuce leaves
  Lemon slices (optional)

1 In a large bowl combine wheat berries, tomato, cucumber, parsley, green onion, and mint.

2 For dressing, in a screw-top jar combine oil, lemon juice, and salt. Cover and shake well (see photos, page 357). Drizzle dressing over wheat berry mixture; toss to coat. Serve immediately or cover and chill for up to 4 hours. Serve in lettuce-lined bowls and, if desired, garnish with lemon slices. Makes 5 side-dish servings.

*Note: Wheat berries are wheat kernels that have had the outer hulls removed. You can find them at any natural foods store. For 2⅔ cups cooked wheat berries, bring one 14-ounce can vegetable broth or chicken broth and ¼ cup water to boiling. Add 1 cup wheat berries. Return to boiling; reduce heat. Simmer, covered, for 45 to 60 minutes or until tender; drain. Cover and chill for up to 3 days.

Per serving: 148 cal., 9 g total fat (1 g sat. fat), 0 mg chol., 295 mg sodium, 17 g carbo., 2 g fiber, 3 g pro.

Bulgur Tabbouleh: Prepare as above, except omit the wheat berries. Place ¾ cup uncooked bulgur in a colander; rinse with cold water and drain. In a large bowl combine bulgur, cucumber, parsley, green onion, and mint. Prepare dressing as above, except add 2 tablespoons water to the dressing. Pour dressing over bulgur mixture; toss to coat. Cover; chill for 4 to 24 hours. Stir tomato into bulgur mixture just before serving in lettuce-lined bowls. Makes 5 side-dish servings.

Tabbouleh Appetizer: Prepare as above, except spoon the tabbouleh mixture into seeded avocado halves and serve on lettuce-lined plates. Makes 6 appetizer servings.

Tabbouleh Wrap or Pita: For a wrap, place several lettuce leaves in the center of an 8-inch flour tortilla. Using a slotted spoon, top lettuce with ½ cup of the tabbouleh mixture. Fold bottom of tortilla halfway over the tabbouleh; fold over sides and secure with a toothpick, forming a pocket. Or for a pita, line pita bread halves with lettuce leaves and fill each with ½ cup of the tabbouleh mixture. Makes 5 wraps or pita halves.

Ask Mom How do I chop a tomato? page 52 / How do I slice green onions? page 43 / How do I snip fresh herbs? pages 42, 328 / What is that oil? page 348 / How do I juice a lemon? pages 30, 80 / How much juice does one lemon yield? page 30 / What is that salad green? page 347 / How do I slice lemons? page 30 / What does drizzle mean? page 79 / What does it mean to toss? page 77 / What does garnish mean? page 79 / How do I seed and peel an avocado? page 36

Mediterranean Beef Salad With Lemon Vinaigrette

  1 pound boneless beef top sirloin steak, cut 1 inch thick

  Salt and ground black pepper

  4 cups torn romaine lettuce

  $\frac{1}{2}$ of a small red onion, thinly sliced and separated into rings ($\frac{1}{2}$ cup)

  1 cup halved cherry or grape tomatoes

  $\frac{1}{2}$ cup pitted kalamata olives

  $\frac{1}{2}$ cup crumbled feta cheese (2 ounces)

  1 recipe Lemon Vinaigrette

1 Preheat broiler. Trim fat from steak. Lightly sprinkle steak with salt and pepper. Place steak on the unheated rack of a broiler pan. Broil 4 to 5 inches from the heat to desired doneness, turning once halfway through broiling. Allow 15 to 17 minutes for medium rare (145°F) or 20 to 22 minutes for medium (160°F). Thinly slice the meat.

2 Divide romaine among four dinner plates. Top with sliced meat, onion, tomato, olives, and cheese. Drizzle with Lemon Vinaigrette. Makes 4 main-dish servings.

Lemon Vinaigrette: In a screw-top jar combine $\frac{1}{4}$ cup olive oil; $\frac{1}{2}$ teaspoon finely shredded lemon peel; 3 tablespoons lemon juice; 1 tablespoon snipped fresh oregano; and 2 cloves garlic, minced (below). Cover and shake well (below). Season vinaigrette to taste with salt and ground black pepper.

Per serving: 363 cal., 24 g total fat (6 g sat. fat), 86 mg chol., 606 mg sodium, 9 g carbo., 3 g fiber, 28 g pro.

Flavor Changes This salad is also delicious made with lamb. Prepare it as above, except substitute 8 lamb rib or sirloin chops, 1 inch thick, for the beef. Broil for 12 to 15 minutes for medium (160°F), turning lamb once halfway through broiling. Cut the meat into strips.

1 Combine vinaigrette ingredients in a jar with a screw top, such as a small canning jar.

2 Screw on the lid tightly and shake to thoroughly combine the vinaigrette ingredients.

Ask Mom What is that cut of meat? pages 220–221 / What is that salad green? page 347 / How do I slice an onion? page 47 / What is a cherry/grape tomato? page 52 / How do I pit olives? page 75 / How do I crumble cheese? pages 71, 90 / How do I shred lemon peel? page 30 / How do I juice a lemon? page 30 / How do I snip fresh herbs? pages 42, 328 / How do I mince garlic? page 40 / What does broil mean? page 68 / How do I use a thermometer? page 74 / What does drizzle mean? page 79

3 Skill Level

Ingredient Info
Prosciutto is a cured, unsmoked Italian ham that is almost always sliced very thin. It is a little pricey but very rich in flavor, so a little goes a long way. Look for it in the deli or specialty meats section of your grocery store.

Steak and Roasted Vegetable Salad

    I pound tiny new potatoes
    I recipe Fresh Herb Vinaigrette
    8 ounces fresh asparagus spears, trimmed
  ¾ cup grape tomatoes
    I teaspoon dried Italian seasoning, crushed
  ¼ teaspoon salt
  ¼ teaspoon ground black pepper
    I pound boneless beef top sirloin steak, cut I inch thick
       Nonstick cooking spray
    6 cups mixed salad greens, such as small romaine lettuce leaves, radicchio, arugula, or leaf lettuce
    I ounce Asiago cheese, shaved

1 Preheat oven to 425°F. Scrub potatoes thoroughly; cut in half. In a 13×9×2-inch baking pan toss potatoes with 2 tablespoons of the Fresh Herb Vinaigrette. Roast potatoes in the pre-heated oven for 30 minutes, stirring once halfway through cooking. Add asparagus, tomatoes, and 2 tablespoons additional Fresh Herb Vinaigrette to pan with potatoes. Roast for 10 minutes more; stir once.

2 Meanwhile, in a small bowl combine Italian seasoning, salt, and pepper. Using your fingers, rub seasoning mixture into the steak. Lightly coat a 10-inch skillet with cooking spray. Preheat skillet over medium-high heat until very hot. Add steak. Do not add any liquid and do not cover the skillet. Reduce heat to medium and cook about 15 minutes for medium rare or until an instant-read thermometer inserted in steak registers 145°F. Turn steak occasionally during cooking. (If steak browns too quickly, reduce heat to medium low.) Remove steak from skillet and thinly slice.

3 To serve, arrange salad greens on a large platter. Arrange potatoes, asparagus, and tomatoes on greens. Top with steak slices and cheese. Serve with remaining Fresh Herb Vinaigrette. Makes 4 main-dish servings.

Fresh Herb Vinaigrette: In a screw-top jar combine ¼ cup olive oil; ¼ cup white wine vinegar; 1 tablespoon finely chopped red onion; 1 tablespoon snipped fresh herb, such as thyme, basil, and/or oregano; 1 clove garlic, minced; ¼ teaspoon Dijon-style mustard; ¼ teaspoon kosher salt; and ⅛ teaspoon ground black pepper. Cover and shake well (see photos, page 357).

Per serving: 424 cal., 22 g total fat (6 g sat. fat), 77 mg chol., 439 mg sodium, 25 g carbo., 4 g fiber, 30 g pro.

Roasted Vegetable Salad: Prepare as above, except omit the steak and seasonings. If desired, top salad with 2 ounces thinly sliced prosciutto, cut into strips. Makes 6 side-dish servings.

Ask Mom What are some potato varieties? page 50 / What is that oil/vinegar? pages 348–349 / How do I chop an onion? page 47 / How do I snip fresh herbs? pages 42, 328 / How do I mince garlic? page 40 / What is Dijon-style mustard? page 379 / What is kosher salt? page 79 / How do I trim asparagus? page 34 / What is a grape tomato? page 52 / What is that cut of meat? pages 220–221 / What is that salad green? page 347 / What is radicchio? page 350 / How do I use a thermometer? page 74

Asian-Style Pork-Noodle Salad

1 3-ounce package pork- or chicken-flavor ramen noodles
½ cup salad oil
⅓ cup rice vinegar
3 cloves garlic, minced
3 tablespoons bottled Thai peanut sauce
¼ teaspoon crushed red pepper
12 ounces boneless pork loin chops, cut ¾ inch thick
4 cups shredded napa or green cabbage
1 cup broccoli florets
½ cup sliced almonds, toasted
½ cup sliced green onion (4)

1 Preheat broiler. Measure ¾ teaspoon seasoning of the seasoning packet (half the packet) from the ramen noodles and reserve the remaining seasoning for another use. In a medium bowl whisk together the ¾ teaspoon seasoning, oil, vinegar, garlic, peanut sauce, and crushed red pepper. Remove 2 tablespoons of the oil mixture for brushing meat.

2 Place chops on unheated rack of broiler pan; brush the 2 tablespoons oil mixture over chops (below). Broil 3 to 4 inches from heat for 9 to 11 minutes or until an instant-read thermometer registers 160°F, turning chops once. Cool slightly. Thinly slice across grain into strips (below).

3 Meanwhile, in a medium saucepan cook ramen noodles in boiling water as directed on the package for 2 minutes; drain. Transfer noodles to a large bowl. Add the pork, cabbage, broccoli, almonds, onion, and remaining oil mixture. Toss to coat (below). Cover and chill for 4 to 24 hours. Makes 4 main-dish servings.

Per serving: 627 cal., 47 g total fat (7 g sat. fat), 50 mg chol., 433 mg sodium, 26 g carbo., 4 g fiber, 27 g pro.

1 It's easier to place the chops on the broiler pan rack before brushing with the seasoned oil mixture.

2 After broiling, place the chops on a cutting board and use a chef's knife to cut the meat into bite-size strips.

3 Toss noodles with other ingredients using salad servers or two large spoons.

Ask Mom What is that oil? page 348 / What is that vinegar? page 349 / What is a garlic clove? page 40 / How do I mince garlic? page 40 / What is that cut of meat? pages 220–221 / How do I shred cabbage? page 350 / How do I trim and cut broccoli? page 36 / How do I toast nuts? page 65 / How do I slice green onions? page 43 / What does it mean to broil? page 68 / How do I use a meat/instant-read thermometer? page 74 / What does it mean to toss? page 77

Maple-Pork **Wilted Salad**

8 cups fresh baby spinach or torn fresh spinach

1 medium cucumber, peeled, seeded, and chopped (about 1½ cups)

⅓ cup thin red onion wedges

12 ounces pork tenderloin

¼ teaspoon salt

¼ teaspoon ground black pepper

2 tablespoons olive oil

2 tablespoons finely chopped shallot (1 medium)

¼ cup cider vinegar

¼ cup pure maple syrup

⅓ cup shredded smoked Gouda or cheddar cheese

¼ cup butter-toffee glaze flavored sliced almonds or toasted sliced almonds

1 In a large bowl combine spinach, cucumber, and onion; set aside. Trim pork tenderloin (see photos, page 362). Cut pork tenderloin crosswise into ¼-inch-thick slices (below). Season slices with salt and pepper. In a large skillet cook pork in 1 tablespoon of the hot oil over medium-high heat for 2 to 3 minutes or until meat is just slightly pink in center, turning once. Add pork to bowl with spinach mixture; set aside.

2 For dressing, in the same skillet cook and stir the shallot in the remaining 1 tablespoon hot oil over medium heat about 2 minutes or until tender. Add the vinegar and maple syrup. Simmer, uncovered, for 1½ to 2 minutes or until slightly thickened (below). Season to taste with additional salt and pepper. Pour dressing over spinach mixture (below); toss to coat. Arrange salad on serving plates. Top with cheese and almonds (page 361). Makes 4 main-dish servings.

Per serving: 325 cal., 15 g total fat (4 g sat. fat), 67 mg chol., 349 mg sodium, 23 g carbo., 3 g fiber, 24 g pro.

1 To get thin slices of pork, you may need to partially freeze the pork until it is firm but not completely frozen.

2 Simmer dressing until slightly thickened. Check the thickness with a wooden spoon used for stirring.

3 Pour dressing over salad in the bowl, using a wooden spoon to scrape out the skillet and to toss ingredients.

Ask Mom What is that salad green? page 347 / How do I cut onion wedges? page 47 / What is that cut of meat? pages 220–221 / What is that oil? page 348? / What is a shallot? page 46 / How do I chop an onion? page 47 / What is that vinegar? page 349 / What's the best way to measure sticky liquids? pages 58, 81 / What is pure maple syrup? page 457 / How do I shred cheese? page 71 / How do I toast nuts? page 65 / What does it mean to toss? page 77

WHAT'S THE BENEFIT OF BABY SPINACH? Well, it is slightly more tender and a little sweeter than mature spinach, but the main benefit of using baby spinach is that you don't have to trim the stems and you don't have to tear the leaves before eating it.

Divide salad evenly among the dinner plates, top with cheese, and sprinkle with almonds. Serve at once because the spinach will wilt as it stands in the hot dressing and the amount of salad will slightly shrink.

Blackberry Salad with Pork

1 12- to 16-ounce pork tenderloin
  Salt and ground black pepper
¼ cup olive oil
¼ cup honey
¼ cup lemon juice
4 ounces Brie cheese
6 cups packaged spring mix salad greens or mesclun
2 cups fresh blackberries, raspberries, and/or sliced strawberries
1 cup grape tomatoes (halved, if desired)
½ cup pine nuts, toasted

1 Preheat oven to 425°F. Trim pork tenderloin (below). Place pork in a shallow roasting pan. Sprinkle with salt and pepper. Roast, uncovered, in the preheated oven for 25 to 35 minutes or until an instant-read thermometer inserted in center of pork registers 155°F. Remove from oven. Cover pork with foil and let stand about 15 minutes or until temperature registers 160°F. Cool slightly. Slice pork ¼ inch thick.

2 For dressing, in a screw-top jar combine oil, honey, lemon juice, and salt and pepper to taste; cover and shake well (see photos, page 357). If desired, remove rind from Brie; cut cheese into thin wedges. To serve, place salad greens in bowls or on plates; top with berries, tomatoes, pine nuts, Brie wedges, and pork slices. Drizzle with dressing. Serve immediately. Makes 4 main-dish servings.

Per serving: 569 cal., 36 g total fat (10 g sat. fat), 95 mg chol., 308 mg sodium, 32 g carbo., 5 g fiber, 37 g pro.

1 Use a utility knife or boning knife to trim fat from the tenderloin.

2 Cut away any tough portions on the tenderloin so the pork will be more tender.

Good to Know An abundance of fresh berries is one of the best things about late spring and early summer. Whichever kind of berries you choose, look for those that are plump and firm—and in the case of raspberries, especially, free from mold. Store them in the refrigerator and wash them just before serving or they'll get mushy.

Ask Mom What is that cut of meat? pages 220–221 / What is that oil? page 348 / What's the best way to measure sticky liquids? pages 58, 81 / How do I juice a lemon/lime? page 30 / How much juice does one lemon/lime yield? page 30 / What is that salad green? page 347 / What is a grape tomato? page 52 / How do I toast pine nuts? page 65 / What does drizzle mean? page 79

Ham and Pea
Wild Rice Salad

- 1 6-ounce package long grain and wild rice mix
- 1 recipe Dried Tomato Vinaigrette*
- 10 ounces cooked ham, beef, or pork, cut into bite-size strips (about 2 cups)
- ½ cup frozen peas, thawed
- ¼ cup sliced green onion (2)

1 Prepare rice according to package directions. Meanwhile, prepare Dried Tomato Vinaigrette.

2 In a large bowl combine the cooked rice mixture, ham, peas, and green onion. Drizzle with Dried Tomato Vinaigrette. Toss lightly to coat. Cover and chill for 2 to 24 hours before serving. Makes 4 main-dish servings.

Dried Tomato Vinaigrette: In a screw-top jar combine ¼ cup white wine vinegar; 2 tablespoons olive oil; 2 tablespoons finely chopped dried tomatoes (oil packed); 1 tablespoon oil from dried tomatoes; 1 tablespoon water; 1 teaspoon snipped fresh thyme or ¼ teaspoon dried thyme, crushed; 1 teaspoon sugar; 1 clove garlic, minced; ¼ teaspoon ground coriander; ¼ teaspoon paprika; and ⅛ teaspoon cayenne pepper. Cover and shake well (see photos, page 357). Serve immediately or cover and store in the refrigerator for up to 1 week. Shake before serving.

*Note: For a shortcut when making this recipe, substitute ⅔ cup bottled dried tomato vinaigrette for the Dried Tomato Vinaigrette.

Per serving: 384 cal., 17 g total fat (4 g sat. fat), 40 mg chol., 1,541 mg sodium, 40 g carbo., 4 g fiber, 18 g pro.

Asian Wild Rice Salad: Prepare as above, except use the cooked beef or pork instead of ham. Substitute one 8-ounce can sliced water chestnuts, drained, for the peas and ⅔ cup bottled ginger vinaigrette salad dressing for the Dried Tomato Vinaigrette. If desired, add ¼ cup shredded radishes to the rice mixture. Makes 4 main-dish servings.

Prosciutto Wild Rice Salad: Prepare as above, except substitute 8 ounces slivered prosciutto for the ham. Add ⅓ cup dried cherries and ⅓ cup chopped walnuts or pecans, toasted, to the cooked rice mixture. Substitute ⅔ cup bottled balsamic vinaigrette salad dressing for the Dried Tomato Vinaigrette. Makes 4 main-dish servings.

Salmon Wild Rice Salad: Prepare as above, except substitute 8 ounces smoked salmon, broken into chunks, for the ham and 1 cup shredded fresh spinach or arugula for the peas. Substitute ⅔ cup bottled Italian salad dressing for Dried Tomato Vinaigrette. Makes 4 main-dish servings.

Ask Mom What is that vinegar? page 349 / What is that oil? page 348 / What are dried tomatoes? page 53 / How do I snip fresh herbs? pages 42, 328 / How do I crush dried herbs? page 78 / What is a garlic clove? page 40 / How do I mince garlic? page 40 / How do I slice green onions? page 43 / What does drizzle mean? page 79 / What is prosciutto? page 358 / How do I chop nuts? page 65 / How do I toast nuts? page 65 / What is that salad green? page 347

Chef's Salad

4 cups torn iceberg lettuce or leaf lettuce

4 cups torn romaine lettuce or fresh spinach

4 ounces cooked ham, chicken, turkey, beef, pork, or lamb, cut into bite-size pieces (about I cup)

4 ounces Swiss, cheddar, American, or provolone cheese, cut into bite-size pieces (I cup)

2 hard-cooked eggs, sliced (see page 436)

2 medium tomatoes, cut into wedges, or 8 cherry tomatoes, halved

I small green or red sweet pepper, cut into bite-size strips ($\frac{1}{2}$ cup)

I cup croutons (optional)

$\frac{1}{2}$ cup bottled French salad dressing, ranch salad dressing, or desired salad dressing

1 In a large bowl toss greens. Divide greens among four large salad bowls or plates. Arrange meat, cheese, eggs, tomato, and sweet pepper on top of greens. If desired, sprinkle with croutons. Drizzle with some of the salad dressing and pass any remaining dressing. Makes 4 main-dish servings.

Per serving: 368 cal., 27 g total fat (9 g sat. fat), 148 mg chol., 730 mg sodium, 15 g carbo., 3 g fiber, 18 g pro.

Italian Chef's Salad: Prepare as above, except use 2 ounces cooked chicken and 4 ounces mozzarella cheese. Omit eggs. Add 2 ounces sliced pepperoni; one 6-ounce jar quartered marinated artichoke hearts, drained; and $\frac{1}{4}$ cup sliced, pitted ripe olives. For dressing, use a bottled Italian salad dressing or creamy Italian salad dressing. Makes 4 main-dish servings.

Mexican Chef's Salad Prepare as above, using cooked chicken, beef, or pork and cheddar or Monterery Jack cheese. Omit eggs. Add one 4-ounce can diced green chile peppers, drained, and $\frac{1}{4}$ cup sliced, pitted ripe olives. Substitute corn chips for croutons. For dressing, stir together $\frac{1}{4}$ cup bottled Thousand Island salad dressing and $\frac{1}{4}$ cup bottled salsa.

Ask Mom What is that salad green? page 347 / How do I cut tomato wedges? page 52 / What is a cherry tomato? page 52 / How do I seed sweet peppers and cut them into strips? page 49 / What does drizzle mean? page 79

1 Skill Level

Chicken Salad

10 ounces cooked chicken or turkey
½ cup chopped celery (1 stalk)
¼ cup thinly sliced green onion (2)
⅓ cup mayonnaise or salad dressing
1 teaspoon snipped fresh basil or ¼ teaspoon dried basil, crushed
¼ teaspoon salt
   Torn mixed salad greens (optional)

Flavor Changes Serve this yummy chicken salad on a bed of baby salad greens or as a sandwich. Here are some sandwich options to consider: whole wheat bread with sliced cucumbers and sliced tomatoes; croissant with leaf lettuce; and multigrain bread with spinach leaves and a sprinkling of dried cranberries.

1 Cube or dice chicken; you will need about 2 cups (below). In a medium bowl combine chicken, celery, and green onion. For dressing, in a small bowl stir together mayonnaise, basil, and salt. Pour dressing over chicken mixture; toss gently to coat. Cover and chill for 1 to 4 hours. If desired, serve on salad greens. Makes 4 main-dish servings.

Per serving: 269 cal., 20 g total fat (4 g sat. fat), 69 mg chol., 318 mg sodium, 1 g carbo., 0 g fiber, 20 g pro.

Curried Chicken Salad: Prepare as above, except for dressing, reduce mayonnaise to ¼ cup and omit the basil. Stir in 2 tablespoons cut-up mango chutney and 1 teaspoon curry powder. Before chilling, stir ¾ cup halved red and/or green seedless grapes or chopped apple into the chicken mixture. Before serving, stir in 2 tablespoons coarsely chopped cashews or almonds, toasted. Makes 4 main-dish servings.

Lemon Chicken Salad: Prepare as above, except substitute ½ cup chopped red or green sweet pepper for the celery. For dressing, substitute 1 teaspoon snipped fresh Italian (flat-leaf) parsley for the basil and stir in 1 teaspoon finely shredded lemon peel and 2 teaspoons lemon juice. Makes 4 main-dish servings.

To cut up the cooked chicken, make crosswise slices. Stack several slices; cut crosswise and lengthwise to make the desired size dice or cube. A smaller dice works better for sandwiches; larger cubes are nice for salads.

Ask Mom How do I chop celery? page 39 / How do I slice green onions? page 43 / How do I snip fresh herbs? pages 42, 328 / How do I crush dried herbs? page 78 / What does it mean to cube or dice? page 64 / What does it mean to toss? page 77 / What is curry powder? page 410 / How do I chop nuts? page 65 / How do I toast nuts? page 65 / How do I seed/chop sweet peppers? page 49 / How do I shred lemon/lime peel? page 30 / How do I juice a lemon/lime? page 30

Chicken and Quinoa Salad
With Roasted Chile Peppers

8 ounces fresh Anaheim chile peppers, poblano chile peppers,
banana chile peppers, and/or red sweet peppers

1 cup quinoa

1 cup water

3 tablespoons lime juice

2 tablespoons olive oil

2 cloves garlic, minced

$\frac{1}{4}$ teaspoon salt

$\frac{1}{4}$ teaspoon ground black pepper

8 ounces shredded cooked chicken or cooked pork

$\frac{1}{2}$ cup coarsely snipped fresh cilantro

$\frac{1}{2}$ cup sliced green onion (4)

$\frac{1}{3}$ cup pine nuts or slivered almonds, toasted

Bibb or Boston lettuce leaves

1 Preheat oven to 425°F. Line a baking sheet with foil; set aside. Halve peppers lengthwise. Remove stems, seeds, and membranes. Place pepper halves, cut sides down, on the prepared baking sheet. Roast peppers in the preheated oven for 20 to 25 minutes or until skins are blistered and dark. Carefully fold foil up and around pepper halves to enclose; let stand about 15 minutes. Use a sharp knife to loosen the edges of the skins; gently and slowly pull off the skin in strips. Discard skins. Cut peppers into bite-size strips. Set aside.

2 In a fine-mesh sieve thoroughly rinse the quinoa with cold water. In a medium saucepan combine quinoa and the 1 cup water. Bring to boiling; reduce heat. Simmer, covered, for 25 minutes. Remove from heat. Uncover and let stand about 30 minutes.

3 For dressing, in a small screw-top jar combine lime juice, olive oil, garlic, salt, and black pepper. Cover and shake well to combine (see photos, page 357).

4 In a large bowl combine roasted pepper strips, quinoa, chicken, cilantro, green onion, and pine nuts. Drizzle with dressing and toss to combine. Line serving plates with lettuce. Top with quinoa mixture. Serve salad at room temperature. Makes 4 or 5 main-dish servings.

Per serving: 454 cal., 22 g total fat (3 g sat. fat), 50 mg chol., 220 mg sodium, 43 g carbo., 5 g fiber, 26 g pro.

Ingredient Info To store butterhead lettuce (Bibb or Boston), cut off the bottom core. Rinse thoroughly in cold water. Pat dry and refrigerate the dry leaves in a resealable plastic bag lined with paper towels for up to 5 days. One 8-ounce head yields about 6 cups torn lettuce.

Ask Mom How do I handle hot chile peppers? page 48 / How do I juice a lemon/lime? pages 30, 80 / What is that oil? page 348 / What is a garlic clove? page 40 / How do I mince garlic? page 40 / How do I snip fresh herbs? pages 42, 328 / How do I slice green onions? page 43 / How do I toast nuts? page 65 / How do I toast pine nuts? pages 65, 245 / How do I line a pan with foil? page 60 / What does simmer mean? page 79 / What does drizzle mean? page 79 / What does it mean to toss? page 77

WHAT'S QUINOA? (KEEN-wah) may be unfamiliar to you, but it is far from new. It was a staple of the Incas and is still important in South American cuisine. It is a superfood of sorts—it contains more protein than any other grain and is lower in carbs than most.

The leaves of Bibb or Boston lettuce are ideal for serving salads such as this one because they form little cups—and they're crisp, sweet, and buttery tasting to boot.

Spinach-Pasta Salad with Shrimp

1 cup dried shell pasta or elbow macaroni

1 pound frozen cooked shrimp, thawed, or 1 pound cooked shrimp

1 cup chopped red sweet pepper (1 large)

⅓ cup bottled creamy onion salad dressing or Caesar salad dressing

2 tablespoons snipped fresh dill (optional)

Salt

Freshly ground black pepper

1 6-ounce package fresh baby spinach

4 ounces goat cheese (chèvre), sliced (below), or feta cheese, crumbled

1 Prepare pasta according to package directions; drain. Rinse pasta under cold running water; drain again (see photos, page 305).

2 In a very large bowl combine pasta, shrimp, and sweet pepper. Drizzle with salad dressing. If desired, sprinkle with dill. Toss to coat. Season to taste with salt and black pepper.

3 To serve, divide spinach among six salad plates or bowls. Top with shrimp mixture and cheese. Makes 6 main-dish servings.

Per serving: 247 cal., 10 g total fat (4 g sat. fat), 156 mg chol., 435 mg sodium, 17 g carbo., 2 g fiber, 23 g pro.

1 Goat (chèvre) cheese is a fresh white cheese made with goat's milk. It is soft and has a tangy yet mild flavor. Often you'll find the cheese shaped in a log.

2 One trick for making thin slices from the log of goat cheese is to use unflavored dental floss. Place a piece under the log and bring up both ends. Pull through the cheese, crossing the ends as you cut through the cheese.

Good to Know Baked goat cheese rounds make a delicious and creamy addition to a simple plate of salad greens. Dip each slice in olive oil, then coat generously in seasoned bread crumbs and place on a baking sheet. Bake in a preheated 400°F oven for 6 to 8 minutes or until bread crumbs turn golden brown. Place the baked cheese on dressed greens and serve immediately.

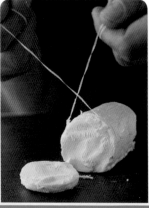

Ask Mom What is that pasta shape? pages 308–309 / How do I seed and chop sweet peppers? page 49 / How do I snip fresh herbs? pages 42, 328 / How do I crumble cheese? pages 71, 96 / What does drizzle mean? page 79 / What does it mean to toss? page 77

bowls of
SOUPS
& stews

What's more soothing than homemade soup? It's good for what ails you—and for what doesn't.

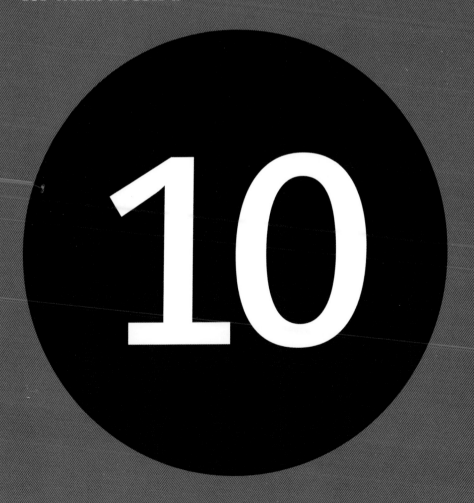

10

2 Skill Level

Garden Fresh Gazpacho

  6 cups coarsely chopped tomato (6 medium)
  1 cup peeled, seeded, and coarsely chopped cucumber (1 medium)
  1 cup coarsely chopped green sweet pepper (1 medium)
  1 cup tomato juice
  ¾ cup beef broth
  ¼ cup red wine
  ¼ cup red onion, finely chopped
  1 fresh jalapeño chile pepper, seeded and finely chopped
  2 tablespoons snipped fresh cilantro
  1 tablespoon red wine vinegar
  4 cloves garlic, minced
    Salt
    Ground black pepper
    Avocado pieces (optional)

Good to Know Be sure the bowl you use to mix this gazpacho is made of a nonreactive material—that is, not aluminum, copper, or cast iron. The acid in the tomatoes reacts with those metals and can give your soup an off taste. Good nonreactive choices include glass, ceramic, and stainless steel.

1 In a very large bowl stir together tomato, cucumber, sweet pepper, tomato juice, broth, wine, onion, jalapeño pepper, cilantro, vinegar, and garlic. Add salt and black pepper to taste. Cover and chill for several hours or overnight.

2 To serve, ladle the gazpacho into bowls. If desired, top with avocado pieces. Makes 12 side-dish servings.

Per serving: 27 cal., 0 g total fat (0 g sat. fat), 0 mg chol., 115 mg sodium, 5 g carbo., 1 g fiber, 1 g pro.

Seafood Gazpacho: Prepare as above, except before serving stir 8 ounces chopped cooked shrimp or 8 ounces lump crabmeat into soup.

Ask Mom How do I chop a tomato? page 52 / How do I seed and chop sweet peppers? page 49 / How do I chop an onion? page 47 / How do I handle hot chile peppers? page 48 / How do I snip fresh herbs? pages 42, 328 / What is that vinegar? page 349 / What is a garlic clove? page 40 / How do I mince garlic? page 40 / How do I seed and peel an avocado? page 36

Guacamole Soup

1 tablespoon cooking oil

1 tablespoon butter or margarine

1 cup chopped red onion (1 large)

6 cloves garlic, minced (2 tablespoons)

3 medium avocados, halved, seeded, peeled, and mashed (1 ¾ cups)

1 14-ounce can chicken broth or vegetable broth

1 ½ cups whipping cream

1 cup bottled salsa

2 tablespoons lime juice

2 tablespoons lemon juice

1 tablespoon ground cumin

Assorted toppers (avocado slices, chopped red or yellow tomato, tortilla chips, lime slices, dairy sour cream, and/or cooked shrimp) (optional)

1 In a 3-quart saucepan heat oil and butter over medium heat; add onion and garlic. Cook and stir onion and garlic about 5 minutes or until tender. Stir in avocado, broth, whipping cream, salsa, lime juice, lemon juice, and cumin; heat through. To serve, ladle soup into bowls. If desired, serve with assorted toppers. Makes 6 to 8 side-dish servings.

Per serving: 349 cal., 33 g total fat (16 g sat. fat), 88 mg chol., 436 mg sodium, 13 g carbo., 4 g fiber, 3 g pro.

Ingredient Info Make this rich and creamy soup as fiery or mild as you like by using hot or mild salsa. You can use either red (tomato-based) or green (tomatillo-based) salsa. There are several good fire-roasted varieties of salsa on the market—this means that the vegetables were grilled before they were chopped and tossed together. Fire-roasting adds another dimension of flavor.

Ask Mom How do I measure butter? pages 58, 59 / How do I chop an onion? page 47 / What is a garlic clove? page 40 / How do I mince garlic? page 40 / How do I juice a lemon/lime? pages 30, 80 / How much juice does one lemon/lime yield? page 30 / How do I seed and peel an avocado? page 36 / How do I slice lemons/limes? page 30

Gingered Pumpkin Soup

    1 tablespoon butter or margarine
    2 15-ounce cans pumpkin
    2 14-ounce cans chicken broth
 1 ½ cups half-and-half, light cream, or milk
   ¼ cup maple syrup
    2 teaspoons grated fresh ginger or ¼ teaspoon ground ginger
   ¼ teaspoon salt
   ¼ teaspoon ground black pepper
       Pumpkin seeds (pepitas), toasted (optional)

1 In a 3-quart saucepan melt butter over medium heat. Stir in pumpkin, broth, half-and-half, maple syrup, and ginger; bring just to boiling. Stir in salt and pepper. To serve, ladle soup into bowls. If desired, top each serving with pumpkin seeds. Makes 8 side-dish servings.

Per serving: 140 cal., 7 g total fat (4 g sat. fat), 22 mg chol., 505 mg sodium, 18 g carbo., 3 g fiber, 3 g pro.

Chipotle Squash Soup: Prepare as above, except substitute two 12-ounce packages frozen cooked winter squash, thawed, for the pumpkin. Omit maple syrup and ginger. Add 1 to 2 chopped chipotle peppers in adobo sauce with the squash. Bring just to boiling; reduce heat. Simmer, uncovered, for 10 minutes.

Curried Squash Soup: Prepare as above, except substitute two 12-ounce packages frozen cooked winter squash, thawed, for the pumpkin and one 14-ounce can unsweetened coconut milk for the half-and-half. Omit maple syrup. Substitute 2 to 3 teaspoons curry powder for the ginger. If desired, substitute chopped cashews or cocktail peanuts for the pumpkin seeds.

Shopping Savvy If you go with the Chipotle Squash variation of this soup, you'll need chipotle peppers. Chipotles are actually dried smoked jalapeños. They are available in two forms—simply dried and sold loose or in packages, as are other dried chiles—or in cans of adobo sauce. Adobo sauce is a piquant sauce made of dried chiles, vinegar, and herbs. Look for canned chipotles in adobo in the Mexican foods section of your supermarket.

Ask Mom How do I measure butter? pages 58, 59 / What's the best way to measure sticky liquids? pages 58, 81 / What is fresh ginger? page 41 / How do I grate fresh ginger? page 41 / How do I toast nuts? page 65 / What does simmer mean? page 79 / What is coconut milk? page 272 / What is curry powder? page 410

WHAT'S A BISQUE? The most elegant of soups, bisque is a rich, creamy concoction of cooked vegetables, seafood, or poultry pureed with cream. Bisque makes a great starter for a fancy dinner.

Good to Know If fresh shiitake mushrooms aren't available, soak dried ones in hot water for 15 minutes. Rinse well and squeeze out the moisture. Two ounces of dried mushrooms equals 1 cup of the fresh.

Shiitake Mushroom–Tomato Bisque

½ cup sliced leek or chopped onion (1 medium)

½ cup sliced celery (1 stalk)

2 cloves garlic, minced

2 tablespoons butter or margarine

1½ cups sliced fresh shiitake mushrooms* or other fresh mushrooms

1 14.5-ounce can diced tomatoes, undrained

1 14-ounce can chicken broth or vegetable broth

½ cup whipping cream

½ teaspoon dried dillweed

⅛ teaspoon ground black pepper

Sauteed mushrooms (optional)

Gearing Up If you love making pureed soups, invest in a handheld immersion blender. An immersion blender can be stuck right in the soup pot to puree the soup rather than doing it in a regular blender, which can be tricky. If that's your only choice, puree only half or one-third at a time—and remove the round plastic piece in the center of the lid to allow steam to escape (see photo, page 377).

1 In a 3-quart saucepan cook and stir leek, celery, and garlic in hot butter until tender (below). Add mushrooms; cook and stir about 5 minutes more or until mushrooms are tender (below). Stir in undrained tomatoes, broth, whipping cream, dillweed, and pepper (below). Bring to boiling; reduce heat. Simmer, covered, for 30 minutes.

2 Let soup cool slightly. Transfer soup mixture, half at a time, to a blender or food processor. Cover and blend or process until smooth (see photo, page 377). (Or use an immersion blender [below].) Return all of the soup mixture to saucepan; heat through. To serve, ladle soup into bowls. If desired, top each serving with additional mushrooms. Makes 4 side-dish servings.

*Note: If using shiitake mushrooms, remove and discard the tough stems before slicing.

Per serving: 193 cal., 13 g total fat (8 g sat. fat), 47 mg chol., 607 mg sodium, 17 g carbo., 2 g fiber, 3 g pro.

4 If you have a handheld immersion blender, you can blend the soup mixture right in the saucepan, which is easier, safer, and less messy.

a wooden spoon to
stir the leek, celery,
in the hot butter
r.

2 Add the sliced shiitake mushrooms to the saucepan; cook and stir until tender.

3 Add the tomatoes, broth, whipping cream, dill, and pepper to the saucepan.

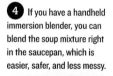
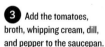
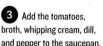

Ask Mom What is a leek? page 43 / How do I slice a leek? page 43 / How do I chop an onion? page 47 / How do I prepare celery? page 39 / What is a garlic clove? page 40 / How do I mince garlic? page 40 / How do I measure butter? pages 58, 59 / What are some mushroom varieties? page 44 / What does it mean to saute? page 69 / What does simmer mean? page 79

Roasted Red
Pepper Soup

- 1 cup chopped onion (1 large)
- 4 cloves garlic, minced
- 1 tablespoon olive oil
- 3 14-ounce cans vegetable broth or chicken broth
- 1 12-ounce jar roasted red sweet peppers, drained and sliced
- 1 cup chopped peeled potato (1 medium)
- 1 tablespoon snipped fresh oregano or 1 teaspoon dried oregano, crushed
- 1 teaspoon snipped fresh thyme or $\frac{1}{2}$ teaspoon dried thyme, crushed
- $\frac{1}{4}$ cup dairy sour cream
- 1 tablespoon snipped fresh chives

1 In a 3-quart saucepan cook and stir onion and garlic in hot oil for 3 to 4 minutes or until tender. Stir in broth, roasted sweet peppers, potato, oregano, and thyme. Bring to boiling; reduce heat. Simmer, covered, for 15 minutes.

2 Let soup cool slightly. Transfer soup mixture, one-third at a time, to a blender or food processor. Cover and blend or process until nearly smooth (page 377). Return all of the soup mixture to saucepan; heat through. (Or use an immersion blender [see photo 4, page 375].)

3 To serve, ladle soup into bowls. Top each serving with sour cream and sprinkle with chives. Makes 4 side-dish servings.

Per serving: 137 cal., 6 g total fat (2 g sat. fat), 5 mg chol., 1,178 mg sodium, 18 g carbo., 2 g fiber, 2 g pro.

GOOD TO KNOW If you don't have fresh chives, green onion tops make a perfectly acceptable substitution in the sour cream—as does finely chopped white or yellow onion.

Ask Mom How do I chop an onion? page 47 / What is a garlic clove? page 40 / How do I mince garlic? page 40 / How do I drain bottled roasted sweet peppers? page 416 / What are some potato varieties? page 50 / How do I prepare potatoes? page 51 / How do I snip fresh herbs? pages 42, 328 / How do I crush dried herbs? page 78 / What does simmer mean? page 79

COULD I MAKE THIS WITH YELLOW PEPPERS? You can: To roast your own peppers, see the method on page 67. Start with about 1 pound of yellow peppers before roasting (this recipe uses 12 ounces, and you'll be removing the stems, seeds, and membranes).

To avoid too much steam buildup in the blender, let the cooked soup cool slightly in the saucepan before you puree it.

Make sure the blender lid is on tightly. Remove the round plastic piece in the center of the lid and hold a kitchen towel over the opening to allow steam to escape during blending.

Always blend soup mixtures on low speed to avoid a dangerous explosion.

WHAT'S STEW MEAT? Stew meat generally comes from the chuck, or the shoulder, of the animal. The shoulder gets a lot of exercise, so it's tougher and more muscular than other cuts. Long, moist cooking renders it fall-apart tender.

1 Drop the dumpling mixture from a kitchen tablespoon, making small mounds on top of the simmering stew.

2 Cover the Dutch oven and simmer until the dumplings are done. Do not lift the cover until you're ready to test the dumplings for doneness.

3 To check for doneness, insert a wooden toothpick into one of the dumplings. When the dumplings are done, the toothpick will come out clean.

Ingredient Info
Whether it is regular or coarse-grain, Dijon-style mustard tastes essentially the same and has the same ingredients: mustard seeds, white wine, herbs, and spices. The only real difference is how finely the mustard seeds are ground. You can use either kind here; you just won't have the textured "bite" of the mustard seeds if you use the creamy kind.

3 Skill Level

Beef Stew with Cornmeal Dumplings

- 1 pound beef stew meat
- 1 tablespoon cooking oil
- 1 14.5-ounce can diced tomatoes, undrained
- 1 14-ounce can beef broth
- 1 8-ounce can tomato sauce
- 2 tablespoons coarse-grain Dijon-style mustard
- $\frac{1}{2}$ teaspoon dried thyme, crushed
- $\frac{1}{4}$ teaspoon salt
- $\frac{1}{4}$ teaspoon dried oregano, crushed
- $\frac{1}{4}$ teaspoon ground black pepper
- 1 clove garlic, minced
- $\frac{1}{2}$ of a 20-ounce package (about 2 cups) refrigerated diced potatoes with onions
- $\frac{1}{2}$ cup packaged peeled fresh baby carrots
- 1 cup frozen cut green beans
- 1 recipe Cornmeal Dumplings

1 Cut any large pieces of stew meat in half. In a 4-quart Dutch oven brown meat, half at a time, in hot oil. Return all of the meat to Dutch oven. Stir in undrained tomatoes, broth, tomato sauce, mustard, thyme, salt, oregano, pepper, and garlic. Bring to boiling; reduce heat. Simmer, covered, for 1 hour.

2 Add potatoes and carrots. Return to boiling; reduce heat. Simmer, covered, for 20 minutes. Stir in green beans. Return to boiling; reduce heat.

3 Drop dumpling mixture from a large spoon into small mounds on top of stew (page 378). Simmer, covered, about 20 minutes or until dumplings are done (page 378). Let stand, uncovered, 10 minutes before serving. To serve, ladle soup into bowls. Makes 6 main-dish servings.

Cornmeal Dumplings: In a medium bowl stir together one $8\frac{1}{2}$-ounce package corn muffin mix, $\frac{1}{2}$ cup shredded cheddar cheese, and $\frac{1}{4}$ cup sliced green onion. Stir in one lightly beaten egg and $\frac{1}{4}$ cup dairy sour cream just until moistened (batter will be thick).

Per serving: 449 cal., 16 g total fat (6 g sat. fat), 95 mg chol., 1,443 mg sodium, 47 g carbo., 6 g fiber, 26 g pro.

Beef Stew with Tortellini: Prepare as above, except omit mustard, thyme, oregano, potatoes, and Cornmeal Dumplings. Add 1 teaspoon dried Italian seasoning, crushed, and $\frac{1}{4}$ cup dry red wine with the tomatoes. When adding green beans, stir in one 9-ounce package refrigerated cheese-filled tortellini or ravioli and 1 cup water. Simmer, covered, for 5 to 10 minutes or until tortellini are tender. Top each serving with grated Parmesan cheese and refrigerated basil pesto.

Ask Mom What is Dijon-style mustard? page 379 / How do I crush dried herbs? page 78 / What is a garlic clove? page 40 / How do I mince garlic? page 40 / What does simmer mean? page 79 / How do I shred cheese? page 71 / How do I slice green onions? page 43 / How do I beat eggs? page 62 / How do I combine wet and dry ingredients? page 63 / What is that pasta shape? pages 308–309 / How do I grate cheese? page 71

Meatball and Vegetable
Soup with Pasta

- 3 14-ounce cans beef broth
- 1 12- to 16-ounce package frozen cooked meatballs
- 1 15- to 16-ounce can Great Northern beans or cannellini beans (white kidney beans), rinsed and drained
- 1 14.5-ounce can diced tomatoes with basil, garlic, and oregano, undrained
- 1 10-ounce package frozen mixed vegetables
- 1 cup dried small pasta (such as macaroni, small shell, mini penne, or rotini)
  Crusty bread (optional)
  Shredded Parmesan cheese (optional)

1 In a 4-quart Dutch oven combine broth, meatballs, beans, undrained tomatoes, and vegetables. Bring to boiling; stir in pasta. Return to boiling; reduce heat. Simmer, uncovered, about 10 minutes or until pasta is tender. To serve, ladle soup into bowls. If desired, serve with bread and sprinkle each serving with Parmesan cheese. Makes 6 to 8 main-dish servings.

Per serving: 319 cal., 5 g total fat (2 g sat. fat), 32 mg chol., 1,552 mg sodium, 45 g carbo., 7 g fiber, 24 g pro.

Beef and Vegetable Soup with Pasta: Prepare as above, except substitute one 17-ounce package refrigerated cooked beef tips with gravy for the frozen cooked meatballs.

Good to Know Soup tastes best when served hot. To keep it from cooling down too quickly, serve soup in warmed bowls. To warm them, preheat your oven to 200°F, turn it off, and put the bowls in it for a few minutes. No more (unintentionally) cold soup!

Ask Mom How do I rinse and drain canned beans? page 390 / How do I shred cheese? page 71 / What is that pasta shape? pages 308–309 / What does simmer mean? page 79

(2) Skill Level

Souper **Spaghetti**

Flavor Changes
Customize this
Italian-style soup to
your taste by trying
different flavors of
spaghetti sauce—with
cheese, garlic,
sausage, mushrooms,
or red wine, for
example. Experiment
with a spicy style,
simple marinara, or
even creamy vodka
sauce—you're sure
to find more than one
variation you love.

1 pound lean ground beef

½ cup chopped onion (1 medium)

½ cup chopped green sweet pepper (1 small)

½ cup chopped celery (1 stalk)

½ cup chopped carrot (1 medium)

2 cloves garlic, minced

2½ cups water

2 14.5-ounce cans diced tomatoes, undrained

1 13- to 15-ounce jar spaghetti sauce

1 tablespoon sugar

½ teaspoon dried Italian seasoning, crushed

½ teaspoon salt

¼ teaspoon ground black pepper

Dash crushed red pepper

2 ounces dried spaghetti, broken into 2-inch pieces

1 In a 4-quart Dutch oven cook ground beef, onion, sweet pepper, celery, carrot, and garlic until meat is brown and vegetables are tender (below). Drain off fat.

2 Stir in the water, undrained tomatoes, spaghetti sauce, sugar, Italian seasoning, salt, black pepper, and red pepper (below). Bring to boiling; add spaghetti (below). Return to boiling; reduce heat. Boil gently, uncovered, for 12 to 15 minutes or until spaghetti is tender. To serve, ladle soup into bowls. Makes 6 main-dish servings.

Per serving: 262 cal., 9 g total fat (3 g sat. fat), 48 mg chol., 962 mg sodium, 28 g carbo., 5 g fiber, 17 g pro.

1 Cook the ground beef and vegetables over medium heat until the beef is brown and the veggies are tender.

2 Add all the remaining ingredients, except the spaghetti, to the Dutch oven.

3 Once the mixture begins to boil, break up the spaghetti and add it to the Dutch oven.

Ask Mom How do I chop an onion? page 47 / How do I seed and chop sweet peppers? page 49 / How do I chop celery? page 39 / How do I peel and cut carrots? pages 37, 64 / What is a garlic clove? page 40 / How do I mince garlic? page 40 / How do I crush dried herbs? page 78 / What is that pasta shape? pages 308–309

One of the coolest things about chili (so to speak) is how customizable it is. Just set out a raft of toppings in individual bowls. Your guests can make their chili as lip tingling, creamy, crunchy, or cheesy as they like.

WHAT GOES WITH CHILI? Besides the obvious accompaniments of a good game, good friends, and cold beer, consider veggies with Creamy Parmesan Dip (page 93), Party Nachos (page 103), Corn Bread (page 154), and Rocky Road Brownies (page 445).

Chili (see recipe, page 384)

A Chopped tomatoes

B Sour cream

C Shredded cheese

D Chopped onions

E Crushed red pepper

A Cool, fresh tomatoes are a nice contrast to spicy, hot chili. See how to chop them on page 52. **B** A spoonful of sour cream on top adds a dimension of richness to the chili and softens the acidity of the tomatoes. You can use regular or light sour cream. **C** What doesn't some melty cheese make better? Good cheese choices for chili include cheddar, Monterey Jack, or a prepackaged Mexican blend. See page 71 for tips on shredding your own. **D** Raw onions add a fresh crunch and piquant taste to chili. Choose yellow onions for a milder flavor and white onions for more fresh-onion punch. See page 47 for how to chop them. **E** Put a shaker of crushed red pepper on the table and guests can make their chili as fiery they want, from mostly mild to four alarm.

Chili

 I pound lean ground beef
 ½ cup chopped green sweet pepper (I small)
 ½ cup chopped onion (I medium)
 4 cloves garlic, minced
 I 15-ounce can tomato sauce
 I 15-ounce can red kidney beans, undrained
 I 14.5-ounce can diced tomatoes, undrained
 2 to 3 teaspoons chili powder
 ½ teaspoon salt
 ½ teaspoon dried basil, crushed
 ¼ teaspoon ground black pepper
   Shredded cheddar cheese (optional)
   Chopped onion (optional)
   Dairy sour cream (optional)
   Crushed red pepper (optional)

1 In a 3-quart saucepan cook and stir ground beef, sweet pepper, ½ cup chopped onion, and the garlic over medium heat until meat is brown and onion is tender. Drain off fat.

2 Stir in tomato sauce, undrained beans, undrained tomatoes, chili powder, salt, basil, and black pepper. Bring to boiling; reduce heat. Simmer, covered, for 20 minutes. To serve, ladle chili into bowls. If desired, top each serving with cheese, chopped onion, and/or sour cream and pass crushed red pepper. Makes 4 main-dish servings.

Per serving: 381 cal., 15 g total fat (6 g sat. fat), 71 mg chol., 1,265 mg sodium, 35 g carbo., 9 g fiber, 32 g pro.

Chili for Two: Prepare as above, except divide all ingredients in half.

Cincinnati-Style Chili: Prepare as above, except omit sweet pepper, basil, and optional garnishes. Add 1 to 2 tablespoons unsweetened cocoa powder, 1 tablespoon cider vinegar, 1 teaspoon Worcestershire sauce, ½ teaspoon ground cinnamon, ½ teaspoon ground allspice, ½ teaspoon ground cumin, and ¼ teaspoon cayenne pepper with the tomato sauce. To serve, place ½ cup hot cooked spaghetti on each of 4 serving plates; make an indentation in center of each portion. Top each serving with some of the chili, 1 to 2 tablespoons shredded cheddar cheese, 1 to 2 tablespoons chopped onion, and/or ¼ cup additional kidney beans.

MEAL MAKER Got leftover chili? You could eat it all week and never have exactly the same thing twice. Serve it over a hot dog or burger, baked potato, or on a cheese omelet.

Ask Mom How do I seed and chop sweet peppers? page 49 / How do I chop an onion? page 47 / What is a garlic clove? page 40 / How do I mince garlic? page 40 / How do I crush dried herbs? page 78 / How do I shred cheese? page 71 / What does simmer mean? page 79 / What is that vinegar? page 349

1 Skill Level

Southwestern
Steak Chili

1 cup frozen whole kernel corn, thawed

1 to 1 ½ teaspoons chili powder

1 tablespoon cooking oil

1 17-ounce package refrigerated cooked beef tips with gravy

1 16-ounce jar mild or medium thick and chunky salsa

1 14- to 16-ounce can pinto beans or red beans,
  rinsed and drained

¼ cup bottled hickory-flavored barbecue sauce

¼ cup dairy sour cream

  Corn muffins or corn bread (optional)

Ingredient Info
Chili powder or chile powder—is there a difference? Well, yes, and it's rather significant. Chile powder is powdered dried chile of a single variety—ancho chile powder is used commonly in Southwest-style cooking. Chili powder is a blend of chile powder and other herbs and spices such as oregano, garlic, cumin, coriander, and cloves.

1 In a 4-quart Dutch oven cook corn and chili powder in hot oil over medium heat for 3 minutes, stirring frequently. Stir in beef tips with gravy, salsa, beans, and barbecue sauce (below). Bring to boiling, stirring occasionally (below); reduce heat. Simmer, covered, about 5 minutes or until heated through. To serve, ladle chili into bowls. Top each serving with sour cream. If desired, serve with corn muffins. Makes 4 main-dish servings.

Per serving: 354 cal., 11 g total fat (3 g sat. fat), 47 mg chol., 1,834 mg sodium, 42 g carbo., 7 g fiber, 25 g pro.

1 After cooking the corn and chili powder, pour the beef tips with gravy into the Dutch oven.

2 Stir the soup mixture with a wooden spoon to break up the beef slightly.

Ask Mom How do I rinse and drain canned beans? page 390 / What does simmer mean? page 79

Cheeseburger Soup

I pound lean ground beef

½ cup chopped onion (I medium)

2 cups cubed potato (2 medium)

I 14-ounce can beef broth

I medium fresh jalapeño chile pepper, seeded and finely chopped (optional)

2 cups milk

3 tablespoons all-purpose flour

I cup shredded American cheese or Monterey Jack cheese with jalapeño peppers (4 ounces)

Good to Know Flour works wonderfully as a thickener for all kinds of soups and sauces, but if you simply dump it into the pot dry, you'll have lumps of cooked flour in your soup. Blending it with milk (or water) prevents this problem—so don't skip this step!

1 In a 4-quart Dutch oven cook and stir ground beef and onion over medium heat until meat is brown and onion is tender. Drain off fat. Stir in potato, broth, jalapeño pepper (if using), and ¼ teaspoon *salt*. Bring to boiling; reduce heat. Simmer, covered, for 15 to 20 minutes or until potato is tender (below).

2 Combine ½ cup of the milk and the flour; stir into meat mixture (below). Stir in remaining milk. Cook and stir until thickened and bubbly (below). Reduce heat to low; add cheese (page 387). Cook, stirring constantly, until cheese melts. To serve, ladle soup into bowls. Makes 4 to 6 main-dish servings.

Per serving: 465 cal., 24 g total fat (13 g sat. fat), 114 mg chol., 1,131 mg sodium, 25 g carbo., 2 g fiber, 35 g pro.

Mushroom Swiss Cheeseburger Soup: Prepare as above, except cook 1 cup sliced fresh mushrooms with the ground beef and onion. Substitute Swiss cheese for the American cheese. If desired, top with sauteed mushrooms and caramelized onions (see page 66).

Blue Cheeseburger Soup: Prepare as above, except decrease American cheese to ½ cup and add ½ cup crumbled blue cheese. If desired, top with caramelized onions (see page 66).

1 To check doneness of potatoes, carefully insert a sharp knife into one of the potatoes. If you can insert and remove it easily, the potatoes are done.

2 Use a screw-top jar to shake together part of the milk and the flour; shake well to combine thoroughly. Add to saucepan along with the rest of the milk, stirring constantly.

3 Use a heat-resistant spatula to cook and stir the soup mixture over medium heat until it's thickened and bubbly.

Ask Mom How do I chop an onion? page 47 / What are some potato varieties? page 50 / What does it mean to cube? page 64 / How do I handle hot chile peppers? page 48 / What is process cheese? page 408 / How do I shred cheese? page 71 / What does simmer mean? page 79 / How do I crumble cheese? pages 71, 96 / What are some mushroom varieties? page 44 / How do I slice fresh mushrooms? page 45 / What does it mean to saute? page 69

WHAT DO I SERVE WITH SOUP? The classic combo of soup, salad, and bread is so satisfying. Consider the flavor and texture of your soup when choosing bread and salad serve-alongs. Cheeseburger Soup, for example, would be great with onion rolls and a fresh tomato-cucumber salad.

Sprinkle—don't dump—the shredded cheese over the soup to ensure it will all blend in nicely and not end up in a big lump. Cook and stir over low heat until all the cheese melts.

Pork and Mushroom Soup

1 pound pork stew meat, cut into 1-inch cubes (below)
2 tablespoons butter or margarine
1 14-ounce can chicken broth
¼ cup dry white wine
3 tablespoons snipped fresh parsley
¼ teaspoon dried thyme, crushed
¼ teaspoon garlic powder
⅛ teaspoon ground black pepper
2 cups frozen small whole onions
1 8-ounce package peeled fresh baby carrots (2 cups)
1 4-ounce can whole mushrooms, drained
1 cup cold water
3 tablespoons all-purpose flour

1 In a 3-quart saucepan brown pork, half at a time, in hot butter. Return all of the pork to the saucepan. Stir in broth, wine, parsley, thyme, garlic powder, and pepper. Bring to boiling; reduce heat. Simmer, covered, for 40 minutes.

2 Stir in onions, carrots, and mushrooms. Return to boiling; reduce heat. Simmer, covered, about 20 minutes more or until vegetables are tender.

3 In a screw-top jar combine water and flour; cover and shake until smooth. Add flour mixture to soup (see photo 2, page 386). Cook and stir over medium heat until thickened and bubbly. Cook and stir for 1 minute more. To serve, ladle soup into bowls. Makes 4 main-dish servings.

Per serving: 317 cal., 14 g total fat (6 g sat. fat), 90 mg chol., 605 mg sodium, 18 g carbo., 4 g fiber, 27 g pro.

If pork stew meat is not available, look for a small pork shoulder roast. Trim off the fat and cut the meat into pieces as directed in the recipe.

Good to Know
Most recipes call for crushing dried herbs before adding them to the rest of the ingredients. Crushing the herbs between your fingers releases their aromatic oils so that they provide maximum flavor to the finished dish.

Ask Mom How do I measure butter? pages 58, 59 / How do I snip fresh herbs? pages 42, 328 / How do I crush dried herbs? page 78 / What does simmer mean? page 79

Italian Pork and Pepper Soup

1½ pounds boneless pork shoulder

2 tablespoons cooking oil

½ cup chopped onion (1 medium)

2 14-ounce cans beef broth

1 14.5-ounce can diced tomatoes with basil, oregano, and garlic, undrained

1 cup bottled roasted red sweet peppers, drained and cut into bite-size strips

2 tablespoons balsamic vinegar

¼ teaspoon ground black pepper

2 cups sliced zucchini

Shredded Parmesan cheese (optional)

1 Trim fat from pork. Cut pork into 1-inch pieces (see photo, page 388). In a 4-quart Dutch oven brown half of the pork in hot oil; remove pork from Dutch oven. Add remaining pork and the onion. Cook and stir until pork is brown and onion is tender. Return all of the pork to the Dutch oven.

2 Stir in broth, undrained tomatoes, roasted sweet peppers, vinegar, and black pepper. Bring to boiling; reduce heat. Simmer, covered, for 50 minutes. Add zucchini. Return to boiling; reduce heat. Cook, covered, about 15 minutes more or until zucchini and pork are tender. To serve, ladle soup into bowls. If desired, sprinkle each serving with Parmesan cheese. Makes 6 main-dish servings.

Slow cooker directions: Prepare and brown pork with onion as above. In a 3½- or 4-quart slow cooker combine pork mixture, broth, undrained tomatoes, roasted sweet peppers, vinegar, and black pepper. Cover and cook on low-heat setting for 6 to 8 hours or on high-heat setting for 3 to 4 hours. If using low-heat setting, turn to high-heat setting. Stir in zucchini. Cover and cook about 15 minutes more or until zucchini is crisp-tender.

Per serving: 217 cal., 7 g total fat (2 g sat. fat), 73 mg chol., 943 mg sodium, 12 g carbo., 1 g fiber, 25 g pro.

Ask Mom What is that cut of meat? pages 220–221 / How do I chop an onion? page 47 / How do I drain bottled roasted sweet peppers? page 416 / What is that vinegar? page 349 / How do I slice summer squash/zucchini? page 54 / How do I shred cheese? page 71 / What does simmer mean? page 79 / What is a slow cooker? page 21 / What does crisp-tender mean? page 79

1 Skill Level

Cuban Black Bean Soup

Ingredient Info
Although there are all kinds of wild salsas on the market—with mangoes and peaches and cherries and berries—authentic Mexican salsa is usually just red or green. Red salsa is tomato-based. Salsa verde or green salsa contains tomatillos (a firm, citrusy Mexican fruit), jalapeño chile peppers, and cilantro. Either type works here.

1 16-ounce jar mild or medium thick and chunky salsa
  or salsa with lime and garlic
1 15- to 16-ounce can black beans, rinsed
  and drained
1 14-ounce can chicken broth
1 ¾ cups water
1 ½ cups cubed cooked ham (8 ounces)
1 teaspoon ground cumin
½ cup dairy sour cream
¼ cup bottled green salsa (optional)
  Crushed lime-flavored tortilla chips (optional)

1 In a 3-quart saucepan combine salsa, beans, broth, water, ham, and cumin. Bring to boiling; reduce heat. Simmer, covered, for 10 minutes.

2 To serve, ladle soup into bowls and top with sour cream. If desired, top each serving with green salsa and crushed tortilla chips. Makes 4 main-dish servings.

Per serving: 251 cal., 11 g total fat (5 g sat. fat), 44 mg chol., 2,095 mg sodium, 25 g carbo., 8 g fiber, 19 g pro.

Cuban Black Bean Soup with Peppers: Prepare as above, except substitute 2 cups frozen peppers and onion stir-fry vegetables for the ham.

Canned beans save time, but they add salt to your recipes. You can eliminate the salty liquid by rinsing the beans in a colander under cold running water; drain well.

Ask Mom What does it mean to cube? page 64 / What does simmer mean? page 79

Beer, Cheese, and Bacon Soup

$\frac{1}{4}$ cup butter or margarine

1 cup finely chopped onion (1 large)

$\frac{1}{2}$ cup all-purpose flour

1 teaspoon dry mustard

1 teaspoon paprika

$\frac{1}{8}$ teaspoon cayenne pepper

4 cups milk

1 12-ounce can beer

1 14-ounce can reduced-sodium chicken broth

$1\frac{1}{2}$ cups shredded sharp cheddar cheese (6 ounces)

6 ounces American cheese, cut up

10 slices bacon, crisp-cooked, drained, and crumbled

1 In a 4-quart Dutch oven melt butter; add onion and cook and stir over medium heat about 4 minutes or until tender. Stir in flour, mustard, paprika, and cayenne pepper until all of the flour is coated. Stir in the milk, beer, and broth all at once. Cook and stir over medium heat until thickened and bubbly; reduce heat to medium low. Gradually stir in cheddar cheese and American cheese until smooth. Stir in bacon; heat through. To serve, ladle soup into bowls. Makes 6 to 8 main-dish servings.

Per serving: 505 cal., 34 g total fat (20 g sat. fat), 101 mg chol., 1,123 mg sodium, 21 g carbo., 1 g fiber, 25 g pro.

Beer Cheese Chili: Prepare as above, except after adding the cheeses, stir in two 15-ounce cans hot and spicy chili beans in chili gravy, undrained; heat through. Omit bacon. If desired, top each serving with dairy sour cream. Makes 8 to 10 main-dish servings.

Beer, Cheese, and Ham Soup: Prepare as above, except substitute 1 cup cubed cooked ham or turkey ham for the bacon.

Spicy Beer Cheese Soup: Prepare as above, except increase cayenne pepper to $\frac{1}{4}$ teaspoon. Substitute Monterey Jack cheese with jalapeño peppers for the cheddar cheese. Omit bacon. If desired, sprinkle each serving with crushed red pepper.

Ingredient Info The most important consideration in choosing a beer to use in this soup is that it's one you like to drink. You can choose any style of beer, including Pilsner, ale, or lager—even a porter or stout if you like that intense molasses flavor. A light beer will lend less beer flavor and body to the soup.

Ask Mom How do I measure butter? pages 58, 59 / How do I chop an onion? page 47 / How do I measure flour? page 58 / What is process cheese? page 408 / How do I shred cheese? page 71 / How do I cook bacon? page 172 / What does it mean to cube? page 64

GET ORGANIZED. The French have a cooking term *mise en place,* which means "setting in place." It means you should have all ingredients chopped, prepped, and measured before you start cooking so everything will go as smoothly as possible.

Both escarole and Swiss chard are hearty winter greens that are absolutely packed with vitamins. Stir them into soup, add them to a salad, or quick-saute them in a little olive oil and garlic as a side.

Baking potatoes

Beef broth

Crushed red pepper

Cannellini bean

Escarole

Stewed tomat

Swiss chard

Minced garlic

Shredded Parmesan

Good to Know If you can't find precooked Italian sausage links, you can buy them raw and cook them yourself. The least messy way to do this is to prick the sausages a few times with a fork, then lay them in a skillet and add about an inch of water. Bring to boiling; reduce heat. Simmer, covered, about 10 minutes or until no longer pink inside. Let cool before slicing.

(1) Skill Level

Quick Minestrone

- 1 19-ounce can cannellini beans (white kidney beans), rinsed and drained
- 2 cups cubed, peeled potato (2 medium)
- 1 14.5-ounce can Italian-style stewed tomatoes, undrained and cut up
- 1 14-ounce can lower-sodium beef broth
- 8 ounces cooked Italian sausage links, cut into $\frac{1}{2}$-inch slices
- $\frac{1}{4}$ teaspoon crushed red pepper
- 4 cloves garlic, minced
- 2 cups chopped escarole or Swiss chard leaves
- $\frac{1}{3}$ cup shredded Parmesan or Asiago cheese

1 In a 4-quart Dutch oven combine beans, potato, undrained tomatoes, broth, sausage, crushed red pepper, and garlic. Bring to boiling; reduce heat. Simmer, covered, for 25 to 30 minutes or until potato is tender (see photo 1, page 386). Stir in escarole.

2 To serve, ladle soup into bowls. Sprinkle each serving with Parmesan cheese. Makes 6 main-dish servings.

Per serving: 256 cal., 12 g total fat (4 g sat. fat), 25 mg chol., 942 mg sodium, 26 g carbo., 6 g fiber, 16 g pro.

Quick Meatball Minestrone: Prepare as above, except substitute one 10-ounce package frozen mixed vegetables for the potato and one 12- to 16-ounce package frozen cooked Italian-style meatballs for the sausage. Increase broth to 2 cans. Omit escarole. Add 1 cup dried macaroni after soup has simmered for 15 minutes. Simmer about 10 minutes more or until pasta is tender.

Quick Chicken Minestrone: Prepare as above, except substitute one 10-ounce package frozen green beans for the potato, reduced-sodium chicken broth for the beef broth, and two 6-ounce packages refrigerated or frozen cooked Italian-style chicken breast strips for the sausage. Reduce cooking time to 15 minutes or until beans are tender. Substitute torn spinach for the escarole.

Ask Mom How do I rinse and drain canned beans? page 390 / What are some potato varieties? page 50 / What does it mean to cube? page 64 / How do I cut up canned tomatoes? page 405 / What is a garlic clove? page 40 / How do I mince garlic? page 40 / How do I shred cheese? page 71 / What does simmer mean? page 79 / What is that pasta shape? pages 308–309

Chicken Noodle Soup

4 1/2 cups chicken broth
    1 cup chopped onion (1 large)
    1 cup sliced carrot (2 medium)
    1 cup sliced celery (2 stalks)
    1 teaspoon dried basil, crushed
    1 teaspoon dried oregano, crushed
 1/4 teaspoon ground black pepper
    1 bay leaf
1 1/2 cups dried medium egg noodles
    2 cups chopped cooked chicken or turkey

1 In a 3-quart saucepan combine broth, onion, carrot, celery, basil, oregano, pepper, and bay leaf. Bring to boiling; reduce heat. Simmer, covered, for 5 minutes. Stir in uncooked noodles. Return to boiling; reduce heat. Simmer, covered, for 8 to 10 minutes or until noodles are tender but still firm and vegetables are just tender. Discard bay leaf. Stir in chicken; heat through. To serve, ladle soup into bowls. Makes 4 main-dish servings.

Per serving: 241 cal., 7 g total fat (2 g sat. fat), 77 mg chol., 1,190 mg sodium, 20 g carbo., 3 g fiber, 24 g pro.

Chicken Tortellini Soup: Prepare as above, except substitute small broccoli florets for the celery and one 9-ounce package refrigerated cheese-filled tortellini for the noodles. Add the broccoli and 1 cup sliced fresh mushrooms when tortellini is added.

Parmesan-Pesto Chicken Noodle Soup: Prepare as above, except substitute 1 small zucchini, halved lengthwise and sliced, for the celery; Italian seasoning for the basil and oregano; and dried small shell macaroni for the noodles. Add 2 cloves garlic, minced, to the broth mixture. Add the zucchini with the macaroni. Meanwhile, spread each of 4 slices Italian bread with 1 tablespoon refrigerated basil pesto; sprinkle each with 1 tablespoon finely shredded Parmesan cheese. Place, pesto sides up, on a baking sheet. Preheat broiler. Broil 3 to 4 inches from the heat about 2 minutes or until cheese melts. Top each serving with a slice of the bread.

GOOD TO KNOW Bay leaves add a wonderful, aromatic flavor to all kinds of foods, but you don't want to eat them—they're bitter and fibrous. Always be sure to remove the bay leaf from whatever you're making before serving.

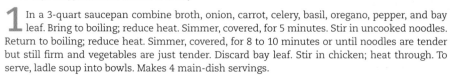

Ask Mom How do I chop an onion? page 47 / How do I peel and cut carrots? pages 37, 64 / How do I prepare celery? page 39 / How do I crush dried herbs? page 78 / What is that pasta shape? pages 308–309 / What does simmer mean? page 79 / How do I trim and cut broccoli? page 36 / How do I slice fresh mushrooms? page 45 / How do I mince garlic? page 40 / How do I slice summer squash/zucchini? page 54 / How do I shred cheese? page 71 / What does it mean to broil? page 68

Chicken Tortilla Soup

1 2- to 2 ¼-pound deli-roasted chicken
2 14-ounce cans chicken broth with roasted garlic
1 15-ounce can chopped tomatoes and green chile peppers, undrained
1 11-ounce can whole kernel corn with sweet peppers, drained
1 small fresh jalapeño chile pepper, seeded and finely
    chopped, or 2 teaspoons bottled finely chopped jalapeño peppers
1 teaspoon ground cumin
2 tablespoons snipped fresh cilantro
1 tablespoon lime juice
   Lime-flavored tortilla chips or regular tortilla chips, broken
   Dairy sour cream (optional)
   Shredded lime peel (optional)

Meal Maker Have some leftover shredded chicken? Mix with barbecue sauce and use to top a pizza; make chicken quesadillas; put it in a taco shell with lettuce, cheese, tomato, and salsa; or mix it with mayo, chopped celery, and minced onion for a quick chicken salad.

395

Soups & Stews

1 Remove chicken meat from chicken (below). Shred enough of the chicken to measure 2 cups (below). Set chicken aside. Reserve any remaining chicken for another use.

2 In a 3-quart saucepan combine broth, undrained tomatoes, corn, jalapeño pepper, and cumin. Bring to boiling; reduce heat. Simmer, covered, for 10 minutes. Stir in the shredded chicken, cilantro, and lime juice; heat through. To serve, ladle soup into bowls and top each serving with tortilla chips. If desired, stir together the sour cream and lime peel; top each serving with some of the sour cream mixture. Makes 6 main-dish servings.

Per serving: 183 cal., 5 g total fat (1 g sat. fat), 43 mg chol., 1,080 mg sodium, 18 g carbo., 2 g fiber, 16 g pro.

1 You can make this soup with any precooked chicken, including a purchased roasted chicken from a deli or supermarket.

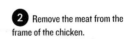

2 Remove the meat from the frame of the chicken.

3 To shred the chicken, pull the meat apart into thin strips with your fingers or with 2 forks.

Ask Mom How do I handle hot chile peppers? page 48 / How do I juice a lemon/lime? pages 30, 80 / How do I shred lemon/lime peel? page 30 / How do I snip fresh herbs? pages 42, 328 / How much juice does one lemon/lime yield? page 30 / What does simmer mean? page 79

② Skill Level

Creamy Turkey And Rice Soup

4 cups chicken broth
¼ teaspoon dried Italian seasoning, crushed
¼ teaspoon ground black pepper
1 10-ounce package frozen mixed vegetables
1 cup quick-cooking white or brown rice
2 cups chopped cooked turkey or chicken
1 14.5-ounce can diced tomatoes, drained
2 tablespoons refrigerated basil pesto
1 8-ounce carton dairy sour cream
2 tablespoons all-purpose flour

Ingredient Info

Purchased pesto is superconvenient, but it doesn't last long once opened. Buy the smallest amount you can so it's always fresh, and use it up fast. Toss it with plain noodles or hot steamed green beans, stir it into mashed potatoes for a side dish, or spread it on bread when making a grilled sandwich.

1 In a 3-quart saucepan combine broth, Italian seasoning, and pepper. Bring to boiling. Stir in vegetables and rice. Return to boiling; reduce heat. Simmer, covered, for 8 to 10 minutes or until vegetables are tender. Stir in turkey, drained tomatoes, and pesto; heat through.

2 Meanwhile, in a small bowl whisk together sour cream and flour (below); add to saucepan (below). Cook and stir until thickened and bubbly. Cook and stir for 1 minute more (below). To serve, ladle soup into bowls. Makes 6 main-dish servings.

Per serving: 245 cal., 12 g total fat (5 g sat. fat), 42 mg chol., 585 mg sodium, 20 g carbo., 2 g fiber, 13 g pro.

Turkey and Rice Soup: Prepare as above, except omit Step 2.

1 Place sour cream in a small bowl. Use a whisk to stir in the flour, 1 tablespoon at a time, until no lumps remain.

2 Add the sour cream mixture to the hot soup.

3 Use the whisk to stir sour cream mixture into soup. Continue cooking, stirring constantly, until soup is thickened and bubbly. Cook 1 minute more to ensure the flour is fully cooked and won't taste starchy.

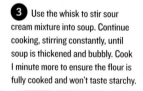

Ask Mom How do I crush dried herbs? page 78 / What does simmer mean? page 79

WHAT'S A ROUX? Gumbo wouldn't be gumbo without roux—a base of flour and fat that's cooked to a deep, coppery brown. Roux adds both a nutty flavor and body to the finished dish. Roux is ready when it's the color of a penny.

Turkey and Barley Vegetable Soup

1 pound uncooked ground turkey or chicken

2 cloves garlic, minced

2 tablespoons cooking oil

5 cups water

1 14.5-ounce can diced tomatoes, undrained

1 cup vegetable juice or hot-style vegetable juice

⅓ cup quick-cooking barley (see photo, page 332)

⅓ cup dry split peas, rinsed and drained

2 teaspoons dried Italian seasoning, crushed

1 to 1½ teaspoons salt

¼ teaspoon ground black pepper

1 cup sliced celery (2 stalks)

1 cup sliced carrot (2 medium)

1 In a 3-quart saucepan cook ground turkey and garlic in hot oil about 5 minutes or until turkey is no longer pink. Drain off fat. Stir in water, undrained tomatoes, vegetable juice, barley, split peas, Italian seasoning, salt, and pepper. Bring to boiling; reduce heat. Simmer, covered, for 30 minutes.

2 Stir in celery and carrot. Simmer, covered, about 30 minutes more until vegetables and barley are tender. To serve, ladle soup into bowls. Makes 6 main-dish servings.

Per serving: 256 cal., 11 g total fat (2 g sat. fat), 60 mg chol., 698 mg sodium, 21 g carbo., 5 g fiber, 18 g pro.

Beef and Barley Vegetable Soup: Prepare as above, except substitute lean ground beef for the ground turkey. Omit cooking oil.

Ingredient Info All ground turkey isn't created equal. Some ground turkey is made from all parts—white meat, dark meat, fat, and skin. Other ground turkey is made only from the breast. The first type is easier to find, but it's also higher in fat. Ground turkey breast is sometimes labeled "diet lean." It will probably be more expensive, but it's better for you.

Ask Mom What is a garlic clove? page 40 / How do I mince garlic? page 40 / How do I crush dried herbs? page 78 / How do I prepare celery? page 39 / How do I peel and cut carrots? pages 37, 64 / What does simmer mean? page 79

Chicken and
Sausage Gumbo

Ingredient Info Okra is a delicious and integral addition to a classic gumbo—the trick is not to overcook it. Cook okra only for the prescribed time so it stays crisp-tender and doesn't turn mushy and (even worse!) slightly slimy.

⅓ cup all-purpose flour

⅓ cup cooking oil

½ cup chopped onion (1 medium)

½ cup chopped green or red sweet pepper (1 small)

½ cup sliced celery (1 stalk)

3 cloves garlic, minced

1½ to 2 teaspoons Cajun seasoning

1 14-ounce can beef broth

1 10-ounce package frozen cut okra* or cut green beans

1½ cups chopped cooked chicken

8 ounces cooked smoked sausage links, sliced

3 cups hot cooked long grain or brown rice (see pages 268 and 324)

1 For roux, in a 3-quart heavy saucepan combine flour and oil until smooth (below). Cook over medium-high heat for 5 minutes, stirring constantly. Reduce heat to medium. Cook and stir constantly for 8 to 10 minutes more or until the roux is dark reddish brown (below).

2 Stir in onion, sweet pepper, celery, and garlic. Cook about 10 minutes or until vegetables are tender, stirring frequently. Stir in Cajun seasoning. Stir in broth and ¾ cup *water* (below). Add okra. Bring to boiling; reduce heat. Simmer, covered, for 15 minutes. Stir in chicken and sausage; heat through. To serve, ladle gumbo into bowls with rice. If desired, top each serving with sliced green onion and pass bottled hot pepper sauce. Makes 6 main-dish servings.

*Note: If you can't find cut okra, buy whole. Thaw slightly and slice.

Per serving: 482 cal., 27 g total fat (7 g sat. fat), 59 mg chol., 900 mg sodium, 34 g carbo., 2 g fiber, 24 g pro.

1 To start the roux, use a wooden spoon to combine the flour and cooking oil until smooth.

2 Roux is ready when its color is similar to a penny. Stir the roux constantly so it doesn't scorch. If it does, it won't thicken the gumbo.

3 Gradually stir the broth and water into the cooked vegetable mixture.

Ask Mom How do I measure flour? page 58 / How do I chop an onion? page 47 / How do I seed and chop sweet peppers? page 49 / How do I prepare celery? page 39 / What is a garlic clove? page 40 / How do I mince garlic? page 40 / What does simmer mean? page 79

② Skill Level

Good to Know Gremolata is usually a minced-up combination of lemon peel, garlic, and parsley. It is best known as the traditional accompaniment to osso bucco, the Italian dish of braised veal shanks, but it adds a fresh, bright flavor to anything it touches. It can be made with other herbs (such as basil) or even orange zest, if you like.

Quick Cioppino with Basil Gremolata

- 6 ounces fresh or frozen cod fillets
- 6 ounces fresh or frozen peeled and deveined shrimp
- 1 cup green sweet pepper strips (1 medium)
- 1 cup chopped onion (1 large)
- 4 cloves garlic, minced
- 1 tablespoon olive oil or cooking oil
- 2 14.5-ounce cans Italian-style stewed tomatoes, undrained and cut up
- ½ cup water
- ¼ teaspoon salt
- ¼ teaspoon ground black pepper
- 3 tablespoons snipped fresh basil
- 1 tablespoon finely shredded lemon peel

1 Thaw cod and shrimp, if frozen. Rinse cod and shrimp; pat dry. Set shrimp aside. Cut cod into 1-inch pieces; set aside.

2 In a 3-quart saucepan cook and stir sweet pepper, onion, and 2 cloves of the garlic in hot oil until tender. Stir in undrained tomatoes, water, salt, and black pepper; bring to boiling. Stir in cod and shrimp. Return to boiling; reduce heat. Simmer, covered, for 2 to 3 minutes or until cod flakes easily when tested with a fork and shrimp turn opaque.

3 For gremolata, combine the remaining 2 cloves of garlic, the basil, and lemon peel. To serve, ladle soup into bowls and sprinkle with gremolata. Makes 4 main-dish servings.

Per serving: 197 cal., 5 g total fat (1 g sat. fat), 83 mg chol., 686 mg sodium, 19 g carbo., 5 g fiber, 19 g pro.

In a small bowl stir together the gremolata ingredients. Sprinkle a little bit over the cioppino before serving.

Ask Mom What other kinds of fish can I use? page 295 / How do I thaw fish? page 73 / How do I seed sweet peppers and cut them into strips? page 49 / How do I chop an onion? page 47 / What is a garlic clove? page 40 / How do I mince garlic? page 40 / How do I cut up canned tomatoes? page 405 / How do I snip fresh herbs? pages 42, 328 / How do I shred lemon/lime peel? page 30 / What does simmer mean? page 79

Hot-and-Sour Soup with Shrimp

12 ounces fresh or frozen peeled and deveined shrimp

4 ounces fresh shiitake mushrooms* or fresh button mushrooms, sliced

1 tablespoon cooking oil

2 14-ounce cans chicken broth

$\frac{1}{4}$ cup rice vinegar or white vinegar

2 tablespoons soy sauce

1 teaspoon sugar

1 teaspoon grated fresh ginger or $\frac{1}{4}$ teaspoon ground ginger

1 tablespoon cornstarch

$\frac{1}{2}$ cup frozen peas

$\frac{1}{2}$ cup shredded carrot (1 medium)

2 tablespoons thinly sliced green onion (1)

1 egg, lightly beaten

1 Thaw shrimp, if frozen. Rinse shrimp; pat dry. Set shrimp aside. In a 3-quart saucepan cook and stir mushrooms in hot oil until tender. Stir in broth, vinegar, soy sauce, sugar, ginger, and $\frac{1}{2}$ teaspoon *ground black pepper*. Bring to boiling; reduce heat. Simmer, covered, for 2 minutes. Stir in shrimp. Return to boiling; reduce heat. Simmer, covered, for 1 minute more.

2 In a small bowl stir together cornstarch and 1 tablespoon *cold water*; stir into saucepan. Cook and stir until slightly thickened and bubbly. Cook and stir for 2 minutes more. Stir in peas, carrot, and green onion. Pour egg into soup in a steady stream, stirring a few times to create shreds (below). To serve, ladle soup into bowls. Makes 4 main-dish servings.

*Note: If using shiitake mushrooms, remove and discard tough stems before slicing.

Per serving: 212 cal., 7 g total fat (1 g sat. fat), 184 mg chol., 1,431 mg sodium, 13 g carbo., 2 g fiber, 22 g pro.

Hot-and-Sour Soup with Tofu: Prepare as above, except substitute one 12-ounce package firm, silken-style tofu (fresh bean curd), cut into bite-size pieces, for the shrimp.

Stir soup gently and keep it just at simmering (not boiling) so the egg forms fine threads rather than turning the soup cloudy.

Ask Mom How do I beat eggs? page 62 / How do I grate fresh ginger? page 41 / How do I shred vegetables? page 20 / How do I slice fresh mushrooms? page 45 / How do I slice green onions? page 43 / What are some mushroom varieties? page 44 / What is fresh ginger? page 41 / What is that vinegar? page 349 / What is tofu? page 331

3 Skill Level

Clam Chowder

4 slices bacon, chopped
2½ cups refrigerated diced potatoes with onions
½ cup chopped celery (1 stalk)
1 8-ounce bottle clam juice
1 cup milk
2 tablespoons all-purpose flour
1 teaspoon dried thyme, crushed
1 teaspoon instant chicken bouillon granules
1 teaspoon Worcestershire sauce
2 cups half-and-half or light cream
2 6.5-ounce cans minced clams, drained

Shopping Savvy
Along with milk and light cream, clam juice—the strained briny liquid of shucked clams—provides liquid for this rich soup. It gives it a great by-the-sea flavor. Look for clam juice at your supermarket near the canned tuna, salmon, and sardines.

1 In a 3-quart saucepan cook bacon until crisp. Remove bacon with a slotted spoon, reserving 2 tablespoons drippings in saucepan. Drain bacon on paper towels; set aside. Add potatoes and celery to hot drippings (below). Cook and stir over medium heat about 4 minutes or until tender. Add clam juice (below). Bring to boiling; reduce heat. Simmer, covered, for 10 minutes.

2 Whisk together milk, flour, thyme, bouillon granules, and Worcestershire sauce (below); stir into saucepan (below). Stir in half-and-half. Cook and stir until thickened and bubbly. Cook and stir 1 minute more (below). Mash potatoes slightly (page 403). Stir in clams; heat through. Season with *salt* and *ground black pepper*. Sprinkle with bacon. Makes 4 main-dish servings.

Per serving: 403 cal., 19 g total fat (10 g sat. fat), 96 mg chol., 886 mg sodium, 32 g carbo., 2 g fiber, 25 g pro.

Cheesy Corn Chowder: Prepare as above, except substitute one 14-ounce can chicken broth for the clam juice and one 15-ounce can whole kernel corn, drained, for the clams. Omit bouillon granules and Worcestershire sauce. Stir in 2 cups shredded cheddar cheese with the corn. Heat and stir until cheese melts. Makes 5 main-dish servings.

1 Add potatoes and celery to hot bacon drippings in saucepan.

2 Pour clam juice into saucepan, stirring to combine.

3 In a 2-cup glass measuring cup whisk together the milk, flour, and the rest of the seasonings.

4 Pour milk mixture saucepan, stirring cons with a wooden spoon.

Ask Mom How do I chop celery? page 39 / How do I crush dried herbs? page 78 / What does simmer mean? page 79

WHAT'S A CHOWDER? Though the name comes from the French *chaudière*—the cauldron fisherman used to cook their fresh fish stews—chowder has come to mean any thick, rich, chunky soup made with fat and/or cream or milk.

5 When the soup becomes thickened and bubbly, use a potato masher to mash the potatoes slightly. Or use the back of a fork to mash the potatoes against the sides of the saucepan.

Ingredient Info Sherry is a fortified wine—a wine that has a small bit of spirit, such as brandy, added to it. The best kind of sherry to cook with is a dry sherry. Cream sherry is sweeter and generally is consumed as an after-dinner drink.

(1) Skill Level

Easy Crab Bisque

2 ¾ cups milk

I 10.75-ounce can condensed cream of asparagus soup

I 10.75-ounce can condensed cream of mushroom soup

I cup half-and-half or light cream

I 6- to 6.5-ounce can crabmeat, drained, flaked, and cartilage removed

3 tablespoons dry sherry or milk

Fresh chives (optional)

1 In a 3-quart saucepan combine milk, asparagus soup, mushroom soup, and half-and-half. Bring just to boiling over medium heat, stirring frequently. Stir in crabmeat and sherry; heat through. To serve, ladle bisque into bowls. If desired, garnish each serving with chives. Makes 6 main-dish servings.

Per serving: 225 cal., 12 g total fat (5 g sat. fat), 51 mg chol., 882 mg sodium, 15 g carbo., 0 g fiber, 12 g pro.

Easy Shrimp Bisque: Prepare as above, except substitute cream of shrimp soup for the cream of mushroom soup and 8 ounces cooked small shrimp for the crabmeat.

Easy Mushroom Bisque: Prepare as above, except cook and stir 2 cups sliced fresh button, shiitake, and/or portobello mushrooms in 2 tablespoons hot butter until tender. Continue as directed, omitting crabmeat. Omit watercress. If desired, garnish each serving with additional sauteed mushrooms and caramelized onions (see page 66).

Ask Mom How do I snip fresh herbs? pages 42, 328 / What does garnish mean? page 79 / What are some mushroom varieties? page 44 / How do I slice fresh mushrooms? page 45 / What does it mean to saute? page 69

1 Skill Level

Ingredient Info Use any firm, meaty fish in this soup. Good options include cod, catfish, whitefish, sea bass, halibut, flounder, pollack, red snapper, mahi mahi, and swordfish.

Cajun Fish Soup

- 12 ounces fresh or frozen fish fillets or peeled and deveined medium shrimp
- 1 14-ounce can vegetable broth or chicken broth
- 1 cup sliced fresh mushrooms
- 1 medium yellow summer squash or zucchini, halved lengthwise and sliced (1¼ cups)
- ½ cup finely chopped onion (1 medium)
- 1 teaspoon Cajun seasoning
- 1 teaspoon dried oregano, crushed
- 2 cloves garlic, minced
- 2 14.5-ounce cans stewed tomatoes, undrained and cut up
- ½ teaspoon finely shredded lemon peel

1 Thaw fish, if frozen. Rinse fish; pat dry. Cut fish into 1-inch pieces; set aside.

2 In a 3-quart saucepan combine broth, mushrooms, summer squash, onion, Cajun seasoning, oregano, and garlic. Bring to boiling; reduce heat. Simmer, covered, for 5 to 7 minutes or until vegetables are tender.

3 Stir in fish and undrained tomatoes. Bring to boiling; reduce heat. Simmer, covered, for 2 to 3 minutes or until fish flakes easily when tested with a fork. Remove saucepan from heat; stir in lemon peel. To serve, ladle soup into bowls. Makes 6 main-dish servings.

Per serving: 106 cal., 0 g total fat (0 g sat. fat), 24 mg chol., 563 mg sodium, 14 g carbo., 2 g fiber, 12 g pro.

Tex-Mex Fish Soup: Prepare as above, except substitute one 10-ounce package frozen corn, thawed, for the summer squash and 2 teaspoons Mexican seasoning for the Cajun seasoning. Omit oregano and lemon peel. If desired, top each serving with dairy sour cream Mexican-flavor dip and snipped fresh cilantro.

Kitchen scissors make quick work of cutting up canned tomatoes. Snip the tomatoes into bite-size pieces while they are still in the can.

Ask Mom What other kinds of fish can I use? page 295 / How do I thaw fish? page 73 / What are some mushroom varieties? page 44 / How do I slice fresh mushrooms? page 45 / What is summer squash? page 54 / How do I slice summer squash/zucchini? page 54 / How do I chop an onion? page 47 / How do I crush dried herbs? page 78 / What is a garlic clove? page 40 / How do I mince garlic? page 40 / How do I shred lemon/lime peel? page 30 / What does simmer mean? page 79

(2) Skill Level

Good to Know
Cooking the onions slowly over medium-low heat caramelizes them; it gently cooks the sugars in the onions, rather than burning them. That's why this soup has such a wonderful, nutty-sweet flavor.

French Onion Soup

¼ cup butter

2½ cups thinly sliced onion (2 large)

2 14-ounce cans beef broth

¼ cup dry sherry or dry white wine

I teaspoon Worcestershire sauce

¼ teaspoon ground black pepper

4 ½-inch slices French bread

⅔ cup shredded Swiss, Gruyère, or Jarlsberg cheese

1 In a 3-quart saucepan melt butter. Add onion and cook, covered, over medium-low heat for 13 to 15 minutes or until tender, stirring occasionally.

2 Uncover saucepan; cook and stir onion over medium-high heat about 10 minutes more or until onion is golden. Stir in broth, sherry, Worcestershire sauce, and pepper. Bring to boiling; reduce heat. Simmer, covered, for 15 minutes.

3 Meanwhile, preheat broiler. Line a baking sheet with foil; arrange bread slices on baking sheet. Broil 4 to 5 inches from heat for 2 to 3 minutes or until toasted, turning once. Sprinkle with cheese (below). Broil for 2 to 3 minutes more or until cheese melts and is light brown.

4 To serve, ladle soup into bowls. Top each serving with a bread slice (below). Makes 4 main-dish servings.

Per serving: 306 cal., 18 g total fat (II g sat. fat), 47 mg chol., 1,023 mg sodium, 24 g carbo., 2 g fiber, IO g pro.

French Onion Soup with Beef: Prepare as above, except add 1 cup chopped cooked beef with the broth.

French Onion Soup with Mushrooms: Prepare as above, except add 2 cups sliced fresh mushrooms to saucepan in Step 2 before adding broth. Cook and stir over medium-high heat about 15 minutes more or until onion is golden and mushrooms are tender. Continue as directed.

1 Divide the shredded cheese among the 4 slices of toasted French bread.

2 Use tongs to transfer each cheesy bread slice to a bowl of soup.

Ask Mom How do I measure butter? pages 58, 59 / How do I slice an onion? page 47 / How do I slice bread? page 64 / How do I shred cheese? page 71 / What does simmer mean? page 79 / What does it mean to broil? page 68 / How do I line a pan with foil? page 60 / What are some mushroom varieties? page 44 / How do I slice fresh mushrooms? page 45

DOES THE KIND OF CHEESE MATTER? Eating French Onion Soup is an experience for both the mouth and the nose. The cheese has to melt easily. A Swiss-style cheese provides that classic nutty flavor and aroma as you revel in your soup.

By adding some chopped cooked beef to this soup—and serving a green salad alongside—you turn a classic bistro-style starter into a full meal. It's just what you want to eat on a cold winter night.

Onion-Swiss Cream Soup

  4 14-ounce cans (7 cups) vegetable broth or chicken broth
  3 cups thinly sliced onion (3 medium)
1½ cups sliced fresh mushrooms
  1 teaspoon dried fines herbes, crushed
  ½ teaspoon ground white pepper
  ⅓ cup all-purpose flour
  6 ounces process Swiss cheese, torn
  1 cup whipping cream
  2 tablespoons snipped fresh parsley
    Sliced green onion (optional)

1 In a 4-quart Dutch oven combine 4¾ cups of the broth, onion, mushrooms, fines herbes, and pepper. Bring to boiling; reduce heat. Simmer, covered, for 15 to 20 minutes or until onion is tender. Cool slightly.

2 Place one-third of the onion mixture in a blender or food processor. Cover and blend or process until smooth (see photo, page 377). Repeat with remaining onion mixture. Return all of the onion mixture to the Dutch oven. Stir in 1 cup of the remaining broth.

3 In a small bowl stir together the remaining 1¼ cups broth and the flour until smooth. Stir into Dutch oven. Stir in cheese. Cook and stir over medium-low heat until slightly thickened and bubbly and cheese melts. Stir in whipping cream and parsley; heat through but *do not boil*. To serve, ladle the soup into bowls. If desired, top each serving with green onion. Makes 6 main-dish servings.

Per serving: 291 cal., 22 g total fat (14 g sat. fat), 78 mg chol., 1,495 mg sodium, 15 g carbo., 1 g fiber, 9 g pro.

Leek, Potato, and Blue Cheese Cream Soup: Prepare as above, except substitute 4 cups sliced leek for the onion, finely chopped peeled potato for the mushrooms, and dried basil for the fines herbes. Reduce Swiss cheese to 4 ounces and add ½ cup crumbled blue cheese. Omit green onion. If desired, top each serving with croutons.

Ingredient Info Process Swiss cheese looks similar to American cheese—only it's white in color, not orange. Unlike the original Swiss, it doesn't have holes and it comes in thin, very soft slices. Process Swiss is milder in flavor than the original and highly meltable, making it a good choice for this soup. Look for it with the other process cheeses (including American) at your supermarket.

Ask Mom How do I slice an onion? page 47 / What are some mushroom varieties? page 44 / How do I slice fresh mushrooms? page 45 / How do I crush dried herbs? page 78 / How do I measure flour? page 58 / How do I snip fresh herbs? pages 42, 328 / How do I slice green onions? page 43 / What does simmer mean? page 79 / What is a leek? page 43 / How do I slice a leek? page 43 / How do I prepare potatoes? page 51 / What does it mean to chop? page 64 / How do I crumble cheese? pages 71, 96

2 Skill Level

Smashed Potato Chowder

3 ½ pounds potatoes, peeled and cut into ¾-inch cubes
¾ cup chopped red or yellow sweet pepper (I medium)
1 ½ teaspoons bottled roasted minced garlic
½ teaspoon ground black pepper
5 cups chicken broth
8 slices bacon, crisp-cooked, drained, and coarsely chopped
2 cups shredded cheddar cheese (8 ounces)
½ cup whipping cream, half-and-half, or light cream
½ cup thinly sliced green onion (4)
½ cup dairy sour cream

1 In a 4-quart Dutch oven combine potato, sweet pepper, garlic, and black pepper. Stir in broth. Bring to boiling; reduce heat. Simmer, covered, for 20 to 25 minutes or until potato is tender (see photo 1, page 386).

2 Use a potato masher to mash potato mixture slightly (see photo, page 403). Stir in bacon, 1½ cups of the cheese, the whipping cream, and green onion; heat through. To serve, ladle soup into bowls. Top each serving with sour cream and remaining cheese. Makes 8 main-dish servings.

Per serving: 363 cal., 21 g total fat (12 g sat. fat), 64 mg chol., 944 mg sodium, 31 g carbo., 3 g fiber, 14 g pro.

Smashed Potato Chowder with Ham: Prepare as above, except substitute 1½ cups chopped cooked ham for the bacon.

Smashed Potato Chowder with Beans: Prepare as above, except substitute shredded carrot for the sweet pepper. Add one 15-ounce can cannellini (white kidney beans) or Great Northern beans, rinsed and drained, after mashing the potato mixture. Substitute 2 teaspoons dried dill-weed for the green onion.

Ask Mom What are some potato varieties? page 50 / How do I prepare potatoes? page 51 / What does it mean to cube? page 64 / How do I seed and chop sweet peppers? page 49 / How do I cook bacon? page 172 / How do I shred cheese? page 71 / How do I slice green onions? page 43 / What does simmer mean? page 79 / How do I rinse and drain canned bean? page 390

Curried Ginger Lentil Soup

   1 cup chopped onion (1 large)
   1 fresh jalapeño chile pepper, seeded and finely chopped
   1 teaspoon grated fresh ginger
   3 cloves garlic, minced
   1 tablespoon olive oil
   2 14-ounce cans vegetable broth
1½ cups chopped tomato (2 medium)
   1 cup dry lentils (see page 327), rinsed and drained
   2 medium sweet potatoes, peeled and cut into ½-inch pieces
   1 cup water
   1 tablespoon curry powder
     Dash salt
     Dairy sour cream (optional)

1 In a 3-quart saucepan cook and stir onion, jalapeño pepper, ginger, and garlic in hot oil over medium heat until tender. Stir in broth, tomato, lentils, sweet potato, water, curry powder, and salt. Bring to boiling; reduce heat. Simmer, covered, for 25 to 30 minutes or until lentils are tender. To serve, ladle soup into bowls. If desired, top each serving with sour cream. Makes 4 to 6 main-dish servings.

Per serving: 328 cal., 5 g total fat (1 g sat. fat), 0 mg chol., 886 mg sodium, 57 g carbo., 19 g fiber, 18 g pro.

Ingredient Info Curry powder is not made from a single element as is, say, cinnamon or nutmeg or paprika. Curry powder is a blend of up to 20 spices, herbs, and seeds—and Indian cooks usually grind their own fresh. The most common ones are cardamom, chiles, cinnamon, cloves, coriander, cumin, fennel seeds, nutmeg, red and black pepper, and turmeric (which gives curry powder its vibrant yellow color). Curry powders have different levels of heat. Those labeled "Madras" are hotter than standard supermarket-variety curry powders.

Ask Mom How do I chop an onion? page 47 / How do I handle hot chile peppers? page 48 / What is fresh ginger? page 41 / How do I grate fresh ginger? page 41 / What is a garlic clove? page 40 / How do I mince garlic? page 40 / How do I chop a tomato? page 52 / What are some potato varieties? page 50 / How do I prepare potatoes? page 51 / What does simmer mean? page 79

that's a wrap, SANDWICH, or pizza

Skip the knife and fork and serve some of the best bites on the planet. Here's to finger foods!

11

Grilled Cheese **Sandwiches**

- 8 slices white or wheat bread
- 2 tablespoons butter, softened
- 2 tablespoons Dijon-style mustard or honey mustard
- 4 ounces thinly sliced American cheese

1 To assemble sandwiches, lightly spread one side of each bread slice with butter (below). Spread other side of each bread slice with mustard (below). Top the mustard sides of 4 of the bread slices with cheese (below). Top with remaining bread slices, mustard sides down.

2 Preheat an indoor electric grill or a 12-inch skillet over medium heat. Place the sandwiches on the grill rack or in the skillet. If using a covered grill, close lid. Grill sandwiches until bread is golden and cheese melts. (For a covered grill, allow 3 to 5 minutes. For an uncovered grill or skillet, allow 6 to 8 minutes, turning once halfway through grilling.) Cut sandwiches in half (below). Makes 4 sandwiches.

Per sandwich: 298 cal., 16 g total fat (10 g sat. fat), 42 mg chol., 984 mg sodium, 27 g carbo., 1 g fiber, 12 g pro.

Cheese variations: Substitute any cheese that melts well for the American cheese, such as farmer, cheddar, Monterey Jack, pepper Jack, Colby and Monterey Jack, mozzarella, provolone, Muenster, or fontina. If you want to use a crumbly cheese such as blue cheese or feta, use 2 ounces and mix it with 2 ounces of a mild, melty cheese such as provolone or mozzarella.

Grilled Meat and Cheese Sandwiches: Prepare as above, except layer thinly sliced ham, salami, or cooked roast beef or shredded chicken or turkey on cheese before topping with remaining bread slices.

Grilled Veggie-Cheese Sandwiches: Prepare as above, except, if desired, substitute bottled ranch salad dressing for mustard. Layer $\frac{1}{2}$ cup sliced cucumber or tomato, $\frac{1}{2}$ cup fresh spinach, and $\frac{1}{4}$ cup thinly sliced red onion on cheese before topping with remaining bread slices.

...e butter stand at ...erature until soft ...spread. Use a table ...ead butter over each bread slice.

2 Place bread slices, butter sides down, on a cutting board or work surface. Spread mustard over each bread slice.

3 Cut or tear cheese slices to completely cover the bread. Place cheese on the mustard sides of four of the bread slices.

4 Cut the sandwiches in half with a long serrated knife. Use a gentle sawing motion to make a good, clean cut.

Ask Mom How do I measure butter? pages 58, 59 / How do I soften butter? page 59 / What is Dijon-style mustard? page 379 / What is process cheese? page 408 / How do I crumble cheese? pages 71, 96 / How do I slice tomatoes? page 52 / How do I slice an onion? page 47

Chicken Panini

8 ½-inch slices hearty multigrain or ciabatta bread

⅓ cup light mayonnaise dressing or salad dressing

1 cup lightly packed fresh basil

1½ cups sliced or shredded purchased deli-roasted chicken (see photo 3, page 395)

½ cup bottled roasted red sweet peppers, drained and cut into strips

2 tablespoons olive oil

1 Preheat an electric sandwich press, a covered indoor grill, a grill pan, or a 12-inch skillet. To assemble sandwiches, spread one side of each bread slice with the mayonnaise. Layer basil, chicken, and roasted sweet peppers on 4 of the bread slices. Top with remaining bread slices, mayonnaise sides down. Brush both sides of each sandwich with oil.

2 Place sandwiches (half at a time, if necessary) in the sandwich press or indoor grill; cover and cook about 6 minutes or until bread is toasted. (If using a grill pan or skillet, place sandwiches on grill pan. Weight sandwiches down* and grill about 2 minutes or until bread is lightly toasted. Turn sandwiches over, weight down, and grill until remaining sides are lightly toasted.) Makes 4 sandwiches.

*Note: Place a heavy skillet or a pie plate with a can of vegetables on top of the sandwiches to weight down.

Per sandwich: 347 cal., 18 g total fat (3 g sat. fat), 53 mg chol., 315 mg sodium, 30 g carbo., 9 g fiber, 22 g pro.

Apple, Ham, and Brie Panini: To assemble sandwiches, spread ½ cup whole cranberry sauce on eight ½-inch slices sourdough bread. Top 4 bread slices evenly with 4 ounces sliced cooked ham; 2 ounces sliced Brie cheese; and ½ of a tart apple, cored and thinly sliced. Top with remaining bread slices, cranberry sauce sides down. Brush with olive oil and cook as directed above.

Deli Panini: To assemble sandwiches, spoon 1½ cups chopped pickled mixed vegetables (giardiniera) or 1 pint marinated vegetable deli salad, drained and chopped (1½ cups), onto the bottoms of 4 onion rolls. Top evenly with 4 ounces deli-sliced pastrami and 2 ounces sliced provolone cheese. Add roll tops. Brush with olive oil and cook as directed above.

Tuna and White Bean Panini: In a medium bowl stir together two 7.1-ounce packages tuna (water pack), drained; one 15-ounce can cannellini (white kidney) beans, rinsed, drained, and slightly mashed; ¼ cup mayonnaise or salad dressing; and 2 cloves garlic, minced. Spread tuna mixture on four ½-inch slices country Italian bread. Top with ¼ cup thinly sliced red onion, 1 thinly sliced tomato, and 4 ounces sliced Havarti or mozzarella cheese. Top each with another bread slice. Brush with olive oil and cook as directed above.

Ask Mom What is ciabatta bread? page 417 / How do I slice bread? page 64 / How do I drain bottled roasted sweet peppers? page 416 / How do I core and slice/chop apples? page 28 / How do I rinse and drain canned beans? page 390 / What is a garlic clove? page 40 / How do I mince garlic? page 40

WHAT'S A PANINI? Rather, it's what's a panino? (*Panini* is plural in Italian for "sandwiches.") Panini are gooey, delicious toasted sandwiches filled with meats, cheeses, vegetables, relishes, and/or condiments. Hearty European-style bread works best.

Deli Panini

Apple, Ham, and Brie Panini

Chicken Panini

Tuna and White Bean Panini

② Skill Level

Smoked Turkey and Prosciutto Panini

Good to Know Here are a few ideas for using up the rest of the bottled roasted red sweet peppers. Layer them on a burger; chop them and add to jarred tomato sauce for pasta; or make a Spanish-style chef's salad: Cut peppers into thin strips and lay them, along with thin strips of ham, green olives, and slivers of Manchego cheese, on a bed of greens.

½ cup mayonnaise or salad dressing
¼ cup bottled roasted red sweet peppers, drained (below)
1 clove garlic, quartered
4 soft French or sourdough (about 7×3 inches)
8 ounces thinly sliced smoked turkey or smoked chicken
2 ounces thinly sliced prosciutto or fontina, Havarti, or pepper Jack cheese
8 ounces sliced provolone or mozzarella cheese
1 cup mesclun or baby lettuce

1 In a blender or food processor combine mayonnaise, roasted sweet peppers, and garlic (below). Blend or process until mayonnaise mixture is almost smooth (below). Transfer mayonnaise mixture to a small bowl (below). Set aside.

2 Preheat an electric sandwich press, a covered indoor grill, a grill pan, or a 12-inch skillet. To assemble sandwiches, split each roll in half horizontally; spread cut sides of rolls with the mayonnaise mixture. Layer turkey, prosciutto, provolone cheese, and mesclun on bottom halves of rolls. Replace top halves of rolls. Place sandwiches (half at a time, if necessary) in the sandwich press or indoor grill; cover and cook about 6 minutes or until cheese melts and rolls are toasted. (If using a grill pan or skillet, place sandwiches on grill pan. Weight sandwiches down [see note, page 414] and grill about 2 minutes or until rolls are lightly toasted. Turn sandwiches over, weight down, and grill until remaining sides are lightly toasted.) Makes 4 sandwiches.

Per sandwich: 842 cal., 49 g total fat (17 g sat. fat), 111 mg chol., 2,465 mg sodium, 59 g carbo., 4 g fiber, 38 g pro.

1 Place peppers in a sieve to drain. Press gently with paper towels to blot liquid from the peppers and push the liquid through the sieve.

2 Place the drained peppers with the mayonnaise and garlic in the blender. You don't need to stir the ingredients together.

3 Pour the blended mixture into a bowl, using a rubber scraper to remove all of it from the bottom and sides of the container.

Ask Mom What is a garlic clove? page 40 / What is prosciutto? page 358 / What is that salad green? page 347

Red, White, and Green Panini

- 1 16-ounce loaf unsliced ciabatta or Italian bread
- 2 tablespoons olive oil
- ¼ cup mayonnaise or salad dressing
- 1 tablespoon purchased basil pesto
- 6 ounces thinly sliced provolone cheese
- 4 ounces thinly sliced cooked ham or coppacola
- 4 ounces thinly sliced salami
- 1 recipe Red Onion Relish
- 2 cups fresh spinach or arugula

1 Cut bread in half horizontally. Brush outside of loaf with oil. Place bottom half of loaf on a piece of waxed paper. Set top aside. In a small bowl mix mayonnaise and pesto; set aside.

2 Preheat an electric sandwich press, covered indoor grill, grill pan, or 12-inch skillet. Place half of the cheese on bottom half of bread. Spread mayonnaise mixture over cheese. Layer with meats, Red Onion Relish, spinach, and remaining cheese. Replace top. Cut into 4 sandwiches. Place sandwiches (half at a time, if necessary) in sandwich press or indoor grill; cover and cook about 6 minutes or until bread is toasted. (If using a grill pan or skillet, place sandwiches on grill pan. Weight sandwiches down [see note, page 414] and grill about 2 minutes or until bread is toasted. Turn sandwiches, weight down, and grill remaining sides.) Makes 4 sandwiches.

Red Onion Relish: Combine 1 medium red onion, halved and thinly sliced; 2 tablespoons olive oil; 1 tablespoon red wine vinegar; and 1 teaspoon snipped fresh oregano. Season with salt and ground black pepper. Cover; let stand at room temperature up to 2 hours. Drain.

Per sandwich: 869 cal., 54 g total fat (16 g sat. fat), 77 mg chol., 2,114 mg sodium, 63 g carbo., 4 g fiber, 32 g pro.

The best bread for making panini is a sturdy European-style bread such as ciabatta, that can be pressed without getting squished. Pronounced "chuh-BAH-tah," ciabatta means "slipper" in Italian, alluding to its shape.

Ask Mom How do I slice bread? page 64 / What is that salad green? page 347 / How do I slice an onion? page 47 / What is that vinegar? page 349 / How do I snip fresh herbs? pages 42, 328

(2) Skill Level

Shopping Savvy There are two types of pita bread. Pita pockets are meant to be cut in half and stuffed. Soft pita—a round, flatbread without a pocket—is meant to be folded around the fillings. That's the type you want to buy for this recipe.

Gyros

I pound ground lamb or beef

2 teaspoons dried minced onion or ¼ cup finely chopped onion

I teaspoon garlic powder

I teaspoon Greek seasoning or dried oregano, crushed

I 6-ounce container plain low-fat yogurt or ⅔ cup dairy sour cream

¼ cup chopped, seeded cucumber

2 teaspoons snipped fresh mint or Italian (flat-leaf) parsley

I clove garlic, minced

4 soft pita bread rounds, warmed*

I medium tomato, thinly sliced

¼ cup very thin red onion wedges

⅓ cup crumbled feta cheese

1 Preheat broiler. In a medium bowl mix together ground meat, onion, garlic powder, Greek seasoning, ½ teaspoon *salt*, and ¼ teaspoon *ground black pepper*. Shape meat mixture into four ½-inch-thick oval patties (below). Place patties on the unheated rack of a broiler pan.

2 Broil patties 4 to 5 inches from heat for 10 to 12 minutes or until meat is no longer pink and juices run clear (160°F), turning patties once (below). Meanwhile, for yogurt sauce, in a small bowl stir together yogurt, cucumber, mint, and garlic; set aside. To serve, layer pitas with tomato, yogurt sauce, onion, feta cheese, and patties; fold pitas. Makes 4 sandwiches.

*Note: To warm pitas, wrap in microwave-safe paper towels. Microwave on 100 percent power (high) about 1 minute or until warm.

Per sandwich: 462 cal., 20 g total fat (9 g sat. fat), 89 mg chol., 868 mg sodium, 41 g carbo., 2 g fiber, 29 g pro.

1 To shape patties, divide the meat into four equal portions. Gently shape each portion into a ball. Flatten the balls to make the patties.

2 To tell when patties are done, insert a thermometer into the side of a patty so the tip touches its center. It should register 160°F.

Ask Mom How do I chop an onion? page 47 / How do I crush dried herbs? page 78 / How do I snip fresh herbs? pages 42, 328 / What is a garlic clove? page 40 / How do I mince garlic? page 40 / How do I slice tomatoes? page 52 / How do I cut onion wedges? page 47 / How do I crumble cheese? pages 71, 96 / What does it mean to broil? page 68 / How do I use a meat/instant-read thermometer? page 74

Pulled Pork Sandwiches

  1 2½- to 3-pound boneless pork shoulder roast
  ½ cup water
  3 tablespoons cider vinegar
  2 tablespoons Worcestershire sauce
  1 teaspoon ground cumin or chili powder
3½ cups bottled barbecue sauce
10 kaiser rolls, hamburger buns, or onion buns, split

1 Trim fat from the roast. If necessary, cut the roast to fit into a 3½- or 4-quart slow cooker. Sprinkle roast with *salt* and *ground black pepper*. In a small bowl stir together the water, vinegar, Worcestershire sauce, and cumin. Pour over roast in slow cooker. Cover and cook on low-heat setting for 8 to 10 hours or on high-heat setting for 4 to 5 hours.

2 Using tongs, remove meat from the cooker; discard cooking liquid. Using two forks, shred the pork (below) and return it to the cooker. Stir in 2 cups of the barbecue sauce. Cover and cook on high-heat setting for 30 to 45 minutes or until heated through. Serve meat mixture in rolls and, if desired, with *thinly sliced onion* and *pickle slices*. Pass remaining barbecue sauce. Makes 10 sandwiches.

Per sandwich: 446 cal., 9 g total fat (3 g sat. fat), 73 mg chol., 1,486 mg sodium, 61 g carbo., 2 g fiber, 30 g pro.

Sliced Beef Sandwiches: Prepare as above, except substitute beef brisket for the pork. Trim off fat layer before adding meat to slow cooker. Thinly slice beef across grain instead of shredding.

Stovetop Directions: Prepare as above, except place meat in a 4-quart Dutch oven. Add 1 cup water, vinegar, Worcestershire sauce, and cumin. Bring to boiling; reduce heat. Cover; simmer for 2 to 2½ hours or until meat is tender. Add 2 cups barbecue sauce; simmer over medium-low heat for 15 to 20 minutes or until heated through, stirring frequently. Serve as above.

Flavor Changes You can use any kind of barbecue sauce you like for these finger-licking sandwiches. Try a North Carolina-style sauce (it's usually a vinegary sauce spiked with black and cayenne pepper) and serve with a helping of cool, crunchy coleslaw inside the sandwich on top of the meat.

1 To shred the pork, cut or break the meat into chunks. With two forks, separate the meat into smaller pieces.

2 Continue pulling the meat apart with the forks until shreds form. Return the meat and 2 cups barbecue sauce to the slow cooker.

Ask Mom What is that cut of meat? pages 220–221 / What is that vinegar? page 349 / What is a slow cooker? page 21 / What does simmer mean? page 79

WHY BOIL BRATS BEFORE GRILLING? Parboiling, or partially cooking, the brats in the seasoned beer first ensures they won't burn on the outside before they're cooked on the inside on the grill. It also adds flavor to the crunchy skin of the brats.

The no-stress relish that finishes off these tasty brats is sweet pickle relish stirred with sweet-tart whole cranberry sauce. Add some caramelized onions and dig in.

Beer-Braised Brats

2 tablespoons butter
$\frac{1}{2}$ cup thinly sliced onion
1 12-ounce bottle or can dark German beer
1 tablespoon packed brown sugar
1 tablespoon vinegar
$\frac{1}{2}$ teaspoon caraway seeds
$\frac{1}{2}$ teaspoon dried thyme, crushed
$\frac{1}{2}$ teaspoon Worcestershire sauce
5 uncooked bratwurst links (1$\frac{1}{4}$ pounds)
5 hoagie buns, bratwurst buns, or other crusty rolls, split and toasted
1 recipe Easy Cranberry-Pickle Relish

1 In a 4-quart Dutch oven heat butter over medium heat. Add onion; cook and stir about 5 minutes or until tender. Add beer, brown sugar, vinegar, caraway seeds, thyme, and Worcestershire sauce. Bring to boiling; reduce heat. Place bratwursts in beer mixture. Cover and simmer for 10 minutes.

2 Using tongs, remove bratwursts from cooking liquid. If desired, reserve cooking liquid. In a grill pan or a 10-inch skillet cook bratwursts over medium heat about 10 minutes or until brown and an instant-read thermometer inserted into bratwursts registers 160°F, turning occasionally. If desired, return bratwursts to cooking liquid to keep warm until serving time.

3 To serve, place grilled bratwursts in buns. Using a slotted spoon, top with onion slices and Easy Cranberry-Pickle Relish. Makes 5 sandwiches.

Easy Cranberry-Pickle Relish: In a small bowl combine $\frac{1}{2}$ cup canned whole cranberry sauce and $\frac{1}{4}$ cup sweet pickle relish.

Per sandwich: 955 cal., 45 g total fat (20 g sat. fat), 89 mg chol., 1,840 mg sodium, 99 g carbo., 5 g fiber, 36 g pro.

Flavor Changes Bratwurst made with pork is most commonly used in these German-style sandwiches, but you can use turkey brats. They're a little less traditional, a little more healthful, and they go well with cranberry too.

Ask Mom How do I measure butter? pages 58, 59 / How do I slice an onion? page 47 / How do I pack brown sugar? page 58 / How do I crush dried herbs? page 78 / How do I toast buns? page 77 / What does it mean to braise? page 68 / What does simmer mean? page 79 / How do I use a meat/instant-read thermometer? page 74

(2) Skill Level

Italian Sausage Grinders

- 1 pound bulk hot or sweet Italian sausage
- 1 14.5-ounce can fire-roasted diced tomatoes, undrained
- 1 14.5-ounce can crushed tomatoes, undrained
- 1 teaspoon dried basil, crushed
- 1 teaspoon balsamic vinegar (optional)
- ½ teaspoon dried oregano, crushed
- ¼ teaspoon salt
- ¼ teaspoon crushed red pepper
- 2 cloves garlic, minced
- 1 small onion, sliced
- 1 small green sweet pepper, seeded and cut into strips
- 2 tablespoons olive oil
- 4 French-style rolls or hoagie buns, split
- 4 slices provolone cheese

Ingredient Info You'll find Italian sausage in several variations. It's sold in bulk (not in a casing) and in links. It also has two basic seasoning styles. Sweet Italian sausage is seasoned primarily with garlic and fennel. Hot Italian sausage has a generous amount of crushed red pepper added. For this recipe, bulk is more convenient—but you can also just remove the casing if links are all you can find.

1 In a 3-quart saucepan cook the sausage over medium heat until no longer pink, stirring break up meat; drain off fat. Stir in diced tomatoes, crushed tomatoes, basil, balsamic v egar (if using), oregano, salt, crushed red pepper, and garlic. Bring to boiling; reduce heat. Simm uncovered, about 30 minutes or until mixture is thickened.

2 Meanwhile, in a 10-inch skillet cook onion and sweet pepper in hot oil over medium he until tender. Set aside and keep warm.

3 Place split rolls on a baking sheet. Spoon the meat mixture onto the bottom halves of t rolls. Top with the onion mixture and cheese. Broil 4 to 5 inches from the heat for 2 3 minutes or until cheese melts and is bubbly. Makes 4 sandwiches.

Per sandwich: 667 cal., 45 g total fat (18 g sat. fat), 106 mg chol., 2,180 mg sodium, 35 g carbo., 4 g fiber, 29 g pro.

Sausage and Pepper Grinders: Prepare as above, except, if desired, omit onion, sweet pepp and olive oil. Top sausage mixture with ½ cup bottled roasted red sweet peppers, drained, a ½ cup bottled sliced banana or pepperoncini peppers, drained.

Ask Mom How do I crush dried herbs? page 78 / What is that vinegar? page 349 / What is a garlic clove? page 40 / How do I mince garlic? page 40 / How do I slice an onion? page 47 / How do I drain bottled roasted sweet peppers? page 416 / What does simmer mean? page 79 / What does it mean to broil? page 68

1 Skill Level

Reubens

- 3 tablespoons butter or margarine, softened
- 8 slices rye and pumpernickel swirl bread, rye bread, or pumpernickel bread
- 3 tablespoons bottled Thousand Island or Russian salad dressing
- 6 ounces thinly sliced cooked corned beef or pastrami
- 4 slices Swiss cheese (3 ounces)
- 1 cup sauerkraut, well drained

1 Spread butter on one side of each bread slice (see photo 1, page 413) and salad dressing on the other. With the buttered sides down, top 4 slices of the bread with corned beef, cheese, and sauerkraut. Top with remaining bread slices, dressing sides down.

2 Preheat an indoor electric grill or a 12-inch skillet over medium heat. Place the sandwiches on the grill rack or in the skillet. If using a covered grill, close lid. Grill sandwiches until the bread is toasted and the cheese melts, turning once. (For a covered grill, allow 3 to 5 minutes. For an uncovered grill or skillet, allow 6 to 8 minutes, turning once halfway through grilling.) Cut sandwiches in half. Makes 4 sandwiches.

Per sandwich: 487 cal., 29 g total fat (13 g sat. fat), 89 mg chol., 1,509 mg sodium, 36 g carbo., 5 g fiber, 20 g pro.

Rachel Sandwiches: Prepare as above, except substitute sliced cooked turkey for corned beef.

Good to Know
Depending on whom you talk to, the Reuben was invented in the early 1900s at Reuben's, a Manhattan deli, or in 1925 by Reuben Kulakofsky at the Blackstone Hotel in Omaha, Nebraska, to feed hungry late-night poker players. Either way, it's just good.

Ask Mom How do I measure butter? pages 58, 59 / How do I soften butter? page 59

Sloppy Joes

1 pound lean ground beef or ground pork
½ cup chopped onion (1 medium)
½ cup chopped green sweet pepper (1 small)
1 8-ounce can tomato sauce
2 tablespoons water
1 to 1½ teaspoons chili powder
1 teaspoon Worcestershire sauce
½ teaspoon garlic salt
   Dash bottled hot pepper sauce
6 kaiser rolls or hamburger buns, split and toasted

1 In a large skillet cook beef, onion, and sweet pepper until meat is brown and vegetables are tender, stirring to break up meat. Drain off fat.

2 Stir tomato sauce, water, chili powder, Worcestershire sauce, garlic salt, and hot pepper sauce into beef mixture in skillet. Bring to boiling; reduce heat. Simmer, uncovered, for 5 minutes, stirring occasionally. Serve on rolls. Makes 6 sandwiches.

Per sandwich: 3II cal., I0 g total fat (3 g sat. fat), 48 mg chol., 632 mg sodium, 35 g carbo., 2 g fiber, 20 g pro.

Pizza Joes: Prepare as above, except substitute one 14-ounce jar pizza sauce for the tomato sauce, water, chili powder, Worcestershire sauce, garlic salt, and hot pepper sauce. Add ½ cup chopped pepperoni. Serve on toasted rolls with slices of mozzarella cheese.

Tex-Mex Joes: Prepare as above, except add ½ cup fresh or frozen whole kernel corn and 1 tablespoon chopped chipotle chile in adobo sauce (see photo, page 373) with the tomato sauce. Serve on toasted rolls with slices of cheddar cheese.

Veggie Joes: Prepare as above, except omit ground beef. Cook onion and sweet pepper in 1 tablespoon hot olive oil over medium heat until tender. Add 2 cups cooked brown rice (see page 324); one 15- to 16-ounce can red kidney beans, rinsed and drained; and ½ cup shredded carrot with the tomato sauce.

Ask Mom How do I chop an onion? page 47 / How do I seed and chop sweet peppers? page 49 / How do I toast buns? page 77 / What does simmer mean? page 79 / How do I rinse and drain canned beans? page 390 / How do I shred vegetables? page 20

ACCESSORIZE YOUR SANDWICH. What's a sloppy joe, really, other than a deconstructed (loose-meat) burger swimming in tangy-sweet barbecue sauce? Anything you put on a burger, you can put on a sloppy joe: mustard, pickles, raw onion, hot pepper Jack cheese.

Meal Maker Sloppy joes got their name for good reason. Serve these saucy sandwiches with potato chips, celery and carrot sticks—and a stack of napkins.

(2) Skill Level

Flavor Changes If you're hankering for a traditional burger, just cut the meat mixture into four sections and form into four patties, leaving the filling out. Top with your favorite condiments.

Burger Bonanza

  1 egg, lightly beaten
  ¼ cup chopped onion
  2 tablespoons ketchup
  ½ teaspoon garlic salt
  ¼ teaspoon ground black pepper
1¼ pounds lean ground beef or turkey
  1 recipe Fiesta Filling or Greek Filling
  4 hamburger buns, toasted, if desired

1 In a large bowl combine egg, onion, ketchup, garlic salt, and pepper. Add beef; mix well. Shape beef mixture into eight 4-inch-diameter patties (below). Place 2 tablespoons of desired filling in center of each of 4 of the patties, spreading filling to within ½ inch of edges. Top with remaining patties, pressing edges together to seal (below).

2 In a grill pan or a 10-inch skillet cook burgers over medium heat for 7 minutes. Turn burgers carefully using a wide spatula; cook for 5 to 8 minutes more or until burgers are done (160°F for beef; 165°F for turkey) (see photo 2, page 418). Serve burgers in buns. Makes 4 sandwiches.

Fiesta Filling: In a small bowl stir together ¼ cup shredded Mexican cheese blend; 2 tablespoons finely chopped tomato; 2 tablespoons finely chopped, seeded jalapeño chile pepper; 2 tablespoons snipped fresh cilantro; and 2 tablespoons thinly sliced green onion.

Greek Filling: In a small bowl stir together ¼ cup finely chopped, seeded tomato; 1 ounce crumbled feta cheese; 2 teaspoons finely chopped onion; 2 teaspoons finely chopped, pitted ripe olives; ¼ teaspoon red wine vinegar; ¼ teaspoon olive oil; and ⅛ teaspoon dried oregano, crushed. Cover; chill for at least 30 minutes before using.

Per sandwich: 556 cal., 35 g total fat (14 g sat. fat), 165 mg chol., 577 mg sodium, 25 g carbo., 1 g fiber, 33 g pro.

1 After mixing the beef mixture, place it on a cutting board or work surface. Shape the beef mixture into a large, flat rectangle.

2 Score the rectangle crosswise into four equal sections. Cut lengthwise down the middle, making eight equal portions of meat.

3 With your hands, lightly but firmly press each portion into a patty.

4 When placing the on the patties, leave a b Top with remaining patt and press the edges tog to seal the filling inside.

Ask Mom How do I beat eggs? page 62 / How do I chop an onion? page 47 / How do I toast buns? page 77 / How do I chop a tomato? page 52 / How do I handle hot chile peppers? page 48 / How do I snip fresh herbs? pages 42, 328 / How do I slice green onions? page 43 / How do I crumble cheese? pages 71, 96 / How do I crush dried herbs? page 78 / How do I use a meat/instant-read thermometer? page 74

French Dips

- 1 3- to 3½-pound boneless beef round rump roast
  Nonstick cooking spray
- 1 14-ounce can onion-flavored beef broth
- 1 large red onion, cut into ½-inch slices
- 8 hoagie buns, split and toasted

1 Trim fat from meat (below). If necessary, cut roast to fit into a 4- to 5-quart slow cooker. Lightly coat a 10-inch skillet with nonstick cooking spray; preheat over medium heat. Brown roast on all sides in hot skillet (below). Place meat in the slow cooker. Pour broth over roast and top with onion.

2 Cover and cook on low-heat setting for 8 to 9 hours or on high-heat setting for 4 to 4½ hours. Using tongs, remove roast from slow cooker and place on a cutting board. Thinly slice meat. Arrange sliced beef on buns. Remove onion from cooking liquid with a slotted spoon and arrange over beef. Top with remaining bun halves.

3 Pour cooking juices into a measuring cup; skim off fat. Drizzle a little of the liquid onto each sandwich and pour the remaining liquid into bowls to serve with sandwiches for dipping. Makes 8 sandwiches.

Per sandwich: 639 cal., 15 g total fat (4 g sat. fat), 89 mg chol., 980 mg sodium, 75 g carbo., 4 g fiber, 50 g pro.

French Dips with Cheese: Prepare as above, except when assembling sandwiches divide 4 ounces sliced provolone cheese among sandwiches, placing the cheese on top of the beef.

French Dips with Mushrooms: Prepare as above, except clean 4 portobello mushrooms (3 to 4 inches in diameter); remove and discard stems. Cut mushrooms into ¼-inch slices. Add to slow cooker with beef.

② Using a sharp knife, slide the blade between the fat and the meat. With a gently sawing motion, trim away the fat.

① Use kitchen scissors to cut the netting from the roast. Be careful not to cut into the meat.

③ Brown the meat in the preheated skillet. Use tongs to occasionally turn the meat so the roast browns evenly on all sides.

Five-Spice Steak Wraps

12 ounces boneless beef round steak

2 cups packaged shredded cabbage with carrot (coleslaw mix)

¼ cup red and/or green sweet pepper cut into thin bite-size strips

¼ cup julienned carrot

¼ cup snipped fresh chives

2 tablespoons rice vinegar

½ teaspoon toasted sesame oil

½ teaspoon five-spice powder

¼ teaspoon salt

Nonstick cooking spray

¼ cup plain low-fat yogurt or light dairy sour cream

4 8-inch flour tortillas

1 If desired, partially freeze steak for easier slicing (see photo 1, page 360). In a medium bowl combine coleslaw mix, sweet pepper, carrot, and chives. In a small bowl combine vinegar and sesame oil. Pour vinegar mixture over coleslaw mixture; toss to coat. Set aside.

2 Trim fat from steak. Thinly slice steak across the grain into ¼-inch-thick strips. Sprinkle steak strips with five-spice powder and salt. Coat an unheated 10-inch nonstick skillet with nonstick cooking spray. Preheat skillet over medium-high heat. Add steak strips; stir-fry for 3 to 4 minutes or until brown.

3 To assemble, spread 1 tablespoon of the yogurt down the center of each tortilla. Top with steak strips. Stir coleslaw mixture; spoon over steak. Fold in sides of tortillas. If desired, secure with wooden toothpicks. Makes 4 wraps.

Per wrap: 237 cal., 7 g total fat (2 g sat. fat), 51 mg chol., 329 mg sodium, 20 g carbo., 2 g fiber, 22 g pro.

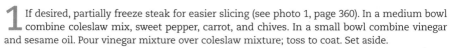

INGREDIENT INFO Five-spice powder is a readily available spice mixture often used in Chinese cooking. It consists of cinnamon, cloves, star anise, fennel seed, and Szechwan peppercorns. Look for it in the spice aisle of your supermarket.

Ask Mom What is that cut of meat? pages 220–221 / How do I seed sweet peppers and cut them into strips? page 49 / How do I peel and cut carrots? pages 37, 64 / How do I snip fresh herbs? pages 42, 328 / What is that vinegar? page 349 / What is toasted sesame oil? page 138 / What does it mean to toss? page 77

Ingredient Info
Horseradish is a spicy, head-clearing root that's a member of the mustard family. You can sometimes find it fresh, but you can always get prepared horseradish in a jar—it's grated and mixed with vinegar or, sometimes, salt, sugar, or cream. Look for it in the condiment section of the supermarket.

② Skill Level

Open-Face
Steak Sandwiches

- 12 ounces beef flank steak
- ½ cup bottled clear Italian salad dressing
- 4 slices sourdough bread, toasted
- ¼ cup mayonnaise or salad dressing
- 1 cup shredded romaine lettuce or baby romaine lettuce leaves
- 1 medium tomato, sliced

1 Trim fat from steak. Score steak on both sides by making shallow cuts at 1-inch intervals in a diamond pattern. Place steak in a resealable plastic bag. Add salad dressing; seal bag. Marinate in the refrigerator for 6 to 24 hours, turning bag occasionally. Drain; discard dressing.

2 Preheat broiler. Place meat on the unheated rack of a broiler pan. Broil steak 4 to 5 inches from heat for 15 to 18 minutes or until desired doneness (160°F for medium), turning steak once halfway through cooking.

3 To serve, thinly slice the steak across the grain. Spread the bread slices evenly with mayonnaise. Top with lettuce and tomato slices. Layer steak slices on top of the tomatoes. Serve warm. Makes 4 sandwiches.

Per sandwich: 397 cal., 26 g total fat (6 g sat. fat), 40 mg chol., 772 mg sodium, 18 g carbo., 1 g fiber, 22 g pro.

Blue Cheese Steak Sandwiches: Prepare as above, except stir ⅓ cup crumbled blue cheese, 1 teaspoon Worcestershire sauce, and 1 teaspoon white wine vinegar into the mayonnaise. Broil and assemble as directed.

Italian Steak Sandwiches: Prepare as above, except omit lettuce and tomato. Top sandwiches with ⅓ cup sliced pickled pepperoncini peppers and/or bottled roasted red sweet peppers cut into strips or bottled pickled vegetables and peppers, chopped. Broil and assemble as directed.

Mustard Steak Sandwiches: Prepare as above, except omit the salad dressing and marinating time. Combine 2 tablespoons Dijon-style mustard; 1 teaspoon packed brown sugar; 1 clove garlic, minced; and ½ teaspoon cracked black pepper. Brush both sides of scored steak with mustard mixture. Broil and assemble as directed.

Steak Sandwiches with Horseradish Sauce: Prepare as above, except stir 1 tablespoon prepared horseradish and ½ teaspoon dried oregano, crushed, into the mayonnaise. Broil and assemble as directed.

Ask Mom What's that cut of meat? pages 220–221 / How do I slice bread? page 64 / What's that salad green? page 347 / How do I slice tomatoes? page 52 / What does score mean? page 79 / What does marinate mean? page 73 / What does broil mean? page 68 / How do I use a thermometer? page 74 / How do I crumble cheese? pages 71, 96 / What's that vinegar? page 349 / What is Dijon-style mustard? page 379 / How do I mince garlic? page 40 / How do I crush dried herbs? page 78

New Orleans-Style Muffuletta

½ cup coarsely chopped, pitted ripe olives

½ cup chopped pimiento-stuffed green olives

1 tablespoon snipped fresh parsley

2 teaspoons lemon juice

½ teaspoon dried oregano, crushed

1 16-ounce loaf ciabatta or unsliced French bread

1 tablespoon olive oil

1 clove garlic, minced

6 lettuce leaves

3 ounces thinly sliced salami, pepperoni, or summer sausage

3 ounces thinly sliced cooked ham or turkey

6 ounces thinly sliced provolone, Swiss, or mozzarella cheese

1 or 2 medium tomatoes, thinly sliced

⅛ teaspoon coarsely ground black pepper

Traditionally the muffuletta is made on a round loaf cut into wedges. Ciabatta or French bread works fine too. The important thing is to hollow out the top to make room for fillings.

Although the olive salad is the classic relish on the muffuletta, you can make a relish with giardiniera (page 431), a piquant, vinegary combo of pickled vegetables.

Ask Mom How do I snip fresh herbs? pages 42, 328 / How do I crush dried herbs? page 78 / How do I juice a lemon/lime? pages 30, 80 / How much juice does one lemon/lime yield? page 30 / What is ciabatta bread? page 417 / What is a garlic clove? page 40 / How do I mince garlic? page 40 / What is that salad green? page 347 / How do I slice tomatoes? page 52 / How do I slice bread? page 64?

WHAT'S A MUFFULETTA? The signature sandwich of the Crescent City, the muffuletta was invented in 1906 at the Italian-owned Central Grocery in New Orleans—hence its layers of Italian meats and cheeses. The olive salad distinguishes it from an ordinary sub.

1 In a small bowl stir together ripe olives, green olives, parsley, lemon juice, and oregano. Cover and chill for 4 to 24 hours, stirring occasionally.

2 To assemble sandwich, using a serrated knife, split loaf of bread horizontally and hollow out the inside of the top half, leaving a ¾-inch-thick shell. Stir together olive oil and garlic. Using a pastry brush, brush the bottom half of the bread with olive oil mixture. Top with lettuce, salami, ham, cheese, and tomato slices. Sprinkle tomato slices with pepper. Stir olive mixture. Mound olive mixture on top of the tomato slices. Add top half of bread. To serve, cut into 6 portions. Makes 6 sandwiches.

Per sandwich: 435 cal., 21 g total fat (8 g sat. fat), 41 mg chol., 1,512 mg sodium, 43 g carbo., 3 g fiber, 20 g pro.

Giardiniera-Style Muffuletta: Prepare as above, except omit the olives, parsley, lemon juice, and oregano and omit Step 1. Drain one 16-ounce jar of pickled mixed vegetables (giardiniera), reserving the liquid. Chop the vegetables, removing any pepperoncini stems if present. In a medium bowl stir together chopped vegetables; 2 tablespoons of the reserved liquid; ¼ cup chopped pimiento-stuffed green olives and/or pitted ripe olives; 1 clove garlic, minced; and 1 tablespoon olive oil. Assemble sandwich as above, spooning the pickled vegetable mixture on top of the tomato slices.

Though the types of salami made in Italy are practically infinite, the most popular kind in this country is called Genoa salami, from the city of Genoa. It's spiked with peppercorns.

1 Skill Level

Turkey-Avocado Wraps

½ cup mayonnaise or salad dressing

1 or 2 canned chipotle peppers in adobo sauce, drained and finely chopped (see photo, page 373)

6 10-inch flour tortillas or flatbread wraps

12 ounces sliced cooked turkey or chicken

1 recipe Black Bean-Corn Salsa

1 avocado, halved, seeded, peeled, and sliced

1 In a small bowl stir together mayonnaise and chipotle pepper. To assemble wraps, spread mayonnaise mixture evenly over tortillas. Top with turkey, Black Bean-Corn Salsa, and avocado slices. Fold bottom one-fourth of tortillas over filling. Fold in one of the sides of each tortilla and roll up, starting from the edge with the filling. If necessary, secure wraps with wooden toothpicks. Serve immediately or wrap each in plastic wrap (see photo 4, page 433) and chill for up to 4 hours. Makes 6 wraps.

Black Bean-Corn Salsa: In a large bowl combine one 15-ounce can black beans, rinsed and drained; 1 cup chopped, seeded tomatoes; ½ cup frozen whole kernel corn, thawed; 2 tablespoons thinly sliced green onion; 2 tablespoons snipped fresh cilantro; 1 tablespoon cooking oil; 1 tablespoon lime juice; ¼ teaspoon salt; ¼ teaspoon ground cumin; and ¼ teaspoon ground black pepper. Cover and chill for 1 to 24 hours, stirring occasionally.

Per wrap: 496 cal., 28 g total fat (5 g sat. fat), 50 mg chol., 608 mg sodium, 39 g carbo., 7 g fiber, 25 g pro.

Meal Maker Serve these Mexican-style wraps with wedges of ripe cantaloupe or slices of fresh pineapple (if you want to get fancy, sprinkle them with a little brown sugar and cinnamon and broil them for a few minutes), and you have dinner.

Ask Mom How do I rinse and drain canned beans? page 390 / How do I seed tomatoes? page 52 / How do I chop a tomato? page 52 / How do I slice green onions? page 43 / How do I snip fresh herbs? pages 42, 328 / How do I juice a lemon/lime? pages 30, 80 / How much juice does one lemon/lime yield? page 30 / How do I seed and peel an avocado? page 36

Salmon and Asparagus Wraps

12 thin fresh asparagus spears, trimmed
½ cup tub-style cream cheese spread with chive and onion
2 teaspoons finely shredded lemon peel
2 tablespoons lemon juice
⅛ teaspoon cayenne pepper
6 ounces smoked salmon, coarsely flaked and skin and bones removed
4 6- to 7-inch whole wheat flour tortillas
2 cups fresh baby spinach leaves
½ of a red sweet pepper, cut into thin bite-size strips

1 In a covered 10-inch skillet cook asparagus spears in a small amount of boiling lightly salted water for 2 to 3 minutes or until crisp-tender (see page 125). Drain and plunge into ice water to cool quickly. Drain again; pat dry with paper towels.

2 In a medium bowl stir together cream cheese, lemon peel, lemon juice, and cayenne pepper. Fold in salmon (below). Spread on tortillas. To assemble wraps, arrange one-fourth of the spinach, 3 of the asparagus spears, and one-fourth of the sweet pepper strips over salmon mixture on each tortilla (below). Roll up tortillas, starting from the edge with the filling (below). If necessary, secure wraps with wooden toothpicks. Wrap in plastic wrap (below). Serve immediately or chill plastic-wrapped wraps for up to 6 hours. Makes 4 wraps.

Per wrap: 225 cal., 14 g total fat (7 g sat. fat), 40 mg chol., 661 mg sodium, 16 g carbo., 9 g fiber, 15 g pro.

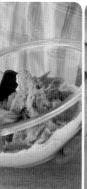
a rubber scraper salmon into the xture. To fold, move a across the bottom side of the bowl.

2 Arrange the spinach over the salmon mixture. Place the asparagus and sweet pepper at one end of the tortilla.

3 Fold the tortilla over the asparagus and sweet pepper. Roll up the tortilla, encasing the veggies. Continue rolling to the end of the tortilla.

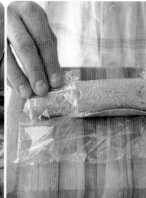
4 Place each wrap on a sheet of plastic wrap. Bring up the plastic wrap to cover the ends, then roll the plastic wrap around the tortilla.

Ask Mom How do I trim asparagus? page 34 / How do I shred lemon/lime peel? page 30 / How do I juice a lemon/lime? pages 30, 80 / How much juice does one lemon/lime yield? page 30 / How do I seed sweet peppers and cut them into strips? page 49 / What does crisp-tender mean? page 79

Easy Fish Sandwiches

8 frozen breaded or battered fish fillets (1.8 to 2.2 ounces each)
4 slices Colby and Monterey Jack cheese or Monterey Jack cheese (4 ounces), halved
2 cups packaged shredded cabbage with carrot (coleslaw mix) or broccoli slaw mix
$\frac{1}{4}$ cup bottled Thousand Island or peppercorn ranch salad dressing
4 hoagie buns, split and toasted, if desired

1 Bake fish according to package directions, placing halved cheese slices on top of the fillets for the last 1 minute of baking.

2 Meanwhile, in a medium bowl stir together coleslaw mix and salad dressing. Place 2 fish fillets on the bottom half of each bun. Top with coleslaw mixture. Add bun tops. Makes 4 sandwiches.

Per sandwich: 916 cal., 42 g total fat (11 g sat. fat), 71 mg chol., 1,832 mg sodium, 102 g carbo., 5 g fiber, 34 g pro.

Fish Sandwiches with Horseradish Sauce: Prepare as above, except omit cheese and salad dressing. In a medium bowl combine $\frac{1}{4}$ cup mayonnaise or salad dressing and 2 to 3 teaspoons prepared horseradish. Stir in coleslaw mix. Divide coleslaw mixture among bun bottoms. Top with fish fillets. Top fish with $\frac{1}{2}$ cup thinly sliced red onion and 4 red-tip leaf lettuce leaves. Add bun tops.

1 Using a spatula, transfer the baked fish fillets to the bun. Use a fork to help slide the fillet from the spatula.

2 Use two forks to place a helping of coleslaw on each fish piece. Try to divide the mixture evenly among the sandwiches.

Ask Mom How do I toast buns? page 77 / What is prepared horseradish? page 429 / How do I slice an onion? page 47 / What is that salad green? page 347

Good to Know To keep cheese fresh, leave it in the rind if it has one. Wrap unused cheese tightly in foil or plastic wrap; seal in a plastic bag or an airtight container. Store in the refrigerator. The softer the cheese, the shorter the storage life. Harder cheese, such as sharp cheddar or Parmesan, will last for weeks in the refrigerator if properly stored.

(2) Skill Level

Roasted Veggie Pitas

- 1 small zucchini (6 ounces), thinly sliced lengthwise
- 1 small yellow summer squash (6 ounces), thinly sliced lengthwise
- 1 medium onion, thinly sliced (½ cup)
- ½ cup sliced fresh mushrooms
- ½ of a red sweet pepper, cut into thin strips (½ cup)
- 2 tablespoons olive oil
- ½ teaspoon salt
- ¼ teaspoon ground black pepper
- 2 large pita bread rounds, halved
- 4 teaspoons bottled vinaigrette or Italian salad dressing
- ¾ cup shredded smoked provolone or mozzarella cheese (3 ounces)

1 Preheat oven to 450°F. In a large bowl place zucchini, summer squash, onion, mushrooms, and sweet pepper. Add oil, salt, and black pepper; toss to coat. Spread vegetable mixture evenly in a 15×10×1-inch baking pan. Roast, uncovered, in the preheated oven for 8 to 10 minutes or until vegetables are tender.

2 Divide roasted vegetables among pita bread halves; drizzle with salad dressing. Top with cheese. If desired, place the filled pitas on a baking sheet and bake in the 450°F oven for 2 to 3 minutes or until cheese melts. Makes 4 sandwiches.

Per sandwich: 270 cal., 16 g total fat (5 g sat. fat), 15 mg chol., 669 mg sodium, 24 g carbo., 2 g fiber, 10 g pro.

Avocado-Veggie Pitas: Prepare as above, except omit salad dressing. In a small bowl mash 1 avocado, halved, seeded, and peeled, with 1 tablespoon lime juice and ¼ teaspoon salt. Spread avocado mixture in pita bread rounds before filling with vegetables.

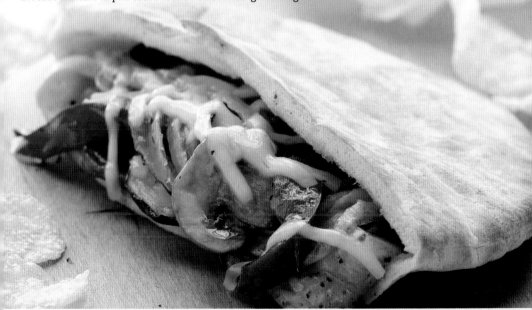

Ask Mom What is summer squash? page 54 / How do I slice an onion? page 47 / What are some mushroom varieties? page 44 / How do I slice fresh mushrooms? page 45 / How do I seed sweet peppers and cut them into strips? page 49 / How do I shred cheese? page 71 / What does it mean to toss? page 77 / What does drizzle mean? page 79 / How do I seed and peel an avocado? page 36 / How do I juice a lime? pages 30, 80 / How much juice does one lime yield? page 30

Egg Salad Sandwiches

4 hard-cooked eggs, chopped (below)

2 tablespoons sweet or dill pickle relish

2 tablespoons finely chopped red sweet pepper

$\frac{1}{4}$ cup mayonnaise or salad dressing

$1\frac{1}{2}$ teaspoons yellow mustard

4 croissants, split

4 leaves red-tip leaf lettuce

4 to 8 slices Colby and Monterey Jack cheese or cheddar cheese (4 to 8 ounces)

1 For egg salad, in a medium bowl stir together eggs, pickle relish, sweet pepper, mayonnaise, and mustard. If desired, cover and chill for up to 6 hours.

2 To assemble sandwiches, layer the bottom halves of the croissants with lettuce leaves. Spread egg salad over lettuce; top with 1 or 2 cheese slices. Add top halves of croissants. If necessary, use wooden toothpicks to secure sandwiches. Makes 4 sandwiches.

Per sandwich: 451 cal., 31 g total fat (12 g sat. fat), 261 mg chol., 695 mg sodium, 30 g carbo., 2 g fiber, 13 g pro.

Curried Egg Salad Sandwiches: Prepare as above, except add $\frac{1}{2}$ to 1 teaspoon curry powder to the egg salad. Cover and chill for 2 to 6 hours.

Honey-Dill Egg Salad Sandwiches: Prepare as above, except substitute honey mustard for yellow mustard and add 1 teaspoon dried dillweed to the egg salad.

Egg Salad Wraps: Prepare egg salad as above. Substitute four 8-inch flour tortillas for croissants. Lay lettuce leaves on tortillas; top with egg salad and roll up.

1 To hard-cook eggs, place eggs in a single layer in a saucepan. Do not stack the eggs. Add enough cold water to cover the eggs by 1 inch.

2 Heat over medium-high heat until the water comes to a rapid boil (water will have large rapidly breaking bubbles). Remove from heat.

3 Cover the saucepan and let stand for 15 minutes. Drain, then run cold water over the eggs or place in ice water until cool.

4 To peel an egg, ge tap it on the counter to the shell. Peel off the sh with your fingers. Use a knife to chop eggs.

Ask Mom How do I work with eggs? page 62 / How do I seed and chop sweet peppers? page 49 / What is that salad green? page 347 / What is curry powder? page 410

EGG SALAD À LA YOU.

One of the best things about a classic egg salad is that you can make it your own. Stir in some fresh dill, sliced green onion, minced raw onion or celery, crumbled cooked bacon, celery seeds, or chopped green olives with pimiento.

Serving your egg salad on croissants is a great "ladies' lunch" thing to do, but really, any kind of soft bread works well, too. Try sourdough, pumpernickel, rye, or multigrain.

① Skill Level

Pizza Your Way

- I pizza crust (I pound frozen pizza dough, thawed; one 13.8-ounce package refrigerated pizza crust; or one 10-inch packaged prebaked pizza crust)
- I 8-ounce can pizza sauce or ¾ cup bottled pasta sauce or Alfredo sauce
- I 8-ounce package (2 cups) shredded Italian blend cheeses, mozzarella cheese, or Monterey Jack cheese or 2 cups shredded Gouda or fontina cheese (4 ounces)
- I cup cooked meat (pepperoni slices, ground beef, bulk sausage, chopped ham, or shredded chicken or turkey)
- I cup vegetables (sliced mushrooms, sliced or chopped onion, sliced or chopped sweet pepper, sliced green or ripe olives, chopped tomato, shredded spinach, and/or small broccoli florets)

1 Preheat oven to 425°F. Pat or roll the dough into a 12-inch circle and place on a greased pizza pan or baking sheet. Or place the pizza crust on a pizza pan or baking sheet. Bake in the preheated oven for 5 minutes. Using a spoon, spread desired sauce over crust. Sprinkle with 1 cup of the cheese. Top with desired meat and vegetables. Sprinkle with remaining 1 cup cheese. Bake for 15 to 20 minutes or until crust is brown and cheese is bubbly. Makes 4 servings.

Per serving: 561 cal., 32 g total fat (14 g sat. fat), 82 mg chol., 1,496 mg sodium, 40 g carbo., 2 g fiber, 28 g pro.

Ask Mom How do I shred cheese? page 71 / How do I slice fresh mushrooms? page 45 / How do I slice an onion?
page 47 / How do I seed and chop sweet peppers? page 49 / How do I chop a tomato? page 52 / How do I shred fresh herbs/
spinach? page 42 / How do I trim and cut broccoli? page 36

DO I HAVE TO COOK MEAT FIRST? Yes—for a couple of reasons. You want to be sure that it cooks thoroughly. Second, cooking the meat allows you to drain off the fat. Cook ground meat until brown, stirring with a wooden spoon to break it into small pieces. Drain it on a plate lined with paper towels.

Shred your cheese—or take preshredded cheese from the refrigerator—right before you plan to use it. As it warms to room temperature, it starts to stick together.

3 Skill Level

Chicago-Style Deep-Dish Pizza

  1 16-ounce loaf frozen whole wheat or white bread dough, thawed
1½ cups shredded mozzarella cheese (6 ounces)
  1 recipe Meaty Pizza Filling
  1 10-ounce package frozen chopped spinach, thawed and well drained
  1 egg, lightly beaten
  1 tablespoon butter or margarine, melted
  2 tablespoons grated Parmesan or Romano cheese

1 Preheat oven to 375°F. On a lightly floured surface, roll two-thirds of the dough into a 12-inch circle. (If necessary, let dough rest once or twice during rolling.) Place circle in a greased 9-inch springform pan, pressing dough 1½ inches up the sides (below). Sprinkle with ½ cup of the mozzarella. Top with Meaty Pizza Filling. Mix spinach, egg, and remaining mozzarella. Spread spinach mixture over Meaty Pizza Filling (below).

2 Roll remaining dough into a 10-inch circle. Cut into 8 wedges. Arrange wedges on spinach mixture, slightly overlapping edges and sealing edges to bottom crust along edge of pan (below). Brush top with melted butter and sprinkle with Parmesan (below).

3 Bake, uncovered, in the preheated oven for 40 to 45 minutes or until filling is hot and crust is done. If necessary, cover with foil the last 10 minutes of baking to prevent overbrowning. Cool on a wire rack for 10 minutes. Remove sides of springform pan. Cut into wedges. Serves 8.

Meaty Pizza Filling: In a large skillet cook 12 ounces bulk Italian sausage and 1 cup chopped onion until sausage is brown; drain. Pat meat with paper towels. Stir in one 8-ounce can pizza sauce; one 4-ounce can mushrooms, drained; one 3.5-ounce package sliced pepperoni; 2 teaspoons dried basil, crushed; and 1 teaspoon dried oregano, crushed.

Per serving: 480 cal., 28 g total fat (11 g sat. fat), 95 mg chol., 1,267 mg sodium, 36 g carbo., 5 g fiber, 24 g pro.

1 With your fingers, press the dough into the pan, taking care to fit the dough into the bottom edge of the pan without any air pockets.

2 Spoon the spinach mixture evenly over the sausage mixture. Spread gently to keep sausage and spinach layers separate.

3 Arrange the dough wedges on top of the spinach mixture. Overlap the wedges as needed to fit. Press edges to the bottom crust to seal.

4 Use a pastry brush to brush the melted butter over the pizza. Sprinkle Parmesan over the buttered top and bake.

Ask Mom How do I shred cheese? page 71 / How do I crush dried herbs? page 78 / How do I drain spinach? page 321 / How do I beat eggs? page 62 / How do I measure butter? pages 58, 59 / How do I grate cheese? page 71 / What is a springform pan? pages 16–17

WHY DO I HAVE TO LET THE DOUGH REST? As you roll out pizza dough, it can shrink and snap back. If that happens, cover it with a clean towel and let it sit for 5 to 10 minutes. The dough will "relax" and be easier to work with.

It's important to bake this hearty pizza in a springform pan rather than a deep-dish pizza pan. The sides of the springform pan are removable, which makes the thick slices much easier to serve.

1 Skill Level

Meatball Pizza

1 10-inch packaged prebaked pizza crust
1 8-ounce can pizza sauce
2 cups shredded fontina cheese (8 ounces)
½ of a 16-ounce package frozen Italian-style meatballs (2 cups), thawed and halved
¼ cup shredded fresh basil leaves
¼ cup finely shredded Parmesan cheese

1 Preheat oven to 425°F. Place pizza crust on an ungreased baking sheet. Spread pizza sauce over crust. Sprinkle with 1 cup of the fontina cheese. Top with meatballs and basil. Sprinkle with remaining 1 cup fontina and the Parmesan cheese. Bake in the preheated oven about 10 minutes or until heated through and cheese melts. Makes 4 servings.

Per serving: 698 cal., 38 g total fat (18 g sat. fat), 110 mg chol., 1,801 mg sodium, 53 g carbo., 5 g fiber, 38 g pro.

Alfredo and Sweet Pepper Pizza: Prepare as above, except omit pizza sauce, meatballs, basil, and Parmesan. Substitute one 8-ounce package 4-cheese Italian blend cheese for the fontina. Stir together ¾ cup refrigerated or bottled Alfredo pasta sauce and ½ teaspoon dried Italian seasoning, crushed. Top with one 16-ounce package frozen pepper stir-fry vegetables (yellow, green, and red peppers and onion), thawed and well drained. Bake as directed.

Asian Pizza: Prepare as above, except substitute ½ cup bottled hoisin sauce for the pizza sauce. Substitute smoked Gouda for the fontina cheese, 8 ounces peeled and deveined cooked shrimp or 2 cups shredded cooked chicken for the meatballs, and ¼ cup sliced green onion for the basil. Add ¼ cup chopped red sweet pepper with the green onion. Omit the Parmesan cheese. Bake as directed.

Buffalo Chicken Pizza: Prepare as above, except in a small bowl stir together ⅓ cup bottled ranch or blue cheese salad dressing and 1 to 2 teaspoons bottled hot pepper sauce. Substitute salad dressing mixture for the pizza sauce. Substitute one 8-ounce package shredded mozzarella cheese for the fontina cheese; one 6-ounce package refrigerated cooked Southwestern chicken breast strips, coarsely chopped, for the meatballs; and ¼ cup sliced green onion for the basil. Omit the Parmesan cheese. Bake as directed. If desired, drizzle the pizza with ⅓ cup warmed bottled barbecue sauce before serving.

Ingredient Info Prebaked pizza crusts or Italian bread shells are real timesavers. Just top them and pop them in the oven and you have a hunger killer. The larger sizes come in a variety of types—including original, thin, and whole wheat. There are also smaller, individual crusts—ideal for a personal pie.

Ask Mom How do I shred cheese? page 71 / How do I shred fresh herbs/spinach? page 42 / How do I crush dried herbs? page 78 / How do I slice green onions? page 43 / How do I seed and chop sweet peppers? page 49

something
SWEET

Have brownies on the brain? Bake a batch—or a birthday cake or a few dozen chocolate cookies. Pass the milk, please.

12

(2) Skill Level

Rocky Road Brownies

2 cups all-purpose flour

2 cups sugar

1 teaspoon baking soda

1 cup butter

$\frac{1}{3}$ cup unsweetened cocoa powder

2 eggs

$\frac{1}{2}$ cup buttermilk or sour milk

1$\frac{1}{2}$ teaspoons vanilla

1$\frac{1}{2}$ cups chopped dry-roasted peanuts

3 cups tiny marshmallows

1 recipe Chocolate Drizzle

Good to Know If you don't have buttermilk, you can make sour milk. Combine 1 tablespoon lemon juice or vinegar with enough milk to make 1 cup total liquid; stir. Let stand for 5 minutes before using.

1 Preheat oven to 350°F. Line a 13×9×2-inch baking pan with foil, leaving about 1 inch of foil extending over the ends of pan. Grease foil; set aside. In a large bowl stir together flour, sugar, baking soda, and $\frac{1}{4}$ teaspoon *salt*; set aside.

2 In a 2-quart saucepan combine butter, 1 cup *water*, and the cocoa. Bring to boiling, stirring constantly. Add to flour mixture; beat with an electric mixer on medium speed (below). Add eggs, buttermilk, and vanilla. Beat for 1 minute. Stir in 1 cup of the peanuts. Pour into prepared pan.

3 Bake in preheated oven about 40 minutes or until a toothpick inserted in center comes out clean. Sprinkle remaining $\frac{1}{2}$ cup peanuts and the marshmallows over hot brownies (below). Top with Chocolate Drizzle (below). Cool in pan on wire rack. Remove brownies from pan, using the overlapping foil to lift brownies. Place on cutting board; cut into bars. Makes 32 brownies.

Chocolate Drizzle: In a medium saucepan combine 1 cup semisweet chocolate pieces, $\frac{1}{4}$ cup whipping cream, and 2 tablespoons butter. Heat and stir over medium-low heat until smooth.

Per brownie: 237 cal., 13 g total fat (6 g sat. fat), 33 mg chol., 119 mg sodium, 27 g carbo., 2 g fiber, 3 g pro.

cocoa mixture into the flour mixture.

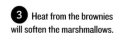
2 Use an electric mixer on medium speed to blend well.

3 Heat from the brownies will soften the marshmallows.

4 Chocolate Drizzle keeps everything on top in its place.

Ask Mom How do I measure flour? page 58 / How do I measure butter? pages 58, 59 / How do I line a pan with foil? page 60 / How do I grease a baking pan/dish? page 61 / What is an electric mixer? page 21 / What does drizzle mean? page 79

(2) Skill Level

Lemon Bars Deluxe

2 cups all-purpose flour
½ cup powdered sugar
1 cup butter, softened
4 eggs
1½ cups granulated sugar
1 tablespoon finely shredded lemon peel (set aside)
⅓ cup lemon juice
¼ cup all-purpose flour
Powdered sugar

Good to Know To dust baked goods with powdered sugar, use a fine-mesh strainer. Put a few spoonfuls of powdered sugar in the strainer, then gently tap the side of it as you move it over the pan to shake some sugar onto the brownies or bars. (Don't add the powdered sugar until just before serving or it will melt.)

1 Preheat oven to 350°F. Line a 13×9×2-inch baking pan with foil, leaving about 1 inch of foil extending over the ends of pan. In a large bowl stir together the 2 cups flour and the ½ cup powdered sugar. Add butter and beat with an electric mixer on low to medium speed just until mixture begins to cling together (below). Press flour mixture into the bottom of prepared baking pan (below). Bake in the preheated oven about 25 minutes or until light brown.

2 In a medium bowl beat eggs with a whisk; whisk in granulated sugar and lemon juice until well mixed. Whisk in the ¼ cup flour and the lemon peel. Pour over baked crust (below).

3 Bake about 20 minutes more or until edges begin to brown and center is set. Cool in pan on a wire rack. Remove bars from pan, using the overlapping foil to lift bars (below). Place on cutting board. Sift powdered sugar over the top of the bars. Cut into bars or into 2×1¾-inch diamonds. Store, covered, in the refrigerator. Makes 30 bars.

Per bar: 147 cal., 7 g total fat (4 g sat. fat), 44 mg chol., 53 mg sodium, 20 g carbo., 0 g fiber, 2 g pro.

1 Use an electric mixer to "cut" butter into flour mixture. It should just start to cling together when ready.

2 Using your fingers, press the flour mixture into the pan. As you press, it will hold together to make a crust.

3 Pour the lemon filling over the hot crust, then immediately return it to the oven to finish baking.

4 Grasp the foil that overlaps the ends of the Lift cooled bars from th transfer to a cutting bo

Ask Mom How do I measure flour? page 58 / How do I measure butter? pages 58, 59 / How do I soften butter? page 59 / How do I shred lemon/lime peel? page 30 / How do I juice a lemon/lime? pages 30, 80 / How much juice does one lemon/lime yield? page 30 / How do I line a pan with foil? page 60 / What is an electric mixer? page 21

1 Skill Level

Chocolate Chip Cookies

¾ cup butter, softened
¼ cup shortening
1 cup packed brown sugar
½ cup granulated sugar
¾ teaspoon baking soda
½ teaspoon salt
2 eggs
1 teaspoon vanilla
2½ cups all-purpose flour
1 12-ounce package (2 cups) semisweet chocolate pieces or miniature candy-coated semisweet chocolate pieces
1½ cups chopped walnuts or pecans, toasted if desired (optional)

Flavor Changes
To make giant chocolate chip cookies, drop ¼-cup mounds of dough 4 inches apart onto cookie sheet; flatten slightly. Bake for 10 to 12 minutes or until edges are light brown.

1 Preheat oven to 375°F. In a large mixing bowl beat butter and shortening with an electric mixer on medium to high speed for 30 seconds. Add the brown sugar, granulated sugar, baking soda, and salt. Beat until combined, scraping sides of bowl occasionally. Beat in eggs and vanilla until combined. Beat in as much of the flour as you can with the mixer. Using a wooden spoon, stir in any remaining flour. Stir in chocolate pieces and, if desired, walnuts.

2 Drop dough by rounded teaspoons 2 inches apart onto an ungreased cookie sheet. Bake in the preheated oven for 8 to 9 minutes or until edges are light brown (see photo, page 75). Transfer to a wire rack and let cool. Makes about 60 cookies.

Per cookie: 94 cal., 5 g total fat (3 g sat. fat), 13 mg chol., 55 mg sodium, 13 g carbo., 1 g fiber, 1 g pro.

Chocolate-Peanut Cookies: Prepare as above, except substitute candy-coated peanut butter-flavor pieces for the chocolate pieces and dry-roasted peanuts for the walnuts.

Macadamia Nut and White Chocolate Chip Cookies: Prepare as above, except substitute white baking pieces for the semisweet chocolate pieces. Stir in one 3.5-ounce jar macadamia nuts, chopped, with the baking pieces.

Ice Cream Cookie Sandwiches: Prepare as above. To make 10 ice cream sandwiches, soften 1 pint of chocolate chip or desired flavor ice cream at room temperature for 10 minutes. Place a scoop (about ¼ cup) of ice cream on the bottoms of 10 cookies. Spread the bottoms of 10 more cookies with about 2 teaspoons each fudge ice cream topping. Place cookies, fudge sides down, on top of ice cream. Press down lightly. Wrap ice cream sandwiches separately in plastic wrap. Freeze for at least 6 hours or until firm. To serve, let ice cream sandwiches stand at room temperature about 10 minutes. Makes 10 sandwiches.

Ask Mom How do I measure butter? pages 58, 59 / How do I soften butter? page 59 / How do I measure shortening? page 58 / How do I pack brown sugar? page 58 / How do I measure flour? page 58 / How do I chop nuts? page 65 / How do I toast nuts? page 65 / What is an electric mixer? page 21 / What does it mean to drop from a teaspoon? page 78

③ Skill Level

Triple Chocolate Cookies

Good to Know

Chocolate melts better when it's in small pieces. To chop it, place the bar or block on a cutting board. With the widest part of a chef's knife, press down on the chocolate to break it into big chunks. To chop it into smaller pieces, hold the tip of the knife in one place and make small chops with the back of the knife, moving side to side.

  7 ounces bittersweet chocolate, chopped
  5 ounces unsweetened chocolate, chopped
  ½ cup butter
  ⅓ cup all-purpose flour
  ¼ teaspoon baking powder
  1 cup granulated sugar
  ¾ cup packed brown sugar
  4 eggs
  ¼ cup finely chopped pecans, toasted
    Chocolate Drizzle (page 449)

1 In a 2-quart saucepan combine chocolates and butter. Heat and stir over low heat until smooth (below). Remove from heat. Let cool for 10 minutes. In a small bowl stir together flour, baking powder, and ¼ teaspoon *salt.* Set aside.

2 In a large mixing bowl combine sugars and eggs. Beat with an electric mixer on medium to high speed for 2 to 3 minutes or until color lightens slightly (below). Beat in melted chocolate. Add flour mixture to chocolate mixture; beat until combined. Stir in pecans. Cover surface of cookie dough with plastic wrap (below). Let stand for 20 minutes (dough thickens as it stands).

3 Preheat oven to 350°F. Line cookie sheets with parchment paper or foil. Drop dough by rounded teaspoons 2 inches apart onto prepared cookie sheets (below). Bake in the preheated oven about 9 minutes or just until tops are set. Let stand for 1 minute on cookie sheet. Transfer to a wire rack; let cool. Spoon Chocolate Drizzle over cookies (page 449). Makes 60 cookies.

Per cookie: 92 cal., 6 g total fat (3 g sat. fat), 18 mg chol., 29 mg sodium, 11 g carbo., 1 g fiber, 1 g pro.

Big Triple Chocolate Cookies: Prepare as above, except drop 3-tablespoon mounds of dough per cookie 3 inches apart onto cookie sheets. Bake for 13 minutes. Makes about 18 cookies.

① Heat chocolates and butter over low heat, stirring with a heat-resistant spatula until melted and smooth.

② Beat the sugars and eggs with an electric mixer until well blended and the color lightens a bit.

③ Press plastic wrap onto surface of dough. Let stand at room temperature so dough sets up.

④ Using a flatware teaspoon, "drop," or push scoop of dough onto coo sheet with a second spo

Ask Mom How do I measure butter? pages 58, 59 / How do I measure flour? page 58 / How do I pack brown sugar? page 58 / How do I chop nuts? page 65 / How do I toast nuts? page 65 / What is an electric mixer? page 21 / What is parchment paper? page 79 / What does it mean to drop from a teaspoon? page 78 / What does drizzle mean? page 79

HOW DO I MAKE A CHOCOLATE DRIZZLE? For this recipe, combine 1 cup semisweet chocolate pieces with 4 teaspoons shortening in a small saucepan over low heat. Stir until the chocolate melts and is smooth. Remove from the heat and drizzle away.

Place cooled cookies on a cookie sheet lined with parchment or waxed paper. Drizzle melted chocolate over tops. Place the entire cookie sheet in the freezer for 4 to 5 minutes or until chocolate is firm.

Coconut Macaroons

2 ⅔ cups flaked coconut (7 ounces)
⅔ cup sugar
⅓ cup all-purpose flour
¼ teaspoon salt
3 egg whites
½ teaspoon vanilla extract or ¼ teaspoon almond extract
2 ounces semisweet chocolate, chopped (optional)
½ teaspoon shortening (optional)

1 Preheat oven to 325°F. Lightly grease and flour a large cookie sheet or line it with parchment paper; set aside. In a medium mixing bowl stir together coconut, sugar, flour, and salt. Using a wooden spoon, stir in egg whites and vanilla.

2 Drop coconut mixture by rounded teaspoons 2 inches apart onto the prepared cookie sheet. Bake in the preheated oven for 20 to 25 minutes or until edges are golden brown. Transfer to a wire rack and let cool. If desired, in a heavy 1-quart saucepan heat and stir chocolate and shortening over low heat until melted and smooth. Dip half of each cookie in melted chocolate or drizzle melted chocolate over cookies. Place cookies on waxed paper and let stand until set. Makes about 30 cookies.

Per cookie: 73 cal., 4 g total fat (4 g sat. fat), 0 mg chol., 57 mg sodium, 10 g carbo., 1 g fiber, 1 g pro.

Chewy, nutty-flavored coconut and rich chocolate are great partners. Present these yummy macaroons three ways: dipped in chocolate, drizzled with chocolate, or au naturel.

Ask Mom How do I measure flour? page 58 / How do I separate eggs? page 62 / How do I grease a baking pan/dish? page 61 / What is parchment paper? page 79 / What does it mean to drop from a teaspoon? page 78 / What does drizzle mean? page 79

2 Skill Level

Sugar Cookie Cutouts

$\frac{2}{3}$ cup butter, softened

$\frac{3}{4}$ cup granulated sugar

1 teaspoon baking powder

$\frac{1}{4}$ teaspoon salt

1 egg

1 tablespoon milk

1 teaspoon vanilla

2 cups all-purpose flour

1 recipe Powdered Sugar Icing (optional)

1 Preheat oven to 375°F. In a large mixing bowl beat butter with an electric mixer on medium to high speed for 30 seconds. Add granulated sugar, baking powder, and salt. Beat until combined, scraping sides of bowl occasionally. Beat in egg, milk, and vanilla until combined. Beat in as much of the flour as you can with the mixer. Using a wooden spoon, stir in any remaining flour. Divide dough in half. If necessary, wrap each half in plastic wrap; chill dough about 30 minutes or until easy to handle.

2 On a lightly floured surface, roll half the dough at a time until $\frac{1}{8}$ inch thick. To roll, start from the center and push dough out toward the edges until it is a uniform thickness. Using a 2$\frac{1}{2}$-inch cookie cutter, cut out shapes. Place shapes 1 inch apart on an ungreased cookie sheet.

3 Bake in the preheated oven for 7 to 8 minutes or until edges are firm and bottoms are very light brown. Transfer to a wire rack and let cool. If desired, frost with Powdered Sugar Icing. Makes about 36 cookies.

Per cookie: 73 cal., 4 g total fat (2 g sat. fat), 16 mg chol., 66 mg sodium, 9 g carbo., 0 g fiber, 1 g pro.

Powdered Sugar Icing: In a small bowl stir together 1 cup powdered sugar, 1 tablespoon milk, and $\frac{1}{4}$ teaspoon vanilla. Stir in additional milk, 1 teaspoon at a time, until icing reaches drizzling consistency.

> To make the cleanest cuts with the cookie cutter, roll out your dough on a lightly floured surface and dip the cutter in flour each time (or every other time) you press it into the dough. You might have to lightly flour the rolling pin too.

Ask Mom How do I measure butter? pages 58, 59 / How do I soften butter? page 59 / How do I measure flour? page 58 / What is an electric mixer? page 21 / What does drizzle mean? page 79

Shortbread

1¼ cups all-purpose flour
3 tablespoons granulated sugar
½ cup butter

1 Preheat oven to 325°F. In a medium bowl stir together flour and sugar. Using a pastry blender, cut in butter until mixture resembles fine crumbs and starts to cling. Using your hands, shape the mixture into a ball and knead until smooth.

2 On a lightly floured surface, roll dough until ½ inch thick.* Using a 1½-inch cookie cutter, cut dough into circles, rerolling scraps as necessary. Place circles 1 inch apart on an ungreased cookie sheet. Bake in the preheated oven for 20 to 25 minutes or until bottoms just start to brown. Transfer to a wire rack and let cool. Makes 16 cookies.

*Note: To make shortbread strips, on a lightly floured surface, roll dough into a 6×4-inch rectangle about ½ inch thick. Using a utility knife, cut rectangle in half lengthwise, then crosswise into 16 pieces. Bake as directed.

Per cookie: 98 cal., 6 g total fat (4 g sat. fat), 16 mg chol., 62 mg sodium, 10 g carbo., 0 g fiber, 1 g pro.

Gearing Up There are two basic styles of rolling pins: the rotating roller type and the rod style or French rolling pin—an elongated stick with tapered ends (similar in shape to a baguette).

French rolling pin   Rotating rolling pin

1 Using a pastry blender, cut butter into flour until mixture looks like coarse crumbs and just begins to stick together.

2 Gently knead the dough by squeezing it and pressing it against the sides of the bowl until smooth. Don't overwork the dough.

3 Lay two clean ½-inch-thick strips of wood on either side of dough. Rest the rolling pin on wood strips and roll dough to a perfect thickness.

4 Use a 1½-inch rou cutter to cut out dough. Reroll scraps as before a continue cutting until all dough is used.

Ask Mom How do I measure flour? page 58 / How do I measure butter? pages 58, 59 / How do I cut in butter? page 63 / How do I finely shred orange peel? page 30 / How do I pack brown sugar? page 58 / How do I chop nuts? page 65 / How do I shred lemon/lime peel? page 30

Spiced Shortbread

Prepare as on page 452, except substitute brown sugar for the granulated sugar and stir $\frac{1}{2}$ teaspoon ground cinnamon, $\frac{1}{4}$ teaspoon ground ginger, and $\frac{1}{8}$ teaspoon ground cloves into the flour mixture.

Cherry-Orange Shortbread

Prepare as on page 452, except add 2 teaspoons finely shredded orange peel with the butter and stir in $\frac{1}{3}$ cup snipped dried cherries after cutting in the butter.

Butter-Pecan Shortbread

Prepare as on page 452, except substitute brown sugar for the granulated sugar. After cutting in butter stir in 2 tablespoons finely chopped pecans. Sprinkle mixture with $\frac{1}{2}$ teaspoon vanilla before kneading.

Lemon-Poppy Seed Shortbread

Prepare as on page 452, except stir I tablespoon poppy seeds into flour mixture and add I teaspoon finely shredded lemon peel with the butter.

Cranberry Shortbread

Prepare as on page 452, except after cutting in butter, stir in $\frac{1}{3}$ cup snipped dried cranberries.

(2) Skill Level

Good to Know
This one-pot-and-a-pan fudge is supereasy and there is no need for a candy thermometer. Just stir, melt, stir some more, pour, and chill.

Peanut Butter and
Chocolate Fudge

   2 cups sugar
  ½ cup evaporated milk
1 ⅓ cups creamy or chunky peanut butter
   1 7-ounce jar marshmallow crème
1 ½ cups semisweet chocolate pieces
  ½ cup coarsely chopped peanuts

1 Line an 8×8×2-inch baking pan with foil, leaving about 1 inch of foil extending over the ends of pan. Butter the foil; set pan aside.

2 In a 2-quart saucepan combine sugar and evaporated milk. Cook and stir over medium-high heat until sugar mixture boils (below). Reduce heat to medium; continue cooking for 3 minutes, stirring occasionally. Remove from heat.

3 Immediately stir in peanut butter, marshmallow crème, and chocolate pieces (below). Stir until chocolate melts and ingredients are well combined. Quickly spread fudge evenly into the prepared pan (below). Sprinkle with peanuts, pressing them lightly into the fudge with a spatula or your hands.

4 Cover and chill for 2 to 3 hours or until firm. When firm, remove fudge from pan, using the overlapping foil to lift fudge. Place on a cutting board; cut fudge into squares (below). Store, covered, in an airtight container in the refrigerator for up to 1 week. Makes about 3 pounds (64 pieces).

Per piece: 91 cal., 5 g total fat (1 g sat. fat), 1 mg chol., 35 mg sodium, 12 g carbo., 1 g fiber, 2 g pro.

1 Using a wooden spoon, stir the sugar and evaporated milk constantly over medium-high heat until boiling.

2 Add the peanut butter, marshmallow crème, and chocolate pieces to hot milk mixture. Stir until smooth.

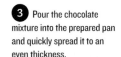

3 Pour the chocolate mixture into the prepared pan and quickly spread it to an even thickness.

4 After the fudge is f lift it from the pan using foil. Use a chef's knife to fudge into squares.

Ask Mom How do I chop nuts? page 65 / How do I line a pan with foil? page 60 / How do I grease a baking pan/dish? page 61

1 Skill Level

Berry Trifle

| 4-serving-size package instant vanilla pudding mix
2 cups milk
| 8-ounce package cream cheese, softened
| 6-ounce container vanilla yogurt
| 10.75-ounce frozen loaf pound cake, thawed and cubed ($\frac{3}{4}$-inch cubes)
6 cups strawberries, quartered
2 cups blueberries and/or raspberries
| recipe Berry Sauce

1 Prepare pudding mix according to package directions using the milk; set aside. In a large mixing bowl beat cream cheese and yogurt with an electric mixer on medium speed until smooth; stir in pudding.

2 To assemble trifle, in a 2$\frac{1}{2}$- to 3-quart glass bowl layer one-third of the cake cubes, one-third of the pudding mixture, and one-third of the strawberries and blueberries. Repeat layers twice. Cover and chill for 4 to 24 hours. Spoon Berry Sauce onto serving plates; top with trifle. Makes 8 to 10 servings.

Berry Sauce: In a blender or food processor combine 2 cups fresh or frozen (thawed) strawberries or raspberries; 2 to 3 tablespoons sugar; and 1 tablespoon raspberry liqueur, rum, or orange juice. Cover and blend or process until smooth. If desired, press sauce through a fine-mesh sieve to remove seeds. Cover and chill until serving time or for up to 24 hours.

Per serving: 425 cal., 20 g total fat (12 g sat. fat), 80 mg chol., 442 mg sodium, 54 g carbo., 4 g fiber, 8 g pro.

FLAVOR CHANGES This light, luscious, summery dessert would be delicious made with other flavors of yogurt too. Try raspberry, lemon, orange, or coconut.

Ask Mom How do I soften cream cheese? page 93 / What is a fine-mesh sieve? page 22 / What is an electric mixer? page 21

Chocolaty Tiramisu Parfaits

1 8-ounce carton mascarpone cheese
1 cup whipping cream
3 tablespoons powdered sugar
1 teaspoon vanilla
⅓ cup chocolate- or coffee-flavored liqueur
1 3-ounce package ladyfingers, cubed
¾ cup brewed espresso or strong coffee
3 ounces bittersweet chocolate, shredded or finely chopped

1 In a large mixing bowl beat mascarpone cheese, cream, powdered sugar, and vanilla with an electric mixer on medium to high speed just until soft peaks form (tips curl). Fold in the liqueur just until combined.

2 Divide half of the ladyfinger cubes among eight 6-ounce parfait glasses or sundae glasses. Drizzle with half of the espresso. Top with half of the mascarpone mixture. Sprinkle with half of the chocolate. Repeat layers once. Cover and chill for 1 to 24 hours before serving. Makes 8 servings.

Per serving: 365 cal., 29 g total fat (17 g sat. fat), 116 mg chol., 47 mg sodium, 21 g carbo., 1 g fiber, 8 g pro.

Shopping Savy Ladyfingers are a type of Italian cookie-cake. These oblong cookies have a delicate, light, and airy texture like that of a spongecake. Look for ladyfingers in the bakery aisle of your supermarket—or buy them at an Italian market.

Ask Mom How do I grate/shred chocolate? page 20 / What is an electric mixer? page 21 / What are soft peaks? page 62

Bread Pudding with Amaretto Sauce

    5 cups cubed cinnamon-swirl bread or sweet bread
    4 egg yolks, lightly beaten
 1½ cups whipping cream*
 1½ cups half-and-half or light cream*
    3 tablespoons sugar
    1 tablespoon vanilla
    1 recipe Amaretto Sauce or ¾ cup warm maple syrup

1 Preheat oven to 300°F. Spread bread cubes in a single layer in a large shallow baking pan. Bake in the preheated oven for 10 to 15 minutes or until the bread cubes are dry, stirring once or twice. Place dry bread cubes in a greased 2-quart square baking dish. Set aside. Increase oven temperature to 325°F.

2 In a medium mixing bowl whisk together egg yolks, cream, half-and-half, sugar, and vanilla. Pour egg mixture over bread. Use the back of a large spoon to gently push down on the bread cubes, making sure the bread absorbs the egg mixture. Cover and chill for 4 hours or overnight.

3 Bake, uncovered, for 45 to 50 minutes or until puffed and a knife inserted near the center comes out clean. Cool slightly. Serve warm with Amaretto Sauce or maple syrup. Makes 9 servings.

Amaretto Sauce: In a heavy 1-quart saucepan stir together ½ cup packed brown sugar, ⅓ cup light-colored corn syrup, and ¼ cup amaretto (almond-flavor liqueur). Cook and stir over medium heat just until boiling. Remove from heat. Stir in ½ teaspoon vanilla. Serve sauce warm with bread pudding.

*****Note:** If desired, omit the whipping cream and use 3 cups total half-and-half or light cream.

Per serving: 461 cal., 27 g total fat (14 g sat. fat), 186 mg chol., 182 mg sodium, 48 g carbo., 1 g fiber, 5 g pro.

Ingredient Info There's a difference between pure maple syrup and maple-flavored syrup. Pure maple syrup is made entirely from the sap of the sugar maple tree. Maple-flavored syrup is largely made of dark corn syrup (which is cheaper than pure maple syrup) with maple flavoring added. Pure maple syrup is more expensive than maple-flavored syrup, but if you have the pennies to spare, it's worth it for the flavor.

Ask Mom How do I make/toast bread cubes? page 79 / How do I separate eggs? page 62 / How do I beat eggs? page 62 / How do I pack brown sugar? page 58 / What's the best way to measure sticky liquids? page 58

WHY BAKE CHEESECAKE IN A BATH? A water bath, or what the French call a bain-marie, keeps the cheesecake from cracking or curdling. Leaving it for an hour in the turned-off oven helps in the same way by allowing it to gently finish cooking.

1 Pour the crumb mixture into the springform pan. Firmly press it over the bottom and about 2 inches up the sides of the pan. Make sure the crust has an even thickness.

Cheesecake

1½ cups finely crushed graham crackers
⅓ cup sugar
⅓ cup butter, melted
3 8-ounce packages cream cheese, softened
1 cup sugar
2 tablespoons all-purpose flour
1 teaspoon vanilla
¼ cup milk
3 eggs, lightly beaten

Good to Know Once you've baked the perfect cheesecake (aren't you proud?), you don't want to mess it up in the serving. To get clean slices, use a long nonserrated knife with a thin blade. Before cutting each slice, dip the knife in hot water and wipe it dry with a towel so it doesn't drag down through the cheesecake.

1 Preheat oven to 375°F. For crust, in a medium bowl stir together crushed graham crackers and the ⅓ cup sugar. Stir in melted butter. Press the crumb mixture onto bottom and about 2 inches up the sides of an 8- or 9-inch springform pan (page 458). Place the crust-lined springform pan on a double layer of 18×12-inch heavy-duty aluminum foil. Bring edges of foil up and mold around sides of pan to form a watertight seal (below).

2 For filling, in a large mixing bowl beat cream cheese, the 1 cup sugar, the flour, and vanilla with an electric mixer on medium speed until combined. Beat in milk until smooth. Stir in eggs (below). Pour into crust-lined pan. Place in a roasting pan and pour enough hot water around pan to reach halfway up the sides (below). Bake in the preheated oven for 40 to 45 minutes for the 8-inch pan (35 to 40 minutes for the 9-inch pan) or until edges of cake are set but center jiggles a bit when pan is gently shaken. Turn oven off and let cheesecake sit in oven for 1 hour.

3 Cool in pan on a wire rack for 15 minutes. Using a small sharp knife, loosen the crust from sides of pan (below); cool for 30 minutes. Remove the sides of the pan; cool cheesecake completely on rack. Cover and chill for at least 4 hours before serving. Makes 12 slices.

Per slice: 405 cal., 27 g total fat (16 g sat. fat), 129 mg chol., 282 mg sodium, 34 g carbo., 0 g fiber, 7 g pro.

the foil as far
s of the pan as
no water gets to

3 Stir the beaten eggs into filling until it is smooth and looks uniform.

4 Place the roasting pan on oven rack before pouring in the water. There's less chance you'll slosh the water.

5 Run a small thin knife between the crust and the pan to loosen the cake before releasing the sides of the pan.

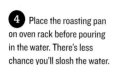

Ask Mom How do I make bread/cracker crumbs? page 76 / How do I measure butter? pages 58, 59 / How do I soften cream cheese? page 93 / How do I beat eggs? page 62 / What is a springform pan? pages 16–17 / What is an electric mixer? page 21 / How do I toast nuts? page 65 / What's the best way to measure sticky liquids? pages 58, 81 / What does drizzle mean? page 79

CAN I USE FLAVORED GRAHAM CRACKERS?
Why not? A cinnamon- or gingerbread-flavored crust would be smashing for a fall or holiday cheesecake—and a chocolate-crusted cheesecake made with chocolate grahams (or a honey-graham crust) is fine for any time of year.

Cheesecake (*see recipe, page 459*)

Good to Know This Fruit-Topped Cheesecake gets a final glaze from heated preserves (marmalade, in this case). If you prefer a smooth glaze with no chunks of fruit or peel, use a seedless jam such as raspberry, blackberry, or blueberry.

Mint and Chip Cheesecake

Prepare as on page 459, except substitute chocolate-flavor graham crackers for the regular graham crackers in the crust. For the filling, add $\frac{1}{4}$ teaspoon mint flavoring with the vanilla and substitute $\frac{1}{4}$ cup green crème de menthe liqueur for the milk. After stirring in the eggs, stir in I cup miniature semisweet chocolate pieces. Bake and cool as directed. Cover and chill for at least 4 hours before serving. If desired, just before serving, drizzle slices with purchased fudge sauce.

Try these toppers

With just a few simple flavor twists, plain cheesecake becomes a completely different dessert.

Chocolate Bar Cheesecake: Before serving, top chilled cheesecake with I cup of one or more flavors chopped chocolate candy bars, such as chocolate-covered peanut butter cups, chocolate-covered English toffee, chocolate-covered nougat bars, milk chocolate, and/or dark chocolate. If desired, drizzle each slice with purchased butterscotch, caramel, mocha chocolate, or chocolate fudge sauce.

Fruit-Topped Cheesecake: In a I-quart saucepan heat $\frac{1}{3}$ cup of Orange marmalade or desired flavor fruit preserves just until spoonable. Top the cheesecake with I to 2 cups fresh fruit such as raspberries, blueberries, halved sweet cherries, or sliced strawberries or peaches; drizzle with heated preserves.

Honey-Nut Cheescake: Before serving, top chilled cheesecake with $\frac{1}{2}$ cup toasted sliced almonds and, if desired, $\frac{1}{2}$ cup fresh raspberries. Drizzle with $\frac{1}{4}$ cup honey. Slice and serve cheesecake as directed.

Turtle Cheescake: Before serving, drizzle slices with $\frac{1}{2}$ to I tablespoon each purchased caramel ice cream topping and chocolate-flavored syrup. Sprinkle each slice with about I tablespoon chopped dry-roasted peanuts.

CAN I USE ANY KIND OF PEAR? The most common kind of pear in the supermarket is probably Bartlett, but this dessert is best made with thin-necked Bosc pears. They hold up best when cooked and have the prettiest shape.

Oven-poached pears are wonderful warm, but they make a light and refreshing dessert when chilled too. After they've cooled, cover them and refrigerate for a few hours—and serve with chilled Raspberry Sauce.

Raspberry-Sauced Pears

4 small pears

2 tablespoons orange juice

2 teaspoons vanilla

$\frac{1}{2}$ teaspoon ground cinnamon

$\frac{1}{2}$ cup Raspberry Sauce

   Mint sprigs

1 Preheat oven to 375°F. Peel pears. If necessary, trim bottoms of pears so they stand upright. Core the pears using a melon baller (below) or a measuring teaspoon, leaving the stems intact. Place pears in a 2-quart square baking dish.

2 In a small bowl stir together the orange juice, vanilla, and cinnamon. Brush onto pears. Pour remaining orange juice mixture over pears. Cover with foil and bake in the preheated oven for 30 to 35 minutes or until pears are tender. Cool slightly. Brush pears again with some of the juices in the dish.

3 Meanwhile, prepare Raspberry Sauce. To serve, spoon sauce onto dessert plates. Place warm pears, stem ends up, on sauce. Garnish with mint sprigs. Serve warm. Makes 4 servings.

Raspberry Sauce: Thaw 3 cups frozen unsweetened raspberries. Do not drain. Place half of the berries in a blender. Cover and blend until berries are smooth. Press berries through a fine-mesh sieve to remove seeds. Repeat with remaining berries. In a 1-quart saucepan stir together $\frac{1}{3}$ cup sugar and 1 teaspoon cornstarch. Add raspberry puree. Cook and stir over medium heat until thickened and bubbly. Cook and stir for 2 minutes more. Transfer to a bowl; cool slightly. Cover and chill leftovers for up to 1 week.

Per serving: 162 cal., 0 g total fat (0 g sat. fat), 0 mg chol., 2 mg sodium, 4l g carbo., 7 g fiber, l g pro.

Chocolate-Raspberry Pears: Prepare as above, except drizzle 1 to 2 tablespoons of purchased chocolate-flavored syrup over each pear.

Menu Maker If you have any Raspberry Sauce left over, drizzle it over ice cream, cheesecake, or pound cake. Make a batch of the sauce to serve with ice cream or purchased cake for a spur-of-the-moment dessert.

Slice the bottoms off the pears so they will stand upright. Use a melon baller to scoop the cores out from the bottoms of the pears. Leave the stems intact but remove all of the cores and seeds.

Skill Level

Saucy Apple Dumplings

½ of a 17.3-ounce package frozen puff pastry (1 sheet), thawed
4 medium Granny Smith apples
1 tablespoon sugar
½ teaspoon ground cinnamon
1 egg
1 teaspoon water
½ cup purchased caramel ice cream topping or Caramel Sauce (see page 468)
⅓ cup chopped pecans, toasted

½ cup purchased caramel ice cream topping or Caramel Sauce (see page 468)

Ingredient Info You can thaw a single sheet of puff pastry one of two ways: at room temperature, covered with plastic wrap, about 30 minutes; or in the refrigerator, covered, about 4 hours. Store puff pastry thawed in the fridge for up to 2 days.

1 Unfold puff pastry on a lightly floured surface. Roll pastry into a 14-inch square. Using a knife, cut pastry into four 7-inch squares (below). Set aside.

2 Preheat oven to 375°F. Peel and core apples. If necessary, trim bottoms of apples so they stand upright. Place an apple in the center of each pastry square. In a small bowl stir together sugar and cinnamon; spoon into centers of apples.

3 In another small bowl beat egg and water with a fork. Moisten the edges of the pastry squares with egg mixture (below); fold corners to center over apples. Pinch to seal, pleating and folding pastry along seams as necessary (below). Place dumplings in a 13×9×2-inch baking pan (below). Using a pastry brush, brush dumplings with egg mixture.

4 Bake dumplings, uncovered, in the preheated oven for 30 to 35 minutes or until apples are tender and pastry is golden. (Test for doneness by sticking the tip of a paring knife into a dumpling.) Meanwhile, combine caramel topping and pecans in a microwave-safe 2-cup glass measure; microwave, uncovered, on 100-percent power (high) for 30 to 60 seconds or until heated through, stirring once. Serve dumplings warm with sauce. Makes 4 dumplings.

Per dumpling: 567 cal., 28 g total fat (1 g sat. fat), 53 mg chol., 362 mg sodium, 77 g carbo., 5 g fiber, 5 g pro.

1 Using a sharp knife, cut the rolled pastry into four equal squares.

2 After filling the apples with the sugar mixture, brush the egg mixture on pastry edges to help seal them.

3 Starting from the corners, pinch the pastry edges together; pleat and fold as necessary.

4 Arrange dumpling a baking pan so they are touching. Brush dumplir with more of the egg mix

Ask Mom How do I peel and core apples? page 28 / How do I chop nuts? page 65 / How do I toast nuts? page 65 / How do I pack brown sugar? page 58 / How do I finely shred orange peel? page 30

DRESS UP YOUR DUMPLINGS. Roll out the second sheet of puff pastry on a lightly floured surface. Cut out leaf shapes with a paring knife (or use small cookie cutters for other shapes). "Glue" them onto the sealed pastry with some egg mixture—then bake.

Apple Dumplings with Cranberry-Sour Cream Filling: Prepare as on page 464, except omit the cinnamon and sugar. In a small bowl combine 2 tablespoons sour cream, 2 tablespoons packed brown sugar, 2 tablespoons dried cranberries, 2 tablespoons chopped toasted pecans, and, if desired, $\frac{1}{2}$ teaspoon finely shredded orange peel. Fill apples with sour cream mixture.

(3) Skill Level

Almond-Cherry Pastry Braids

Flavor Changes Make this flaky, almond-and-fruit-filled pastry with any kind of preserves. Try cherry or raspberry, of course, or peach, apricot, blackberry, or blueberry—even marmalade. (Orange and almond flavors are wonderful together.)

I 17.3-ounce package frozen puff pastry, thawed (2 sheets)
I 8-ounce can almond paste
¼ cup sugar
I egg, separated
½ cup cherry or raspberry preserves
¼ cup sliced almonds
 Coarse or granulated sugar

1 Preheat oven to 375°F. Line 2 large baking sheets with parchment paper. Unfold puff pastry sheets; place 1 pastry sheet on each prepared baking sheet. Set aside.

2 For filling, in a medium bowl beat almond paste, sugar, and egg white with an electric mixer on medium speed until combined. Spread half the filling in a 3-inch-wide strip lengthwise down the center of each sheet, leaving a ½ inch on ends. Spread preserves over filling (below).

3 Using a sharp knife, make 3-inch-long cuts at 1-inch intervals in pastry on each side of the filling (below). Starting at one end, alternately fold opposite strips of dough at an angle over the filling, overlapping ends of strips in the middle (below). Press down gently on strips.

4 Beat egg yolk with 1 tablespoon *water*. Brush over braids. Sprinkle with almonds and coarse sugar (below). Cover lightly with plastic wrap and let stand for 20 minutes. Uncover.

5 Bake, one braid at a time, in the preheated oven for 30 to 35 minutes or until tops and bottoms are golden brown. Cool braids on baking sheets on a wire rack at least 15 minutes before cutting. Cut each braid into 6 slices. Makes 2 braids (6 servings each).

Per serving: 344 cal., 20 g total fat (I g sat. fat), 18 mg chol., 165 mg sodium, 38 g carbo., I g fiber, 5 g pro.

1 Spread preserves down the center of the pastry, completely covering the almond filling.

2 Using a knife, cut pastry on both sides of the filling at I-inch intervals right up to the filling.

3 Starting at one end, crisscross the strips at a slight angle over the filling to make the braid.

4 Sprinkle sliced alr and coarse sugar over brushed braids for look texture, and flavor.

Ask Mom How do I separate eggs? page 62 / What is parchment paper? page 79 / What is an electric mixer? page 21

(1) Skill Level

Dessert Fruit **Pizza**

Good to Know To make this dessert a few hours ahead of serving, prepare the crust, the cream cheese mixture, and the fruit. Cool and wrap the crust in plastic wrap and refrigerate the cream cheese mixture and the fruit separately. Don't assemble the pizza until right before serving to keep the crust from getting soggy.

1   16- to 18-ounce roll refrigerated sugar cookie dough
1   8-ounce package cream cheese, softened
¼   cup amaretto*
2   tablespoons packed brown sugar
⅓   cup finely chopped almonds, toasted
2   cups assorted fresh fruit, such as halved green and/or
    red grapes, sliced kiwifruit, sliced mango, sliced or chopped
    melon, sliced peaches, raspberries, and/or sliced strawberries
2   tablespoons honey (optional)

1 Preheat oven to 375°F. For crust, line a 12-inch pizza pan with foil. Pat cookie dough evenly onto foil-lined pan. Build up edges slightly. Bake in the preheated oven for 15 to 20 minutes or until edges are light brown and center appears set. Cool in pan on a wire rack.

2 Invert cooled crust onto a baking sheet; remove foil (below). Place a serving platter over inverted crust; invert platter and crust together (below).

3 In a medium mixing bowl beat cream cheese, amaretto, and brown sugar with an electric mixer on medium speed until smooth. Stir in the almonds. Spread the cream cheese mixture evenly over the top of the cookie crust, leaving a 1-inch border around the edges. Top with assorted fresh fruit (below). If desired, drizzle with honey. Makes 8 servings.

*Note: If desired, substitute ¼ cup milk and ½ teaspoon almond extract for the amaretto.

Per serving: 438 cal., 24 g total fat (9 g sat. fat), 48 mg chol., 326 mg sodium, 50 g carbo., 1 g fiber, 6 g pro.

1 Turn the baked crust upside down onto a baking sheet and carefully peel foil off the bottom.

2 Place a serving platter on inverted crust, then turn the baking sheet, crust, and platter over together so the crust is right side up again.

3 Spread the cream cheese mixture over crust, leaving a 1-inch edge, then arrange fresh fruit over top.

Ask Mom How do I soften cream cheese? page 93 / How do I pack brown sugar? page 58 / How do I chop nuts? page 65 / How do I toast nuts? page 65 / How do I line a pan with foil? page 60 / What is an electric mixer? page 21

(2) Skill Level

Flavor Changes
Apples aren't the only fruit that works in this no-bake dessert. Try fresh ripe peaches, pitted and sliced; fresh ripe pears, cored and sliced; or chunks of fresh pineapple.

Mock Apple Crisp

1 recipe Caramel Sauce

3 tablespoons butter

2 teaspoons sugar

$\frac{1}{2}$ teaspoon ground cinnamon

4 cups sliced, peeled cooking apples (see page 212)

1$\frac{1}{2}$ cups coarsely crushed cookies, such as biscotti, pecan shortbread, oatmeal, snickerdoodle, or chocolate chip (about 3 ounces)

Sweetened whipped cream (optional)

1 Prepare Caramel Sauce. In a 10-inch skillet melt butter over medium heat. Stir in sugar and cinnamon. Stir in apple slices. Cook, uncovered, for 8 to 10 minutes or until apple slices are tender and slightly brown, stirring occasionally.

2 Place cooked apple slices in serving bowls. Top evenly with crushed cookies. Drizzle Caramel Sauce over top. If desired, serve with sweetened whipped cream. Makes 8 servings.

Caramel Sauce: In a heavy 2-quart saucepan combine $\frac{1}{2}$ cup whipping cream, $\frac{1}{2}$ cup butter, $\frac{3}{4}$ cup packed dark brown sugar, and 2 tablespoons light-colored corn syrup. Bring to boiling over medium-high heat (about 5 to 6 minutes), whisking occasionally. Reduce heat to medium. Boil gently for 3 minutes more. Remove from heat. Stir in 1 teaspoon vanilla. Let sauce cool for 15 minutes before serving with apple crisp. Cover and chill any leftovers for up to 2 weeks. (If chilled, let stand at room temperature for 1 hour before serving.)

Per serving: 361 cal., 23 g total fat (14 g sat. fat), 66 mg chol., 160 mg sodium, 39 g carbo., 2 g fiber, 2 g pro.

Raisins and apples go together like peas and carrots, right? (Maybe even better.) If you're a raisin lover, sprinkle a few over the apples and cookies before you douse them with Caramel Sauce and top them with whipped cream.

Ask Mom How do I measure butter? pages 58, 59 / How do I peel and slice apples? page 28 / How do I pack brown sugar? page 58 / How do I make sweetened whipped cream? page 59

Caramel Nut Tart

- 1 recipe Pastry for Single-Crust Pie (see page 471)
- ½ cup butter
- ½ cup packed brown sugar
- 3 tablespoons light-colored corn syrup
- 2 cups mixed roasted and salted nuts
- 1 teaspoon vanilla
  Sweetened whipped cream (optional)

1 Preheat oven to 450°F. Prepare Pastry for Single-Crust Pie. Wrap pastry circle around the rolling pin. Unroll it into a 9-inch tart pan with a removable bottom. Ease pastry into pan without stretching it. Press pastry into fluted sides of tart pan and trim edges (below). Prick pastry with a fork. Line pastry with a double thickness of foil. Bake in the preheated oven for 8 minutes. Remove foil. Bake for 5 to 6 minutes more or until golden. Cool on a wire rack. Reduce oven temperature to 375°F.

2 In a heavy 1-quart saucepan combine butter, brown sugar, and corn syrup. Bring to boiling over medium heat, stirring frequently. Remove from heat. Stir in nuts and vanilla. Pour filling into cooled crust, spreading evenly. Place tart pan on a baking sheet.

3 Bake in the 375°F oven for 20 minutes. Cool on a wire rack for 15 minutes. Remove sides of pan (see Trick #9, page 81). Cool completely. If desired, serve with sweetened whipped cream. Makes 10 servings.

Per serving: 413 cal., 30 g total fat (9 g sat. fat), 24 mg chol., 134 mg sodium, 32 g carbo., 3 g fiber, 6 g pro.

Ingredient Info Use any combination of nuts in this rich, dense tart. Or use just one kind of nut. Consider walnuts, almonds, hazelnuts, or pecans.

1 Gently ease the 12-inch circle of dough into tart pan. Do not stretch dough. Press it into fluted sides of pan.

2 Trim the excess pastry by pressing through it along the top edges of the pan.

Ask Mom How do I measure butter? pages 58, 59 / How do I pack brown sugar? page 58 / How do I make sweetened whipped cream? page 59

HOW DO I ROLL A PIECRUST? To get your piecrust into an even thickness, start by flattening the ball of dough slightly. Then begin rolling from the center of the dough ball out to the edges, rolling forward and backward in all directions.

1 Using a pastry blender, cut shortening into the flour until the pieces are about the size of a pea.

2 Sprinkle cold water, l tablespoon at a time, over the flour mixture, tossing mixture with a fork to mix.

3 After all the flour is just moistened, gently press and form the dough into a ball.

4 On a lightly f roll the doug circle. Wrap around the r transfer it to

5 Gently ease the pastry into the pie plate, being careful not to stretch the dough.

6 Lightly press the circle over bottom and sides of plate. Using kitchen scissors, trim excess dough to 1/2 inch beyond edge of the plate.

7 Fold edges of extra pastry under along the edges of the pie plate.

8 Crimp the ed pastry. An ea press the thu hand agains the other har

Skill Level 3

Pumpkin Pie

1 recipe Pastry for Single-Crust Pie or half of a 15-ounce
  package of rolled refrigerated unbaked piecrust (1 crust)

1 15-ounce can pumpkin

½ cup sugar

1½ teaspoons pumpkin pie spice

2 eggs, lightly beaten

¾ cup half-and-half, light cream, or evaporated milk

1 Preheat oven to 375°F. Prepare Pastry for Single-Crust Pie or follow package directions for refrigerated piecrust.

2 For filling, in a large bowl stir together pumpkin, sugar, and pumpkin pie spice. Add eggs; beat lightly with a fork until combined. Gradually add half-and-half. Stir with fork just until combined. Pour filling into pastry-lined pie plate.

3 Bake in the preheated oven about 45 minutes or until a knife inserted in the center comes out clean. Cool on a wire rack for 2 hours. Cover and chill to store. Makes 8 servings.

Pastry for Single-Crust Pie (page 470): In a medium bowl stir together 1¼ cups all-purpose flour and ¼ teaspoon salt. Using a pastry blender, cut in ⅓ cup shortening until pieces are pea size. Sprinkle 1 tablespoon cold water over part of the flour mixture; gently toss with a fork. Push moistened dough to one side of the bowl. Repeat moistening flour mixture, using 1 tablespoon water at a time, until all the flour mixture is moistened (about 4 to 5 tablespoons cold water). Form pastry into a ball. On a lightly floured surface, roll dough into a circle about 12 inches in diameter. Wrap pastry circle around the rolling pin to transfer it; unroll circle into a 9-inch pie plate. Ease into pie plate without stretching it. Trim pastry to ½ inch beyond edges of pie plate. Fold under extra pastry. Crimp edges as desired.

Per serving: 262 cal., 13 g total fat (4 g sat. fat), 61 mg chol., 103 mg sodium, 33 g carbo., 2 g fiber, 7 g pro.

Cheese-Swirled Pumpkin Pie: Prepare as above, except in a small mixing bowl place one 3-ounce package cream cheese, softened; ¼ cup light-colored corn syrup; and ½ teaspoon vanilla. Beat with an electric mixer on medium speed until smooth. Pour pumpkin filling into piecrust; drop cream cheese mixture by spoonfuls onto filling. Swirl mixtures gently with a thin metal spatula or table knife. Bake and cool as directed.

Chocolate-Toffee Pumpkin Pie: Prepare as above, except before adding the filling to the pastry-lined pie plate, sprinkle ½ cup semisweet chocolate pieces over the bottom of the pastry. Over the top of the filling, sprinkle three 1.25-ounce chocolate-covered toffee bars, coarsely chopped. Bake and cool as directed.

Pecan-Topped Pumpkin Pie: Prepare as above, except bake pie for 35 minutes. Meanwhile, in a small bowl stir together 1 cup coarsely chopped pecans, ¼ cup packed brown sugar, and 2 tablespoons melted butter. Sprinkle pecan mixture evenly over partially baked pie. Bake about 10 minutes more or until filling appears set. Cool as directed. If desired, drizzle servings with maple syrup.

Flavor Changes
Crown your achievement of a homemade pumpkin pie by topping each slice with a spoonful of sweetened whipped cream and a sprinkle of chopped nuts.

Ask Mom How do I measure flour? page 58 / How do I measure shortening? page 58 / How do I beat eggs? page 62 / How do I chop nuts? page 65 / How do I pack brown sugar? page 58 / How do I measure butter? pages 58, 59 / How do I soften cream cheese? page 93 / What's the best way to measure sticky liquids? pages 58, 81 / How do I make sweetened whipped cream? page 59

(2) Skill Level

Rustic Peach Tart

- 1 recipe Pastry for Single-Crust Pie (see page 471)
- 1/8 teaspoon ground nutmeg (optional)
- 1/4 cup granulated sugar
- 4 teaspoons all-purpose flour
- 4 cups sliced, peeled fresh peaches or unsweetened frozen peach slices
- 1 tablespoon rum or lemon juice
- 1 egg, beaten
- 1 tablespoon water
  Peach or apricot preserves, melted (optional)
  Powdered sugar

Good to Know Part of the charm of this country-style tart is that the crust is intentionally freeform—it doesn't have to be a perfect round with smooth edges. If you were served a similar tart in the French countryside baked by an expert baker, it would look just like this. Pretty cool, huh?

1 Line a large baking sheet with parchment paper. Set aside. Prepare Pastry for Single-Crust Pie, except, if desired, add ground nutmeg with the salt. Roll pastry into a 13-inch circle; place on the prepared baking sheet (below).

2 In a large bowl stir together granulated sugar and flour. Add peaches and rum; toss gently until coated. If using frozen peaches, let stand about 45 minutes or until fruit is partially thawed but still icy.

3 Preheat oven to 375°F. Mound peach mixture in center of pastry (below), leaving a 2-inch border. Fold border up over peaches, pleating pastry gently as needed to hold in juices (below). In a small bowl beat the egg and water with a fork; brush onto the top and sides of the pastry.

4 Bake in the preheated oven for 35 to 45 minutes or until pastry is golden and filling is bubbly. If necessary to prevent overbrowning, cover edges with foil during the last 5 to 10 minutes of baking. Cool on the baking sheet for 30 minutes. If desired, brush filling with melted preserves. Dust pastry edges with powdered sugar (below). Serve warm. Makes 8 servings.

Per serving: 225 cal., 10 g total fat (2 g sat. fat), 26 mg chol., 82 mg sodium, 31 g carbo., 2 g fiber, 4 g pro.

1 Use a rolling pin to transfer pastry to parchment-lined baking sheet.

2 Mound peach mixture in the center of the pastry circle.

3 Fold, pleat, and pinch pastry over edges of filling.

4 Tap powdered su through a sieve to dust of pastry.

Ask Mom How do I peel peaches? page 66 / How do I juice a lemon/lime? pages 30, 80 / How much juice does one lemon/lime yield? page 30 / How do I beat eggs? page 62 / What is parchment paper? page 79 / What does it mean to toss? page 77

Petite Fruit Tarts

    2 cups all-purpose flour
   1/3 cup granulated sugar
   3/4 cup cold butter
    2 egg yolks, beaten
   1/4 cup dairy sour cream
    3 tablespoons ice water
   2/3 cup granulated sugar
   1/4 cup all-purpose flour
    6 to 8 cups fresh fruit, such as blackberries, blueberries,
       coarsely chopped apples, sliced nectarines,
       raspberries, and/or sliced apricots
   1/4 to 1/3 cup granulated sugar
       Powdered sugar (optional)

1 In a medium bowl stir together the 2 cups flour and the 1/3 cup granulated sugar. Using a pastry blender, cut butter into flour mixture until pieces are pea size. In a small bowl stir together egg yolks, sour cream, and ice water. Gradually stir egg yolk mixture into flour mixture. Using your fingers, gently knead the dough just until a ball forms (see photo 2, page 452). Cover dough with plastic wrap; chill about 1 hour or until dough is easy to handle.

2 Preheat oven to 375°F. Divide dough into 8 portions. On lightly floured pieces of parchment paper, roll dough portions into 6- to 7-inch circles. Transfer circles, on parchment, to baking sheets.

3 In a small bowl stir together the 2/3 cup granulated sugar and the 1/4 cup flour. Sprinkle a scant 2 tablespoons of the sugar mixture on each pastry circle to within 1/2 inch of the edges. In a large bowl combine fruit and the 1/4 to 1/3 cup granulated sugar; toss gently to coat.

4 Spoon 3/4 to 1 cup of the fruit mixture into the center of each dough circle. Fold pastry edges over the edges of fruit (see photo 3, page 472). Bake tarts for 20 to 25 minutes or until fruit is tender and pastry is golden brown. If desired, dust pastry edges with powdered sugar (see photo 4, page 472). Makes 8 tarts.

Per tart: 467 cal., 21 g total fat (10 g sat. fat), 102 mg chol., 136 mg sodium, 66 g carbo., 3 g fiber, 5 g pro.

GOOD TO KNOW Mom may have taught you to share, but be honest: What's better than your very own dessert? Serve these little beauties warm with a scoop of vanilla bean ice cream. You will be a hero.

Ask Mom How do I measure flour? page 58 / How do I measure butter? pages 58, 59 / How do I separate eggs? page 62 / How do I cut in butter? page 63 / How do I beat eggs? page 62 / How do I core and slice/chop apples? page 28 / What is parchment paper? page 79 / What does it mean to toss? page 77

Phyllo Cups

Nonstick cooking spray
8 sheets frozen phyllo dough (14×9-inch), thawed
4 teaspoons sugar
1 recipe Honey Filling with Berries, Espresso Coconut-Macadamia Filling,
 or Lemon Cheesecake Filling (page 475)

1 Preheat oven to 350°F. Lightly coat twelve $2^1/_2$-inch muffin cups with cooking spray. Set aside. Lay out 1 sheet of phyllo dough (keep remaining phyllo covered with plastic wrap to prevent it from drying out). Lightly coat phyllo with cooking spray; sprinkle with some of the sugar (below). Top with another sheet of phyllo. Lightly coat with cooking spray and sprinkle with sugar. Repeat layering with two more sheets of phyllo, the cooking spray, and sugar (using 4 sheets for one stack). Repeat with remaining sheets of phyllo, cooking spray, and sugar for a second stack.

2 Cut each stack in half lengthwise. Cut crosswise into thirds (below). (There should be a total of 12 rectangles.) Press 1 rectangle into each prepared muffin cup, pleating phyllo as necessary to form a cup (below). Bake in the preheated oven about 8 minutes or until golden. Cool for 5 minutes in pan. Remove from pan; cool completely. Fill with desired filling. (Cups may be filled up to 1 hour before serving.) Makes 12 cups.

Per cup with Honey Filling with Berries: 161 cal., 8 g total fat (4 g sat. fat), 22 mg chol., 148 mg sodium, 20 g carbo., 1 g fiber, 3 g pro.

1 Lay a phyllo sheet on the work surface. Lightly coat the phyllo sheet with cooking spray.

2 Lightly sprinkle sugar over entire sheet of phyllo. Top with another phyllo sheet. Spray and sprinkle 4 sheets per stack.

3 Using a sharp knife, cut stacks in half lengthwise. Then cut crosswise into thirds, making 6 rectangles per stack for a total of 12.

4 Press each recta[ngle] stack into prepared mu[ffin] pleating sides as neede[d] form cups.

Ask Mom How do I soften cream cheese? page 93 / What are stiff peaks? page 62 / What does drizzle mean? page 79 / How do I chop nuts? page 65 / How do I toast coconut? page 65 / What does garnish mean? page 79

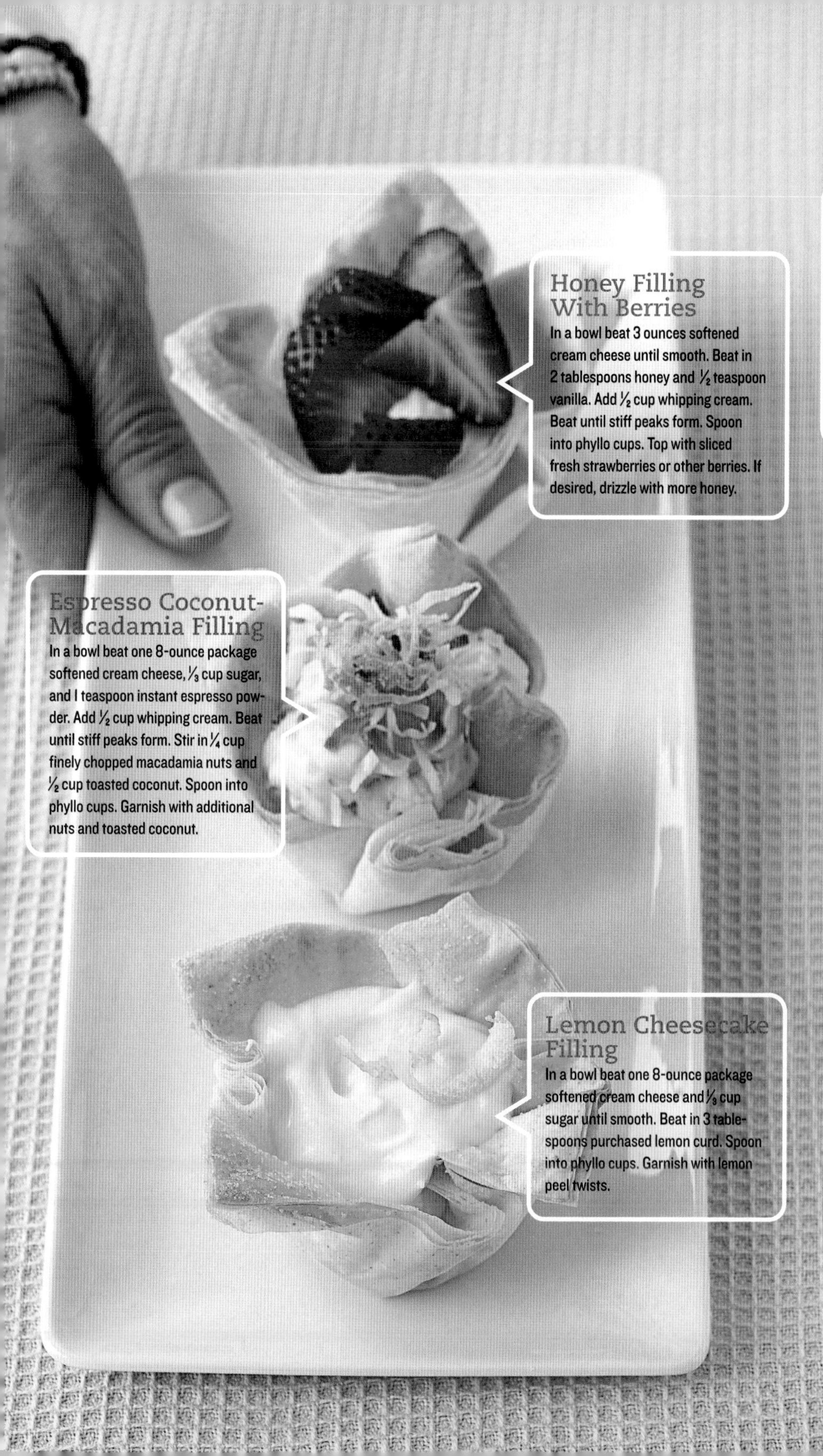

Honey Filling With Berries

In a bowl beat 3 ounces softened cream cheese until smooth. Beat in 2 tablespoons honey and $\frac{1}{2}$ teaspoon vanilla. Add $\frac{1}{2}$ cup whipping cream. Beat until stiff peaks form. Spoon into phyllo cups. Top with sliced fresh strawberries or other berries. If desired, drizzle with more honey.

Espresso Coconut-Macadamia Filling

In a bowl beat one 8-ounce package softened cream cheese, $\frac{1}{3}$ cup sugar, and 1 teaspoon instant espresso powder. Add $\frac{1}{2}$ cup whipping cream. Beat until stiff peaks form. Stir in $\frac{1}{4}$ cup finely chopped macadamia nuts and $\frac{1}{2}$ cup toasted coconut. Spoon into phyllo cups. Garnish with additional nuts and toasted coconut.

Lemon Cheesecake Filling

In a bowl beat one 8-ounce package softened cream cheese and $\frac{1}{3}$ cup sugar until smooth. Beat in 3 tablespoons purchased lemon curd. Spoon into phyllo cups. Garnish with lemon peel twists.

(2) Skill Level

Strawberry **Shortcakes**

1 ½ cups all-purpose flour
¼ cup sugar
1 teaspoon baking powder
¼ teaspoon baking soda
¼ teaspoon salt
⅓ cup cold butter
1 egg, lightly beaten
½ cup dairy sour cream
2 tablespoons milk
5 cups sliced strawberries
3 tablespoons sugar
   Sweetened whipped cream

Flavor Changes If you're wild for all kinds of berries, make these shortcakes with a jumble of them. Simply use 5 cups of mixed fresh berries such as raspberries, blueberries, and/or blackberries instead of the 5 cups of strawberries—and prepare as directed.

1 Preheat oven to 400°F. Lightly grease a baking sheet; set aside. In a medium bowl stir together flour, the ¼ cup sugar, the baking powder, baking soda, and salt. Using a pastry blender, cut in butter until mixture resembles coarse crumbs (see photo 1, page 470). In a small bowl combine egg, sour cream, and milk. Add to flour mixture; stir with a fork just until moistened (below).

2 Drop dough into 8 mounds onto prepared baking sheet (below). Bake in the preheated oven for 12 to 15 minutes or until golden. Transfer to a wire rack and let cool.

3 Meanwhile, in a large bowl combine 4 cups of the strawberries and the 3 tablespoons sugar. Using a potato masher, mash berries slightly; set aside. To serve, halve shortcakes (below); fill with strawberries and sweetened whipped cream. Top with remaining sliced strawberries. Makes 8 shortcakes.

Per shortcake: 373 cal., 23 g total fat (14 g sat. fat), 93 mg chol., 226 mg sodium, 39 g carbo., 3 g fiber, 5 g pro.

1 Pour sour cream mixture into flour mixture, stirring with a fork just until the flour is moistened. Don't overstir.

2 "Drop" dough onto baking sheet by scooping it with one spoon and pushing it off with another spoon.

3 Slice strawberries to fill shortcakes and to place on top of whipped cream as a garnish.

4 Use a knife to sp[l] shortcakes in half cros[s] Spoon strawberries an[d] cream between halves.

Ask Mom How do I measure flour? page 58 / How do I measure butter? pages 58, 59 / How do I cut in butter? page 63 / How do I beat eggs? page 62 / How do I make sweetened whipped cream? page 59

Easy Topped Cupcakes

1 recipe Butter Pecan Ice Cream "Frosting" or Banana Split "Frosting"
1 package 2-layer-size desired flavor cake mix

1 Prepare and freeze desired ice cream "frosting." Meanwhile, line twenty-four 2½-inch muffin cups with paper bake cups or lightly grease muffin cups; set aside.

2 Prepare and bake cake mix according to package directions for cupcakes using prepared muffin cups. Cool cupcakes in pans on wire racks for 5 minutes. Remove cupcakes from pans; cool completely on wire racks.

3 Remove paper bake cups, if using, from 12 of the cupcakes. Save remaining cupcakes for another use. Place the 12* cupcakes on serving plates or in shallow bowls. Top each cupcake as directed in the "frosting" recipes below. Serve immediately. Makes 12 topped cupcakes.

*Note: Assemble only as many desserts as you are serving. Store unfrosted cupcakes in an airtight container for up to 3 days or freeze for up to 3 months. Thaw cupcakes before assembling.

Butter Pecan Ice Cream "Frosting": Line a large baking sheet with waxed paper; set aside. Using a 2- to 3-inch-diameter ice cream scoop, drop 12 scoops of butter pecan ice cream onto prepared baking sheet. Cover and freeze for 4 hours or up to 3 days. To serve, place a scoop of ice cream on each cupcake. Top evenly with ¾ cup caramel ice cream topping or Caramel Sauce (see page 468) and ¾ cup chopped toasted pecans.

Per cupcake with Butter Pecan Ice Cream "Frosting" : 437 cal., 21 g total fat (5 g sat. fat), 65 mg chol., 393 mg sodium, 58 g carbo., 1 g fiber, 6 g pro.

Banana Split "Frosting": Prepare Butter Pecan Ice Cream "Frosting" as above, except substitute strawberry or banana split ice cream for the butter pecan ice cream. Top ice cream with ¾ cup chocolate fudge ice cream topping, 1 cup chopped banana, and ¾ cup chopped dry-roasted peanuts instead of the caramel topping and pecans.

Chocolate-Lover's Cake

¾ cup butter

2 eggs

⅔ cup unsweetened cocoa powder

⅔ cup boiling water

⅔ cup buttermilk or sour milk (page 445)

2 teaspoons vanilla

2¼ cups all-purpose flour

1½ teaspoons baking soda

⅛ teaspoon salt

¾ cup granulated sugar

¾ cup packed brown sugar

1 recipe Chocolate Butter Frosting

1 Let butter and eggs stand at room temperature for 30 minutes. Grease and flour two 9-inch round cake pans; set aside. In a medium bowl whisk together cocoa powder and boiling water until smooth. Let cool for 10 minutes. Whisk in buttermilk and vanilla (below); set aside. In a medium bowl stir together flour, baking soda, and salt; set aside.

2 Preheat oven to 350°F. In a mixing bowl beat butter with electric mixer on medium speed for 30 seconds. Add sugars; beat until combined. Add eggs, one at a time, beating until combined after each addition (below). Beat in one-third of the flour mixture on low speed just until combined (below). Beat in half of buttermilk mixture. Mixture may look curdled. Beat in half of the remaining flour mixture, then the remaining buttermilk mixture, and, finally, the remaining flour mixture.

3 Divide batter between prepared pans; spread evenly. Bake about 30 minutes or until toothpick inserted near centers comes out clean. Cool in pans on wire rack 10 minutes. Remove cakes from pans. Let cool on wire rack. Assemble as below and on page 479. Makes 16 servings.

Chocolate Butter Frosting: In a very large mixing bowl beat ¾ cup butter, softened, and ½ cup unsweetened cocoa powder with an electric mixer on medium speed until smooth. Gradually beat in 2 cups powdered sugar until well combined. Gradually beat in ½ cup milk and 2 teaspoons vanilla until well combined. Gradually beat in 6 cups powdered sugar. If necessary, beat in additional milk, 1 teaspoon at a time, to reach spreading consistency.

Per serving: 559 cal., 19 g total fat (12 g sat. fat), 73 mg chol., 288 mg sodium, 97 g carbo., 2 g fiber, 5 g pro.

1 In a medium bowl whisk buttermilk and vanilla into cooled cocoa mixture.

2 Add eggs, one at a time, beating in completely after each addition.

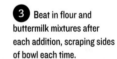 3 Beat in flour and buttermilk mixtures after each addition, scraping sides of bowl each time.

 4 Place first cake la... on a serving plate. Spre... 1½ cups frosting over t... of the layer.

Ask Mom How do I measure butter? pages 58, 59 / How do I soften butter? page 59 / How do I measure flour? page 58 / How do I pack brown sugar? page 58 / How do I grease a baking pan/dish? page 61 / What is an electric mixer? page 21

WHY SHOULD EGGS BE AT ROOM TEMPERATURE?

For almost any kind of baking (and it's especially important for cakes), room-temperature eggs beat up fluffier and with more volume than do cold eggs. The result: lighter, higher, fluffier cakes. Can't beat that.

Top frosted first layer with second cake layer, top side up. Frost top and sides of entire cake with remaining Chocolate Butter Frosting.

Chocolate Cherry Cake

Prepare Chocolate-Lover's Cake as on page
478, except stir $\frac{1}{2}$ cup coarsely chopped,
well-drained maraschino cherries into the batter
at the end of Step 2. To assemble, place one cake
layer on a serving plate, top side up. Spread with
I cup of the Chocolate Butter Frosting. Snip any
large cherry pieces in $\frac{1}{2}$ cup cherry preserves.
Spread preserves on top of frosting on first cake
layer, leaving a I-inch space around the top edges
of the cake. Top with second cake layer, top
side up. Use the remaining Chocolate Butter
Frosting to frost the top and sides of the whole
cake. If desired, garnish the top of the cake with
well-drained whole maraschino cherries.

Malted Milk Shake Cake

Prepare Chocolate-Lover's Cake as on page
478, except stir in $\frac{1}{3}$ cup malted milk powder
with the flour, baking soda, and salt in Step
I. Prepare the Chocolate Butter Frosting as
directed, except add $\frac{1}{4}$ cup malted milk powder
with the first 2 cups powdered sugar. If desired,
garnish cake with I cup coarsely chopped malted
milk balls.

IS THERE A DIFFERENCE IN COCOA POWDERS?

There are two kinds: natural—usually labeled
"unsweetened cocoa powder"—and Dutch-process
cocoa powder. Dutch-process is milder in flavor than
natural and deep red—not brown—in color. Use
natural if you like a more intense chocolate flavor.

Good to Know With just a few minor tweaks, this basic chocolate cake becomes a whole new thing entirely. This version has chopped maraschino cherries in the batter and a glaze of cherry preserves in the filling. The combo of cherry and chocolate is a classic; this is very similar to Bavarian Black Forest Cake.

Chocolate-Lover's Cake (see recipe, page 478)

② Skill Level

Butterscotch Crunch Squares

Flavor Changes For a fun fall or holiday dessert that celebrates the pumpkin in a whole new way, try making this with pumpkin ice cream rather than butter brickle, chocolate, or vanilla ice cream. Grab it while you can: Pumpkin ice cream is available seasonally in most supermarkets.

I cup all-purpose flour
¼ cup quick-cooking rolled oats
¼ cup packed brown sugar
½ cup butter
½ cup chopped pecans or walnuts
½ cup butterscotch-flavor or caramel ice cream topping
½ gallon butter brickle, chocolate, or vanilla ice cream

1 Preheat oven to 400°F. In a medium bowl stir together flour, oats, and brown sugar. Using a pastry blender, cut in butter until mixture resembles coarse crumbs. Stir in pecans. Pat mixture lightly into an ungreased 13×9×2-inch baking pan. Bake in the preheated oven for 10 to 15 minutes or until light brown. Remove from oven. While still warm, stir nut mixture to crumble it (below). Cool.

2 Spread half of the crumbled nut mixture in a 9×9×2-inch pan; drizzle about half of the ice cream topping over crumbs in pan. Place ice cream in a chilled large bowl; stir to soften. Spoon softened ice cream carefully over crumbs in pan (below). Drizzle with remaining topping; sprinkle with the remaining crumbs (below). Cover and freeze for at least 6 hours or until firm. Let stand at room temperature for 5 to 10 minutes before serving. Use a sharp knife to cut into squares. Makes 12 squares.

Per square: 450 cal., 28 g total fat (15 g sat. fat), 112 mg chol., 156 mg sodium, 46 g carbo., 1 g fiber, 5 g pro.

Strawberry Crunch Squares: Prepare as above, except substitute fudge ice cream topping for the butterscotch-flavor topping and strawberry ice cream for the butter brickle ice cream.

1 Use a spoon to stir the baked nut mixture to coarsely crumble it.

2 Carefully spoon softened ice cream over crumbs in pan, then smooth the top.

3 Sprinkle the remaining crumbs evenly over the top of the ice cream and topping.

Ask Mom How do I measure flour? page 58 / How do I pack brown sugar? page 58 / How do I measure butter? pages 58, 59 / How do I cut in butter? page 63 / How do I chop nuts? page 65 / What's the best way to measure sticky liquids? pages 58, 81 / What does drizzle mean? page 79

Index

Boldfaced page references indicate photographs of finished recipes.

Boldfaced page references indicate photographs of finished recipes.

Boldfaced page references indicate photographs of finished recipes.

Boldfaced page references indicate photographs of finished recipes.

Boldfaced page references indicate photographs of finished recipes.

Metric Information

The charts on this page provide a guide for converting measurements from the U.S. customary system, which is used throughout this book, to the metric system.

Product Differences

Most of the ingredients called for in the recipes in this book are available in most countries. However, some are known by different names. Here are some common American ingredients and their possible counterparts:
• Sugar (white) is granulated, fine granulated, or castor sugar.
• Powdered sugar is icing sugar.
• All-purpose flour is enriched, bleached or unbleached white household flour. When self-rising flour is used in place of all-purpose flour in a recipe that calls for leavening, omit the leavening agent (baking soda or baking powder) and salt.
• Light-colored corn syrup is golden syrup.
• Cornstarch is cornflour.
• Baking soda is bicarbonate of soda.
• Vanilla or vanilla extract is vanilla essence.
• Green, red, or yellow sweet peppers are capsicums or bell peppers.
• Golden raisins are sultanas.

Volume and Weight

The United States traditionally uses cup measures for liquid and solid ingredients. The chart below shows the approximate imperial and metric equivalents. If you are accustomed to weighing solid ingredients, the following approximate equivalents will be helpful.
• 1 cup butter, castor sugar, or rice = 8 ounces = $\frac{1}{2}$ pound = 250 grams
• 1 cup flour = 4 ounces = $\frac{1}{4}$ pound = 125 grams
• 1 cup icing sugar = 5 ounces = 150 grams
• Canadian and U.S. volume for a cup measure is 8 fluid ounces (237 ml), but the standard metric equivalent is 250 ml.
• 1 British imperial cup is 10 fluid ounces.
• In Australia, 1 tablespoon equals 20 ml, and there are 4 teaspoons in the Australian tablespoon.
• Spoon measures are used for smaller amounts of ingredients. Although the size of the tablespoon varies slightly in different countries, for practical purposes and for recipes in this book, a straight substitution is all that's necessary. Measurements made using cups or spoons always should be level unless stated otherwise.

Common Weight Range Replacements

Imperial / U.S.	Metric
$\frac{1}{2}$ ounce	15 g
1 ounce	25 g or 30 g
4 ounces ($\frac{1}{4}$ pound)	115 g or 125 g
8 ounces ($\frac{1}{2}$ pound)	225 g or 250 g
16 ounces (1 pound)	450 g or 500 g
1$\frac{1}{4}$ pounds	625 g
1$\frac{1}{2}$ pounds	750 g
2 pounds or 2$\frac{1}{4}$ pounds	1,000 g or 1 Kg

Oven Temperature Equivalents

Fahrenheit Setting	Celsius Setting	Gas Setting
300°F	150°C	Gas Mark 2 (very low)
325°F	160°C	Gas Mark 3 (low)
350°F	180°C	Gas Mark 4 (moderate)
375°F	190°C	Gas Mark 5 (moderate)
400°F	200°C	Gas Mark 6 (hot)
425°F	220°C	Gas Mark 7 (hot)
450°F	230°C	Gas Mark 8 (very hot)
475°F	240°C	Gas Mark 9 (very hot)
500°F	260°C	Gas Mark 10 (extremely hot)
Broil	Broil	Grill

*Electric and gas ovens may be calibrated using celsius. However, for an electric oven, increase celsius setting 10 to 20 degrees when cooking above 160°C. For convection or forced air ovens (gas or electric), lower the temperature setting 25°F/10°C when cooking at all heat levels.

Baking Pan Sizes

Imperial / U.S.	Metric
9×1$\frac{1}{2}$-inch round cake pan	22- or 23×4-cm (1.5 L)
9×1$\frac{1}{2}$-inch pie plate	22- or 23×4-cm (1 L)
8×8×2-inch square cake pan	20×5-cm (2 L)
9×9×2-inch square cake pan	22- or 23×4.5-cm (2.5 L)
11×7×1$\frac{1}{2}$-inch baking pan	28×17×4-cm (2 L)
2-quart rectangular baking pan	30×19×4.5-cm (3 L)
13×9×2-inch baking pan	34×22×4.5-cm (3.5 L)
15×10×1-inch jelly roll pan	40×25×2-cm
9×5×3-inch loaf pan	23×13×8-cm (2 L)
2-quart casserole	2 L

U.S. / Standard Metric Equivalents

$\frac{1}{8}$ teaspoon = 0.5 ml	
$\frac{1}{4}$ teaspoon = 1 ml	
$\frac{1}{2}$ teaspoon = 2 ml	
1 teaspoon = 5 ml	
1 tablespoon = 15 ml	
2 tablespoons = 25 ml	
$\frac{1}{4}$ cup = 2 fluid ounces = 50 ml	
$\frac{1}{3}$ cup = 3 fluid ounces = 75 ml	
$\frac{1}{2}$ cup = 4 fluid ounces = 125 ml	
$\frac{2}{3}$ cup = 5 fluid ounces = 150 ml	
$\frac{3}{4}$ cup = 6 fluid ounces = 175 ml	
1 cup = 8 fluid ounces = 250 ml	
2 cups = 1 pint = 500 ml	
1 quart = 1 litre	

WHAT'S NEXT? Now that you've learned the basics thanks to *Anyone Can Cook,* take your culinary skills to the next level. Check out the updated version of a trusted American classic, the *Better Homes and Gardens® New Cook Book,* for more mouthwatering recipes!

New Features

- All-new 20-Minute Meals chapter— more than 45 quick meal solutions
- New "Essentials" section located at the front of each chapter ensures cooking success
- Simple menu ideas featured in each main dish chapter

More Value

- 800 NEW recipes—1,400 in all— including tried-and-true classics an fresh new flavors tested in the Bette Homes and Gardens® Test Kitchen
- More than 400 quick and easy recipes
- More than 800 beautiful color photos

ALSO AVAILABLE IN COMB BOUND AND TRADEPAPER FORMATS!

Available where quality books are sol

ADT02